CONSTRUCTION LAW, COSTS AND CONTEMPORARY DEVELOPMENTS

Lord Justice Jackson's retirement in March 2018 concluded a career of almost 20 years on the bench. His judicial career has seen a remarkable transformation of construction law, construction law litigation and the litigation landscape more generally. *Drawing the Threads Together* is a Festschrift which considers many of the important developments in these areas during the Jackson era.

The Festschrift discusses most of the leading construction cases decided by Lord Justice Jackson, with subject matter including statutory adjudication, fitness for purpose obligations, consideration, delays and extensions of time, liquidated damages, time bar provisions, the prevention principle, neighbour rights, limitation clauses, negligence, good faith, bonds and guarantees and concurrent duties of care. It also includes a discussion of the background to the Jackson Review of Civil Litigation Costs (2009–2010) and its impact on litigation, as well as considering the development of the Technology and Construction Court during and subsequent to Mr Justice Jackson's tenure as judge in charge of that court.

Construction Law, Costs and Contemporary Developments: Drawing the Threads Together

A Festschrift for Lord Justice Jackson

Edited by
Julian Bailey

·HART·
OXFORD · LONDON · NEW YORK · NEW DELHI · SYDNEY

HART PUBLISHING

Bloomsbury Publishing Plc

Kemp House, Chawley Park, Cumnor Hill, Oxford, OX2 9PH, UK

HART PUBLISHING, the Hart/Stag logo, BLOOMSBURY and the Diana logo are
trademarks of Bloomsbury Publishing Plc

First published in Great Britain 2018

A catalogue record for this book is available from the British Library.

Library of Congress Cataloging-in-Publication data

Names: Jackson, Rupert M., honouree. I Bailey, Julian, editor.

Title: Construction law, costs, and contemporary developments : drawing the threads together :
a festschrift for Lord Justice Jackson / edited by Julian Bailey.

Description: Oxford [UK] ; Portland, Oregon : Hart Publishing, 2018. I Includes index.

Identifiers: LCCN 2018031649 (print) I LCCN 2018032318 (ebook) I
ISBN 9781509919956 (Epub) I ISBN9781509919949 (hardback)

Subjects: LCSH: Construction industry—Law and legislation—Great Britain. I Construction
contracts—Great Britain. I Construction industry—Great Britain—Costs. I Jackson, Rupert M.

Classification: LCC KD2435 (ebook) I LCC KD2435 .C68 2018 (print) I DDC 343.4107/8624—dc23

LC record available at https://lccn.loc.gov/2018031649

ISBN: HB: 978-1-50991-994-9
       ePDF: 978-1-50991-996-3
       ePub: 978-1-50991-995-6

Typeset by Compuscript Ltd, Shannon

To find out more about our authors and books visit www.hartpublishing.co.uk.
Here you will find extracts, author information, details of forthcoming events
and the option to sign up for our newsletters.

PREFACE

This *Festschrift* has been prepared to mark Lord Justice Jackson's retirement from the bench in March 2018, having reached the statutory retirement age. The *Festschrift* reflects upon his contribution to the law, primarily in relation to construction law, including the reform of the Technology and Construction Court, as well as the reform of civil litigation costs in England and Wales.

Each of the contributors to the *Festschrift* is warmly thanked for their efforts and patience. Most contributors faced considerable time pressures from their "day jobs", hence finding the opportunity to put pen to paper, or fingers to keyboard, has not always been easy. But the fruits of each time-oppressed contributor are – and I hope the reader will agree – stimulating, and collectively they offer a fine tribute to one of the more influential judges in England and Wales of recent years.

Thanks also to the publishers, Hart, for their support and hard work in putting the *Festschrift* into shape for publication.

The royalties from the *Festschrift* will be donated to the Personal Support Unit, the only court-based charity in England and Wales which offers non-legal emotional and practical support to people who come to court, unable to afford to pay for legal advice and ineligible for legal aid (see www.thepsu.org). Lord Justice Jackson has supported this charity over many years, having acted as the liaison judge for the PSU at the Royal Courts of Justice, and having shorn millimetres off the soles of his trainers on several London Legal Walks.

Julian Bailey
9 April 2018

CONTENTS

PART I
INTRODUCTION

PART II
THE TECHNOLOGY AND CONSTRUCTION COURT

PART III
COSTS

PART IV
CONSTRUCTION ADJUDICATION

PART IX
PERFORMANCE BONDS

PART X
TIME AND LIQUIDATED DAMAGES

TABLE OF CASES

TABLE OF STATUTES, TREATIES
AND REGULATIONS

Regulations

LIST OF CONTRIBUTORS

Julian Bailey is a solicitor and partner at White & Case LLP; Adjunct Professor of Law at Hamad bin Khalifa University, Doha, Qatar.

Professor Philip Britton is a former Visiting Professor and Director, Centre of Construction Law & Dispute Resolution, Dickson Poon School of Law, King's College London; Senior Fellow, Melbourne Law School.

Professor Mindy Chen-Wishart is a Professor of the Law of Contract at Oxford University and a Tutorial fellow at Merton College.

Lord Clarke of Stone-cum-Ebony is a former justice of the Supreme Court of the United Kingdom, and was Master of the Rolls 2005–2009.

Michael Curtis QC is a barrister practising at Crown Office Chambers, London.

Lord Justice Coulson is a Lord Justice of Appeal (England and Wales), and was judge in charge of the Technology and Construction Court 2016–2018.

Sir Antony Edwards-Stuart is a former judge of the Technology and Construction Court, and was judge in charge of that court 2013–2016.

Karim Ghaly QC is a barrister practising at 39 Essex Chambers, London.

Riaz Hussain QC is a barrister practising at Atkin Chambers, London.

Shy Jackson is a solicitor and partner at Pinsent Masons.

Mrs Justice Jefford DBE is a High Court judge, nominated to hear cases in the Technology and Construction Court.

Professor Doug Jones AO RFD is an independent international arbitrator based in London, Sydney and Toronto.

Professor Anthony Lavers is a barrister and counsel at White & Case LLP; Visiting Professor of Law at King's College, London.

Manus McMullan QC is a barrister practising at Atkin Chambers, London.

Vincent Moran QC is a barrister practising at Keating Chambers, London.

Rachael O'Hagan is a barrister practising at 39 Essex Chambers, London.

Fiona Sinclair QC is a barrister practising at 4 Pump Court Chambers, London.

Steven Walker QC is a barrister practising at Atkin Chambers, London.

Adrian Williamson QC is a barrister practising at Keating Chambers, London.

Richard Wilmot-Smith QC is a barrister practising at 39 Essex Chambers, London.

PART I

Introduction

1

A Judicial Career of Many Parts

JULIAN BAILEY

I. Introduction

The focus of this *Festschrift* is upon three areas of the law in which Lord Justice Jackson[1] has made a substantial contribution, being:

- the development of the Technology and Construction Court (TCC);
- civil litigation costs, including by recommending measures to reform the legal system of England & Wales to ensure that litigation is cost effective; and
- the development of construction law.

This chapter discusses those matters, as well as the man for whom this *Festschrift* has been written.

There is always a risk that a biographical exposition may read as an extended entry in *Who's Who* or Wikipedia, and in some respects the backgrounds and paths to the bench for most senior judges are tessellated with familiar fact patterns. The traditional route of university, call to the bar, taking silk and (after a few outings as a Recorder or a Deputy High Court Judge) appointment to the High Court (and, for some, upwards) makes for a career of great distinction, but not necessarily one that warrants or necessitates any special recognition from one's colleagues or members of a profession. Something more is needed, and I believe we find it here with Lord Justice Jackson.

What follows is intended to provide some details and vignettes of the man, his background, and his progression to the High Court bench and then to the Court of Appeal. Interwoven in this are aspects of his career, first at the bar, and more predominantly when on the bench, which highlight key areas of law and legal developments in which he was involved, usually at the forefront.

---

[1] References in this *Festschrift* are to 'Lord Justice Jackson', as he has usually been referred to during his time as a Court of Appeal judge. For a brief period, that is from 4 October 2017 (when Sir Peter Jackson was appointed to the Court of Appeal) until 7 March 2018 (the retirement date of Sir Rupert Jackson), the correct nomenclature was 'Lord Justice Rupert Jackson'. As the publication of this *Festschrift* post-dates his retirement from the bench, Lord Justice Jackson is now 'Sir Rupert Jackson'; however, for convenience the appellate appellation will be maintained.

II. School Days

Rupert Jackson's school days were spent at Christ's Hospital, in West Sussex.[2] One of his contemporaries at Christ's Hospital was Christopher Ennis, who would go on to become a well-known quantity surveying expert and Chairman of the Society of Construction Law (UK). Mr Ennis shared this reflection with me: 'Above all I remember his kindness, approachability and civility to all, young and old ... In many ways he has hardly changed, and high office has not made him any less approachable and personable'.

It was perhaps these lifelong virtues – including his humility, good humour and generous spirit – that endeared him to fellow students and later in life to professional colleagues, clients and counsel appearing before him in court.

III. University and Early Days at the Bar

In keeping with the Nazarene nomenclature, education at Christ's Hospital was followed by four years at Jesus College, Cambridge (1967–1971), where he studied classics (graduating with a first) and law (graduating with a 2:1). At Cambridge, Rupert Jackson met someone who would become his lifelong friend and collaborator: one John Powell. Jackson and Powell were both involved with the Cambridge Union, with Rupert Jackson becoming President of the Cambridge Union in Easter 1971.[3] His immediate successor as President was Ariadnē-Anna Stasinopoúlou, now better known by her married name of Arianna Huffington, of *Huffington Post* fame. Though he knew her well at university, their paths diverged thereafter, with Ms Stasinopoúlou pursuing a career in journalism and music, whereas Rupert Jackson entered the less burnished world of the law.

---

[2] Incidentally, the school itself was involved in construction litigation in the early Victorian period, when the school was located in Newgate Street in central London: *Bradbee v Christ's Hospital* (1842) 4 Man & G 714; 134 ER 294. The school owned a row of eight houses in a part of the City, and wished to pull them down to build new ones. The owner of a neighbouring property, who ran a business (as a 'fancy-trimming, lace, and fringe manufacturer'), brought an action in nuisance against the school, on the basis that the school had taken an unreasonable amount of time to pull down the property next door. He alleged that the hoarding the school put in place for the demolition had been there for too long, blocking the footpath in front of the plaintiff's business and thus causing damage to that business. He also alleged that the house next door was pulled down in a negligent manner, causing damage to his own property and business. In what was evidently hard-fought litigation in the Court of Common Pleas, the school met with mixed success.

[3] Former Presidents of the Cambridge Union include a number of current political grandees, including Kenneth Clarke, Vince Cable and Michael Howard. Going back even further, one of Rupert Jackson's predecessors as President was the father of English legal history, the unequalled FW Maitland, who was President for the Lent term of 1873.

Rupert Jackson was called to the bar in 1972, at the Middle Temple. After pupillage at the chambers of Ralph Gibson QC,[4] he took up tenancy at those chambers in 1973, based at Crown Office Row, Temple. In 1974, Rupert Jackson's friend from Cambridge, John Powell, also joined chambers as a tenant, and some eight years later they would publish the book[5] which made their names in the law.

The urge to write was evidently present from the earliest days of Rupert Jackson's career at the bar, if not before.[6] Three contributions from this time are extant, and bear brief mention to bring out the varied interests of the young legal mind.

A case note from 1973 'Can Clubs Discriminate?'[7] considered section 2(1) of the Race Relations Act 1968, which made it unlawful 'for any person concerned with the provision to the public or a section of the public ... of any goods, facilities or services to discriminate against any person seeking to obtain those goods, facilities or services' on the basis of the latter's 'colour, race or ethnic or national origins'. The case in question[8] concerned an application by a Mr Shah, a Conservative of Indian origin, to join the East Ham South Conservative Club. Mr Shah's application to join the club had been rejected due to his colour. The club's defence – which succeeded in the House of Lords – was that section 2(1) did not apply to it because, as a *private* club, it was not providing goods, facilities or services to the *public*.[9] Unsurprisingly, Rupert Jackson's note in the *Modern Law Review* was unsupportive of this outcome.[10]

In the same year, Rupert Jackson authored a 'review of reviews' in the journal *Quis Custodiet?*[11] of the article 'Civilised Violence' by Friar Thomas Gilby OP,[12] being a meditation on the causes of and possible justifications for violence in societies, including violence by and against the state. Rupert Jackson's review of

---

[4] Later Lord Justice Ralph Gibson. At chambers, Rupert Jackson was a pupil of Ian Kennedy, later Mr Justice Kennedy. As a judge, Kennedy J sat as part of the Court of Criminal Appeal in *R v Seymour* (1987) 9 Cr App R (S) 395, which involved the prosecution of the 8th Marquess of Hertford for ploughing through the remains of the Roman town of Alcester, which happened to be located on Lord Hertford's estate at Ragley Hall, Warwickshire. The Court of Criminal Appeal reduced Lord Hertford's fine from £10,000 to £3,000. Although it is purely a matter of speculation, it may be conjectured that if Kennedy J's former pupil Rupert Jackson (a devotee of all things Roman in Britain) had been a member of the court, the fine may well have been increased substantially.

[5] Jackson & Powell, *Professional Negligence* (London, Sweet & Maxwell, 1982). *Jackson & Powell* is discussed further below.

[6] There are surviving letters to the editor of *The Spectator*, from 1969, on the subject of Cambridge University colleges becoming co-educational. The 21-year-old Rupert Jackson was in favour of co-educational colleges, whereas other *Spectator* correspondents were dead against the idea: see www.archive.spectator.co.uk.

[7] R Jackson, 'Can Clubs Discriminate?' (1973) 36 *Modern Law Review* 529.

[8] *Charter v Race Relations Board* [1973] AC 868.

[9] The Race Relations Act was later amended to overcome this lacuna in the legislation: see *Watt v Ahsan* [2008] 1 AC 696 at 705 [20]–[21], per Lord Hoffmann.

[10] '[A] local Conservative or working men's club should not be permitted to discriminate blatantly against coloured persons who seek to join': (1973) 36 *Modern Law Review* 529 at 531.

[11] 'Quis custodiet ipsos custodes?' or 'Who will watch the watchmen?': from the Roman poet Juvenal.

[12] T Gilby, 'Civilised Violence' (1973) 38 *Quis Custodiet* 25.

Friar Gilby's pamphlet concluded in slightly withering terms: 'The moral force of law and the legitimacy of revolution is a vast subject, upon which Mr Gilby could only touch briefly at the end of his article. One hopes he will develop it in the future'.

Two years later in the *Modern Law Review* appeared a book review of 'Who becomes delinquent?',[13] a study based on data compiled over 10 years of 411 delinquent children from a working class area of London. As noted in the book review, the data gathered revealed that '[t]he hard core juvenile recidivists usually come from certainly clearly recognisable home situations.' The review also recommended that '[o]ur community, it is suggested, should devote substantially more of its resources' to intervening to ensure that children in those recognisable situations were not led down some inexorable path to perdition.

IV. Development at the Bar

The early years of Rupert Jackson's career at the bar were typical for the time. His practice was a general one, involving criminal cases in the Magistrates' Courts and Crown Courts, civil and family cases in the County Courts, employment cases before industrial tribunals (now called Employment Tribunals), periodic forays into the High Court, some education cases before various tribunals, and occasional ventures into the Court of Appeal.

Early reported cases of his included a solicitors' disciplinary case[14] and a social security appeal,[15] both of which saw him appear before Lord Denning MR in his final year as a judge. A variety of other cases ensued, including a prosecution concerning an unlicensed vehicle,[16] and a case about a fire at a fish-and-chip shop.[17]

However, it was only natural that Rupert Jackson's practice would develop in his nascent area of specialisation – professional negligence. Not only did his practice grow rapidly, but he quickly became the leader at the professional negligence bar, taking silk in 1987. The development of a professional negligence practice stemmed from early and consistent briefs from firms of solicitors who were usually defending such claims, often on behalf of insurers. His practice, and that of his chambers, flourished. This growth and success saw both Rupert Jackson and John Powell become heads of chambers in the 1990s, and the chambers grew and moved to their present location at 4 New Square in Lincoln's Inn.

Inevitably, the work of a sought-after barrister leaves an indelible record in the judgments of the courts in which he or she has appeared. Even a brief survey of the case law from the 1980s and 1990s in the construction or professional negligence

---

[13] DJ West and DP Farrington, *Who Becomes Delinquent?* (Heinemann, 1973), reviewed at (1975) 38 *Modern Law Review* 108.
[14] *R&T Thew Ltd v Reeves (No 2)* [1982] QB 1283 (CA).
[15] *Crewe v Anderson* [1982] 1 WLR 1209.
[16] *Guyll v Bright* (1987) 84 Cr App R 260.
[17] *Salmon v Seafarer Restaurants Ltd* [1983] 1 WLR 1264 (Woolf J).

fields will turn up Rupert Jackson's name with regularity. Some of the notable cases in which he appeared as counsel during this period include the following:

- *Northern Regional Health Authority v Derek Crouch Construction Co Ltd*,[18] a controversial Court of Appeal decision on the reviewability of architects' certificates;[19]

- *London Borough of Merton v Leach*,[20] a landmark case on the duties of contract administrators in carrying out their functions under construction and engineering contracts;

- *Eagle Star Insurance Company Ltd v National Westminster Finance Australia Ltd*,[21] being one of the last Privy Council appeals from Australia, concerning a valuable stallion named 'Asian Beau' that died after bouts of colic;

- *Anglian Water Authority v RDL Contracting Ltd*,[22] which considered the ability of a contract administrator to delegate its functions;

- *Mercers v New Hampshire Insurance Co Ltd*,[23] on the interpretation and operation of an advance payment guarantee;

- *Clark Boyce v Mouat*,[24] a New Zealand appeal to the Privy Council concerning conflicts of interest affecting solicitors in that country;

- *Machin v Adams*,[25] on whether an architect assumed responsibility in negligence to a third party who relied upon the architect's 'letter of comfort' that works had been completed satisfactorily;

- *Stanton v Callaghan*,[26] on the immunity from suit of expert witnesses;[27] and

- *Arthur JS Hall & Co v Simons*,[28] in the Court of Appeal, on the immunity from suit of advocates.

As if these and other cases were not sufficient to occupy his waking hours, Rupert Jackson added to his workload considerably through wading into the world of legal publications.

---

[18] *Northern Regional Health Authority v Derek Crouch Construction Co Ltd* [1984] 1 QB 644.

[19] Fourteen years later, and after much academic discussion concerning the correctness of *Crouch* and subsequent cases which followed it (see, eg, Duncan Wallace, 'Construction Contracts: The Architect, the Arbitrator and the Courts' (1986) 2 *Construction Law Journal* 13), the case was overruled by the House of Lords in *Beaufort Developments (NI) Ltd v Gilbert-Ash NI Ltd* [1999] 1 AC 266.

[20] *London Borough of Merton v Leach* (1985) 32 BLR 51 [Vinelott J].

[21] *Eagle Star Insurance Company Ltd v National Westminster Finance Australia Ltd* [1985] UKPC 2. The very last Privy Council appeal from Australia came two years later, in *Austin v Keele* (1987) 10 NSWLR 283.

[22] *Anglian Water Authority v RDL Contracting Ltd* (1988) 43 BLR 98 [OR, HHJ Fox-Andrews QC].

[23] *Mercers v New Hampshire Insurance Co Ltd* (1992) 60 BLR 26 (CA). This case is discussed by Mr Wilmot-Smith QC in Chapter 17 of this volume.

[24] *Clark Boyce v Mouat* [1994] 1 AC 428.

[25] *Machin v Adams* (1997) 84 BLR 83 (CA).

[26] *Stanton v Callaghan* [2000] 1 QB 75 (CA).

[27] Although the position of English law on the immunity of expert witnesses was later refined in *Jones v Kaney* [2011] 2 AC 398.

[28] *Arthur JS Hall & Co v Simons* [1998] EWCA Civ 1943. By the time the matter reached the House of Lords ([2002] 1 AC 615), Rupert Jackson QC had been appointed to the High Court bench. His replacement in the House of Lords was Jonathan Sumption QC, now Lord Sumption JSC.

V. *Jackson & Powell*

Much of the early and rapid success that Rupert Jackson found at the bar arose from the publication, in 1982, of *Professional Negligence*, co-authored with his friend John Powell.

The rationale for such a book was self-evident to its authors and indeed to the community of English lawyers: there was a need for such a book. Much had been written in other countries, especially the United States,[29] on the subject-matter, but there was no contemporary English text that addressed this evolving and burgeoning area of law. This was not to say that professional negligence was new territory in English law. Almost 30 years before *Professional Negligence* was first published, there had been a book of the same title authored by JP Eddy QC,[30] but this was long out of print, and of limited use, given that it pre-dated the landmark case of *Hedley Byrne & Co Ltd v Heller & Partners Ltd*,[31] let alone subsequent authorities. No doubt Mr Eddy QC's monograph served its purpose in the 1950s, but by the 1980s any attempts to rely upon it would have been as fruitful as using a 1950s road map of Buckinghamshire to navigate the grid roads of Milton Keynes.

Rupert Jackson and John Powell's monograph quickly cornered the professional negligence market, and went into subsequent editions to meet the ongoing demand for updated texts in this important area. '*Jackson & Powell*', as it is universally known, was (and is) *the* go-to text on professional negligence. Today, some 36 years after it was first published, *Jackson & Powell* is in its eighth edition, published in 2016. Its title has changed from 'Professional Negligence' to 'Professional Liability', as a subtle but important shift of emphasis to recognise that, for professional persons, liability in their business activities does not arise purely in tort, but also under contract, statute and occasionally for unjust enrichment. And whereas the first edition of the book consisted of 344 pages of text, prepared by its industrious authors alone, the lucubratory eighth edition expands to 1,465 pages, has two general editors[32] and 26 editors, with Lord Justice Jackson himself contributing as a 'consultant editor'.[33] The chapter on 'construction professionals' alone (chapter 9) runs to 169 pages.

This exponential growth of the text in the book and the number of contributors to it reflects at least two things. First, it evidences the rapid growth of professional negligence as a specialist area of law since 1982. Indeed, most of the cases referred

---

[29] Eg Roady and Andersen (eds), *Professional Negligence* (Vanderbilt University Press, 1960); *Restatement (Second) of Torts* § 299A (1965).

[30] Eddy, *Professional Negligence* (Stevens & Sons, 1955) – with a foreword written by the Rt Hon Sir Alfred Denning, as he then was.

[31] *Hedley Byrne & Co Ltd v Heller & Partners Ltd* [1964] AC 465 (HL(E)).

[32] John Powell QC and Roger Stewart QC, although John Powell QC has now retired from legal practice.

[33] The first two editions of *Jackson & Powell* were written by the eponymous authors themselves. Subsequent editions were opened up to members of their chambers, and thus the work became a 'chambers book'.

to in the eighth edition of *Jackson & Powell* post-date the publication of the first edition of the book. Secondly, and consequently, we may conclude that *Jackson & Powell* succeeded not only because of a gap in the market for such a book in the 1980s, but because professional negligence was an area of law that was on the cusp of enormous development. *Jackson & Powell* was therefore published in the right place, at the right time.

VI. The Woolf Review

As yet a further extra-curricular activity, Rupert Jackson QC acted as one of Lord Woolf's 'assessors' in the 'Official Referees' Working Group' as part of his Lordship's review of the legal system in England and Wales, culminating in the report *Access to Justice – Final Report* (1996). The Woolf review ultimately led to the enactment of the Civil Procedure Rules (1998), which inter alia sought to simplify the civil litigation system, including by modernising rules of court that had been in place since the Judicature Act reforms of the 1870s. For Official Referees' Business, as it was then known, the specific recommendations were limited and modest, and indeed one of Lord Woolf's recommendations was that the pre-action protocol that was pioneered before the Official Referees be rolled-out to other parts of the civil litigation system.[34]

Although the Woolf Review did produce radical and much-needed changes to the civil litigation system, it could not guard against all future eventualities that might necessitate a further review (or reviews) of the system. As mentioned below, more than a decade later Lord Justice Jackson himself would be called upon to undertake an exercise of a similar magnitude to that of Lord Woolf, in relation to troubling issues arising from the cost of civil litigation.

VII. Judicial Career

Rupert Jackson QC was appointed to the High Court bench in January 1999, leaving many satisfied solicitor clients searching for substitute leading counsel. As was reported at the time 'A chorus of regrets were expressed over the departure of Rupert Jackson QC'.[35] The bar's loss was therefore the bench's gain.

The newly-appointed Mr Justice Jackson was assigned to the Administrative Court of the Queen's Bench Division of the High Court. The spectrum of cases encountered by Jackson J, both in the QBD and in the Court of Appeal (Criminal Division), was both varied and interesting. Over a period of five years,

---

[34] Lord Woolf's recommendation 273 was: 'An extended civil litigation protocol should be developed for use across the entire civil justice system, building on the protocol developed by the Official Referees' Solicitors' Association [now the Technology and Construction Solicitors Association]'.

[35] *The Lawyer*, 15 March 1999 (www.thelawyer.com).

Jackson J sat in cases involving such diverse matters as Arsenal ticket touts,[36] the conviction of a burglar on the basis of an ear-print he left at the crime scene,[37] the sentencing of Liverpool pickpockets,[38] a claim by Lady Archer against her former secretary for breach of confidence,[39] the right of property developer Nicholas van Hoogstraten to be visited in Belmarsh Prison by his putative Italian counsel,[40] whether the inquiry into the murders committed by Dr Harold Shipman would be held in public,[41] and Moors murderer Ian Brady's claimed 'right to die'.[42] As an *outremer* excursion during this period, Sir Rupert Jackson also found himself sitting as an ad hoc judge of the European Court of Human Rights in a poll-tax case.[43]

Attention grabbing as these cases may be, however, it must also be recognised that the more usual type of case was a grinding encounter that would presumably make one despair at the state of society, if not the human condition itself. That is, cases involving rape and other sexual offences, child abuse and paedophilia, burglary, robbery, arson, fraud, drugs, murder, assault, dangerous driving – all part of the diet of a High Court judge in his position. But after a period of five years as a judge in the Administrative Court, Jackson J's career took a different direction.

A. The Technology and Construction Court

Mr Justice Jackson became the judge in charge of the Technology and Construction Court (TCC) in 2004. At the time, the TCC suffered from certain reputational and similar issues, arising from the individual and collective experiences of users of the court. The extent of the disquiet amongst the construction law community was significant, in that prominent members of the community openly expressed views that:

- 'the perception amongst users had been that the TCC had lost its way';

---

[36] *R (on the application of Brown) v Inner London Crown Court* [2003] EWHC 3194 (Admin).

[37] *R v Kempster* [2003] EWCA Crim 3555.

[38] *R v McGee* [2003] EWCA Crim 2627.

[39] *Archer v Williams* [2003] EWHC 1670 (QB). 'Mary Archer tells court of "betrayal" over her face lift' – the headline in *The Independent* on 30 June 2003.

[40] *R (van Hoogstraten) v The Governor of HMP Belmarsh* [2002] EWHC 2015 (Admin). Mr van Hoogstraten's counsel of choice was Mr Giovanni di Stefano, who described himself as a 'Professione Avvocato'. The Wikipedia entry for Mr di Stefano states: 'Di Stefano used the Italian title "avvocato" ("advocate", analogous to an English lawyer) on his business card, and misled clients and the courts into believing that he was a qualified lawyer. On 27 March 2013 he was convicted on 25 charges including deception, fraud and money laundering between 2001 and 2011 by a jury at Southwark Crown Court in London. During the trial he had told the court of his links to Robert Mugabe, Osama bin Laden, Saddam Hussein (whom he described as a "nice guy") and his "friendship" with the daughter of Slobodan Milosevic'.

[41] *R v Secretary of State for Health, ex parte Associated Newspapers* [2001] 1 WLR 292.

[42] 'Brady: My fight goes on', 9 June 2001: www.news.bbc.co.uk/2/hi/uk_news/1380047.stm. Brady died in 2017.

[43] *Perks v United Kingdom* (ECtHR, Applications nos 25277/94, 25279/94, 25280/94, 25285/94, 28048/95, 28192/95 and 28456/95, judgment delivered 12 October 1999).

- 'judgments had taken too long to be handed down'; and
- 'the TCC appeared to be quiet, yet it was not always accessible.'[44]

This unsatisfactory state of affairs is brought out in Chapter two of this *Festschrift* by Lord Justice Coulson, who recounts in unalloyed terms that 'It is impossible to convey to younger lawyers just how low the reputation of the TCC had sunk when Rupert became the Judge in Charge in the summer of 2004'.[45]

Indeed, there was even discussion at the time about the possibility of *closing the TCC*, and merging its work into that of other parts of the High Court. In one sense this would have been the path of least resistance, and eminently feasible to implement. But it was through the persistent lobbying of Jackson J, supported by representatives of the construction bar and construction solicitors, that the TCC was salvaged from this existential crisis, and subsequently its fortunes were turned around. How was this done?

Principally, the measures which restored court users' faith in the TCC were the fact that they now had a judge-in-charge of the court who led by example, combined with the phasing out of Senior Circuit Judges, and the introduction of High Court judges, as permanent judges of the TCC in London.[46] The changes made by Mr Justice Jackson to the TCC also included revamping the TCC Guide,[47] a modest but emblematic recognition that court users would benefit from having an up-to-date, practical guide to the workings of TCC business, and that the court was very much considering their interests.

---

[44] 'Does the TCC meet the needs of the construction industry?', a note (prepared by Hamish Lal) of a panel discussion at a meeting of the Society of Construction Law in London on 1 November 2005 to discuss the Technology and Construction Court Guide (the panel consisting of HHJ Coulson QC (as he then was), Paul Darling QC, Henry Sherman and Christopher Miers) (see: www.scl.org.uk).

[45] The damage to the TCC's reputation was also perceived within senior circles of the judiciary. See, by way of illustration, *Co-operative Group (CWS) Ltd v International Computers Ltd* [2003] EWCA Civ 1955, an appeal from a TCC judge, where the Court of Appeal held (at [84]–[88]): 'we have concluded, much to our regret, that we have no alternative but to recognise that the judge has erred so fundamentally in his approach to this trial as to have lost, or at least given the appearance of losing, his ability to try CWS' claim with an objective judicial mind ... In the result the trial was unfair ... what is so troubling is that the judge has made findings of bad faith and false evidence, against CWS and its principal witness, Mr Brydon, and against Mr Melmoth who was not even a witness when no bad faith had been pleaded or suggested ... Finally, we have not said anything about the wounding and sarcastic comments which the judge made about Mr Mawrey and CWS' other legal advisors. We cannot help feeling that these comments were informed by the same unfair view which the judge took of CWS' case. If the allegation of bad faith had been pleaded and put in issue during the hearing, counsel and solicitors would have been able to address it and would have been open to criticism if they had not done so. As it was we think that the judge's comments about them were unfair'. The legal press at the time was no less excoriating of the judge in question 'After [the judge's] attack on Co-op, who's judging the judges?', *The Lawyer*, 2 February 2004 (www.thelawyer.com).

[46] See Lord Justice Coulson's Chapter two for a further account of this. Lord Justice Coulson was himself a judge in charge of the TCC, and replaced Lord Justice Jackson in the Court of Appeal upon his retirement.

[47] There was previously a TCC Guide, but it was somewhat out of date. The 2nd edition of the TCC Guide was prepared as a project under the guidance of Mr Justice Jackson, and was published on 3 October 2005.

Mr Justice Jackson stepped down as judge in charge of the TCC on 31 August 2007, and was succeeded by Mr Justice Ramsey. In a period of three years, Mr Justice Jackson had managed to reverse the negative image of the TCC. By the time he left it the TCC had become a court which litigants and their legal advisers were confident would deliver sound and efficient justice. It may be difficult to find any other modern parallel to such a profound transformation of a failing court in such a short period of time.

B. Judgment Structure, Style and Delivery

Justice Benjamin Cardozo wrote that: 'For quotable good things, for pregnant aphorisms, for touchstones of ready application, the opinions of the English judges are a mine of instruction and a treasury of joy'.[48]

Judgments are not required to adopt any particular structure, or indeed any structure at all. Nevertheless, throughout his judicial career an identifiable formula, of simplicity and elegance, has been deployed in Lord Justice Jackson's judgments.[49] Each judgment commences by identifying the number of parts constituting the judgment, and the particular matter covered by each part. Part 1 will be the introduction, identifying the parties and the general background to the matters before the court. Part 2 then sets out the relevant facts and the evidence. Subsequent Parts of the judgment are then created to address the issues arising, the relevant legal principles, the application of those principles to the facts, and a conclusion. The sub-title of this *Festschrift* – 'Drawing the Threads Together' – alludes to a concluding phrase (perhaps a 'catchphrase') that has been used by Lord Justice Jackson in almost 200 judgments,[50] ie 'Let me now draw the threads together'.

For practitioners and even judges, perhaps the greatest utility of these judgments has been in their distillation of the relevant propositions of law, so that they can then be applied subsequently without the need to rehearse or review earlier judgments on the particular subject-matter. As Cardozo noted, judges are 'expounding a science',[51] and as with the scientist the judge needs to be clear – so that others may be clear – on the principles which operate in the self-defining universe of the law. Judges' gnomic utterances or musings may have a certain value as esoteric miscellany, but in the cold, practical world of the law, above all else the espousal of clear, readily-applicable principles is essential.

One of the other defining features of Lord Justice Jackson's judgments has been the speed at which they were handed down. With the exception of the

---

[48] Cardozo, 'Law and Literature' (1939) 48 *Yale Law Journal* 489 at 498.

[49] This is also reflected upon by Mr Wilmot-Smith QC in Chapter 17 of this volume.

[50] The earliest of which was *R v Bristol City Council, ex parte DL Barrett & Sons* [2001] 3 LGLR 11 at [64], and the last was *Amey Birmingham Highways Ltd v Birmingham City Council* [2018] EWCA Civ 264 at [73].

[51] Cardozo, 'Law and Literature' (1939) 48 *Yale Law Journal* 489 at 507.

Multiplex v Cleveland Bridge behemoth, mentioned below, all other judgments by Jackson J in the TCC were delivered immediately after the conclusion of the particular hearing.[52] This celerity had a profound effect, not only on the parties to the immediate litigation, who would obtain near-instant justice of the highest quality, as opposed to waiting weeks or even many months for their judgment. But this measure also served to restore and then enhance the reputation of the TCC itself, to raise the value of its stocks in the eyes of the principal users of the court, through knowing that justice would not be delayed (and therefore not denied).[53]

C. Wembley Stadium

Several of the chapters of this *Festschrift* focus upon construction cases decided by Mr Justice Jackson when in the TCC. However, probably the most notable case of all is not discussed, which may seem anomalous to some. The case is *Multiplex Construction (UK) Ltd v Cleveland Bridge UK Ltd*, which involved a dispute between the main contractor (Multiplex) for the construction of the new Wembley stadium, and its steelwork subcontractor (Cleveland Bridge). The litigation attracted considerable media interest, including from the mainstream media, largely because it involved the jewel in the crown of English football.[54]

The *Multiplex v Cleveland Bridge* litigation produced no fewer than seven judgments from Jackson J from 2006–2008.[55] Two of those judgments stand out. The first is a decision on 10 preliminary issues delivered in 2006, where the judgment

---

[52] It may be hard to find modern parallels for this rapid disposition of business. Indeed, perhaps the closest comparator is the great Victorian Master of the Rolls Sir George Jessel, of whom it was written: 'As a judge of first instance Jessel was a revelation to those accustomed to the proverbial slowness of the Chancery Courts and of the Master of the Rolls who preceded him. He disposed of the business before him with rapidity combined with correctness of judgment, and he not only had no arrears himself, but was frequently able to help other judges to clear their lists … In the Rolls Court he never reserved a judgment, not even in the Epping Forest case (*Commissioners of Sewers v. Glasse*, L.R. 19 Eq 134; *The Times*, 11th November 1874), in which the evidence and arguments lasted twenty-two days (150 witnesses being examined in court, while the documents went back to the days of King John), and in the Court of Appeal he did so only twice, and then in deference to the wishes of his colleagues': *Encyclopaedia Britannica*, 1911, vol 15, p 336.

[53] In Chapter 16 of this *Festschrift*, Mrs Justice Jefford DBE pays tribute to the speed at which Jackson J delivered judgment in the *Midland Expressway* litigation, in which Mrs Justice Jefford appeared as junior counsel. No doubt dozens of similar expressions of amazement at the speed of judgment delivery could be given by the parties and legal counsel in the cases before Jackson J in the TCC.

[54] Mainstream press articles at the time include 'Multiplex accused of trying to torpedo subcontractor' (*The Guardian*, 12 January 2006) and 'Wembley was delayed by the use of 'wrong concrete'' (*The Guardian*, 13 January 2006): www.theguardian.com. It is not known whether Mr Justice Jackson read these articles in *The Guardian*, or indeed whether he has ever read that newspaper.

[55] The first judgment in the Wembley saga was from HHJ Wilcox, in *Cleveland Bridge (UK) Ltd v Multiplex Constructions (UK) Ltd* [2005] EWHC 2102 (TCC), which actually involved an application by the Australian Broadcasting Corporation to be given access to the pleadings in the litigation. Multiplex Constructions UK Limited was a wholly-owned subsidiary of Multiplex Limited, which was listed on the Australian Stock Exchange. It may also be noted that the Wembley stadium project produced other TCC litigation involving Multiplex and other parties, including *Multiplex Constructions*

runs to 667 paragraphs.[56] Mr Justice Jackson concluded his judgment with the following propitious words:

> Both parties have had a measure of success on the preliminary issues. Neither party has won an outright victory. With the assistance of this court's decision on the ten prelimi-nary issues, it may now be possible for both parties to arrive at an overall settlement of their disputes, either through negotiation or else with the help of a mediator, who is unconnected with this court.[57]

Mr Justice Jackson's optimism went unrewarded, as the litigation rumbled onwards, concluding in a 2½ month trial in March–May 2008, following which he handed down his second stand-out judgment. For many lesser judges such a long trial may have necessitated judgment being delivered in, say, mid-2009 at the earliest – possibly even later. However, Mr Justice Jackson delivered his 1,693 paragraph judgment on 29 September 2008, a mere four months after the end of the trial.[58]

Although the *Multiplex v Cleveland Bridge* judgments involved the discussion and application of many points of construction law, the abiding reflection one may make from this hard-fought, disproportionate[59] litigation was the dexterous and diligent way in which it was managed by Jackson J.

The end of the Wembley litigation represented Jackson J's last outing as a TCC judge, before being elevated to the Court of Appeal in October 2008. However, upon appointment to the Court of Appeal the newly-minted Jackson LJ's path immediately took an unexpected detour.

VIII. Civil Litigation Costs Reviews

A. Review of Civil Litigation Costs (Late 2008–Early 2010)

No sooner had Sir Rupert Jackson been appointed to the Court of Appeal, when he was hurtled into the world of law reform. In 1996, he had assisted Lord Woolf with his review of civil litigation, which paved the way for the Civil Procedure Rules and associated reforms. Now, in late 2008, he (like Cincinnatus) was called from his plough to address troubling issues arising from the cost of litigation,

---

(UK) Ltd v Honeywell Control Systems Ltd (No 2) [2007] BLR 195 (discussed by Professor Jones in Chapter 19 of this volume).

[56] *Multiplex Constructions (UK) Ltd v Cleveland Bridge UK Ltd* [2006] EWHC 1341 (TCC) (appeal dismissed: [2007] EWCA Civ 443).

[57] *Multiplex Constructions (UK) Ltd v Cleveland Bridge UK Ltd* [2006] EWHC 1341 (TCC) at [666].

[58] *Multiplex Constructions (UK) Ltd v Cleveland Bridge UK Ltd (No 6)* [2008] EWHC 2220 (TCC). An appeal from this decision was subsequently made, and allowed in part: *Cleveland Bridge UK Ltd v Multiplex Constructions (UK) Ltd* [2010] EWCA Civ 139. The judgment of the Court of Appeal was given by Sir Anthony May P, who acknowledged Jackson J's 'monumental judgment' (at [8]).

[59] *Cleveland Bridge UK Ltd v Multiplex Constructions (UK) Ltd* [2010] EWCA Civ 139 at [8], per Sir Anthony May P.

which had emerged since the Woolf reforms, that were making certain types of litigation an unduly (if not outrageously) expensive exercise. The terms of reference given for Lord Justice Jackson's review of civil litigation costs were expressed in beguilingly simple terms, unrevealing of what really lay behind the costs review. Lord Justice Jackson was requested, within the period of one year (2009): 'To carry out an independent review of the rules and principles governing the costs of civil litigation and to make recommendations in order to promote access to justice at proportionate cost'.[60]

By late 2008 there was a perception that civil litigation was too expensive. But was this so in all cases? Or only in certain types of case? The open-ended scope of the costs review did not presuppose that one type of litigation was more expensive than another, or that certain measures would be needed to streamline the civil litigation system.

Nor was it contemplated that the costs review be conducted as some kind of desktop exercise. Instead, like the *legati* of William the Conqueror's Domesday survey of 1085–86, Lord Justice Jackson was to go out into the land[61] to see what litigation was really like, how much it was costing, and to work out what the cost drivers were, and how they could be reined in if they were leading to disproportionate costs. This he duly did.[62]

Despite the broad remit of enquiry, it became plain that a central focus for the costs review would be conditional fee agreements (CFAs) which, when combined with their complementary after-the-event insurance (ATE) insurance, could lead to the legal costs payable by a defendant becoming wholly disproportionate to the amount at stake in the litigation. The background story to the emergence of CFAs as a form of litigation funding was the government eradicating legal aid for civil cases. To fill the gaping hole in funding for civil litigation for people of limited means, the laws concerning the charging and recovery of costs and disbursements in civil litigation were changed. Under the revised system, solicitors would be entitled to represent claimants on a contingent basis, such as 'no win, no fee'. If the case failed, the solicitor would be unpaid; but if the case succeeded, the claimant would be entitled to recover his solicitor's 'usual' fee, plus a success fee on top of up to 100 per cent of the usual fee.

As part of the funding arrangement, the solicitor would arrange for ATE insurance to be taken out, to cover the possibility that the claim would fail, and the claimant being ordered to pay the defendant's costs. For a claimant of limited means, the possibility of being ordered to pay the defendant's costs could ground

---

[60] Press release from Sir Anthony Clarke MR (as he then was), 3 November 2008. Lord Clarke (as he now is) discusses the background to the costs review in Chapter 3 of this volume.

[61] And indeed into other lands – Lord Justice Jackson visited judges, practitioners and academics in France, Germany, Australia, New Zealand, the United States and Canada to gain a better understanding of civil litigation costs in those jurisdictions.

[62] See Lord Justice Jackson, *Review of Civil Litigation Costs: Preliminary Report* (TSO, May 2009), Vol 1, Chapter 10, which sets out the various meetings around England and Wales attended by Lord Justice Jackson in the early part of 2009, as well as the views of stakeholders and court users.

an application by the defendant that the claimant provide security for costs – which many claimants would simply be unable to do, thus stopping the claim from continuing. ATE insurance therefore operated as a form of security for costs.

The issue which was created by these arrangements was that they had the potential to lead to unsuccessful defendants regularly being required to pay out significant sums *as legal costs* to claimants' solicitors in what were often 'routine' cases, for personal injuries, and the like. A claimant's solicitor could take on a meritorious claim from a claimant of slender means, on a 'no win, no fee' basis, and when the claim succeeded the unsuccessful defendant (often, in effect, an insurer) would be required to pay not only the claimant's solicitor's 'regular' or 'usual' legal costs, but also (i) the solicitor's 'success fee' (which would often be 100 per cent of the solicitor's 'regular' costs); plus (ii) the ATE premium for the claimant's claim, which could also be in a sum approaching the amount of the claimant's solicitor's legal fees, or something of that order. In simple terms, instead of the unsuccessful defendant being required to pay '£X' (ie the claimant's solicitor's 'regular' fee), it could be '£3X'. This kind of outcome was perverse,[63] yet it was ensuing on a daily basis, usually in little-noticed smaller cases in the County Courts, which nevertheless, like dark matter in the universe, make up the vast bulk of civil litigation in England and Wales.

I had the good fortune to be one of Lord Justice Jackson's assistants for the costs review, both for the preparation of the *Preliminary Report* and then the *Final Report*. I came to see first-hand the great work ethic and diligence he brought to his Herculean labours. Plaudits have rightly been bestowed for his industriousness during the 2009 costs review.[64] If I can add one point to these deserved accolades, it would be to reflect on his politeness, patience and good nature in the face of what were often heated and personal criticisms of himself, seemingly driven by those who saw their vested commercial interests threatened by the costs review.[65]

---

[63] As Professor Zuckerman noted shortly after the publication of Lord Justice Jackson's *Preliminary Report*, 'the recoverability of hourly fees plus a success fee of up to 100 per cent of the hourly fees, plus ATE premiums, creates perverse economic incentives and unacceptable distortions which no other country in the world has ever been foolish enough to introduce, let alone tolerate': Zuckerman, 'Lord Justice Jackson's Review of Civil Litigation Costs – Preliminary Report (2009)' (2009) 28 *Civil Justice Quarterly* 435 at 447.

[64] For example, as Lord Clarke writes in Chapter 3 of this *Festschrift*, the costs review 'was a massive piece of work, which few, if any, of Rupert's colleagues could have achieved. I certainly could not'.

[65] See also Jackson, 'Was it all worth it?' (a lecture to the Cambridge Law Faculty, 5 March 2018, www.judiciary.gov.uk) paragraph 1.4. Of course, Lord Justice Jackson is not unique amongst members of the senior judiciary (including retired members) for such criticisms. In recent times, there have been at least two such prominent attacks on judges. The first is in the context of the Brexit litigation before the UK courts in 2016–17: *R (Miller) v Secretary of State for Exiting the European Union* [2016] EWHC 2768 (Admin) [Divisional Court] and then [2017] UKSC 5. Following the handing down of the judgment of the Divisional Court (constituted by Lord Thomas of Cwmgiedd CJ, Sir Terence Etherton and Sales LJ), *The Daily Mail* reported the story on 3 November 2016 with the headline: 'Enemies of the people: Fury over "out of touch" judges who have "declared war on democracy" by defying 17.4m Brexit voters and who could trigger constitutional crisis' (www.dailymail.co.uk). A second example concerns Sir Martin Moore-Bick, a former Court of Appeal judge, who at the time of writing is chairing an inquiry into the disastrous fire at Grenfell Tower, London, on 14 June 2017. Sir Martin spoke at a press conference

B. The Final Report and Law Reform

The recommendations made by Lord Justice Jackson in his *Final Report* were published in January 2010.[66] Principal among these was the suggestion that 'success fees and ATE insurance premiums should cease to be recoverable'.[67] This was hardly a surprising recommendation, given that the existing requirement for an unsuccessful defendant to pay a successful claimant's lawyer's success fee, as well as the claimant's ATE insurance premium, was postulated at the outset of the costs review as being the main driver of high legal costs.

Although the review was published in January 2010, the UK government's reaction to the *Final Report* was not immediate. Perhaps this was to be expected, given the breadth and scale of the Jackson review, and the number and detail of the recommendations made by Lord Justice Jackson. However, in March 2011 the government made its position clear, namely that:

> the Government believes that the right way forward is to abolish the recoverability of CFA success fees and ATE insurance premiums. In implementing the primary recommendations of Sir Rupert's report set out in the consultation paper, the Government agrees that these proposals should be taken forward as a package, and that the connected constituent parts should be implemented together.[68]

After a further period of reflection and gestation by the government, this primary recommendation was implemented through the medium of Part 2 of the Legal Aid, Sentencing and Punishment of Offenders Act 2012, the relevant provisions of which took effect on April Fool's Day, 2013.

Sir Antony Edwards-Stuart in Chapter four of this *Festschrift* discusses the Jackson reforms and their impact on TCC litigation. It is fair to say that the Jackson reforms concerning TCC litigation were focused on making subtle, incremental improvements to what was generally an effective system in the TCC – effective, that is, in dispensing justice in TCC cases in a proportionate timeframe and cost for the issues in the case.

By contrast, the major reforms that took effect in 2013 involved dismantling the previous system of permitting success fees and ATE insurance premiums to be recoverable. This was a profound change to the civil litigation system, particularly

---

in July 2017 to outline the nature and scope of his inquiry. The headline from *The Telegraph* summarises the reception he faced: 'Grenfell Tower inquiry chairman heckled as he is met with angry response from residents' (7 July 2017).

[66] Jackson, *Review of Civil Litigation Costs: Final Report* (TSO, December 2009). Years later, Lord Justice Jackson wrote a student text, describing the background to the costs review, and the rationale for the recommendations made in his *Final Report*: Jackson, *The Reform of Civil Litigation* (London, Sweet & Maxwell, 2016). A second edition of this book was published in 2018, co-authored by Stephen Clark.

[67] Jackson, *Review of Civil Litigation Costs: Final Report* (TSO, December 2009) p xvi, para 2.2.

[68] 'Reforming Civil Litigation Funding and Costs in England and Wales – Implementation of Lord Justice Jackson's Recommendations – The Government Response' (Ministry of Justice, Cm 8041, March 2011) (www.gov.uk).

for those types of litigation in which CFAs and ATE insurance were widely used.[69] The pyroclastic flows of these reforms had a real impact, but principally upon the business models of those who had conducted claimant-led litigation on a 'no win, no fee' basis, or similar. With the passing of some five years since these major aspects of the Jackson reforms took effect, it may be observed that access to justice has not been impeded, as was predicted by some in 2009 during the Jackson review. Instead, claimants with legitimate claims may still bring those claims to court. Claimants with legitimate claims will usually find a lawyer to take on their case.[70] And, in the event of the claim succeeding, the unsuccessful defendant is required to pay the claimant's reasonable and proportionate costs; not some unreasonable or perverse amount.

We may conclude that in this important respect alone, the Jackson reforms have been a success.[71] But the business of law reform, like the law itself, never reaches a stasis, so it was perhaps inevitable that, during his tenure as a Court of Appeal judge, further costs issues would arise for consideration.

One area in particular which was ripe for review was that of the use of fixed costs in civil litigation. Fixed costs regimes are found in many countries, including those of Continental Europe. There are at least two attractive aspects to utilising a fixed-costs regime in civil litigation. First, it gives litigating parties certainty as to the measure of their financial exposure in the event of being unsuccessful in the litigation, and hence being ordered to pay the successful party's costs. Secondly, the fixing of recoverable costs to a pre-defined amount ensures that a successful party is not able to foist upon the unsuccessful party the burden of having to pay an uncapped, and potentially disproportionate, amount. Put simply, legal costs as between litigating parties can never become disproportionate because they are fixed to a proportionate figure.

In the *Final Report*, Lord Justice Jackson recommended that costs be fixed for relatively low-value personal injuries litigation in the fast track, where the sum claimed is £25,000 or less.[72] The question, left open in the *Final Report* for future consideration, was whether fixed costs should be applied in a broader range of litigation.[73] Lord Justice Jackson returned to that question many years later.

C. The 2017 Costs Review

In the first half of 2017, Lord Justice Jackson undertook a further costs review, which essentially built on the 2009 costs review in relation to fixed costs.

---

[69] Being mainly personal injuries litigation, road traffic cases and similar matters. CFA agreements were only used to a limited extent in TCC litigation, so the impact of this aspect of the Jackson reforms was not widely felt in TCC cases.

[70] Cf Jackson, *Review of Civil Litigation Costs: Final Report* (TSO, December 2009) p 42, para 2.8.

[71] Cf Jackson, 'Was it all worth it?' (a lecture to the Cambridge Law Faculty, 5 March 2018, www.judiciary.gov.uk) para 1.5.

[72] Jackson, *Review of Civil Litigation Costs: Final Report* (TSO, December 2009) p xviii, para 2.9.

[73] Jackson, *Review of Civil Litigation Costs: Final Report* (TSO, December 2009) p 173, para 4.1.

The terms of reference for the 2017 costs review were relevantly: 'To develop proposals for extending the present civil fixed recoverable costs regime in England and Wales so as to make the costs of going to court more certain, transparent and proportionate for litigants'.[74] By contrast with the 2009 costs review, the 2017 review – although a substantial undertaking – had a narrower focus than the review of some eight years previous.

Lord Justice Jackson issued his *Supplemental Report* in July 2017, recommending that the regime for fixed recoverable costs be extended 'across those parts of the fast track where costs are still at large and across the lower regions of the multi-track'.[75] As matters currently stand, the recommendations made in the *Supplemental Report* have not been responded to by the UK government in any formal way. Nevertheless, as with the *Final Report* published in 2010, the ruminations of government may not yield any decision, let alone any reforming statute, for a little while.[76]

It would be easy to develop the impression, based purely upon his prodigious output (reports, articles and lectures) in the field, that Lord Justice Jackson's working life as a judge has been consumed by tackling the issues of the day in relation to civil litigation costs. Such an impression would be understandable, but ultimately wrong. Lord Justice Jackson's career on the bench has been devoted primarily to the serious business of hearing and deciding cases. This *Festschrift* cannot, and therefore does not, attempt to give an overview of the full nature of the cases coming before Lord Justice Jackson. Instead, the focus is upon an area of law with which he is closely associated, namely construction law.

IX. The Development of Construction Law

A. Introduction

The influence that Lord Justice Jackson has had on the development of construction law in a judicial capacity divides into three periods.

The first period was during his time as a Recorder, ie before his appointment to the High Court bench. The role of a Recorder is an occasional one, which typically involves a barrister or solicitor sitting as a judge as an interlude of sorts from his or her private practice. Rupert Jackson QC sat as a Recorder over a number of years, and two judgments decided in his capacity as a Recorder are discussed in Chapters nine and twelve respectively.

---

[74] From the terms of reference issued by the Lord Chief Justice and the Master of the Rolls on 11 November 2016.

[75] Jackson, *Review of Civil Litigation Costs: Supplemental Report, Fixed Recoverable Costs* (TSO, July 2017) p 12, para 1.8.

[76] See also Jackson, 'Was it all worth it?' (a lecture to the Cambridge Law Faculty, 5 March 2018, www.judiciary.gov.uk) paras 3.22–3.23.

The second period is from 2004–07, when Jackson J was the judge in charge of the TCC. Aside from the revolutionary change to the structure and administration of the TCC that Jackson J brought about, his judgments whilst judge in charge also had a notable impact in several areas of construction law, including in shaping the nascent jurisprudence concerning the application of Part II of the Housing Grants, Construction and Regeneration Act 1996.

The third period is from 2010 until his retirement from the bench in 2018, when he was for a period the only Court of Appeal judge with a background in construction law. Deliberately and inevitably, the major appeals from the TCC would come to a Court of Appeal constituted by Lord Justice Jackson and two other judges, with Lord Justice Jackson usually delivering the leading judgment of the court.

Chapters five to twenty of this *Festschrift* consider the more significant cases of Lord Justice Jackson across these three periods of time. When viewed in isolation, each case is notable, or perhaps of profound importance, in its own way. When grouped together, the cases display the evolutionary changes across the spectrum of construction law, spanning a period of almost three decades. From this, and from the details of the chapters discussed below, we can see the scale and importance of the impact Lord Justice Jackson has had on the development of construction law.

B. Construction Adjudication

In Chapter five, Adrian Williamson QC considers two principal decisions, separated by a decade, being *Quietfield Ltd v Vascroft Contractors Ltd*[77] and *Harding v Paice*.[78] The title of Mr Williamson QC's chapter 'A Second Bite', refers to adjudications brought under Part II of the Housing Grants, Construction and Regeneration Act 1996 which either seek to re-argue an issue that was decided in a previous adjudication (as was the case in *Quietfield*), or which seek to challenge an amount that is deemed under the 1996 Act (as amended) to have become due to a contractor because a valid 'pay less' notice was not issued against the contractor's claim. As established through this jurisprudence, the legislative scheme of the 1996 Act contemplates adjudication being conducted as a fast-track form of dispute resolution, following which money may be paid pursuant to an adjudicator's decision. The losing (and paying) party will, however, have an opportunity to claw its money back (and have a 'second bite'), but the forum for seeking to do so is not usually adjudication – it will be a *final* form of dispute resolution, such as TCC litigation, or arbitration.

---

[77] *Quietfield Ltd v Vascroft Contractors Ltd* [2006] EWHC 174 (TCC) (Jackson J) and then [2007] BLR 67 (CA).
[78] *Harding v Paice* [2016] 1 WLR 4068.

The issue, as Mr Williamson QC elucidates, is perhaps more nuanced insofar as payment obligations under the amended 1996 Act are concerned. Under the amended legislation, giving valid payment notices is paramount, and an employer's failure to give a 'pay less' notice against a contractor's payment notice leads to the employer being obliged to pay the full amount claimed by the contractor, whether or not the full amount claimed represents the sum to which the contractor is ultimately entitled. *Harding v Paice*, in which Jackson LJ gave the leading judgment, establishes that an employer may use the vehicle of adjudication to have a 'second bite' if it failed to give a 'pay less' notice, *at least insofar as final account disputes are concerned*. The unresolved issue from this case was whether adjudication may be used by a payer to redress the fact that it did not give a 'pay less' notice against a contractor's *interim* payment claim. Subsequent authority, however, suggests that adjudication can be so used.[79]

Statutory adjudication is further considered in Chapter six by Steven Walker QC, who examines broader aspects of Lord Justice Jackson's contributions to the law concerning statutory adjudication during its infant years. The title of Mr Walker QC's chapter – 'Of Special Character' – comes from *Speymill Contracts Ltd v Baskind*,[80] where Jackson LJ pithily summarised the position the law had reached regarding the status of adjudicators' decisions:

> In a series of decisions over the last twelve years both the Technology and Construction Court and this court have emphasised the special character of adjudicators' decisions and the policy considerations which underlie section 108 of the 1996 Act. In essence, the adjudicator's decision provides an interim resolution of the referred dispute. If both parties are content with that interim resolution, they can agree to treat it as final. If any of the parties are discontented, they can litigate or arbitrate, in order to achieve the correct determination of the matters in issue.[81]

Once it is understood that this is the essence of the regime for statutory adjudication, the approach taken by the courts to challenges, whether direct or collateral, to the adjudication process becomes broadly predictable. Adjudication is not designed to produce the 'correct determination of the matters in issue'. It may well lead to such a determination, but given the exiguous timetables for adjudications, it cannot be expected (and nor can the legislature be taken to have expected) that an 'incorrect' decision will not be enforced *pro tem*. As Mr Walker QC demonstrates in Chapter six, both the TCC (including especially through the judgments of Jackson J, as he then was) and the Court of Appeal have upheld such an approach, time and time again. What this then leaves is *limited* scope for impugning the adjudication process, based on what might be considered to be technical or 'fringe' grounds.

---

[79] *Grove Developments Ltd v S&T (UK) Ltd* [2018] EWHC 123 (TCC) at [86]–[89] and [95]–[96], per Coulson J.

[80] *Speymill Contracts Ltd v Baskind* [2010] EWCA Civ 120.

[81] [2010] EWCA Civ 120 at [30].

One such ground is that an adjudication was commenced before a 'dispute' was extant. Only a 'dispute' may be referred to adjudication. If the parties' communications had not reached such a position that a 'dispute' had crystallised, it follows that there would be no jurisdictional basis for the adjudication thus brought. But as we see in Chapter six, from early days such arguments were narrowly circumscribed, as the TCC and the Court of Appeal took a broad (and practical) approach to when a 'dispute' comes into existence.[82]

In Chapter seven, Rachael O'Hagan considers a further aspect of statutory adjudication whose (implicit) nuances have been worked-out by the courts, heavily influenced by the jurisprudence of Jackson LJ. Ms O'Hagan considers the Court of Appeal case of *Lanes v Galliford Try Infrastructure Ltd*,[83] where Jackson LJ gave the leading judgment of the court. One of the principal issues in *Lanes* was that of natural justice in statutory adjudications – an issue on which Part II of the Housing Grants, Construction and Regeneration Act 1996 is completely silent. As *Lanes* confirms,[84] the general requirements of natural justice are common across statutory adjudication, arbitration and litigation. Shortly stated, adjudicators (and courts / tribunals) are required to proceed with matters before them by giving each party a fair opportunity of presenting its position, and furthermore the adjudicator (or court / tribunal) must not give the appearance of being unduly partial in favour of or against a particular party. In *Lanes* itself, the issue was whether the adjudicator, by expressing what he described as a 'Preliminary View' on the underlying dispute, had in fact closed his mind at that point so that he would not give fair and due weight to any later submissions made by the parties before rendering his 'final' decision. Cases where such allegations are made are invariably fact sensitive,[85] so whether *Lanes* creates any new principle of law applicable to statutory adjudications is largely moot. But as an example of the sensitivity of the appellate courts to the somewhat 'rough and ready' nature of the adjudication process, *Lanes* perhaps demonstrates that judicial intervention will usually only be forthcoming in those cases where a major mistake has been made in the adjudicative process.

C. Construction Contracts

It is relatively rare (although unsurprisingly so) for construction cases to reach the highest appellate levels. In the United Kingdom in the last 11 years, only four such cases have been decided by the House of Lords and subsequently the

---

[82] See *Amec Civil Engineering Limited v Secretary of State for Transport* [2004] EWHC 2339 (TCC) (Jackson J); [2005] EWCA Civ 291; [2005] BLR 227 (CA).

[83] *Lanes v Galliford Try Infrastructure Ltd* [2011] EWCA Civ 1617.

[84] Perhaps as a 'background legislative assumption': compare, in an analogous context, *Probuild Constructions (Aust) Pty Ltd v Shade Systems Pty Ltd* [2018] HCA 4 at [104], per Edelman J.

[85] Compare *Town & City Properties (Development) Ltd v Wiltshier Southern Ltd* (1988) 44 BLR 109 at 115–17, per Sir William Stabb QC.

Supreme Court.[86] Construction cases that make it through the appellate gateway to the apex court must therefore possess unusual or vexing features. Commonly, this may be because the case gives rise to a novel or important point of legal principle, or because the case concerns a matter of some complexity on which there have been divided views in the lower courts. *MT Højgaard A/S v E.On Climate & Renewables UK Robin Rigg East Ltd*[87] (discussed by Michael Curtis QC in Chapter eight) is the most recent case in this quartet.

The issue in *MT Højgaard* was easy to state, but difficult to resolve. Did a contract for the design and construction of an offshore wind farm include a warranty from the contractor that the foundations would have a lifetime of 20 years? The contract in question, as noted by Lord Neuberger PSC, was 'complex, diffuse and multi-authored'.[88] It consisted of a number of documents, including one which imposed upon the contractor an obligation to 'design … the foundations [to] ensure a lifetime of 20 years in every aspect without planned replacement'. A further contractual provision required the work as a whole to be 'fit for its purpose'. Other parts of the contract imposed upon the contractor an obligation to carry out its design so that it met particular standards for offshore wind turbines, including standards published by a Norwegian classification society. As it happened, and unbeknownst to the contractor at the time, the relevant Norwegian standard contained an error which meant that even if the standard was followed (as it had been), the piles for the wind turbine would not be of sufficient strength. Once this problem was discovered, expensive remedial works were commissioned. The economic issue in the case was which party took the contractual risk of such matters.

The Supreme Court, upholding the decision of the trial judge (Edwards-Stuart J), allowed the appeal from the Court of Appeal, in which Jackson LJ gave the leading judgment,[89] and held that the contract imposed 'fitness for purpose' obligations upon the contractor, meaning that the contractor was liable for the hugely expensive remedial works, even though it had not committed any particular error itself.[90] Construction and engineering contracts are often vast, composite documents, and the potential for the type of interpretative issue in *MT Højgaard* to reappear before the courts is a certainty. And the very fact that a distinguished Court of Appeal took a different view on the correct interpretation of the contract brings into sharp relief the binary differences which may arise when courts are

---

[86] The first three being *Melville Dundas Ltd v George Wimpey UK Ltd* [2007] 1 WLR 1136, *Reinwood Ltd v L Brown & Sons Ltd* [2008] 1 WLR 696 and *Aspect Contracts (Asbestos) Ltd v Higgins Construction Plc* [2015] UKSC 38 – each case considering aspects of the operation of Part II of the Housing Grants, Construction and Regeneration Act 1996.

[87] *MT Højgaard A/S v E.On Climate & Renewables UK Robin Rigg East Ltd* [2017] UKSC 59.

[88] [2017] UKSC 59 at [29].

[89] *MT Højgaard A/S v E.On Climate & Renewables UK Robin Rigg East Ltd* [2015] EWCA Civ 407. Underhill LJ delivered a short judgment, and Patten LJ concurred with the judgments of Jackson and Underhill LJJ.

[90] But, then again, nor had the employer.

confronted with a diffuse, composite contract. A possible solution, as suggested by Michael Curtis QC, is for contracts to contain a clear 'overriding obligation' which prescribes the standard of performance called for by the contract, ie 'reasonable skill and care' (which requires proof of fault or negligence for breach) or the more burdensome 'fitness for purpose' (which simply requires proof of failure of the supplied article or works).

In Chapter nine, Professor Mindy Chen-Wishart explores the earliest of Rupert Jackson's cases in a judicial capacity, namely *Williams v Roffey Bros*, which was heard at the Kingston-upon-Thames County Court by the newly-minted Assistant Recorder Rupert Jackson QC. The case is probably the most well-known of all of his cases, at least in legal circles; however its fame (or notoriety) stems from the fact that it went to the Court of Appeal,[91] and indeed the judgment given by Assistant Recorder Rupert Jackson QC has apparently been lost for all time. The issue in that case was whether a further agreement between a contractor and an apparently impecunious subcontractor, to be paid *further amounts* for completing work which the subcontractor was contractually required to perform, was legally enforceable. Central to this issue was the question: what consideration moved from the subcontractor to make the further agreement enforceable, if the contractor was simply agreeing to do what it was already bound to do? Both the Assistant Recorder and the Court of Appeal held that the further agreement was indeed legally binding. The issue which has vexed courts and academics since 1989 is *why*, as a matter of legal theory, such an agreement should be enforceable.

On Professor Chen-Wishart's analysis, the logic of *Williams v Roffey Bros*, and indeed many subsequent cases, is that such an agreement will be enforceable (as a unilateral collateral contract) if it *actually yields* a practical benefit to the promisor (who agrees to pay an additional sum). There is an instinctive logic and good sense in such an outcome. If A offers to pay B an additional amount (perhaps described as a 'bonus') for performing its obligations in a timely way, and B then does so, surely the mutual expectation of both parties is that the additional payment will be made. The position may well be different if a party (B) deliberately withholds performance to try to put pressure on its counterparty (A), so as to extract additional payment made under pressure. But such cases aside (and there is no suggestion *Williams v Roffey Bros* was such a case), should not the reasonable expectations of honest people be upheld?[92]

The third case considered in the 'construction contracts' section of the *Festschrift* is *Mid Essex Hospital Services NHS Trust v Compass Group UK and*

---

[91] *Williams v Roffey Brothers & Nicholls (Contractors) Ltd* [1989] EWCA Civ 5, [1990] 1 QB 1.

[92] As Lord Steyn observed extra-judicially: 'The court [in *Williams v Roffey Bros*] was obviously concerned that the doctrine of consideration should not restrict the ability of commercial contractors to make periodic consensual modifications, and even one-sided modifications, as the work under a construction contract proceeded. The reasonable expectations of the parties prevailed over technical and conceptualistic reasoning': see 'Contract law: fulfilling the reasonable expectations of honest men' (1997) 113 *LQR* 433 at 437–38.

Ireland Ltd,[93] discussed by Shy Jackson in Chapter ten, together with other recent authorities on the application of 'good faith' notions to commercial contracts, including construction contracts. *Mid Essex* concerned a catering contract for a hospital, as part of a PFI scheme. The contract contemplated the catering contractor being paid according to the service it provided, whereby deductions from payment could be made if the quality of catering fell short of particular standards. The extent of the deductions could be enormous, and indeed the hospital sought to deduct £84,450 because a chocolate mousse was discovered in the contractor's fridge that was one day past its expiry date. Deductions of a similar financial magnitude, for other minor transgressions, were also made.

The contract in *Mid Essex* contained an express good faith obligation; however it was not *general* in nature. It provided that:

> the [hospital] Trust and the Contractor will co-operate with each other in good faith and will take all reasonable action as is necessary for the efficient transmission of information and instructions and to enable the Trust or, as the case may be, any Beneficiary to derive the full benefit of the Contract.

As the Court of Appeal held (Jackson LJ giving the leading judgment), this was a narrow and specific obligation, relating to the transmission of information and instructions, and not anything else (such as the making of payment deductions for shortcomings in services rendered). Accordingly, despite the magnitude of the deductions made by it, the hospital was not found to have acted in breach of any good faith obligation. To a person unfamiliar with PFIs, the facts of the *Mid Essex* case, and in particular the eye-watering deductions made for trivial matters, must seem bewildering. But as Shy Jackson observes in Chapter ten, 'good faith arguments are sensitive to context'.

The day has not yet come when 'good faith' has been embraced as a universal, overarching principle of English contract law, and perhaps this makes English law appear something of a legal Galápagos, cut off from the many nations of the world who write good faith into their civil and commercial codes. We may only speculate as to whether this impacts upon standards of commercial behaviour where English law applies.[94]

D. Negligence and Nuisance

If construction contracts assume centre-stage in construction and engineering projects, non-contractual rights and obligations, such as those in tort, sometimes

---

[93] *Mid Essex Hospital Services NHS Trust v Compass Group UK and Ireland Ltd* [2013] EWCA Civ 200.

[94] In this regard, perhaps the spirit of British commerce, or at least certain quarters of it, is encapsulated in a quote attributed by Eddie Jordan to Formula One impresario Bernie Ecclestone: 'A great philosophy of Bernie Ecclestone's was "Shake my hand and you've got a deal for life. Sign me a contract and I'll find a way around it"': *The Telegraph*, 3 July 2016.

fall upon the fringes. This, in many respects, is both unwarranted and perhaps even dangerous, for parties seeking to manage legal risk. Before a risk can be managed it must be known about. And in order for it to be known about there must be a clear and practically-minded statement of what, in legal terms, that risk is and when it arises.

One of the hallmarks of the jurisprudence of Lord Justice Jackson has been to recognise the need for clarity, particularly in those areas of the law which are untidy, if not a complete mess. In this regard, the messiest area of construction law is that concerned with the law of negligence. Two negligence cases are considered in this *Festschrift*.

The first negligence case is *Robinson v PE Jones (Contractors) Ltd*[95] – a landmark in the law of negligence as it applies in the construction paradigm – where Jackson LJ gave the leading judgment (discussed by Fiona Sinclair QC in Chapter eleven). The principal issue in this case was beguilingly simple to state: if a contractor is engaged pursuant to a contract to perform building work for an employer, and the work is performed in a defective manner, does the contractor owe a duty of care to the employer in respect of the defective work? The answer that *Robinson v Jones* gives is 'no'. The 'no duty of care' answer is predicated on two matters.

First, if there are contractual rights between the employer and the contractor which give the employer the ability to hold the contractor accountable for its defective work, there is no need for the law of tort to, as it were, step in and impose a concurrent duty of care. Or, to use the language of Jackson LJ, if a contractor and an employer entered into a 'normal contract whereby the defendant would complete the construction of a house for the claimant to an agreed specification and the claimant would pay the purchase price',[96] the contractor would not ordinarily be taken to 'assume responsibility' in tort to the owner for the quality of its work,[97] thus the law would not impose a duty of care.

Secondly, whereas an architect or an engineer providing design (or similar) services may be regarded as a 'professional' who will be taken (without more) to owe a duty of care, a contractor is not a 'professional', and will not therefore owe a duty of care to an employer in respect of pure economic loss unless the contractor has specifically assumed responsibility to the employer for such matters.[98]

The attractiveness of this reasoning is that it proffers clarity as to the existence of contractors' obligations in tort to those who employ them pursuant to construction or engineering contracts. Such clarity is sorely needed in an area of law so bogged down in, and overwhelmed by, a seemingly interminable procession of

---

[95] *Robinson v PE Jones (Contractors) Ltd* [2012] QB 44 (CA).

[96] *Robinson v PE Jones (Contractors) Ltd* [2012] QB 44 at [83].

[97] Only, however, insofar as the contractor's carelessness caused defects in the works which resulted in pure economic loss to employer. The position is different where a contractor's carelessness leads to defects (or other issues) resulting in harm or injury to persons or property.

[98] See also *Lejovarn v Burgess* [2017] EWCA Civ 254 at [86], per Hamblen LJ.

inconclusive case law and abstract terminology.[99] Reading all the cases leaves one's head spinning. But whether *Robinson v PE Jones* represents the final word (assuming there will *ever be* a final word) is a matter of conjecture.[100]

The second of the negligence cases is *Jacobs v Morton*,[101] a decision of Mr Recorder Jackson QC, as he then was, which is discussed by Karim Ghaly QC in Chapter twelve. *Jacobs v Morton* considers the application of the so-called 'complex structure theory', which finds its origins in the speech of Lord Bridge in *D&F Estates Ltd v Church Commissioners for England*.[102] 'Complex structure theory' has arisen out of the almost Byzantine contortions that the law of negligence in England underwent between the 1970s and the 1990s. Put simply, a builder who performs work may owe no duty of care to anyone in respect of defects in his work which do not cause any harm or injury to anyone or their property.[103] But where a part of the builder's work causes actual damage to another part of the same property where the work is being performed, the builder may be held to owe a duty of care in respect of such damage to 'other property', at least in cases where the structure in question is 'complex', such that it is not 'a single indivisible unit'. This 'complex structure theory' therefore poses a risk for contractors, and an avenue of redress for employers, for defective structures where there is a relevant degree of independence or separation between components of the structure. However, as Mr Ghaly QC notes, the circumstances in which the 'complex structure theory' may be called upon in aid of an employer are limited. The existential question facing the 'complex structure theory' is whether it should even form part of the law of negligence at all.

Liability in negligence is at the heart of Chapter thirteen, although the issue considered in that chapter by Manus McMullen QC is the extent to which such liability may be curtailed by contractual wording. Mr McMullen QC considers two Court of Appeal cases on this subject in which Jackson LJ gave the leading judgments – *Persimmon Homes Ltd v Ove Arup & Partners Ltd*[104] and *Greenwich Millennium Village Ltd v Essex Services Group Plc*.[105] *Persimmon* concerned a limitation clause in a consultant's contract of appointment, whereas *Greenwich*

---

[99] 'Assumption of responsibility' being but one prominent example of the opaque expressions used in the duty of care calculus. The law has not sought to define, let alone describe, what an 'assumption of responsibility' is and how one determines whether or not it exists. 'Proximity' is also a term which appears in negligence cases (although perhaps less so these days). It, too, is something of an elusive concept.

[100] Compare Bailey, *Construction Law*, 2nd edn (London, Informa, 2016) Vol II, paras 10.86–10.88; *Jackson & Powell on Professional Liability*, 8th edn (London, Sweet & Maxwell, 2016) para 9-046.

[101] *A Jacobs v Morton & Partners* (1994) 72 BLR 92.

[102] *D&F Estates Ltd v Church Commissioners for England* [1989] 1 AC 177 at 206–07 (see also per Lord Oliver, at 214). And see Duncan Wallace, 'Negligence and Defective Buildings: Confusion Confounded?' (1989) 105 *LQR* 46; Duncan Wallace, 'Negligence and Complex Structures' (1990) 106 *LQR* 11.

[103] Indeed, this is the very logic underpinning *Robinson v PE Jones (Contractors) Ltd* [2012] QB 44 (CA), mentioned above and discussed by Fiona Sinclair QC in Chapter 11 of this volume.

[104] *Persimmon Homes Ltd v Ove Arup & Partners Ltd* [2017] EWCA Civ 373.

[105] *Greenwich Millennium Village Ltd v Essex Services Group Plc* [2014] EWCA Civ 960.

Millennium Village involved an indemnity provision. One of the issues before the Court of Appeal in the *Greenwich* case was whether the indemnity could be relied upon by the indemnitee in circumstances where the indemnitee's own negligence caused the particular loss for which it sought to invoke the indemnity. As Mr McMullen QC observes in Chapter thirteen, the approach taken by Jackson LJ in both *Greenwich* and *Persimmon* was to construe the relevant clauses in their particular commercial context, without applying any rigid or artificial rules of interpretation. This is very much the modern approach to contractual interpretation, and increasingly limitation, exclusion and indemnity clauses in commercial contracts are not singled out for special treatment from any of the other clauses of the contract. To describe such an approach as 'modern' may sound odd, given that exclusion, limitation and indemnity provisions are now an established (and indeed necessary) feature of the landscape of construction and engineering projects. But this was not always so, and as a sign of how far the world has moved in a relatively short period of time, it is apposite (if not startling) to recall this sentence from the first edition of *Jackson & Powell*: 'Professional men do not normally seek to exclude or restrict their liability to clients'.[106]

The fourth of the tort chapters is Chapter fourteen, in which Professor Philip Britton considers a trio of nuisance cases involving neighbours (either contiguous or otherwise in the vicinity of each other) at loggerheads with each other. The first case, which went to the Supreme Court, related to speedway noise.[107] The other two cases concern unauthorised party-wall work constituting both a nuisance and a trespass.[108] As Professor Britton percipiently notes in his conclusion, the unifying feature of these cases – apart from the fact that in them Jackson LJ delivered the leading judgments of the Court of Appeal – is the apparent eagerness of the parties to litigate issues which could be resolved by discussions between them, or at least by the use of some ADR process.[109] How relatively small matters that could reasonably be addressed by neighbourly courtesy and some 'give-and-take' can spiral into deep-seated enmity and full-blown litigation is not a matter on which courts are likely to dwell. But it is a matter that will (it seems) continue to cause judges to put their heads in their hands in despair, and may indeed properly be the subject of a PhD thesis on the irrational psychology of human beings.

---

[106] Jackson & Powell, *Professional Negligence* (London, Sweet & Maxwell, 1982) para 1.40.

[107] *Coventry (t/a RDC Promotions) v Lawrence* [2012] EWCA Civ 26, [2012] 1 WLR 2127, [2012] 3 All ER 168, 141 Con LR 79; and later *Coventry v Lawrence (No 1)* [2014] UKSC 13, [2014] 1 AC 822.

[108] *Yeung v Potel* [2014] EWCA Civ 481; *Rashid v Sharif* [2014] EWCA Civ 377.

[109] See also *Oliver v Symons* [2012] EWCA Civ 267 at [1], per Elias LJ: 'This is a dispute about the extent of a right of way on farmland in County Durham. The disputed part of the right of way is

E. Contract Administration

It is one of the peculiar features of construction and engineering contracts that they create the special role of a 'contract administrator', to use a neutral term. The parties to the contract agree that the contract administrator is to discharge particular functions – valuing the contractor's payment and extension-of-time applications, reviewing the adequacy of the contractor's work (and requiring the contractor to repair defects), instructing the contractor (at the employer's behest) to change aspects of the works, and certifying when the works have been completed in accordance with the contract, among other things.

One of the recurring issues that arises with regard to contract administrators is what might be abbreviated to the notion of 'impartiality'. The contract administrator fulfils a number of roles under a contract, including adjudicating on the employer's and the contractor's respective financial obligations towards each other. Typically, the contract administrator will be a consultant engaged by the employer itself, and therefore someone who is paid by the employer. A contract administrator will rarely, therefore, be 'independent' of the parties, in the sense of having no financial links with any of them. Notwithstanding this, the law permits a person who is paid by the employer to act as contract administrator, but the law also requires that the contract administrator discharge his or her contractual functions in a manner which is fair or impartial as between the parties. It is occasionally a difficult high-wire for a professional consultant to walk.

In Chapter fifteen, Professor Anthony Lavers discusses three judgments[110] from Jackson J's tenure as judge in charge of the TCC, which consider aspects of the contract administrator's duty to act fairly between the parties – to 'hold the scales even'. These cases reinforce and refine the principles developed by English law over a period dating back to the nineteenth century, which have evolved to a point where it may be said that a contract administrator's duty is to act neutrally and impartially between the parties when making binding determinations of rights and obligations under the contract. In practice, however, what does this actually mean? No precise answer or guidelines may be given. Nevertheless, it seems that if a contract administrator acts *professionally* and exercises *professional judgement*, and in doing so he or she duly considers what *each party* has to say on particular issues for decision or determination, there may not be any more than one can expect (or that the law can expect) of a contract administrator.

---

little more than 100 metres in length. The costs of the litigation are enormous and wholly out of proportion to the practical importance of the issue: the appellants alone have expended in the region of £150,000.00 for their costs. This is a case which was crying out for mediation, even assuming that it could not have been settled more informally than that. It ought never to have come near a court, and with a modicum of good will on both sides, it would not have done so'.

[110] Being *AMEC Civil Engineering Ltd v Secretary of State for Transport* [2004] EWHC 2339 (TCC); *Costain Ltd v Bechtel Ltd* [2005] EWHC 1018 (TCC) and *Scheldebouw BV v St James Homes (Grosvenor Dock) Ltd* [2006] EWHC 89 (TCC).

F. Private Finance Initiatives

Lord Justice Jackson's career as a judge witnessed the emergence of a new type of case, arising from a new type of procurement. The new type of procurement is the opaquely-named 'Private Finance Initiative' or 'PFI', which was developed in the UK in the 1990s and deployed by successive governments as a means of delivering public infrastructure or services.

The basic concept of a PFI is straightforward enough. Under a PFI scheme, a government (or emanation thereof) arranges for private sector businesses to build and then operate/maintain a road, a hospital, a school, etc. The government pays the private sector businesses for the asset or services provided. The government is only liable to make payment for the infrastructure or services actually provided to it, and so in a general sense it incurs no liability to pay for those assets or services *until* they are provided.

The PFI concept has its supporters and its detractors. Whichever view one may take of PFIs, what is beyond argument is that the number, length and complexity of contracts required to effect a PFI project are vast, certainly by comparison with the contractual arrangements traditionally used by public works departments for the construction of eg, a road. As a consequence of this, the risk of inconsistencies and errors – and therefore the potential for claims and disputes – is always there in PFI contracts.

In Chapter sixteen, Mrs Justice Jefford DBE discusses the *Midland Expressway* litigation in which she was involved as junior counsel, both in the TCC before Jackson J and also in the Court of Appeal.[111] The *Midland Expressway* litigation concerned a PFI project for the construction and operation of a toll road in the Midlands. The litigated issues concerned contractual allocations of risk – matters that could only be determined from the cloying detail of the PFI contracts themselves. The diverse and specific matters before the court included responsibility for the appropriate speed limit on the approach to toll stations, and the height of coin baskets, among other things. At first blush such matters may appear trivial or plain weird subjects for expensive High Court litigation.[112] However in the context of PFI contracts the scope for the cost of such matters to add up to tens or hundreds of thousands of pounds (or more) over the life of a PFI project is very real.

Given this, and given that PFI projects represent long-term commitments by both the public and private sector participants, there is clearly an imperative for issues arising under PFI projects to be dealt with by the parties with a large measure of pragmatism, as opposed to antagonism. In this vein, and as a parting

---

[111] *Midland Expressway Limited v Carillion Construction Ltd* [2005] EWHC 2810 (TCC); [2005] EWHC 2963 (TCC); [2006] EWHC 1505 (TCC); on appeal [2006] EWCA Civ 936.

[112] Similar matters of superficially small import were considered in *Mid Essex Hospital Services NHS Trust v Compass Group UK and Ireland Ltd* [2013] EWCA Civ 200, discussed by Shy Jackson in Chapter 10 of this volume.

exhortation on PFI contracts, Jackson LJ held in *Amey Birmingham Highways Ltd v Birmingham City Council*[113] that:

> Any relational contract of this character is likely to be of massive length, containing many infelicities and oddities. Both parties should adopt a reasonable approach in accordance with what is obviously the long-term purpose of the contract. They should not be latching onto the infelicities and oddities, in order to disrupt the project and maximise their own gain.[114]

G. Performance Bonds

Like insurers, guarantors (including guarantors under performance bonds) have traditionally held a special place in the law. A guarantor of a contractor's obligations agrees to accept financial responsibility for the contractor becoming insolvent, or not performing its contractual obligations, based on certain risk assumptions. If the beneficiary of a guarantee (or performance bond) conducts itself so as to prejudice the position of the guarantor, such as by advancing money to the contractor that it has not earned and which is not due, this may be enough, in law, to shatter the fragile, crystalline legal bond between the guarantor and the beneficiary.[115]

As Richard Wilmot-Smith QC recounts in Chapter seventeen, he and Lord Justice Jackson grappled together with the somewhat arcane law concerning bonds and guarantees on two occasions during their careers: the first in *Mercers v New Hampshire Insurance Co Ltd*[116] when Mr Wilmot-Smith was Rupert Jackson QC's junior, and then some two decades later in *Aviva Insurance Ltd v Hackney Empire Ltd*,[117] with Lord Justice Jackson sitting in the Court of Appeal, and giving the leading judgment of that court. It may be difficult to detect clear patterns from these cases, or indeed other ones where guarantors/bondsmen have called upon the courts to extricate them from liability, *deus ex machina*. But perhaps we may deduce that a prominent factor for the court will be *the commercial purpose* for which the security was provided. What is the purpose of the bond? It is to provide financial security to the employer in the event of the contractor defaulting in the performance of its obligations, or becoming insolvent. Did the contractor default or become insolvent? If 'yes', then the intuitive starting point (and possibly also the outcome) may be that the bond or guarantee should be available to the employer

---

[113] *Amey Birmingham Highways Ltd v Birmingham City Council* [2018] EWCA Civ 264. Whereas the *Midland Expressway* case was concerned with the construction and operation of a toll road in the Midlands, the *Amey Birmingham Highways* case concerned a PFI project for the repairing of pot holes and the like in Birmingham.

[114] [2018] EWCA Civ 264 at [93].

[115] This is often referred to, compendiously, as the rule in *Holme v Brunskill* (1878) 3 QBD 495.

[116] *Wardens and Commonalty of the Mystery of Mercers of the City of London v New Hampshire Insurance Co Ltd* (1992) 60 BLR 26.

[117] *Aviva Insurance Ltd v Hackney Empire Ltd* [2012] EWCA Civ 1716, [2013] BLR 57.

for recourse purposes, unless there is a good reason why it should not. Otherwise, the bond or guarantee would be a thing of no value at all.[118]

H. Time and Liquidated Damages

Construction and engineering projects are commonly beset by delay. The courts themselves are sometimes directly impacted by delayed construction projects.[119] The construction of the Royal Courts of Justice on the Strand in London was significantly delayed during the 1870s, principally due to strikes. And the current home in London of the TCC in the High Court – the Rolls Building – was delayed in its construction, leading (with no small measure of irony) to significant litigation, involving Jackson LJ himself, as discussed by Vincent Moran QC in Chapter eighteen.

Chapter eighteen considers *Carillion Construction Ltd v Emcor Engineering Services Ltd*,[120] a case concerned with the operation of an extension-of-time clause in a DOM/2 form of subcontract. The particular issue before the Court of Appeal, where Jackson LJ gave the leading judgment, was a relatively straightforward one; yet one on which there was (surprisingly) no previous authority. The issue was this: if a subcontractor is required to complete its works by date X, and it fails to do so without legal excuse, yet during this period of delay it is *then* delayed by the main contractor – and so entitled to an extension of time – (a) does the extension of time only operate during the period when the main contractor caused the delay; or (b) is it to be added contiguously to the completion date (date X) so that, for contractual purposes, the subcontractor may be exculpated from any liability to pay damages during a period when, as a matter of fact, its works were in culpable delay? The issue may be of significance because during the particular period immediately after date X, where the subcontractor's tardiness was causing delay to the project, the main contractor, in turn, may have faced a liability to the employer to pay liquidated damages, and additionally the main contractor itself may have incurred costs due to the subcontractor's delay.

The answer given by Jackson LJ to the 'exam question' before the court was that the period of the extension of time (Y) was to be added contiguously to date X, so that the revised completion date would be X + Y. Such a conclusion was reached as a matter of interpretation of the relevant provisions of the DOM/2 form.

On the wording of the DOM/2 form, such a conclusion 'seems straightforward enough', as Vincent Moran QC notes. A residual issue, that will be for another

---

[118] See, most recently in the TCC, the observations of Coulson J in *Ziggurat (Claremont Place) LLP v HCC International Insurance Co PLC* [2017] EWHC 3286 (TCC) at [43] and [57].

[119] And, indeed, professional negligence claims arising from the construction of court buildings: see, eg, *Driver v William Willett (Contractors) Ltd* [1969] 1 All ER 665, which concerned the construction of a law courts building in Worthing, Sussex.

[120] *Carillion Construction Ltd v Emcor Engineering Services Ltd* [2017] BLR 203; 170 Con LR 1.

day, and a different case, is whether a subcontractor in the posited scenario may be liable to a main contractor for losses suffered by the main contractor during the period of delay immediately after date X, where the subcontractor is subject to a *separate and distinct* obligation to prosecute its works with 'due diligence and without delay'. Although the subcontractor may be entitled to an extension of time attributable to the period immediately after (and contiguous with) date X, it is conceivable that, during this particular period, it may actually have been in breach of its obligation to work in an expeditious manner.[121]

The complexities of the law concerning damages for delay do not end there. One of the more controversial areas of the law concerning the imposition of liquidated damages is whether an employer is (or *should be*) entitled to claim liquidated damages from a contractor in circumstances where the *employer itself* is factually responsible for some, if not all, of the relevant delay. Under the simplest of contracts (with no extension-of-time clause), the answer as a matter of English law is tolerably clear: the employer is not entitled to claim liquidated damages for the relevant period where the employer prevented the contractor from completing its works in a timely manner.[122]

The legal position becomes more complicated, however, where (as is now often the case) a construction contract includes:

(a)   an extension-of-time clause, entitling the contractor to claim more time for completion in the event that the employer's conduct prevents (or will prevent) it from completing the works by the contract date for doing so; and

(b)   a time-bar provision, which requires the contractor to notify the employer and/or the contract administrator of the employer's delay (and the contractor's extension-of-time claim) within a stated period of it first occurring (eg, 28 days), failing which any later entitlement to an extension of time will not accrue – in other words, the contractor's claim will be 'time barred'.

The origin of the controversy in modern construction law is a judgment of the Supreme Court of the Northern Territory (Australia) in 1999,[123] in which the judge[124] took a broad view of the operation of the so-called 'prevention principle', holding that a 'time-bar' clause could not preclude the invocation of the 'prevention principle', meaning (in effect) that a contractor would be able to defeat an

---

[121] See *Bovis Construction (Scotland) Ltd v Whatlings Construction Ltd* (1995) 75 BLR 1 (HL(Sc)); *Hometeam Constructions Pty Ltd v McCauley* [2005] NSWCA 303 at [159]–[160], per McColl JA.

[122] However, even then this principle may need to be qualified, albeit to a limited extent in practice. An employer *is* entitled to claim liquidated damages in such circumstances if it is clear from the contract that the employer should be so entitled: see, eg, *Jones v St John's College* (1870) LR 6 QB 115; *Reynolds v Strelitz* (1901) 3 WALR 143; *Scottish Power plc v Kvaerner Construction (Regions) Ltd* 1999 SLT 721.

[123] *Gaymark Investments Pty Ltd v Walter Construction Group Ltd* [1999] NTSC 143.

[124] Bailey J (no relation to the editor of this *Festschrift*).

employer's claim for liquidated damages even if the contractor had not given notice of the employer's 'prevention' within the stipulated period for doing so (hence, the contractor was not, under the wording of the contract, entitled to an extension of time). In Chapter nineteen, Professor Doug Jones makes a powerful case for the adoption of such an approach, which has also garnered the support of some commentators in Australia and indeed elsewhere.

The countervailing view is that a 'time-bar' clause applies according to its wording, and if (as is often the case) that wording is clear a 'time-bar' provision may be used to negate a contractor's appeal to the 'prevention principle'. This view was propounded by Jackson J in *Multiplex Constructions (UK) Ltd v Honeywell Control Systems Ltd (No 2)*.[125] With respect, this conclusion must be right. The 'prevention principle' is not some inviolable principle of law, as if enshrined in Magna Carta. It may be modified or displaced by the agreement of the parties.[126] Thus, 'time bar' provisions, when clearly worded, produce in their application a modification or displacement of the 'prevention principle'. Be that as it may, we should still recognise the scope for the application of extra-contractual laws and influences, including (where relevant) concepts such as good faith, which may preclude reliance upon a 'time bar' provision in circumstances where the employer caused the contractor to be delayed.

Attacks on the enforceability of 'time bar' provisions may be seen as a sub-set of the broader topic of legal challenges to the enforcement of liquidated damages clauses. In Chapter twenty, Riaz Hussain QC discusses this important matter using the judgment of Jackson J in *Alfred McAlpine Capital Projects Ltd v Tilebox*[127] as a focal point. *Tilebox* concerned the redevelopment of an office building in Guildford. The main issue in the case was whether the liquidated damages clause in the construction contract between the developer and the contractor constituted a penalty. In *Tilebox*, as in most other cases concerning challenges to liquidated clauses as putative penalties, the attack was predicated upon the amount of liquidated damages stipulated by the contract not representing a 'genuine pre-estimate' of the developer's likely loss in the event of the contractor's works being in culpable delay.

On the findings of fact made by Jackson J, the contractor's thesis was correct. His Lordship found that the likely weekly loss to the developer, in the event of the contractor being late, was in the order of £30,000, whereas the liquidated damages payable under the contract were stipulated to be £45,000 per week. However, as a matter of English law, it did not follow that the liquidated damages clause would be 'struck down as a penalty'. The clause was upheld, largely on the basis that the

---

[125] *Multiplex Constructions (UK) Ltd v Honeywell Control Systems Ltd (No 2)* [2007] EWHC 447 (TCC); [2007] BLR 195.

[126] *Probuild Constructions (Aust) Pty Ltd v DDI Group Pty Ltd* [2017] NSWCA 151 at [117], per McColl JA; *North Midland Building Ltd v Cyden Homes Ltd* [2017] EWHC 2414 (TCC) at [19]–[20], per Fraser J; *North Midland Building Ltd v Cyden Homes Ltd* [2018] EWCA Civ 1744.

[127] *Alfred McAlpine Capital Projects Ltd v Tilebox* [2005] BLR 271.

amount of liquidated damages payable was not grossly disproportionate to the likely loss in the event of delay. The legal test of a penalty, applied by Jackson J in *Tilebox*, was that there be a 'substantial discrepancy' between the liquidated damages payable under the contract and the loss likely to be suffered due to its breach.

As subsequent English case law has emphasised,[128] in cases of alleged penalties, context may also be a determining factor, including the relative bargaining positions of the parties and where their respective commercial interests lie. In the end, the difficulty with penalties, which may never be resolved, is not in identifying 'obvious' cases of abusive or 'over-the-top' clauses, the terms of which may be postulated;[129] but in pinpointing where along the financial spectrum a pre-agreed sum changes from one legal characterisation (an 'enforceable liquidated damages provision') to another (an 'unenforceable penalty').

X. Other Contributions

There have been numerous other ways in which Lord Justice Jackson has contributed to the legal community. Notable amongst these contributions has been in his position (accepted with alacrity) as President of the Society of Construction Law, an office which he has held since 2012 upon succeeding Sir Anthony May.[130] The role of SCL President is largely a ceremonial one, formally requiring little contribution by the incumbent President to the life of the Society. However, as with all his activities (curricular and extra-curricular), Lord Justice Jackson dedicated substantial time to his role, reflecting not only his conscientiousness at 'doing a good job', but also his genuine eagerness for supporting the Society's activities. He could be relied upon to deliver a lecture at SCL events, whether in the UK or at international conferences, and also to provide after-dinner perorations – all *ex tempore* – which invariably drew guffaws or at least wry smiles at the orator's dry wit.

On the legal publications side, he was an editor of the 'White Book'[131] from 2000, becoming editor-in-chief in 2010 on the retirement of the previous editor, Sir Mark Waller. And he continues to be a consultant editor of his joint masterpiece, *Jackson & Powell*.

---

[128] *Cavendish Square Holdings BV v Talal Makdessi* and *Parking Eye Ltd v Beavis* [2015] UKSC 67.

[129] For example, in *Clydebank Engineering and Shipbuilding Co Ltd v Don José Ramos Yzquierdo y Castaneda* [1905] AC 6 at 10, the Earl of Halsbury LC referred to a hypothetical (and extreme) illustration: '[I]f you agreed to build a house in a year, and agreed that if you did not build the home for £50, you were to pay a million of money as a penalty, the extravagance of that would be at once apparent'.

[130] In 2018, Lord Justice Coulson succeeded Lord Justice Jackson as President of the SCL.

[131] *Civil Procedure* (Sweet & Maxwell), generally referred to as the 'White Book'. The White Book contains the sources of law relating to the practice and procedures of the High Court and the County Court for the handling of civil litigation.

XI. Drawing the Threads Together

Judicial legacies are by no means immediate, nor indeed are they inevitable. A judge who is celebrated in his or her own career or lifetime may later be rendered a minor footnote in legal history, or even forgotten altogether.[132]

When I approached each of the contributors for this *Festschrift* to see whether there was interest in participating in the project, the response I received was both immediate and overwhelming. Mr Justice Coulson (as he then was) said it was a 'brilliant idea', and others responded to similar effect. Why was this? There may have been a multitude of reasons, however my distinct impression is that two stand out above all.

First, because it is recognised that Lord Justice Jackson possesses the virtues traditional in the judiciary: learning, wisdom, fair-mindedness and a deep sense of public duty.

Secondly, he has brought to the law and legal life an energy, a work ethic and an uplifting approach which has not only improved our legal system, but has reinforced our belief that the system – through the hard work of those within it – is and can be great, and therefore that our work in the law is worthwhile.

---

[132] Cf David Foxton QC, reviewing Lentin, *Mr Justice McCardie (1869–1933): Rebel, Reformer, and Rogue Judge* (Cambridge Scholars Publishing, 2016), at (2017) 133 *LQR* 683 at 684 (referring to 'the fickle nature of judicial reputation').

PART II

The Technology and
Construction Court

2

Lord Justice Jackson and the Evolution of the Technology and Construction Court[1]

LORD JUSTICE COULSON[2]

I. Introduction

It is difficult now to imagine the TCC as anything other than a success story. It has six ticketed judges, all of whom did TCC work at the Bar. Two of those six judges are presiding judges and another is a former presider. And the TCC is the first part of the High Court to be gender equal – three women and three men.

In addition to the straightforward construction work, and the related professional negligence work concerned with architects, engineers and surveyors, the last decade has seen a huge growth of other work in the TCC. One area has, of course, been construction adjudication where, even now that the law on enforcement is relatively settled, there is still at least one significant and contested adjudication enforcement hearing every week. The TCC has made the law from scratch in this major new area of dispute resolution.

Side by side with that has been the explosion of public procurement work. Originally this work came to the TCC because of the court's experience with the tender processes for major infrastructure contracts. But now the court is the natural home for all kinds of procurement disputes, relating to areas as diverse as the provision of healthcare, social services and legal aid.

It all sounds very satisfactory, doesn't it? It is something of which those of us who have been involved in this field of law for the last 30 years can be justifiably proud. And yet …

---

[1] Some of the material in this chapter was first used in the author's TECBAR/SCL lecture at The Law Society on 2 November 2017.

[2] Sir Peter Coulson: Judge in Charge of the TCC from 2016 to 2018. Currently Deputy Head of Civil Justice.

And yet, it is no exaggeration to say that this happy state of affairs is primarily the responsibility of just one person: Sir Rupert Jackson.

II. The Dark Ages

It is impossible to convey to younger lawyers just how low the reputation of the TCC had sunk when Rupert became the Judge in Charge in the summer of 2004. In the '80s and early '90s, the Official Referees had gone about their work quietly and efficiently. Although they did not have the rank of High Court Judges, much of the work that they did was equal to the most difficult Commercial Court and Chancery Division disputes. What is more, there were some excellent judges undertaking the work, like Judge John Hicks QC, Judge John Loyd QC and Judge Humphrey LLoyd QC.

But when another of this judicial 'A team', Judge Thayne Forbes QC, rightly became a High Court Judge (the first Official Referee in modern times to achieve that distinction), the Lord Chancellor's Department (which was then in charge of judicial appointments) appeared to assume that anyone could do the work, regardless of their previous experience or indeed reputation. Thereafter they made some surprising choices. The reaction of the Bar to one of them was 'Who?'; and to another it was, 'Surely they could have found someone better than him?' (Just in case you don't remember, there were no 'hers' in the days of the Lord Chancellor's Department).

Three months after I became a TCC Judge in the summer of 2004, there was an article about the court in the magazine *Legal Business*. It was devastating in its criticism of the judges of the court I had just joined. Nothing was omitted: their perceived rudeness in court (one was described as 'bloody tetchy'); their alleged inconsistencies; and their apparent failure to grapple with the realities of case management. It even went so far as to list the number of appeals from each judge and the proportion that had been allowed. One judge did well because the article ended its review of him with the words 'he attracted no real criticism'.

I think it is safe to say that no article in any UK magazine has ever been as critical of one group of judges. Even today, when I show others a copy of the article, they are staggered by how personal the criticisms were.

Some of the criticisms were undoubtedly unfair. And there have been more recent examples of judicial conduct which has been much worse than the behaviour of those criticised in the TCC. But those are individuals, not a whole court. And it has to be said, they were/are High Court Judges, for whom it sometimes feels that different rules apply.

But in any event, unfair criticism is a part and parcel of a job in the public eye: you are criticised because people do not like your decision or the way in which you have reached it, regardless of the underlying merits. And let's be honest: those of us who remember the TCC in 2004 will recall that the article was well-researched and reflected very widely-held views. In its grading of the judges, for example, the order in which they were ranked, many felt it was impossible to take issue.

The article ends with a reference to Rupert becoming the Judge in Charge of the TCC. It said:

> Mr Justice Jackson's appointment has been greeted with near-universal enthusiasm … he is regarded as a formidable intellect with a sterling pedigree at the Bar and on the Bench. While his plans at present remain confidential, it is known that he has an agenda for change. A sceptical constituency is keen to see results.

And that is what they got: results, the principal one being the successful court we have today. But how did Rupert achieve those results? What principles guided him and what obstacles did he have to surmount on the way? And what can we learn from those events and what do we need to do to ensure a bright future for the TCC in the next 20 years?

III. Getting to Grips with a Failing Court

The first point to make is that Rupert is a single-minded man. If he sets his mind on doing something then he will do it. Protestations will be considered but often ignored. Distractions ruthlessly shut out. That became apparent to everyone, if it had not been before, during his illness in 2012 when, at one point, he was at risk of losing his leg. Now, because he stuck so rigidly to the prescribed exercises, you would never know that he had ever had anything wrong. So it was with the TCC: he had that 'agenda for change' and he was determined to implement it.

Secondly, as everyone knows, Rupert is a prodigiously hard worker. During his four years as the Judge in Charge of the TCC he worked unstintingly, both in court on the cases that were before him, and out of court, on the changes to the whole way in which the TCC undertook its work. Only when it was simply impossible for Rupert to undertake a particular task – in view of all the other things that he was doing – would he ever ask someone else for assistance. I never minded doing things for Rupert because I knew that, if he could, he would be doing it himself.

Thirdly, Rupert wanted the TCC to work. He believed in the Court and the importance of the work that it did. This is a very important point, and one that many at the time simply missed. Although Rupert's principal background was in professional negligence and insurance work, he came to do more and more construction work during his years as a QC. He had done his share of lengthy arbitrations around the world, often with less-than-riveting subject-matter. He had appeared regularly in the TCC, sometimes in front of the very judges for whom he was now responsible. He knew from his own experience that the Court was not as good as it had been 10 years before. He also knew that, with the right people, the Court could actually be made better than it had ever been.

That was why Rupert was such a fabulous appointment in the summer of 2004. His determination and drive, his appetite for hard work, and his unshakeable belief in the importance of the TCC all combined to make him the only person at the time capable of rescuing the Court.

That might strike the reader as over-dramatic. But it is not. By the autumn of 2004, there was a very real possibility that the TCC would effectively be closed down, that the judges would be dispersed, and the work would be done by way of a construction list in the general Queen's Bench (QB) list. At the TCC Conference in December 2004, attended by the then Lord Chief Justice and the then President of the Queen's Bench Division, the latter (Lord Judge) indicated that the perception was that the TCC 'was a failing court'.

IV. What Rupert did Next

The first thing that Rupert did was to announce that, in future, the bigger TCC cases would be heard exclusively by High Court Judges. Since he was the only High Court Judge attached to the TCC at the time, he identified five QB Judges as Nominated Judges of the TCC, who would undertake the work as and when required. Inevitably nicknamed the Jackson Five, some of them, such as the wonderful Sir Christopher Clarke, heard a large number of TCC cases, but most of the rest did very few.

This was largely because Rupert was doing the majority of the bigger cases himself. He was in court solidly from Monday to Friday every week, doing trial after trial and then producing extempore judgments immediately after the case had finished. I would venture to suggest that no High Court Judge has ever done quite so many back-to-back, difficult trials in this way. At the time, I had the room two floors above his and I was very new, so I needed to pad down to his room and ask him a lot of questions (which he always patiently answered). So I know – perhaps better than anyone – the sheer scale of the work that he got through during an average working week.

Slowly, the reliance on the Jackson Five was eased with the appointment of High Court Judges directly to the TCC. Sir Vivian Ramsey became a judge of the Court in 2005, and Sir Robert Akenhead followed in the autumn of 2007. Three months later, in January 2008, I became the fourth full time High Court Judge in the TCC and Sir Antony Edwards-Stuart followed the next year.

That all sounds fine, but what of the existing TCC judges at the time of these changes? They were, of course, bitterly disappointed and upset to be side-lined in this way. A number retired. Some were moved away from the TCC into more general QB work. One or two remained, underused and unhappy, until their own retirements.

It would be impossible to pretend that these events did not lead to real confrontation. Some of the existing judges refused to accept the validity of any of the criticisms, so were extremely unhappy about their treatment and sought to argue the matter out with Rupert. I know that these confrontations were very stressful for him, but he stuck to his guns. Indeed, looking back, it is extraordinary to remember how quickly resistance melted away. The fact of the matter was that the changes were popular with the users, and the volume and quality of TCC work started to pick up. It was impossible to argue with the results.

Rupert successfully re-launched the court using a number of different weapons. One was the TCC Conference to which I have already referred, which had the effect of bringing home to everyone just how grave the crisis was. But it was also very useful from a wider perspective, because there were a number of papers on a variety of topics which then formed the basis of the revamped TCC Guide.

Rupert concluded that a good way to re-launch the Court was to re-launch the TCC Guide. The first edition of the Guide was quite short and there were many areas of practice and procedure where clearer and fuller guidance was plainly required. Using the Conference papers as a foundation, Rupert and I then set about revamping the TCC Guide. He asked for my help only because he was so busy doing so many other things. But the second edition of the Guide was greatly expanded from the first, and was and remains the basis of all TCC procedure. I learned so much just by working with him on the detailed provisions of the Guide.

Thirdly, Rupert made the TCC users' committee meetings much more of a two-way dialogue, rather than a monologue from the Bench. He actively encouraged participation. He carefully considered suggestions that were made as to how the TCC procedures could be improved and made everyone feel that they had a real stake in the future of the Court.

Fourthly, he never refused an invitation to give a talk, present a lecture, or undertake any public speaking about or on behalf of the TCC. He was not just the public face of the TCC: he *was* the TCC.

The fifth area where Rupert made significant changes concerned the giving of judgments. It had become the practice in the TCC for judgments at the end of trials to be reserved, regardless of the length of the trial or nature of the subject-matter. It was an uncomfortable truth that judgments were often reserved for many, many months.

Rupert's solution was simple: at the end of a trial he would usually give an extempore judgment, which would then be typed up and corrected for its final version. It was extremely rare for Rupert to delay longer than one or two days after a trial before giving judgment in this way. Of course, because he was doing the lion's share of the TCC High Court Judge work in the early days of his reforms, he was obliged to work in this way in order to ensure that one case was completed before the next one began. The pressure of the workload was immense. But this change meant that parties in the TCC got their answer quickly: the days of the 18-month wait were over.

This has always been the one area of judicial practice where Rupert and I have slightly different views. Unlike him, I think that there are some cases (by no means all) which benefit from a reserved judgment, where there can be real time for judicial reflection. But I understand how and why, between 2004 and 2007, there was so little time for him to reserve any judgments at all.

A final change concerned the role of the Judge of the TCC. Hitherto, as a QB Judge, the Judge in Charge of the TCC had been there for half of each term, and had gone out on circuit (or gone across the road to the Royal Courts of Justice to sit in other parts of the QB, the Court of Appeal Criminal Division or the Divisional Court). Rupert concluded that, in order to see his reforms through, it was imperative that he was in the TCC every working day. All of his predecessors have adopted the same methodology: the Judge in Charge of the TCC is in the TCC full time.

This may seem like a small change but, in truth, it was revolutionary. In the short term, it meant that Rupert was on hand to see that his reforms were carried through and that there was no back-sliding when he was away on circuit. But in the longer term it has made for continuity and consistency. These days the TCC runs pretty well and, although being the Judge in Charge adds about eight to ten hours a week to the existing workload (and sometimes more), it is very rewarding. There is usually something that requires the Judge in Charge's decision every single day and a daily discussion with the court manager is vital. Having the Judge in Charge based in London full time is therefore an extremely important feature of the Court.

V. Conclusions

As Lord Judge said in 2004, perception is everything. To change the perception of the TCC so quickly and so markedly was largely down to Rupert. He would be the first to say that he had considerable help from Paul Darling QC, then Chairman of TECBAR, and Caroline Cummins, the President of TeSCA. But the buck stopped with Rupert, so he should take the plaudits.

The changes that Rupert introduced, taken together as a package, changed the perception of the Court. The recruitment of Sir Vivian Ramsey, Sir Robert Akenhead and Sir Antony Edwards-Stuart to be full time judges of the court, and in their time the Judge in Charge of the Court, gave the changes still further momentum. But by the time Rupert went to the Court of Appeal in 2008, the task was well in hand and the TCC has never looked back.

There are advantages and disadvantages of being part of a small court like the TCC. The disadvantage is that, if one or two of the judges in the Court are the subject of properly sustained and fundamental criticism, then, no matter what is done by the other judges, the perception of the Court is disproportionately affected. That is what was happening by 2004. Conversely, with some good appointments, a solid procedural structure and a real sense of identity, a small court can punch above its weight and be a remarkably enjoyable place to work. As I leave it after nearly 14 years, I am in no doubt that the TCC is all of that and more. And I also know who we have to thank for bringing that about.

PART III

Costs

3

The Jackson Review: Its Rationale and Objectives

LORD CLARKE OF STONE-CUM-EBONY

I. Introduction

We all know that Sir Rupert Jackson is a walking phenomenon. I was at the Bar from 1965 to 1993. I was never in a case in which Rupert was on the other side. I can well imagine that to argue a case against Rupert would be a daunting prospect. His attention to detail, his prodigious hard work and his intellect are second to none. He had an unrivalled reputation at the Bar for his ability to master the facts in any case, however substantial, and for hard work. It was said that he often spent the night in chambers sleeping on a camp bed and that he only went to bed after a detailed discussion well into the night with his junior or juniors.

When I was Master of the Rolls between 2005 and 2009, I was also Head of Civil Justice and was Chairman of the Civil Justice Council (and indeed the Rules Committee). Lord Woolf had carried out a detailed analysis of civil procedure comparatively recently and the Civil Justice Council had decided that substantial work was required in order to improve the approach to the costs of civil litigation.

It was left to me as MR to identify a suitable person to carry out the work. Rupert was by this time Lord Justice Jackson and in the Court of Appeal. Enquiries as to who should be asked to carry out the work soon led to Lord Justice Jackson. I hope that he will not mind if I call him Rupert in this chapter. The way that he set about the work was, I like to think, good evidence that the right person had been chosen. This can be seen from the early parts of his report and the way he approached it.

II. The Review

In paragraph 1.4 of the Introduction to his Review[1] he noted that on 3 November 2008 I had appointed him to lead a fundamental review into the costs of civil litigation, in these terms:

> The review will commence in January 2009, and the findings are due to be presented to the Master of the Rolls in December 2009. Lord Justice Jackson will be the sole author of the final report, but he will be assisted in the review by a small group of 'assessors', drawn from the judiciary, legal profession and an economist. The review group are due to meet monthly to discuss issues and findings.

He correctly added that the review was being undertaken because I was concerned at the costs of civil litigation and believed that the time was right for a fundamental and independent review of the whole system. The review had the support of the Ministry of Justice. Its objective was to carry out an independent review of the rules and principles governing the costs of civil litigation and to make recommendations in order to promote access to justice at proportionate cost.

As is recorded in paragraph 1.2,[2] the terms of reference provided that in conducting the review, Rupert would:

- Establish how present costs rules operate and how they impact on the behaviour of both parties and lawyers.
- Establish the effect case management procedures have on costs and consider whether changes in process and/or procedure could bring about more proportionate costs.
- Have regard to previous and current research into costs and funding issues; for example any further Government research into Conditional Fee Agreements – 'No win, No fee' – following a scoping study.
- Seek the views of judges, practitioners, Government, court users and other interested parties through both informal consultation and a series of public seminars.
- Compare the costs regime for England and Wales with those operating in other jurisdictions.
- Prepare a report setting out recommendations with supporting evidence by 31 December 2009.

Rupert agreed to carry out the review on the basis that it would be completed in one year. Indeed, as I recall, he would only agree to carry it out on that basis. I cannot think of anyone else who would have insisted on a defined period to carry out such a major operation. Moreover, he insisted upon being responsible for the whole report himself. He divided the calendar year 2009 into three phases as follows:

- Phase 1 (January to April): Fact finding, preliminary consultation and preparation of Preliminary Report ('PR').

---

[1] Lord Justice Jackson, *Review of Civil Litigation Costs: Final Report* (TSO, December 2009) p 1.
[2] Lord Justice Jackson, *Review of Civil Litigation Costs: Final Report* (TSO, December 2009) pp 1–2.

- Phase 2 (May to July): Consultation.
- Phase 3 (September to December): Analysis of material received and preparation of Final Report.

In his foreword to the Final Report dated 21 December 2009 he expressed this general conclusion: 'In some areas of civil litigation costs are disproportionate and impede access to justice. I therefore propose a coherent package of interlocking reforms, designed to control costs and promote access to justice.'[3]

His approach to the work was unique. He was intent upon being the person responsible for the report. However, he appreciated that he would require expert advice on various aspects of what was bound to be a magnum opus. He identified seven assessors, who gave him the benefit of their advice, which he much appreciated. They were Mr Justice Cranston, Professor Paul Fenn, Senior Costs Judge Master Peter Hurst, Jeremy Morgan QC, Michael Napier CBE QC (Hon), Andrew Parker and Colin Stutt.

A. Phase 1

Phase 1 involved much fact finding and preliminary consultation and resulted in the Preliminary Report, which was published on 8 May 2009.[4] As he put it in paragraphs 2.3 and 2.4,[5] in that report he endeavoured to marshal the available facts and evidence, to identify the issues for consideration and to set out the relevant factors and competing arguments. Where he had formed tentative opinions, he set these out in the Preliminary Report. He invited those who disagreed to explain why such opinions were wrong. As he put it, many respondents accepted this invitation with alacrity. The Preliminary Report provided background material for the consultation exercise during Phase 2.

B. Phase 2

Phase 2 was a major piece of work. He set up four major seminars across the country. He also set up eight informal seminars. They covered the following disparate topics:

- After-the-event (ATE) insurance, success fees and conditional fee agreements.
- Contingency Legal Aid Funds (CLAFs), Supplementary Legal Aid Schemes (SLASs) and contingency fees.

---

[3] Lord Justice Jackson, *Review of Civil Litigation Costs: Final Report* (TSO, December 2009) p i.
[4] Lord Justice Jackson, *Review of Civil Litigation Costs: Preliminary Report* (TSO, May 2009), Vols 1 and 2.
[5] Lord Justice Jackson, *Review of Civil Litigation Costs: Final Report* (TSO, December 2009) p 3.

- Fixed costs (a) in the fast track and (b) above the fast track.
- Chancery litigation.
- Judicial review and environmental claims.
- Business disputes involving SMEs.
- Case management and costs management.
- The assessment of costs.

In addition, two pilot exercises on costs management were carried out and a number of working groups were set up. There was a separate group for each type of case, each comprising experts in their field. They were set up to consider particular issues in depth, and included calibration of software systems for assessing personal injury general damages, fixed costs of insolvency proceedings, costs management of insolvency proceedings, disclosure, libel, assessment of costs and costs management, including third-party funding: see paragraphs 3.9 to 3.16.[6]

C. Phase 3

In paragraph 4.1,[7] Rupert identified his principal task during Phase 3, which covered September to December 2009, as being to analyse the evidence and arguments gathered during Phase 2. It is plain that this was a mammoth exercise. A consideration, in the terms of the title to this chapter, of the rationale and objectives of the Jackson Review shows that this was a massive piece of work, which few, if any, of Rupert's colleagues could have achieved. I certainly could not. The purpose of this chapter is to give a glimpse of Rupert's expertise, intellect and hard work. It is not to explain or analyse it. There have been examples in the past of judges being asked to investigate a difficult problem who shirked the responsibility of setting out an executive summary. Rupert did not.

D. Executive Summary

In his introduction to the Executive Summary,[8] Rupert recognised that the terms of reference required him to review the rules and principles governing the costs of civil litigation and to make recommendations in order to promote access to justice at proportionate cost. They also required him to review case management procedures; to have regard to research into costs and funding; to consult widely; to compare our costs regime with those of other jurisdictions; and to prepare a report setting out recommendations with supporting evidence by 31 December 2009.

---

[6] Lord Justice Jackson, *Review of Civil Litigation Costs: Final Report* (TSO, December 2009) pp 5–7.
[7] Lord Justice Jackson, *Review of Civil Litigation Costs: Final Report* (TSO, December 2009) p 7.
[8] Lord Justice Jackson, *Review of Civil Litigation Costs: Final Report* (TSO, December 2009) p xvi.

In his paragraph 1.3,[9] under the heading 'Recommendations' he said that in some areas of litigation, costs were neither excessive nor disproportionate, so he did not recommend substantial changes. In other areas costs were excessive or disproportionate and he did recommend substantial changes. He also made recommendations in respect of funding regimes, in order to promote access to justice at proportionate cost. He added that funding regimes affect costs and the costs rules impact upon funding. Neither topic can be considered in isolation.

The Executive Summary then set out Rupert's major recommendations in these terms in paragraphs 2.1 to 2.11,[10] which I will set out in detail because they include the thrust of his conclusions:

> 2.1 <u>No win, no fee agreements.</u> Conditional fee agreements ('CFAs'), of which 'no win, no fee' agreements are the most common species, have been the major contributor to disproportionate costs in civil litigation in England and Wales. There are two key drivers of cost under such agreements, being (i) the lawyer's success fee; and (ii) the after-the-event ('ATE') insurance premium that is usually taken out when a CFA is entered into (to cover the claimant against the risk of having to pay the defendant's costs). Both the success fee and the ATE insurance premium are presently recoverable from an unsuccessful defendant.

> 2.2 <u>Success fees and ATE insurance premiums should cease to be recoverable.</u> I recommend that success fees and ATE insurance premiums should cease to be recoverable from unsuccessful opponents in civil litigation. If this recommendation is implemented, it will lead to significant costs savings, whilst still enabling those who need access to justice to obtain it. It will be open to clients to enter into 'no win, no fee' (or similar) agreements with their lawyers, but any success fee will be borne by the client, not the opponent.

> 2.3 <u>Consequences for personal injuries litigation.</u> The importance of ensuring that successful claimants are properly compensated for their injuries or losses was rightly emphasised to me during the Costs Review. Indeed, it must be acknowledged that one of the benefits of the current CFA regime is that it is geared towards ensuring that claimants receive proper compensation. This, however, comes at a heavy price for defendants, who often have to bear a disproportionate costs burden. If the current regime is reformed along the lines I have proposed, so that success fees are no longer recoverable from an opponent in litigation, lawyers will still be able to agree CFAs with their clients, but any success fee will be payable by the client. This is likely to mean that the success fee comes out of the damages awarded to the client.

> 2.4 <u>Increase in general damages.</u> In order to ensure that claimants are properly compensated for personal injuries, and that the damages awarded to them (which may be intended to cover future medical care) are not substantially eaten into by legal fees, I recommend as a complementary measure that awards of general damages for pain, suffering and loss of amenity be increased by 10%, and that the maximum amount of

---

[9] Lord Justice Jackson, *Review of Civil Litigation Costs: Final Report* (TSO, December 2009) p xvi.
[10] Lord Justice Jackson, *Review of Civil Litigation Costs: Final Report* (TSO, December 2009) pp xvi–xviii.

damages that lawyers may deduct for success fees be capped at 25% of damages (excluding any damages referable to future care or future losses). In the majority of cases, this should leave successful claimants no worse off than they are under the current regime, whilst at the same time ensuring that unsuccessful defendants only pay normal and proportionate legal costs to successful claimants. It will also ensure that claimants have an interest in the costs being incurred on their behalf.

2.5 Referral fees. It is a regrettably common feature of civil litigation, in particular personal injuries litigation, that solicitors pay referral fees to claims management companies, before-the-event ('BTE') insurers and other organisations to 'buy' cases. Referral fees add to the costs of litigation, without adding any real value to it. I recommend that lawyers should not be permitted to pay referral fees in respect of personal injury cases.

2.6 Qualified one way costs shifting. ATE insurance premiums add considerably to the costs of litigation. Litigation costs can be reduced by taking away the need for ATE insurance in the first place. This can occur if qualified one way costs shifting is introduced, at least for certain categories of litigation in which it is presently common for ATE insurance to be taken out. By 'qualified' one way costs shifting I mean that the claimant will not be required to pay the defendant's costs if the claim is unsuccessful, but the defendant will be required to pay the claimant's costs if it is successful. The qualifications to this are that unreasonable (or otherwise unjustified) party behaviour may lead to a different costs order, and the financial resources available to the parties may justify there being two way costs shifting in particular cases.

2.7 If it is accepted in principle that CFA success fees and ATE insurance premiums should cease to be recoverable, and qualified one way costs shifting should be introduced, there will need to be further consultation on which categories of litigation should involve qualified one way costs shifting. I can certainly see the benefit of there being qualified one way costs shifting in personal injuries litigation. It seems to me that a person who has a meritorious claim for damages for personal injuries should be able to bring that claim, without being deterred by the risk of adverse costs. The same could be said of clinical negligence, judicial review and defamation claims. There may be other categories of civil litigation where qualified one way costs shifting would be beneficial.

2.8 Overall result. If the package of proposed reforms summarised above is introduced, there will be five consequences:

- Most personal injury claimants will recover more damages than they do at present, although some will recover less.
- Claimants will have a financial interest in the level of costs which are being incurred on their behalf.
- Claimant solicitors will still be able to make a reasonable profit.
- Costs payable to claimant solicitors by liability insurers will be significantly reduced.
- Costs will also become more proportionate because defendants will no longer have to pay success fees and ATE insurance premiums.

2.9 Fixed costs in fast track litigation. Cases in the fast track are those up to a value of £25,000, where the trial can be concluded within one day. A substantial proportion of civil litigation is conducted in the fast track. I recommend that the costs recoverable for fast track personal injury cases be fixed. For other types of case I recommend that there be a dual system (at least for now), whereby costs are fixed for certain types of case, and in other cases there is a financial limit on costs recoverable (I propose that £12,000 be the limit for pre-trial costs). The ideal is for costs to be fixed in the fast track for all types of claim.

2.10 There are several advantages to the fixing of costs in lower value litigation. One is that it gives all parties certainty as to the costs they may recover if successful, or their exposure if unsuccessful. Secondly, fixing costs avoids the further process of costs assessment, or disputes over recoverable costs, which can in themselves generate further expense. Thirdly, it ensures that recoverable costs are proportionate. There is a public interest in making litigation costs in the fast track both proportionate and certain.

2.11 Costs Council. If a fixed costs regime is adopted for the fast track, the costs recoverable for the various types of claim will need to be reviewed regularly to make sure that they are reasonable and realistic. I propose that a Costs Council be established to undertake the role of reviewing fast track fixed costs, as well as other matters.

In paragraph 3 of the Executive Summary,[11] Rupert focused on BTE insurance, contingency fees and CLAFs and SLASs under the heading 'OTHER FUNDING ISSUES'. As to BTE, or legal expenses insurance, he said in paragraph 3.1 that it was underused but that, if it was used more widely, it could produce benefits for small and medium enterprises (SMEs) and individuals.

As to contingency fees, which were not permissible in 'contentious' business when Rupert wrote his report, he recommended, as summarised in paragraphs 3.2 and 3.3 of his Executive Summary, that lawyers should be able to enter into contingency fee agreements with clients for contentious business, provided that:

- the unsuccessful party in the proceedings, if ordered to pay the successful party's costs, is only required to pay an amount for costs reflecting what would be a conventional amount, with any difference to be borne by the successful party; and
- the terms on which contingency fee agreements may be entered into are regulated, to safeguard the interests of clients.

He added that permitting the use of contingency fee agreements increases the types of litigation funding available to litigants, which should thereby increase access to justice. This would be of especial importance if (as proposed) the current CFA regime were reformed.

As to CLAFs and SLASs, he expressed some concern for their financial viability but nevertheless recommended that their use be kept under review.

In paragraph 4,[12] he focused on PERSONAL INJURIES LITIGATION, including process and procedure and clinical negligence; and then in paragraph 5[13]

---

[11] Lord Justice Jackson, *Review of Civil Litigation Costs: Final Report* (TSO, December 2009) pp xviii–xix.
[12] Lord Justice Jackson, *Review of Civil Litigation Costs: Final Report* (TSO, December 2009) pp xix–xx.
[13] Lord Justice Jackson, *Review of Civil Litigation Costs: Final Report* (TSO, December 2009) pp xx–xxii.

he identified some specific types of litigation, notably intellectual property litigation, small business disputes, housing claims, large commercial claims, Chancery litigation, Technology and Construction Court litigation, judicial review, nuisance cases, defamation and related claims, collective actions and appeals. Each topic was given a separate chapter in the Report. I could not possibly refer in detail to each of these topics. Suffice it to say that each chapter is a brilliant piece of work.

Finally, in paragraph 6[14] he examined CONTROLLING THE COSTS OF LITIGATION, which involved an analysis of pre-action protocols, ADR, disclosure, witness statements and expert evidence, case management, costs management, offers, IT and summary and detailed assessments of costs. Each of those is a substantial topic in itself. The recommendations were stated with Rupert's natural clarity.

For example, in paragraph 6.9[15] he recommended a number of measures, as he put it, to enhance the court's role and approach to case management including:

- where practicable, allocating cases to judges who have relevant expertise;
- ensuring that, so far as possible, a case remains with the same judge;
- standardising case management directions; and
- ensuring that case management conferences and other interim hearings are used as effective occasions for case management, and do not become formulaic hearings that generate unnecessary cost (e.g. where directions could easily have been given without a hearing).

III. The Aftermath

Rupert was true to his word and delivered his report on time. Of course, not every recommendation was received with acclaim, but the quality of his work was recognised throughout the system and he himself was keen to play a part in the implementation of the Report. I would like to repeat here my admiration for him and his work. I cannot think of anyone else who could have done it.

In order to keep this chapter within reasonable limits it is not feasible to discuss all the topics covered in Rupert's report. I shall focus on only one, which was central to his thesis. It arises out of his analysis of the question whether success fees and ATE insurance premiums should be recoverable under costs orders from losing parties. In paragraph 4.2 of Chapter 10 of his Final Report[16] he noted that recoverability was introduced to coincide with the substantial retraction of legal

---

[14] Lord Justice Jackson, *Review of Civil Litigation Costs: Final Report* (TSO, December 2009) pp xxii–xxiv.

[15] Lord Justice Jackson, *Review of Civil Litigation Costs: Final Report* (TSO, December 2009) p xxiii.

[16] Lord Justice Jackson, *Review of Civil Litigation Costs: Final Report* (TSO, December 2009) p 108.

aid and the establishment of a new system of public funding which occurred as from 1 April 2000. As Rupert put it, the stated intention of recoverability was fourfold:

- To ensure that the compensation awarded to a successful party was not eroded by any uplift or premium – the party in the wrong would bear the full burden of costs.
- To make conditional fees more attractive, in particular to defendants and to claimants seeking non-monetary redress.
- To discourage weak cases and encourage settlements.
- To provide a mechanism for regulating the uplifts that solicitors charge.

In his paragraph 4.7,[17] Rupert highlights four flaws in the recoverability regime. The first flaw is described in his paragraphs 4.8–4.12.[18] It includes what he describes as tree-root claims, commercial claims and consumer disputes. As he put it in paragraph 4.12, the first flaw in the recoverability regime is that it is unfocused. There is no eligibility test for entering into a CFA, provided that a willing solicitor can be found.

The second flaw is described in paragraph 4.13[19] and is that the party with a CFA generally has no interest in the level of costs being incurred in his or her name. Whether the case is won or lost, the client will usually pay nothing. If the case is lost, the solicitors waive their costs and pay the disbursements, in so far as not covered by ATE insurance. If the case is won, the lawyers will recover whatever they can from the other side either (a) by detailed or summary assessment or (b) by negotiation based upon the likely outcome of such an assessment. In his paragraph 4.14,[20] Rupert added that that means that the client exerts no control (or, in the case of a no win, no fee agreement, little control) over costs when they are being incurred. The entire burden falls upon the judge who assesses costs retrospectively at the end of the case, when it is too late to 'control' what is spent.

The third flaw in the recoverability regime is that the costs burden placed upon opposing parties is excessive and sometimes amounts to a denial of justice. If one takes any large block of cases conducted on CFAs, the opposing parties will end up paying more than the total costs of both parties in every case, regardless of the outcome of any particular case: see paragraph 4.15.[21] Rupert added in paragraph 4.16 that, if the opposing party contests a case to trial (possibly quite reasonably) and then loses, its costs liability becomes grossly disproportionate. Indeed the costs consequences of the recoverability rules can be so extreme as to drive opposing parties to settle at an early stage, despite having good prospects of

---

[17] Lord Justice Jackson, *Review of Civil Litigation Costs: Final Report* (TSO, December 2009) p 109.
[18] Lord Justice Jackson, *Review of Civil Litigation Costs: Final Report* (TSO, December 2009) pp 109–10.
[19] Lord Justice Jackson, *Review of Civil Litigation Costs: Final Report* (TSO, December 2009) p 110.
[20] Lord Justice Jackson, *Review of Civil Litigation Costs: Final Report* (TSO, December 2009) p 111.
[21] Lord Justice Jackson, *Review of Civil Litigation Costs: Final Report* (TSO, December 2009) p 111.

a successful defence. This effect is sometimes described as blackmail, even though the claimant is using the recoverability rules in a perfectly lawful way.

The fourth flaw is described by Rupert in paragraphs 4.17 to 4.19 in these terms:[22]

> 4.17 If claimant solicitors and counsel are successful in only picking 'winners', they will substantially enlarge their earnings. As Professor Zander pointed out at the London seminar, if the claimant solicitor wins a case with a 100% success fee, he or she receives an additional 300% profit. As the Senior Costs Judge explained at the same seminar, it is not possible for costs judges effectively to control success fees retrospectively.
>
> 4.18 Of course, not all lawyers are good at picking winners and some suffer losses on that account. Nevertheless, one repeated criticism of the recoverability regime, which I have heard throughout the Costs Review, is that some claimant lawyers 'cherry pick'. In other words they generally conduct winning cases on CFAs, they reject or drop at an early stage less promising cases and thus generate extremely healthy profits. Obviously the financial records of individual solicitors firms and barristers are confidential. Moreover, even if one such set of accounts were made public, that would tell us nothing about all the others. Nevertheless, the one point that can be made about the CFA regime is that it presents the opportunity to cherry pick. If lawyers succumb to that temptation, they will greatly increase their own earnings and they will do so in a manner which is entirely lawful.
>
> 4.19 Having worked in the legal profession for 37 years, I have a high regard for my fellow lawyers, both solicitors and counsel. The fact remains, however, that lawyers are human. As Professor Adrian Zuckerman has forcefully pointed out both during the Woolf Inquiry and during the present Costs Review, work tends to follow the most remunerative path. In my view, it is a flaw of the recoverability regime that it presents an opportunity to lawyers substantially to increase their earnings by cherry picking. This is a feature which tends to demean the profession in the eyes of the public.

Those points seem to me to have considerable force. Rupert expressed his view in paragraph 4.20 in these terms.[23] The proper course, he said, was to abolish recoverability and to revert to old style CFAs, as they existed before April 2000. Those arrangements were satisfactory and opened up access to justice for many individuals who formerly had no such access: see paragraph 16.3.2 of his Preliminary Report.[24] During 1996, the Association of Personal Injury Lawyers (APIL) confirmed that those arrangements provided access to justice for personal injury claimants and that those arrangements were satisfactory: see paragraph 25 of Chapter 2 of Lord Woolf's Final Report on Access to Justice.[25]

---

[22] Lord Justice Jackson, *Review of Civil Litigation Costs: Final Report* (TSO, December 2009) p 111.

[23] Lord Justice Jackson, *Review of Civil Litigation Costs: Final Report* (TSO, December 2009) p 112.

[24] Lord Justice Jackson, *Review of Civil Litigation Costs: Preliminary Report* (TSO, May 2009) Volume 1, Chapter 16, pages 168–169.

[25] Lord Woolf, *Access to Justice – Final Report* (HMSO, 1996).

There followed in section 5[26] a series of follow-on questions, first on the assumption that his recommendations to abolish recoverability were accepted. He set out his proposed measures relating to personal injuries litigation, other litigation brought by individuals, claimants' offers, and the level of success fees. Secondly, he considered the position if his recommendations were not accepted. Then in section 6,[27] under the heading RECOMMENDATIONS, on the footing that his recommendations were accepted, he made these two recommendations in paragraph 6.1 as follows:

> (i) Section 58A(6) of the CLSA 1990[28] and all rules made pursuant to that provision should be repealed.

> (ii) The level of general damages for personal injuries, nuisance and all other civil wrongs to individuals should be increased by 10%.

He noted in paragraph 6.2 that if the recommendations in Chapter 10 were rejected, then alternative proposals to limit the impact of section 58A(6) of the 1990 Act were set out in section 5 of Chapter 10 of the Final Report.

I have referred to the recoverability section of the Final Report in some detail because it was an important part of the Final Report and has attracted some judicial comment and, indeed, decision. See, for example, the discussion in the Supreme Court in *Times Newspapers Limited v Flood*,[29] where the Supreme Court discussed in some detail the relevant principles in the United Kingdom by comparison with those applied by the European Court of Human Rights in Strasbourg. There is no time to discuss those differences here. I have not therefore considered the European jurisprudence as it stands at present, save to say that I feel sure that Strasbourg will have regard to the views expressed by Rupert.

IV. Lord Justice Jackson's Harbour Lecture 2015

Rupert himself played a significant part in the aftermath of the Final Report. It included his 2015 Harbour Lecture,[30] in which he noted that the cost management regime had been in place for two years and that the purpose of his 2015 Lecture was to review how it was working and to suggest how the rules might be developed in the light of experience. He noted in paragraph 1.8 that between January 2010 and April 2012 he had the lead role in implementing the reforms

---

[26] Lord Justice Jackson, *Review of Civil Litigation Costs: Final Report* (TSO, December 2009) pages 112–116.

[27] Lord Justice Jackson, *Review of Civil Litigation Costs: Final Report* (TSO, December 2009) page 116.

[28] Courts and Legal Services Act 1990.

[29] *Times Newspapers Limited v Flood* [2017] 1 WLR 1414.

[30] 'Confronting Costs Management – Harbour Lecture' (13 May 2015). The lecture is downloadable at www.judiciary.gov.uk.

recommended in the Final Report, subject to the supervision of the Judicial Steering Group (which comprised Lord Neuberger MR, Maurice Kay LJ, Moore-Bick LJ and Rupert himself) to which he reported every fortnight. After April 2012, Rupert was in some respects unwell but that meant, as he put it, that he could watch what was happening with a measure of detachment. That did not, however, mean that he could play no part at all. On two occasions he gave lectures drawing attention to where he thought things were going wrong: see note 4 to paragraph 1.9 of his Harbour Lecture.

He entitled paragraph 2 'WHEN DONE PROPERLY COSTS MANAGEMENT WORKS WELL'. In summary he concluded (in paragraph 2.1) that the first and most important conclusion to be drawn from the experience of the last two years was the same as that which was drawn from the pilots. Costs management works. When an experienced judge or master costs manages litigation with competent practitioners on both sides, the costs of the litigation are controlled from an early stage. Although some practitioners and judges regard the process as tiresome, it brings substantial benefits to court users. In paragraphs 2.2 to 2.4 he described the first benefit of costs management as the knowledge by both parties of the financial position.

The remainder of paragraph 2 set out the reasons for that conclusion. In paragraph 2.5 he identified the second benefit of costs management, namely the encouragement of early settlement, and set out the reasons for that conclusion given by practising lawyers and judges. The third benefit was that costs are controlled (paragraph 2.6). In addition, in paragraph 2.7 he stressed the interface with the new rules on proportionate costs. He did so by reference to Chapter 40 section 7 of his Report and the new Rule 44. In particular, he noted that Rule 44.3(5) contains a new definition of proportionate costs. Rule 44.3(2) provides that when costs are assessed on the standard basis no more than proportionate costs will be recoverable. Therefore the judge at the costs management stage applies the proportionality test and limits the recoverable costs accordingly. It is by no means unusual for a judge to say that (regardless of hourly rates or numbers of hours) no more than £x is proportionate for a particular phase or that no more than £y is proportionate for the case as a whole. Absent an order for indemnity costs, no losing party should be ordered to pay more than proportionate costs to its adversary.

In paragraph 2.8 he asked whether it was a problem that the winner might recover less costs than in the past. His answer was no. He pointed to extensive academic literature and research to demonstrate that the costs-shifting rule tended to drive up costs: see Chapter 9 of the Preliminary Report. If the 2013 civil justice reforms made a modest inroad into that rule, it was no bad thing. He concluded in clear terms that once people knew that they would only recover proportionate costs if they won, they would have a greater incentive to be economical.

His fourth benefit of costs management (expressed in paragraph 2.9) was that it focused attention on costs at the outset of litigation. He noted that a number of solicitors and judges regarded that as a major factor, because costs are a major factor in the majority of cases. As Rupert put it on the basis of evidence before him, a failure by the victor to recover sufficient costs may render the whole litigation futile. He added that the costs burden on the loser may be crushing, quite regardless of the damages which he may have to pay or the property rights which he may forfeit. It was therefore necessary that all concerned should be forced to focus on the costs involved at the outset.

In paragraph 2.9 Rupert described the fifth benefit of costs management as 'an old chestnut conquered'. The summons for directions under the pre-1999 Rules of the Supreme Court was intended to be an occasion when the court would get a grip on the issues and give effective directions. The habitual complaint was that in practice this never happened. Summonses for directions were formulaic and ineffectual. The new-style 'case management conference' (CMC) introduced by Lord Woolf was intended to overcome all that and be a real occasion for effective case management. The evidence which Rupert received during the 2009 Costs Review was that, outside the specialist courts, this still wasn't happening. CMCs were simply becoming formulaic occasions.

Rupert added that it was for that reason that he put forward a series of proposals in Chapters 37 to 39 of his Final Report to convert CMCs into effective occasions when the judge 'takes a grip on the case, identifies the issues and gives directions which are focused on the early resolution of those issues'. He concluded that one consequence of costs management was that that was now happening. With price tags attached to the work, everyone was taking more interest. He concluded that there was serious debate about what work was really necessary, what disclosure was required, what experts were needed and so forth. He added that even practitioners who disliked the recent reforms reluctantly conceded that that was the position.

In paragraphs 2.11 and 2.12 Rupert then described the sixth and seventh benefits of costs management respectively as elementary fairness and the prevention of legal catastrophes. He subsequently produced evidence of others and the perception of parties (in paragraphs 2.13–2.17 and 2.18 respectively). He analysed a number of objections and the answers to them in paragraphs 2.19–2.23. In short, his conclusions remained positive.

The remainder of Rupert's lecture identified various problems that had emerged and set out his detailed responses to them. I recommend the reader to consider carefully his optimistic analysis, as set out in pages 8 to 30. They contain a further detailed analysis of many of the problems.

V. Lord Dyson MR's Harbour Lecture

On the same day, 13 May 2015 (which happens to be my birthday), Lord Dyson, who was then Master of the Rolls, gave a short Harbour lecture.[31] As they say in

---

[31] 'Confronting Costs Management – Harbour Lecture' (13 May 2015). The lecture is downloadable at www.judiciary.gov.uk.

appellate courts (including the Supreme Court and the Court of Appeal), I agree with his conclusions and there is nothing I can usefully add. In spite of that general principle, I would like to quote the views he expressed as part of this *Festschrift*. Lord Dyson's lecture reads as follows:

> It gives me [ie Lord Dyson] great pleasure to add a short contribution to this important topic. At the very outset, I want to make it clear that I strongly support costs management. As Sir Rupert says, the new regime is in the public interest and is here to stay. That is not to say that the current system is perfect. It is unsurprising that the experience of the first two years of the Jackson reforms has revealed some problems. It would have been remarkable had the position been otherwise. That is why the sub-committee of the Civil Procedure Rule Committee chaired by Coulson J has been established to examine the extent of the problems and to make recommendations for improvement. It is also why a seminar organised by the senior QB Master was held in March 2015 on costs budgeting in clinical negligence cases.
>
> The Jackson Report was a brilliant piece of work. It was the product of a huge amount of research. But there is no substitute for testing civil justice reforms in the crucible of the real world of civil litigation. This was a luxury that was denied to Sir Rupert apart from a few pilots. We do now have the benefit of seeing how the reforms have been working in practice. In many respects, the cost management aspects of the reforms have been successful. I greatly welcome the fact that the percentage of cases (other than person injury and clinical negligence cases) in which costs budgets are agreed is steadily rising; and that, for the most part, solicitors are not collaborating to agree inflated budgets.
>
> Judges and practitioners are becoming more familiar with the process of cost budgeting and are getting better at it. That is only to be expected, but is nevertheless encouraging and welcome too.
>
> We are indeed fortunate that Sir Rupert has found the time to produce a detailed report on the working of the costs management regime two years after its introduction. His lecture this evening is a carefully researched and clear review of the current situation as he sees it. It is a valuable piece of work. But it is not appropriate for me to comment on each of the points that he makes, not least because, as Head of Civil Justice, I would not wish to commit myself without taking account of the views of other interested parties. I am also conscious of the central role of the Rule Committee in all of this. There are, however, some aspects of what Sir Rupert has said on which I would like to comment.
>
> The benefits of cost management are obvious and, I believe, not controversial. They tend to be overlooked. The focus of the attention of judges and practitioners alike tends to be on the problems. That is inevitable. Sir Rupert has identified a number of the main objections that are levelled against coats management. I agree with his answers to them.
>
> He has also identified eight particular problems which have emerged and proposed solutions to them. I agree with him that the solution to the problem of inconsistency of judicial approach lies in judicial training. Inconsistency of judicial approach undermines public confidence in the justice system and encourages forum shopping. His proposals for a standard form of costs management order; for an amendment to the rules in relation to the time for lodging costs budgets; and for changes to precedent H should be given careful consideration by the Rule Committee.

Nobody disputes that there is a problem of delay in clinical negligence cases in London and some (but not all) of the regional centres. There has been a massive increase in the number of clinical negligence cases in London in the last few years, but no increase in judicial resources to deal with the case and costs management of them. As Sir Rupert says, the waiting time for a first case management conference in London is now about nine months. This is unacceptable. He proposes that the way to resolve the impasse is by granting a one-off release and coupling this with the repeal of parts of rule 3.15 and [Practice Direction] 3E. These are proposals that are worthy of the most careful consideration. But I have real concern about them. The key proposal seems to be that the Rule Committee should issue new criteria to guide courts in deciding whether or not to make a costs management order; and these should be formulated bearing in mind principles which include that 'the court should not manage costs in any case if it lacks the resources to do so without causing significant delay and disruption to that or other cases.' I do not doubt that, if the rule/practice direction were amended to reflect this principle, judges would do their best conscientiously to apply it. But I fear that the lack of resources card would be played in many cases and that there is a real danger that costs management would become the exception, and not the rule, in clinical negligence cases. As Sir Rupert points out, there are now two fewer QB masters than there were in 2009 when he recommended that an additional QB master be appointed to deal with clinical negligence cases. The massive increase in clinical negligence cases in London since 2009 has made the case for an additional QB master even more powerful than it was when Sir Rupert first made his recommendation. It may be that, without more judicial resources, the costs management of clinical negligence cases may have to be abandoned in a significant number of cases. I await the recommendations of the Coulson report with great interest.

I agree with what Sir Rupert says about the desirability of having a single case and costs management hearing and the advantages of what he refers to as 'an iterative process'.

Sir Rupert makes a number of useful points on the subject of GHRs [guideline hourly rates for solicitors]. I agree that it is unsatisfactory that the rates have not been revised since 2010. But new rates must be firmly evidence-based. I think everyone accepts that. Thus far, obtaining reliable evidence on which to base new rates has proved to be elusive. Neither the Ministry of Justice nor the Law Society has been willing to fund the necessary survey. I agree that other possible avenues should be explored. Sir Rupert suggests that foundations which support socio-legal research or universities might be willing to undertake the work. But the difficulties should not be underestimated. First, the success of the exercise would depend on the willingness of solicitors to provide the necessary information. Secondly, I was advised that the cost of conducting an effective survey and analysing the results would be very considerable.

Sir Rupert has repeated his plea for an extension of the fixed recoverable costs regime to all fast-track cases as well as to the smaller multi-track cases. I take this opportunity to support him on this. I have been urging it publicly for a considerable period of time. There has been no public response from the [Ministry of Justice]. I do not know whether there are any objections in principle to it. So far as I am aware, there are none. I can see that, if the proposal were accepted in principle, there would be battles over the levels at which the fees were set and as to the cut-off point for fixed fees in multi-track cases. I can also see that there would have to be a provision for disapplying the regime in exceptional circumstances. But in my view, the time has come for the Ministry of Justice to say that it accepts in principle that the fixed costs regime should be extended. At a stroke, this reform would surely reduce disputes about costs and also reduce the cost of a large swathe of civil litigation more generally.

Finally, I wish to express my admiration of Sir Rupert for his Harbour lecture. We are fortunate that the author of the reforms which have done so much to improve civil justice in this country has been willing to undertake this review. He has made a number of valuable suggestions which will be taken into account in deciding on the way forward.

For the reasons I have given above, I too would like to express my admiration for Rupert, both in his Review and in his Harbour lecture. I also note that work continues on many of these (and other) topics, not only by Rupert but by Lord Briggs and by Sir Terence Etherton MR.

Rupert himself continues work on fixed costs: see in particular in his IPA Annual lecture delivered on 28 January 2016 which is entitled 'Fixed Costs – The Time Has Come.'[32] For the reasons which Rupert gives, I agree. Although I have not consulted Lord Dyson on fixed costs, it seems reasonably clear from his views on fixed costs quoted above that he is also likely to agree.

I wish Rupert every happiness in his retirement.

---

[32] The speech is downloadable at www.judiciary.gov.uk.

4

The Jackson Reforms and Technology & Construction Court Litigation

SIR ANTONY EDWARDS-STUART

I. A Brief History of the Technology and Construction Court

Those who practised at the Construction Bar in the early 1980s will remember, perhaps with some nostalgia, the Official Referees' corridor on the third floor of the West Wing of the Royal Courts of Justice. That is where the eight Official Referees sat in courts which more closely resembled classrooms than the oak panelled Victorian courts two floors below.

In those days construction disputes were long drawn-out affairs – trials of eight or more weeks were quite common. Under the shadow of Donald Keating QC, new silks were beginning to carve out their practices – amongst them Humphrey LLoyd, Anthony May and John Dyson, to name just three. Although the Official Referees were regarded by many in the senior judicial establishment as the cadet branch of the High Court, they were a continuing source of innovation in trial procedure.

It had to be so: if witnesses were to be examined in chief at great length in the customary way, the trials would have become unmanageable. So the Official Referees were the first judges to introduce the practice of witnesses giving evidence by tendering previously exchanged witness statements, with the result that the bulk of the oral evidence took the form of cross-examination. Of course, this placed a huge burden on counsel for defendants, but they learned to cope with it. It was alleviated to some extent by the court's practice (like the Commercial Court) of hearing trials on four days a week only, leaving Fridays to case management.

In this way the judges took greater control of the management of cases. There were no Masters in the Official Referees' corridor and so the judges did all the case management themselves. The very high settlement rate of these large cases, about 85 per cent, meant that the court could list cases as a first, second, third and sometimes even a sixth fixture. It was reasonably likely that the hearing of a case listed as a second or third fixture would start on the listed date or, at least, within a few days of it.

During the past quarter of a century the Court has seen four major changes. The first was the move, at the end of the 1980s, into a purpose-built court building, St Dunstan's House, in Fetter Lane. There were eight large courts on the top four floors of the building, each with a judge's room nearby. The second change came in October 1998 when the court was renamed the 'Technology and Construction Court' (the TCC) and Mr Justice Dyson was appointed Judge in Charge.

This change coincided with the introduction of compulsory adjudication into construction contracts, and so the Court had to adapt itself rapidly to meet the changing demands presented by this new form of dispute resolution. A body of case law quickly developed and the basic ingredients of the current procedure were established. Today, decisions of adjudicators that are not complied with are regularly enforced by judges of the TCC. Applications to enforce adjudicators' decisions, which typically take half a day or a day to hear, are heard by the TCC within four to five weeks of the issue of the claim form. The approach of the Court is robust and the vast majority of decisions are upheld (but still only on an interim basis, pending final resolution by litigation or arbitration).

The third change, and perhaps the most important, was the decision in 2004 to transform the TCC into an all High Court Judge court. No further Circuit Judges were appointed and the first High Court Judge under the new regime, Sir Vivian Ramsey, was appointed in 2005. Sir Rupert Jackson was by then the Judge in Charge. The burden fell on him to implement the new regime, and there is no question but that it was a very heavy one: the changes were not universally well received by the existing incumbents.

That first appointment was soon followed by others and the Court now has six designated High Court Judges. Thanks to the introduction of adjudication the workload of the Court, in terms of sitting days, has been reduced drastically. However, the breadth of work now handled by the Court has increased enormously. By way of example, a relatively recent class of work to come within the jurisdiction of the TCC is public procurement. Although these cases often have nothing to do with construction or engineering, the TCC has become the court of choice because it has been able to adjust its procedures to meet the needs of this specialist area of work.

The fourth change, and perhaps the most symbolic, was the move into the Rolls Building in 2011 alongside the Chancery Division and the Commercial Court. If the TCC was once thought to be the Cinderella of the High Court, it has now firmly taken its place alongside the ugly sisters.

II. The Need for the Jackson Reforms in the TCC

As Rupert Jackson himself acknowledged, the TCC is a court that had already taken many steps to improve its procedures and to reduce the cost of High Court litigation. In *Harding v Paice*,[1] he described it as a court 'well known for its speed and efficiency'.[2] In his Final Report,[3] Rupert Jackson observed, in relation to the TCC:[4] 'Litigation in the [TCC] is often conducted in a proportionate manner, and I make only modest recommendations concerning the operation of that court. I do, however, recommend that there be a fast track in the TCC.'

In his Final Report, Chapter 29, paragraph 1.9, he said:

> Complacency is dangerous for obvious reasons. On the other hand, given the tenor of responses received during Phase 2, I should be extremely cautious before recommending any significant changes to the existing procedures of the TCC. The TCC is now named as the dispute resolution forum in a number of overseas contracts. Therefore, in respect of the TCC (as in respect of the Commercial Court) it is important not to make procedural changes which will be unacceptable to overseas litigants who choose London as their forum.

However, Rupert Jackson did make a recommendation that there should be a Fast-Track procedure in the TCC for small building disputes.

Perhaps one of the most effective aspects of the Court's procedure is the early fixing of the trial date. A case management conference takes place at an early stage in the litigation, the date for which is set shortly after the acknowledgement of service of the claim form by the defendant, and this usually (but not always) means that it takes place shortly after service of the Defence: accordingly when the first CMC is heard the Court is in a good position to identify the real issues in the case. The parties are required to provide the Court with an estimate of the length of the trial, and in the light of the parties' estimates the Court determines the likely the length of the trial and then the trial date is fixed having regard to availability in the court diary. For a typical two to three-week case, the hearing is usually set for a date about 12 months after the first CMC. It would be only in a very unusual case that this period would be longer, although different considerations will apply to cases with estimates much longer than three weeks. It is a firm rule that the trial is not allowed to overrun, so it is essential that the parties cooperate from the outset to produce a timetable that allows the trial to be conducted in a fair and orderly way during the period fixed.

This fixing of a trial date at a relatively early stage in the litigation is crucial. Whilst it might be thought from a theoretical perspective that in any particular case the steps required, and the resources required to complete them, would be capable of identification in advance with a fair amount of precision, with the result that the time available to complete them would not make much difference, this is not the case. Experience has shown that the costs of litigation increase in direct proportion to the length of the process – another demonstration of the working

---

[1] *Harding v Paice* [2015] EWCA Civ 1231.
[2] [2015] EWCA Civ 1231 at [36].
[3] Lord Justice Jackson, *Review of Civil Litigation Costs: Final Report* (TSO, December 2009).
[4] *Review of Civil Litigation Costs: Final Report*, Executive Summary, paragraph 5.7.

of Parkinson's Law. Quite simply, the more time available for inter-solicitor correspondence and jockeying for tactical advantage, the more of it there will be.

On 1 October 2015 a pilot of two schemes, the Shorter Trials Scheme and the Flexible Trials Scheme, was introduced for a trial period of two years in all courts in the Rolls Building. Whilst this was a welcome initiative, I did not anticipate that it would be much used in the TCC, given that the Court's existing procedures for short cases already permitted them to be heard in a similar timescale. This appears to have been the case: so far as I am aware, the schemes have been little used in the TCC.

Another area in which the TCC has adapted its procedures effectively is that of expert evidence.

Whilst judges of the TCC are always concerned to respect party autonomy in the conduct of litigation, they adopt a reasonably firm approach to the scope of expert evidence. CPR 35 provides that permission will not be given unless the Court is satisfied that the evidence is 'reasonably required'. In practice, judges of the TCC interpret this test quite strictly: the TCC Guide refers to expert evidence being limited to 'what is necessary for the requirements of the case'. Sometimes at the CMC the judge will refuse permission for an expert of a particular discipline to be heard but give the requesting party permission to re-apply at a later stage should the case for evidence in the particular discipline in question turn out to be stronger than initially thought.

The TCC has also developed its own procedures in relation to the holding of experts' meetings and preparation of reports. The approach most commonly favoured in the TCC today is for the experts to meet first to discuss the issues in the case, then to prepare a note of matters agreed (and not agreed) and, finally, to prepare and exchange reports. The conventional approach is the reverse of this procedure, by which the experts exchange their reports first and then hold discussions afterwards. Experience in TCC litigation has shown that with the latter procedure there is a danger that experts will nail their colours to their respective masts without having had any proper opportunity to consider and take into account the merits of the opposing expert's views: there seems to be a better chance of issues narrowing if the experts can discuss them with each other before committing themselves to paper. It seems that this approach is now finding some favour in the Commercial Court. However, flexibility still needs to be the watchword: there are cases in which it is more appropriate to adopt the conventional approach in order to prevent the experts' discussions degenerating into a form of horse trading.

In terms of the way in which expert evidence is given at the trial, the TCC judges are prepared to be flexible and, where it may shorten the trial or lead to a more objective presentation of the evidence, to direct that the evidence of the experts is to be given concurrently, either in the form suggested in the post-Jackson CPR 35, PD 35 paragraph 11 or in one of the ways mentioned in section 13 of the TCC Guide, or some variant of it.

However, adopting this approach places a greater burden on the judge. In effect, he or she has to be as well prepared as counsel who is about to cross-examine.

Since the judge is inevitably on a much steeper learning curve than counsel for the parties, the difficulties that he or she faces if this procedure is to be adopted cannot be underestimated.

I think that the third area in which valuable progress has been made in the TCC concerns e-disclosure. Thanks to a protocol[5] drafted a few years ago by the Technology & Construction Solicitors Association (TeCSA), with assistance from members of the Technology & Construction Bar Association (TECBAR) and the Society for Computers & Law, e-disclosure now gives rise to relatively few disputes in case management terms. The introductory paragraphs to the Protocol (2nd Edition) explain its purpose clearly:

> (1) This Protocol should be used to record the result of discussion between the parties on disclosure which is required by CPR Rule 31.5(5) and PD31B, and this Protocol should so far as possible be finalised not less than 7 days prior to the first Case Management Conference.
>
> (2) Except where otherwise expressly stated, this Protocol is not a contractually binding legal agreement between the parties. It is recognised that circumstances may arise which may make it appropriate for there to be variations to the matters set out in this Protocol. Such variations should be agreed with the other party or parties or may be the subject of an application to the Court for further directions. However, it should be recognised that departure from the areas of agreement on disclosure recorded in this Protocol may have costs consequences.
>
> (3) The matters set out in this Protocol are subject to review by the Court in accordance with the Court's case management powers. Matters which cannot be agreed by the parties should be referred to the Court for directions.

In most cases where there is a substantial volume of material to be disclosed, the parties, following the guidance in the Protocol, agree on matters such as the identity of the appropriate custodians, keywords and the date ranges to be searched. The Protocol is adapted where necessary to fit the circumstances of the particular case, and it is seldom that the parties resort to the Court to resolve any disagreements. That was not the position before the Protocol came into force, when disputes about the scope or procedure for e-disclosure occurred on a fairly regular basis.

A particularly valuable provision in the Protocol, which may go some way to explaining why it has become so widely accepted, is a 'clawback' provision to deal with cases where privileged documents have been disclosed inadvertently. This provides as follows:

> (1) If any party receives material from another party which the receiving party knows or reasonably ought to know was inadvertently produced, or if the producing party notifies the receiving party that it has inadvertently produced to the receiving party a privileged or confidential document, the receiving party will
>
> (a) immediately cease to review that material,
> (b) promptly return that material to the producing party or destroy it, and

---

[5] 'TeCSA/SCL/TECBAR eDisclosure Protocol' version 0.2, 9 January 2015: see www.tecsa.org.uk.

(c)   make no use of that material or its contents for any purpose, unless (i) the Court rejects the asserted ground for withholding production or decides that the disclosure was not inadvertent, or (ii) the claim to be entitled to withhold production is withdrawn by the producing party.

(2) The parties have agreed that the inadvertent disclosure of such material will not amount to a waiver of privilege.

The existence of this provision – which is not one that a court could order – is one of the reasons why the Protocol has to take the form of a separate agreement rather than being incorporated into a court order.

So in each of these three areas I do not think that there was much more that could be done to reduce costs of litigation in the TCC or to improve its procedures. But that is not to say that there is no need for any aspects of the Jackson Reforms in the TCC. So let me now turn to the ways in which the Jackson Reforms have made a difference to the work of the TCC.

III. The Jackson Reforms and their Impact on the TCC

Two areas which have been particularly influenced by the reforms are (1) the extent of disclosure to be ordered and (2) costs budgeting.

CPR 31.5(7) now provides for a menu of disclosure options, which ranges from dispensing with disclosure altogether to making 'any other order in relation to disclosure that the court considers appropriate'. Standard disclosure is simply one of six options. The second option is what is often known as IBA or 'Redfern Schedule disclosure', which is commonly used in international arbitrations. That is the production by each party of the documents on which it relies, whilst at the same time requesting any specific disclosure that it requires from the other party.

Whilst these provisions introduce much more flexibility, and are therefore to be welcomed, it is questionable how much practical use they now have in the world of e-disclosure (in which progress has advanced by leaps and bounds since these changes to CPR 31.5 were introduced). Those service providers who offer packages to deal with e-disclosure have developed sophisticated algorithms to analyse documents electronically and select them for relevance. These can, in effect, provide tailor-made standard disclosure on an issue-by-issue, or custodian-by-custodian, basis, with the result that the menu options in CPR 31.5 are perhaps becoming obsolete. The burden and cost of disclosure is of huge concern to large corporations, and these new advances in e-disclosure will at least reduce the cost of the process if not its intrusiveness.

It is costs management and budgeting that has probably made the most significant difference to the day-to-day case management of litigation in the TCC. Before the first CMC the parties have to prepare their budgets in the approved form (at the risk of dire sanction if they do not) and these, if not agreed, are the subject of scrutiny and revision at the CMC.

In a substantial proportion of cases the parties agree each other's budgets and so the Court has to do no more than record its approval of them. However, there are many cases in which the parties do not agree the costs budgets of the others. If the objections are limited and focused, then the court can usually deal with them at the CMC. But if there are major disagreements, or there are several parties with different interests, then there is often insufficient time to deal with all the costs budgets of the parties at the CMC, still more so where the level of costs in some of the budgets is very high: an exhaustive analysis of one party's budget alone can take 45 minutes.

Where there are serious and profound disputes between the parties about their costs budgets, so that there is not time to deal with them at the CMC, a solution that is sometimes adopted by the judges in the TCC is to direct that each party is to revise its budget in the light of the comments made by the other and to exchange those revised budgets within, say, seven days. Within a further seven days each party is to comment on the other's revised budget unless, of course, it agrees it. Failing agreement, the parties are to file and exchange, within a further seven days, the final versions of their budgets and then, seven days after that, each party is to file with the Court its remaining objections to the other side's final budget. The Court will then, if it thinks it appropriate, deal with any remaining objections on paper. However, unfortunately in some cases it is necessary to hold a further hearing in order to set the budgets.

Whilst all this may seem as if it is no more than an exercise in putting off the evil day, it is my experience that by the end of this process the parties have quite often agreed each other's budgets or, at least, narrowed the objections very significantly. In this situation, the Court can usually deal with those remaining objections on paper. Of course, this represents an added workload for the judges, but that is unfortunately unavoidable.

Of course, there is a risk that the tail can wag the dog: a costs management hearing involving several parties and a full day of court time adds its own substantial costs to the cost of the litigation. But fortunately these are fairly few and far between.

One of the biggest single difficulties facing judges dealing with costs budgets in substantial cases arises where one or both parties have spent enormous sums of money prior to the CMC. Whilst the judge has power to revise and adjust the total figure in the budget for any future stage of the proceedings, there is no such power in respect of historic costs. All that the judge can do is to make any appropriate comments and then take those costs into account when assessing what amount is reasonable and proportionate for each of the remaining stages.

But, of course, another question that the judge must decide is: what is a proportionate sum for each party's costs as a whole? What is the judge to do when he or she concludes that this figure is less than the sum already spent to date? Logically, the conclusion ought to be that the sum to be allowed for each stage going forward should be nil.

This was the problem faced by Coulson J in *CIP Properties (AIPT) Ltd v Galliford Try Infrastructure Ltd*.[6] That was a case in which the judge decided that the claimant's costs budget was an entirely unreliable document and that both the costs already incurred and the estimated future costs were disproportionate and unreasonable. He concluded that a reasonable and proportionate figure for the entirety of the claimant's costs of the action was roughly equivalent to the sum that it said it had already spent. At paragraphs 92–95 of his judgment, in relation to what was described as 'Option 3', Coulson J said this:

> 92. This would involve putting the figure for all phases of future costs at 'nil'. The defendant and the additional parties were in favour of this option, which seems similar to the approach in *Redfern* (paragraph 9 above). They say that, if I refused to allow any further costs beyond those which have been incurred, because that figure is broadly in line with what I consider to be a reasonable figure for the claimant's costs in this case overall, then that would be an appropriate and just solution. It would also mean that the future risks as to costs would be borne by the claimant, which is the party who are, in that sense, in default.

> 93. The potential difficulty with this course is the one that I myself identified during the hearing. If I did not allow any further costs beyond those which have already been incurred, then there is nothing to stop the defendant, at the assessment of the costs already incurred, seeking to reduce those figures considerably. The claimant may then be doubly penalised because its costs incurred would be the subject of significant reduction on assessment, and it would not have got anything further in relation to the costs to be incurred because I would have set its prospective costs at nil.

> 94. I am not persuaded that this difficulty is alleviated by CPR 3.18, despite Mr Constable QC's submissions to the contrary. If I set the prospective costs budget at nil because of the size of the costs incurred to date, then it might be difficult for the claimant to modify that result by making an application under CPR 3.18. After all, all the relevant information is available now. That might be unfair in the result, for the reasons given.

> 95. Regrettably, I conclude that this makes Option 3 (which would otherwise have been the best alternative because it put the risks where they belong, with the claimant) unworkable.

This case is an example of how disruptive the costs management process can be if a particular party is being unreasonable and puts forward a budget that is wholly disproportionate. It involved a full day's hearing attended by five parties, followed by reserved judgment.

There is no doubt that costs management has added a substantial burden to the workload of the judges (and, of course, to the parties also), but the consequent reduction in the levels of costs in commercial litigation generally probably makes it worth it.

But what of the future? I suspect that during the next five years or so the biggest challenge that will arise in the conduct of litigation in the TCC, and the other

---

[6] *CIP Properties (AIPT) Ltd v Galliford Try Infrastructure Ltd* [2015] EWHC 481 (TCC).

commercial or business courts in the Rolls Building, will be the increasing use of electronic document management systems. These will, I am sure, be used in all substantial trials within a few years. They have numerous advantages, not least the saving of paper and the removal of the need to transport many dozens of files, either to and from court or within the Rolls Building itself.

The difficulty with such systems, particularly for the judge, is that they are not easy to operate whilst at the same time listening to evidence or submissions. As these systems exist at present it can be difficult to have two parts of the same document (for example, a long pleading) open at the same time or to find quickly a passage in a document that was being looked at a few minutes before.

A great advantage is that the transcript can be linked to the documents, so that when reading the transcript out of court the document under discussion can be called up – just as one had it on the bench when the evidence was being given. But one problem, which is particularly irritating in construction disputes, is that drawings can take quite a long time to load so that sometimes there can be a pause of nearly half a minute before the document appears on screen. However, this is probably just a matter of capacity and computer speed and I am sure that it will be overcome very shortly, if this has not been done already.

At present these systems are very expensive, which is why they are only used in the largest cases. But as the systems become more sophisticated they will, somewhat counter-intuitively, become less expensive.

IV. Conclusions

The answer to the question 'How have the Jackson reforms affected the conduct of litigation in the TCC?' is, probably, not very much, except in relation to costs management.

However, the extent to which active costs management will in practice reduce the costs of litigation in the TCC remains to be seen. Certainly, it will in many cases reduce a party's exposure to other parties' costs; but the extent to which it will reduce the amount paid by a party to its own solicitors is less apparent. But it is at least likely that it will reduce the need for the receiving party's costs to be referred to detailed assessment. That itself would be a significant improvement.

PART IV

Construction Adjudication

5

A Second Bite

ADRIAN WILLIAMSON QC

I. Introduction

My first experience of serious construction litigation was in the long hot summer of 1989, as junior to Rupert Jackson, then a young silk. We were instructed for the plaintiffs in an extremely tedious final account dispute before the then senior Official Referee, Lewis Hawser.[1] The case proceeded for five weeks, with counsel sweating horribly under their wigs and gowns. We then adjourned part heard, having made little progress, until October of the following year. Unfortunately, the judge then died, and we faced the prospect of starting all over again, whereupon, through a stroke of good fortune, the case settled. This was an extreme, but not wholly untypical, illustration of how such disputes were then conducted.

Over lunch one day, Rupert observed that there must surely be a better way of dealing with these things, but that this would require legislation. His proposal was that cases should be entrusted to senior specialist silks, who would be given inquisitorial powers and required to produce a binding result within a short time-frame. A few years later, the Latham Report proposed change along these lines in the form of adjudication.[2] The Major Government then introduced the Housing Grants, Construction and Regeneration Act 1996 ('the Act') to give effect to the Latham proposals, albeit in somewhat less ambitious terms than Rupert had proposed over lunch.

It was clear from the outset that this new framework for dispute resolution had to combine various features if it was to be effective. On the one hand, parties needed to be able to access the system easily, quickly and cheaply, for otherwise the new system would simply replicate the faults of the old. Decisions had to be enforced speedily, so that the victors received their spoils. On the other hand, there had to be some restrictions upon these rights, for otherwise respondents might be harassed by endless re-litigation of the same issues and paying parties

---

[1] This formed part of long-running litigation between these parties arising out of the Broadgate development: see, inter alia, *Smallman Construction v Redpath Dorman Long (No 1)* (1988) 47 BLR 15.

[2] Sir Michael Latham, *Constructing the Team* (London, HMSO, July 1994), section 9.

might be required to pay sums following a summary procedure which were not in truth due, without any means of righting this injustice.

It is in this area – allowing adjudication to flourish, whilst preventing injustice and discouraging re-litigation – that Jackson (J and LJ) has made a major contribution. In this chapter, I begin by setting the legislative scene, before considering the effect of the two leading cases of *Quietfield* and *Harding*.

II. The Legislative Framework

Section 108 of the Act provides that:

> (1) A party to a construction contract has the right to refer a dispute arising under the contract for adjudication under a procedure complying with this section.
>
> For this purpose 'dispute' includes any difference.
>
> (2) The contract shall–
>
> (a) enable a party to give notice at any time of his intention to refer a dispute to adjudication …
>
> (3) The contract shall provide that the decision of the adjudicator is binding until the dispute is finally determined by legal proceedings, by arbitration (if the contract provides for arbitration or the parties otherwise agree to arbitration) or by agreement …

The Scheme for Construction Contracts (England and Wales) Regulations 1998[3] as amended by the Scheme for Construction Contracts (England and Wales) Regulations 1998 (Amendment) (England) Regulations 2011[4] (the Scheme) states in Part I that:

> 9. – (1) An adjudicator may resign at any time on giving notice in writing to the parties to the dispute.
>
> (2) An adjudicator must resign where the dispute is the same or substantially the same as one which has previously been referred to adjudication, and a decision has been taken in that adjudication …
>
> 20. The adjudicator shall decide the matters in dispute …
>
> 23. …
>
> (2) The decision of the adjudicator shall be binding on the parties, and they shall comply with it until the dispute is finally determined by legal proceedings, by arbitration (if the contract provides for arbitration or the parties otherwise agree to arbitration) or by agreement between the parties.

The combined effect of all these provisions is roughly as follows. A party has an unrestricted right to adjudicate at any time. A winning party is entitled to the fruits

---

[3] SI 1998/649.
[4] SI 2011/2333.

of victory pending final determination. However, the right to adjudicate is subject to this limitation: you cannot have a second bite at the same cherry.

III. Natural Justice and *Quietfield*

These provisions obviously contain within them potential tensions. There is a danger that an overly narrow approach to attempts by parties to raise new issues may lead to injustice and to the undermining of the above scheme. If, however, the courts were too liberal in this respect, adjudication would cease to be the swift and simple process envisaged by Latham and the Act. Parties must, therefore, be able to adjudicate at any time, provided only that they are not going over old ground.

These potential conflicts arose in *Quietfield Ltd v Vascroft Contractors Ltd*.[5] The facts were that Quietfield had employed Vascroft as contractor under a contract in a JCT 1998 standard form with amendments. Clause 25 thereof provided for fair and reasonable extensions of time for delays caused by relevant events. Vascroft twice applied to the architect for extensions of time, first in a letter dated 2 September 2004, and secondly in a letter dated 22 April 2005. The architect refused both requests. On 1 August 2005 Vascroft referred to adjudication disputes including their claims for extensions of time. The adjudicator found that Vascroft had failed to establish that they were entitled to any extension of time. Quietfield then began a further adjudication, for which the same adjudicator was appointed. The dispute included claims for damages in respect of Vascroft's failure to complete by the contractual completion date. Vascroft resisted the claim on the ground that they were entitled to an extension of time for reasons set out in a 400-page document included as appendix C in their response. The adjudicator decided as a preliminary issue that he was not able to have regard to the matters set out in appendix C because they amounted to an attempt by Vascroft to rely for a second time on the same matters as they had unsuccessfully relied on in the first adjudication, but on different evidential bases, and that he was bound by his earlier decision.

Quietfield had, therefore, an open goal in the adjudication. Vascroft had been denied the opportunity to put forward their only possible defence to the damages claim, namely their own claim for an extension of time. Quietfield duly succeeded and then sought to enforce decision through an application for summary judgment. The matter came before Jackson, J in the TCC.[6] Vascroft argued that judgment should not be granted because they had been denied natural justice by the adjudicator: he had not allowed them to put forward their real defence.

---

[5] *Quietfield Ltd v Vascroft Contractors Ltd* [2006] EWHC 174 (TCC) (Jackson J) and then [2007] BLR 67 (CA).
[6] [2006] EWHC 174 (TCC).

Quietfield disputed this: the extension of time issues had been decided in the first adjudication and could not be reopened. This case, therefore, raised starkly the question of what did and did not amount to re-litigation of the same issues.

Jackson J concluded that the adjudicator had been wrong to shut out Vascroft from relying upon their appendix C case. His lucid exposition began with an analysis of the provisions of the Act and the Scheme which I have set out above:

> 34. The effect of these provisions is that once a dispute has been determined by adjudication, there cannot be another adjudication about that same dispute. The adjudicator's decision will remain binding upon the parties unless and until that decision is overtaken by a judgment of the court, an arbitral award or a settlement agreement between the parties.

> 35. The question then arises as to how section 108(3) of the 1996 Act and paragraphs 9 and 23 of the Scheme interrelate with the usual contractual provisions for extension of time. Clause 25 of the contract in this case and the corresponding clause in many other forms of construction contract expressly permit the contractor to make multiple applications for extensions of time. The contractor may apply for an extension of time on one ground and be refused. The contractor may then apply for an extension of time on another ground (possibly in respect of the same period of delay) and be successful.

> 36. If either the employer or the contractor is dissatisfied with the decision of the architect or the contract administrator concerning extension of time, then that party has a right to refer the matter to adjudication. It therefore follows that multiple adjudications concerning extensions of time must be permissible, provided only that each adjudication arises from a separate dispute.

The judge then turned to the previous cases in which this issue had arisen. From these cases, he distilled the following principles:

> 42. From this review of the 1996 Act, the Scheme and previous decisions I conclude that the following four principles apply when there are successive adjudications about extension of time and/or the deduction of damages for delay:

> (i)   Where the contract permits the contractor to make successive applications for extension of time on different grounds, either party, if dissatisfied with the decisions made, can refer those matters to successive adjudications. In each case the difference between the contentions of the aggrieved party and the decision of the architect or contract administrator will constitute the 'dispute' within the meaning of section 108 of the 1996 Act.

> (ii) If the contractor makes successive applications for extension of time on the same grounds, the architect or contract administrator will, no doubt, reiterate his original decision. The aggrieved party cannot refer this matter to successive adjudications. He is debarred from doing so by paragraphs 9 and 23 of the Scheme and section 108(3) of the 1996 Act.

> (iii) Subject to paragraph (iv) below, where the contractor is resisting a claim for liquidated and ascertained damages in respect of delay, pursued in adjudication proceedings, the contractor may rely by way of defence upon his entitlement to an extension of time.

(iv) However, the contractor cannot rely by way of defence in adjudication proceedings upon an alleged entitlement to extension of time which has been considered and rejected in a previous adjudication.

The judge then applied those principles to the fact before him:

50. Vascroft's claim for an extension of time in the third adjudication is contained in Appendix C to its response, as previously mentioned. Appendix C is a far cry from the two application letters dated 2nd September 2004 and 22nd April 2005. It is perhaps regrettable that Appendix C was not advanced in the first adjudication. Appendix C identifies a number of causes of delay which do not feature in the two application letters. Further, Appendix C appears to be a structured and logical document, which sets out to demonstrate what the critical path was and how individual events did or did not impact upon the final date for completion. Whether, at the end of the day, the submissions in Appendix C will prevail, I do not know. This will be a matter for the adjudicator or, possibly, for the arbitrator to decide. I am, however, quite satisfied that Vascroft's alleged entitlement to an extension of time as set out in Appendix C is substantially different from the claims for extension of time which were advanced, considered and rejected in the first adjudication.

51. For these reasons I come to the conclusion that in the third adjudication the adjudicator ought to have considered Vascroft's substantive defence, but he failed to do so. In those circumstances, as Quietfield have very fairly conceded, the adjudicator's decision cannot be enforced because he failed to abide by the rules of natural justice. Indeed, in my view, if the adjudicator's decision is enforced, Quietfield may receive a substantial sum of money to which it is not entitled, even on an interim basis.

Jackson J had, therefore, steered a fair and sensible course through the hazards created by the Act. On the one hand, his statement of principle made clear that parties would not be allowed to return to issues which had been ventilated before and decided by a previous adjudicator. On the other hand, there was nothing to stop a party putting forward in a subsequent adjudication, matters which had not been so decided, and which were necessary to that party's claim or defence.

Quietfield appealed and the Court of Appeal dismissed the appeal.[7] May LJ was satisfied that:

34. In the present case, the judge correctly analysed the documents relevant to the scope of the first adjudication ...

37. In the result, in my judgment both the dispute referred for adjudication and the dispute which the adjudicator decided in the first adjudication was Vascroft's disputed claims for extension of time in the two letters. Since Vascroft's Appendix C in the third adjudication identified a number of causes of delay which did not feature in the two letters and was substantially different from the claims for extension of time which were advanced, considered and rejected in the first adjudication, the adjudicator was wrong in the third adjudication not to consider Appendix C.

---

[7] [2006] EWCA Civ 1737, [2007] BLR 67.

The judgment of May LJ was largely confined to the facts of the instant case. However, Dyson LJ reviewed (and slightly glossed) the broader principles which Jackson J had enunciated. In truth, his gloss essentially amounted to the proposition that each case required a careful investigation of the facts so as to give effect to those principles:

> 43. So much for the position under clause 25. The judge's first principle may appear to suggest that every dispute arising from the rejection of an application for an extension of time may be referred to adjudication. I do not consider that that is necessarily the case. The question whether a contractor may make successive applications for extensions of time depends on the true construction of clause 25 and any term necessarily to be implied. The question whether disputes arising from the rejection of successive applications for an extension of time may be referred to adjudication depends on the effect of section 108(3) of the 1996 Act and paragraph 9(2) of the Scheme.
>
> 44. There are obvious differences between successive applications for extensions of time under the contract and successive referrals of disputes to adjudication. In the real world, there is often a regular dialogue between contractor and architect in relation to issues arising from clause 25. If an architect rejects an application for an extension of time pointing out a deficiency in the application which the contractor subsequently makes good, it would be absurd if the architect could not grant the application if he now thought that it was justified. To do so would be part of the architect's ordinary function of administering the contract. But referrals to adjudication raise different considerations. The cost of a referral can be substantial. No doubt that is one of the reasons why the statutory scheme protects respondents from successive referrals to adjudication of what is substantially the same dispute.
>
> 45. Paragraph 9(2) provides that an adjudicator must resign where the dispute is the same or substantially the same as one which has previously been referred to adjudication and a decision has been taken in that adjudication. It must necessarily follow that the parties may not refer a dispute to adjudication in such circumstances.
>
> 46. This is the mechanism that has been adopted to protect respondents from having to face the expense and trouble of successive adjudications on the same or substantially the same dispute. There is an analogy here, albeit an imperfect one, with the rules developed by the common law to prevent successive litigation over the same matter: see the discussion about *Henderson v Henderson* (1843) 3 Hare 100 abuse of process and cause of action and issue estoppel by Lord Bingham of Cornhill in *Johnson v Gore Wood & Co (a firm)* [2002] 2 AC 1, 30H–31G.
>
> 47. Whether dispute A is substantially the same as dispute B is a question of fact and degree. If the contractor identifies the same Relevant Event in successive applications for extensions of time, but gives different particulars of its expected effects, the differences may or may not be sufficient to lead to the conclusion that the two disputes are not substantially the same. All the more so if the particulars of expected effects are the same, but the evidence by which the contractor seeks to prove them is different.
>
> 48. Where the only difference between disputes arising from the rejection of two successive applications for an extension of time is that the later application makes good shortcomings of the earlier application, an adjudicator will usually have little difficulty in deciding that the two disputes are substantially the same.

49. In the present case, I am in no doubt that the judge reached the right conclusion. The first disputed claim which was the subject of the first adjudication was substantially different from the second disputed claim. The written notices which formed the basis of the second claim identified Relevant Events which were substantially more extensive than those which formed the basis of the first claim. The particulars of expected effects were very different too. There will be some borderline cases where it is a matter of judgment whether the two claims are substantially the same and where there may be room for more than one view. In my view, this is not a borderline case.

This has become the template for subsequent decisions. In *HG Construction Ltd v Ashwell Homes (East Anglia) Ltd*,[8] Ramsey J, Jackson J's successor as Judge in Charge of the TCC, had to consider a similar point. The judge was dealing with clause 39A.7.1 of a JCT Contract which provided that

The decision of the Adjudicator shall be binding on the Parties until the dispute or difference is finally determined by arbitration or by legal proceedings or by an agreement in writing between the parties made after the decision of the Adjudicator has been given.

Following *Quietfield*, the judge laid down these propositions:

38. ... the effect of clause 39A.7.1 is that:

(1) the parties are bound by the decision of an adjudicator on a dispute or difference until it is finally determined by a court or adjudication proceedings or by an agreement made subsequently by the parties.

(2) The parties cannot seek a further decision by an adjudicator on a dispute or difference if that dispute or difference has already been the subject of a decision by an Adjudicator.

(3) As a matter of practice, an adjudicator should consider (based either on an objection raised by one of the parties or on his own volition) whether he is being asked to decide a matter on which there is already a binding decision by another Adjudicator. If so he should decline to decide that matter or, if that is the only matter which he is asked to decide, he should resign.

(4) The extent to which a decision or a dispute is binding will depend on an analysis of

(a) the terms, scope and extent of the dispute or difference referred to adjudication and

(b) the terms, scope and extent of the decision made by the adjudicator.

(5) In considering the terms, scope and extent of the dispute or difference the approach has to be to ask whether the dispute or difference is the same or substantially the same as the relevant dispute or difference.

(6) In considering the terms, scope and extent of the decision, the approach has to be to ask whether the Adjudicator has decided a dispute or difference which is the same or fundamentally the same as the relevant dispute or difference.

(7) As accepted by Mr Bartlett, the approach must involve not only the 'same' but also 'substantially the same' dispute or difference. The reason for this, in my judgement, is

---

[8] *HG Construction Ltd v Ashwell Homes (East Anglia) Ltd* [2007] EWHC 144 (TCC) [2007] BLR 175.

that disputes or differences encompass a wide range of factual and legal issues. If there had to be complete identity of factual and legal issues then the ability to 're-adjudicate' what was in substance the same dispute or difference would deprive Clause 39A.7.1 of its intended purpose. As Dyson LJ pointed out in *Quietfield* at para 44: 'The cost of a referral can be substantial. No doubt that is one of the reasons why the statutory scheme protects respondents form successive referrals to adjudication of what is substantially the same dispute.' The expense and trouble of successive adjudications on the same or substantially the same dispute or difference in relation to adjudication which provides a temporarily binding decision is something which is to be discouraged and is the purpose behind the provisions of Clause 39A.7.1

(8) Whether one dispute is substantially the same as another dispute is a question of fact and degree: see para 46 of *Quietfield* per Dyson LJ.

IV. Interim and Final Payments

Quietfield therefore very largely settled the re-litigation issue. However, there has since arisen controversy as to the question of payment. The intention of the Latham Report and the Act was clearly 'pay now, argue later': sums should be paid for cash-flow purposes and the merits debated later, if necessary. Was there, however, any constraint on the timing and nature of that debate? If so, how did this relate to an unlimited right to adjudicate? This is the point which *Harding* addressed, and to appreciate the issues which arose in that case, it is first necessary to trace the legislative background and the preceding cases. Under the Act, sections 109 to 113 related to payment in construction contracts. Section 109 established that 'a party to a construction contract is entitled to payment by instalments, stage payments, or other periodic payments for work under the contract' unless the work was to take less than 45 days. It remained open to the parties to agree the amounts and the intervals at which such payments became due, although if there was no agreement then the relevant provisions of the Scheme would apply.

Section 110 required every construction contract to provide for the giving of notice from the paying party 'not later than five days after the date on which payment becomes due from him' specifying the amount of the payment made or proposed to be made, and the basis on which that amount was calculated. Under section 111, a party was prohibited from withholding payment after the final date for payment of a sum due unless it had given effective notice of its intention to withhold payment. An effective notice specified the amount proposed to be withheld and the ground(s) for doing so. It was for the parties to agree by when a notice should be given in order to be effective.

These provisions gave rise to criticism in that it was thought that they did not give sufficient effect to the aspirations of the Latham Report to improve cash-flow for payees. It was still possible for paying parties to evade their responsibilities by exploiting obscurities within the Act.

The Local Democracy, Economic Development and Construction Act 2009 therefore heavily amended the payment provisions in the Act, both clarifying and altering the regime. Section 110 was amended, and whilst the requirement for an adequate mechanism (understandably) remains, the substance of that requirement is substantially reformulated. The adequate mechanism requirement is not satisfied if payment is conditional on the performance of obligations under another contract (apart from obligations to make payment). Neither is the adequate mechanism requirement satisfied where payment is dependent on a notice being given to the party entitled to payment.

A number of new provisions were introduced into the Act. Section 110A requires that the contract obliges either the payer (or specified person) or the payee to give a notice specifying the sum it considers to be due at the payment due date. Such a payment notice is to be given not later than five days after the payment due date, and it is immaterial that the sum is zero. Section 110B builds on section 110A, and addresses the situation where the payer was required to give a payment notice but none was forthcoming. In such a situation, generally the payee can instead give a payment notice at any time after the payer was supposed to have provided a payment notice. The final date for payment is accordingly pushed back.

Section 111 establishes the obligation that the payer must pay the notified sum (to the extent not already paid) on or before the final date for payment. The notified sum is the sum contained in a compliant payment notice. Section 111 goes on, however, to make provision for payless notices, that is a notice given by the payer or a specified person of an intention to pay less than the notified sum. A payless notice must specify 'the sum that the payer considers to be due on the date that the notice is served, and the basis on which that sum is calculated'. A payless notice must not be given later than the prescribed period before the final date for payment and, in situations where the payee serves the payment notice, a payless notice cannot pre-date the payment notice. If a valid payless notice is given, then the sum specified therein is now treated as the notified sum.

These provisions were, therefore, aimed at improving the position of payees: if the paying party did not give the correct notice, the payee could do so and was then entitled to the sum notified, save where a compliant payless notice had been given.

The first significant case on payment applications and notified sums under the amended Act was *ISG Construction Ltd v Seevic College*.[9] ISG had submitted a valid interim application which was not met with a payless notice from Seevic. Accordingly, at the first adjudication on the issue, it was held that ISG was entitled to full payment of the notified sum of about £1 million. Seevic then commenced a second adjudication seeking to ascertain the value of ISG's works as at the date of the interim application. The adjudicator valued the works as around £300,000, and therefore ordered ISG to repay over £750,000.

---

[9] *ISG Construction Ltd v Seevic College* [2014] EWHC 4007 (TCC) [2015] BLR 233.

ISG brought proceedings before Edwards-Stuart J, seeking a declaration that enforced the first adjudication and ruled that the second adjudication was invalid for want of jurisdiction. Edwards-Stuart J agreed, commenting that 'if the employer fails to serve any notices in time it must be taken to be agreeing the value stated in the application, right or wrong'.[10]

This decision gave the contractor a very valuable weapon.[11] Provided he submitted his application on time, he was entitled to every penny applied for unless the employer issued a valid payless notice – even if nothing, or much less, was in fact due. Anecdotal evidence suggests that many contractors took this route, and many contract administrators got into difficulties with late or defective notices. Moreover, the employer could not challenge the sum applied for in adjudication because the amount actually due had been determined once and for all, subject only to lengthy and expensive litigation.

On one view, this took the construction industry back to 1989. Cash-flow might be improved for payees, but for paying parties (and therefore, in the long run, payees as well) the vista of never-ending litigation appeared to open up. The difficulties with the *ISG* approach soon became apparent and the TCC made inroads into this somewhat strict approach.

In *Galliford Try v Estura*,[12] another decision of Edwards-Stuart J, the contractor issued an interim application which was described as the 'Indicative Final Account and Valuation Summary' and, the employer having failed to serve a payless notice, this sum was held to be due by an adjudicator. In considering the summary judgment application to enforce that decision, Edwards-Stuart J had little difficulty in concluding that there was no defence to the application, but nevertheless granted a partial stay on the basis that there was a risk of manifest injustice. The reasons which prompted this discretionary response included the fact that the sum payable was almost the same as the likely final value of the works, and so there was little incentive for the contractor to submit its final account (at which point the sum could be challenged and re-assessed). Further, the contract was close to completion and the prejudice which would be suffered by the employer outweighed that suffered by the contractor by a delay in payment. This final point was magnified by the weak financial position of the employer.

A further inroad or exception was made in *Severfield (UK) Ltd v Duro Felguera UK Ltd*.[13] Severfield was engaged to carry out design, supply and erection works as part of a project to construct two power generation plants. Some of the works fell within the definition of construction operations under the Act, and some were excluded because they related to power generation. In December 2014 Severfield submitted an application notice which did not differentiate between

---

[10] At [28].
[11] Permission to appeal to the Court of Appeal was granted by Jackson LJ but the parties resolved their differences before the appeal could be heard.
[12] *Galliford Try v Estura* [2015] BLR 321.
[13] *Severfield (UK) Ltd v Duro Felguera UK Ltd* [2015] EWHC 3352 (TCC).

works which fell under the Act and those which did not. When full payment was not made, Severfield submitted the dispute to adjudication, and it was which held that payment was due. However, Stuart-Smith J refused to enforce that decision, commenting: 'the consequences of obtaining an award which includes matters that are not construction operations is that the award cannot be enforced'.[14]

Undeterred, Severfield submitted a refined interim application, asserting that they had stripped out any claims for payment in respect of excluded operations. Coulson J nevertheless rejected Severfield's application for summary judgment. The principal reason for this was that it was not possible to say that the claim being made was, for all intents and purposes, the interim payment claim notified in December 2014. Even if he was wrong on that, the payment notice of December 2014 did not clearly identify the stripped out sum due or how it had been calculated, and therefore this was not a claim for a sum which was indisputably due. Coulson J commented that 'because of the potentially draconian consequences, the TCC has made it plain that the contractor's original payment notice, from which its entitlement springs, must be clear and unambiguous'.[15]

This then was the (somewhat confused and unsatisfactory) state of play when *Harding v Paice*[16] reached the Court of Appeal. The contractor, Harding, had lawfully terminated the contract and was therefore entitled to submit a termination account. Harding valued the work done at just under £800,000, with the balance owing being around £400,000. Paice, the employer, failed to serve a payless notice on time, and so Harding submitted the dispute to adjudication. Unsurprisingly, following *Seevic*, the adjudicator decided that Harding was entitled to the £400,000 balance, which was then paid. Paice then commenced a new adjudication concerning the value of the works: it was Paice's submission that the true value was much lower than the £800,000 claimed by Harding. The new adjudicator agreed and decided that Harding should repay £325,000.

Harding appealed against the decision of Edwards-Stuart J who had decided that the second adjudicator had jurisdiction to determine the value of the works, even though a decision that payment was due had already been made. The Court of Appeal rejected Harding's argument, concluding that the decision of the first adjudicator (that payment was due because no payless notice was served) was a different decision to one of valuation. Therefore, because the issue had not previously been decided, the question of valuation was open for decision by the second adjudicator.

Harding advanced two main arguments. The first was that, on a literal reading of paragraph 9(2) of the Scheme, the second adjudicator should have resigned, since the dispute before him was the same or substantially the same as the one which had previously been referred to adjudication and *a* decision had been taken

---

[14] [2015] EWHC 3352 (TCC) at [14].
[15] [2015] EWHC 3352 (TCC) at [24].
[16] *Harding (t/a MJ Harding Contractors) v Paice* [2016] 1 WLR 4068.

in that adjudication (even if that decision did not deal with the matters sought to be raised in the second adjudication). The second ground of appeal was that the first adjudicator had in fact decided the question which was then sought to be put before the second adjudicator, namely how much was due.

Jackson LJ gave the sole reasoned judgment in the Court of Appeal. He concluded that *Quietfield* essentially resolved the first point:

> 57. It is quite clear from the authorities that one does not look at the dispute or disputes referred to the first adjudicator in isolation. One must also look at what the first adjudicator actually decided. Ultimately it is what the first adjudicator decided, which determines how much or how little remains available for consideration by the second adjudicator.
>
> 58. In my view Mr Sears's argument is correct.[17] The word 'decision' in paragraph 9(2) means a decision in relation to the dispute now being referred to adjudication. I arrive at this interpretation as a matter of construction rather than implication. It is what the paragraph obviously means. Parliament cannot have intended that if a claimant refers 20 disputes or issues to adjudication but the adjudicator only decides one of those disputes or issues, future adjudication about the other matters is prohibited.

As to the second point, Jackson LJ took the view that the first adjudication had raised two separate issues but that only one of these had been resolved in that adjudication. Thus it was open to the second adjudicator to embark on the valuation issues, as he had done:

> 63. … On a proper analysis of the notice of adjudication and the referral document in the third adjudication, I think that Harding referred to Mr Linnett a dispute involving two alternative issues …
>
> 64. The first issue is a contractual one. The second issue is one of valuation. The adjudicator dealt with the contractual issue. He did not need to deal with the valuation issue. He made that abundantly clear in para 185 of his determination where he said:
>
>> 'For the avoidance of doubt, I stress that I have not decided on the merits of Harding's valuation and have not decided that £397,912·48 represents a correct valuation of the works. The parties made submissions in this adjudication about the proper valuation but these did not fall to be considered by me because of the rule relating to a notified sum becoming automatically due in the absence of a valid pay less notice.'
>
> …
>
> 78. In my view the employer's failure to serve a pay less notice (as held by the previous adjudicator) had limited consequences. It meant that the employer had to pay the full amount shown on the contractor's account and argue about the figures later. The employer duly paid that sum, as ordered by the previous adjudicator. The employer is now entitled to proceed to adjudication in order to determine the correct value of the contractor's claims and the employer's counterclaims. Therefore the judge's decision was correct.

---

[17] Counsel for Paice.

Given this approach, there was strictly speaking no need for the Court to review the *ISG* line of cases. Nonetheless, Jackson LJ analysed the two relevant streams of authority. The first comprised cases such as *Rupert Morgan Building Services (LLC) Ltd v Jervis*.[18] In that case, the Court of Appeal held that payment on an interim certificate

> does not preclude the client who has paid from subsequently showing he has overpaid. If he has overpaid on an interim certificate the matter can be put right in subsequent certificates. Otherwise he can raise the matter by way of adjudication or if necessary arbitration or legal proceedings.[19]

The second line of authority was the 'more recent cases [where] Edwards-Stuart J took a somewhat different line', namely *ISG* and *Estura*.

His conclusion was as follows:

> 69. I do not need to decide whether or not that passage is correct in relation to interim valuations and interim payments. In almost all construction contracts special contractual provisions apply to interim payments. Mistakes can usually be put right at a later stage, although that was not possible in the Galliford Try case because the contract prevented negative valuations.

> 70. The important point for present purposes is that the quoted passage (whether right or wrong in relation to interim valuations) does not apply to final accounts. Edwards-Stuart J said so in the Galliford Try case at para 25, where he emphasised the 'fundamental difference' between payment obligations which arise on an interim application and those that arise on termination.

> 71. In the present case we are concerned with a final account following termination of the construction contract. Clause 8.12.5 of the contract conditions requires an assessment of the amount which is 'properly due in respect of the account'. The clause expressly permits a negative valuation. Mr Linnett did not carry out any such valuation exercise in the third adjudication. Therefore PS were entitled to refer that dispute for resolution in the abortive fourth adjudication. They will be entitled to do so again in the proposed fifth adjudication.

> 72. This conclusion is consistent with the reasoning of Judge Humphrey Lloyd QC in *Watkin Jones* and the reasoning of the Court of Appeal in *Rupert Morgan*. Nothing in *ISG* or *Galliford* contradicts this conclusion.

The effect of this decision is that, whilst payment may become due upon a compliant payment notice to which there is no payless notice in reply, that does not prevent the employer from subsequently challenging the valuation underlying the application. The Court of Appeal were emphatic in stressing that their judgment applied only to final accounts. They noted, as Edwards-Stuart J had in *Seevic*, that in interim payments there remains scope to change valuations in subsequent payment cycles, whereas that was not the case where the payment represented the final account.

---

[18] *Rupert Morgan Building Services (LLC) Ltd v Jervis* [2004] 1 WLR 1867.
[19] ibid, para 14.

The judgment in *Harding* nonetheless left *Seevic* in an uncertain position. Their Lordships were much taken by the judgment in *Rupert Morgan Building Services (LLC) Ltd v Jervis*[20] – another Court of Appeal decision, though decided under the original Act – where it was held that an employer had seemingly a number of options. An overpayment on an interim certificate could be put right in subsequent certificates, or through adjudication, or if necessary, arbitration or legal proceedings. Further, some implicit doubt can be seen in the way Jackson LJ dealt with *ISG* itself: 'Edwards-Stuart J took a somewhat different line.'[21] Since this was a 'different line' to that decided in a strong decision of the Court of Appeal, this could scarcely be regarded as a ringing endorsement.

Harding has been widely followed and indeed seems to have drawn the threads together in this area of the law. In *Brown v Complete Buildings Solutions Limited*[22] the Court of Appeal said as follows:

> 23. As was made clear from the recent decision of this Court in *Matthew Harding (trading as M J Harding Contractors) v. Paice and Springhall* [2015] EWCA Civ 1281, Jackson LJ at [57],
>
> > 'It is quite clear from the authorities that one does not look at the dispute or dispute referred to the first adjudicator in isolation. One must look at what the first adjudicator actually decided. Ultimately it is what the first adjudicator decided which determines how much or how little remains for consideration by the second adjudicator.'
>
> 24. The terms of paragraph 9.2, the approach in the *Quietfield* case of both May LJ at [32] and Dyson LJ at [48], and that of Jackson LJ in the *Harding* case at [57], indicate that the starting point is the Adjudicator's view of whether one dispute is the same or substantially the same. This has often been described (see for example in the *Quietfield* case at [47]) as being 'a question of fact and degree'; and it is important that the Court gives due respect to the adjudicator's decision, see for example, *Carillion Construction Ltd v. Devonport Royal Dockyard Ltd* [2005] EWCA Civ 1358, Chadwick LJ at [85].

The position was not quite so clear in regard to interim payments. *Harding* expressly did not decide this. However, the first instance decisions that followed *Harding* left *ISG* hanging by a thread.[23] The industry has been waiting with bated breath for the Court of Appeal to apply the coup de grâce. In the meanwhile, Coulson, J (in his final judgment before ascending to that august body) has declined to follow *ISG* and *Estura*, so that these cases have little, if any, remaining authority.[24] He held, in reliance upon both first principles and the decisions in *Rupert Morgan* and *Harding*, that:

> 90. … it seems to me to be clear that an employer in the position of Grove must pay the sum stated as due, and is then entitled to commence a separate adjudication addressing the 'true' value of the interim application …

---

[20] [2004] 1 WLR 1867.

[21] At [68].

[22] *Brown v Complete Buildings Solutions Limited* [2016] EWCA Civ 1, [2016] BLR 98.

[23] See, in particular, *Imperial Chemical Industries Ltd v Merit Merrell Technology Ltd* [2017] EWHC 1763 (TCC); 173 Con LR 137, Fraser J, paras 217–23.

[24] *Grove Developments Limited v S&T (UK) Limited* [2018] EWHC 123 (TCC).

103. … In my view, the Court of Appeal authorities all point the same way. An employer who has failed to serve its own payment notice or pay less notice has to pay the amount claimed by the contractor because that is "the sum stated as due". But the employer is then free to commence its own adjudication proceedings in which the dispute as to the 'true' value of the application can be determined …

122. Accordingly, I do not believe that either ISG or Galliford Try deals directly with the submission that Grove now make to me, which is that, following payment of the sum stated as due, the employer should be able to commence an adjudication as to the 'true' value of the interim application. To the extent that the judgments in those cases answer that question in the negative, I consider that they are contrary to first principles (Section 6.2 above) and contrary to the adjudication authorities in the Court of Appeal (Section 6.3 above). They are a 'different line', as Jackson LJ described them, and in my view, they should not be followed.

V. Conclusions

Jackson LJ has contributed significantly to the implementation of the objectives for a streamlined form of dispute resolution in the construction industry which he sketched out nearly 30 years ago. If the right to adjudicate is to be meaningful, then parties must have recourse to that right whenever an issue arises which cannot be resolved amicably. They should therefore be allowed as many bites as necessary, provided only that they are not going over the same ground as has already been decided. That is the principle which emerges from both *Quietfield* and *Harding* and it surely what Parliament had in mind in enacting the Latham recommendations. As Dyson J (as he then was) observed in the first adjudication case to reach the courts, it was 'clear that Parliament intended that the adjudication should be conducted in a manner which those familiar with the grinding detail of the traditional approach to the resolution of construction disputes apparently find difficult to accept.'[25]

However, in order to avoid unnecessary descent into 'grinding detail', and associated expense, it is also essential that the courts should facilitate rather than obstruct the use of adjudication to resolve complex disputes. The decision in *ISG* seemed to herald much reduced access to adjudication for valuation issues, since it was held that 'the employer cannot bring a second adjudication to determine the value of the work at the valuation date of the interim application in question.'[26] *Harding* did not decide this point in terms, but it is apparent that Jackson LJ was out of sympathy with the restrictive approach suggested by *ISG*. The other TCC

---

[25] *Macob Civil Engineering Ltd v Morrison Construction Ltd* [1999] BLR 99 para 14.
[26] *ISG* as explained at para 20 of *Estura* (n 12 above).

judges have declined to follow the 'somewhat different line' taken by Edwards-Stuart, J but have instead accepted that

> the default notice mechanism under the Act might result in unfairness or hardship to an employer in circumstances where the contractor received a windfall from the employer's procedural failure. However, it simply regulates the cash flow as between the parties and does not affect their substantive rights.[27]

This is very much in line with the approach which Jackson, J and LJ, has indicated.

---

[27] *Kersfield Developments (Bridge Road) Ltd v Bray & Slaughter Ltd* [2017] EWHC 15 (TCC), (2017) 170 Con LR 40, para 96, O'Farrell, J.

6

Of Special Character

STEVEN WALKER QC

I. Introduction

The main aims of the Housing Grants, Construction and Regeneration Act (HGCRA) were to regulate payment in many (but not all) construction contracts and to provide a quick and cost-effective means of enforcing rights under such contracts. The means of enforcement adopted in the HGCRA is to require that construction contracts allow any dispute to be referred to an adjudicator. A number of textbooks provide a comprehensive examination of the case law relating to the enforcement of adjudicators' decisions, and this chapter does not attempt such an examination, but instead considers the development of the law with particular reference to the significant contribution made by Sir Rupert Jackson. It is respectfully suggested that Sir Rupert's contribution to the law in this field is perhaps most notable in relation to the following areas:

(i) The meaning of 'dispute' and the argument known as the 'no dispute' or 'the crystallisation argument': *Amec Civil Engineering v Secretary of State for Transport*.[1]

(ii) The application of the rules of natural justice in the context of construction adjudication: *Carillion Construction v Devonport*.[2]

(iii) Issues of forum shopping: *Lanes Group v Galliford Try*.[3]

After addressing the above cases, Sir Rupert's contribution to the possible reform of the HGCRA will be discussed. Before discussing the above it is appropriate to recall the key cases that went before them by way of background.

---

[1] *Amec Civil Engineering v Secretary of State for Transport* [2004] EWHC 2339 (TCC) (and subsequently: [2005] 1 WLR 2339 (CA)).
[2] *Carillion Construction Ltd v Devonport Royal Dockyard Ltd* [2005] BLR 310 (TCC), and subsequently: [2005] EWCA Civ 1358.
[3] *Lanes Group plc v Galliford Try Infrastructure Ltd (t/a Galliford Try Rail)* [2011] EWCA Civ 1617 [2012] BLR 121 (CA).

II. Background

Section 108(2) of the HGCRA provides as follows:

> The contract shall provide that the decision of the adjudicator is to be binding until the dispute is finally determined by legal proceedings, by arbitration (if the contract provides for arbitration or the parties otherwise agree to arbitration) or by agreement. The parties may agree to accept the decision of the adjudicator as finally determining the dispute.

The intention is that the parties must comply with the adjudicator's decision pending final resolution of the dispute. In *Speymill Contracts Ltd v Baskind*,[4] the Court of Appeal considered the effect of fraud upon adjudicators' decisions. Jackson LJ's judgment, with which the other Lord Justices agreed, explains why adjudicators' decisions are different from judgments or arbitration awards. He said this:

> 37.   Counsel have also cited numerous authorities concerning the effect of fraud upon judgments and arbitration awards. For my part I do not find these authorities to be of direct assistance. Judgments of the court and arbitration awards are of permanent effect unless and until reversed on appeal or set aside on some ground such as fraud. An adjudicator's decision, however, under the 1996 Act or equivalent contractual provisions is of a different character. The adjudicator's decision merely establishes the position from which the parties shall start their arbitration or litigation. This judgment is not the place to review the policy considerations underlying the adjudication system or the Latham Report on which that system is based. It is sufficient for the purposes of this appeal to state that I agree with Akenhead J's analysis of the effect of fraud upon adjudication decisions.

Where an adjudicator's decision is not complied with, the forum where such non-compliance can be addressed is the TCC. The TCC will enforce an adjudicator's decision, whether right or wrong, by giving summary judgment save where the adjudicator lacked jurisdiction to make the decision or where the adjudicator failed to observe the rules of natural justice. It is fair to say when such grounds for resisting enforcement are raised those grounds are scrutinised carefully by the courts lest the aims of the HGCRA be frustrated. As Jackson LJ has stated, 'The courts have not allowed "technical" arguments to undermine the adjudication system'.[5]

III. The Enforcement of Adjudicators' Decisions

According to HH Judge LLoyd QC,[6] the judges of the TCC (then called Official Referees) were not consulted, officially, about the HGCRA before it was passed.

---

[4] *Speymill Contracts Ltd v Baskind* [2010] EWCA Civ 120; [2010] BLR 257.
[5] 'The Construction Act in the Courts'. A paper by Sir Rupert Jackson for the DTI Conference on 1 June 2005.
[6] 'The Construction Act – How it has been viewed by the Courts.' A paper by HH Judge LLoyd QC, for the DTI Conference on 14 February 2006.

Judge LLoyd suggested that the HGCRA was unique because, aside from consumer legislation, there had never before been legislation (other than in a state of emergency) which intervened to regulate the freedom of contract in a sector of the economy which should be capable of looking after itself, and this gave rise to a degree of wariness when questions about the meaning of the HGCRA and the Scheme came before the courts.

So far as questions of the enforcement process were concerned, the decision in *Macob Civil Engineering Limited v Morrison Construction Limited*[7] provided the first indication of the Court's willingness to support the adjudication system introduced by the HGCRA. Three key points emerged from this case. Firstly, the purpose of the adjudication system was addressed by Dyson J (as he then was) in *Macob* in the following much quoted passage:

> The intention of Parliament in enacting the Act was plain. It was to introduce a speedy mechanism for settling disputes in construction contracts on a provisional interim basis, and requiring the decisions of adjudicators to be enforced pending the final determination of disputes by arbitration, litigation or agreement: see s 108(3) of the Act and paragraph 23(2) of Part 1 of the Scheme. The timetable for adjudications is very tight (see s 108 of the Act). Many would say unreasonably tight, and likely to result in injustice. Parliament must be taken to have been aware of this. So far as procedure is concerned, the adjudicator is given a fairly free hand. It is true (but hardly surprising) that he is required to act impartially (s 108(2)(e) of the Act and paragraph 12(a) of Part 1 of the Scheme). He is, however, permitted to take the initiative in ascertaining the facts and the law (s 108(2)(f) of the Act and paragraph 13 of Part 1 of the Scheme). He may, therefore, conduct an entirely inquisitorial process, or he may, as in the present case, invite representations from the parties. It is clear that Parliament intended that the adjudication should be conducted in a manner which those familiar with the grinding detail of the traditional approach to the resolution of construction disputes apparently find difficult to accept. But Parliament has not abolished arbitration and litigation of construction disputes. It has merely introduced an intervening provisional stage in the dispute resolution process. Crucially, it has made it clear that decisions of adjudicators are binding and are to be complied with until the dispute is finally resolved.[8]

Secondly, the decision in *Macob* was significant because it gave the HGCRA precedence over the Arbitration Act 1996. Dyson J said that the defendant had an election to make if it wished to challenge the validity of the decision. One course open to it was to treat it as a decision within the meaning of the contract, and refer the dispute to arbitration. The other was to contend that it was not a decision at all within the meaning of the contract, and to seek to defend the enforcement proceedings on the basis that the purported decision was not binding or enforceable because it was a nullity. What the defendant could not do was to assert that the decision was a decision for the purposes of being the subject of a reference to arbitration, but was not a decision for the purposes of being binding and

---

[7] *Macob Civil Engineering Limited v Morrison Construction Limited* [1999] EWHC 254 (TCC); [1999] BLR 93.
[8] [1999] EWHC 254 (TCC) at [14].

enforceable pending any revision by the arbitrator. Once the defendant elected to treat the decision as one capable of being referred to arbitration, he was bound also to treat it as a decision which was binding and enforceable unless revised by the arbitrator.

Thirdly, *Macob* addressed the appropriate procedure for enforcing adjudicators' decisions. The Court stated that the usual remedy for failure to pay in accordance with an adjudicator's decision will be to issue proceedings claiming the sum due, followed by an application for summary judgment.

Later in 1999, the TCC had to decide whether to intervene where the adjudicator's decision contained an arithmetical error that resulted in payment being determined to be due to a subcontractor when the correct calculation would have resulted in a sum due the other way: *Bouygues (UK) Limited v Dahl-Jensen (UK) Limited*.[9] The TCC and the Court of Appeal declined to interfere.[10] At first instance Dyson J said this:

> Mr Furst submits that, if Dahl-Jensen is permitted to enforce a decision which is plainly erroneous, Bouygues will suffer an injustice, and this will bring the adjudication scheme into disrepute. But as I said in *Macob*, the purpose of the scheme is to provide a speedy mechanism for settling disputes in construction contracts on a provisional interim basis, and requiring the decisions of adjudicators to be enforced pending final determination of disputes by arbitration, litigation or agreement, whether those decisions are wrong in point of law or fact. It is inherent in the scheme that injustices will occur, because from time to time, adjudicators will make mistakes. Sometimes those mistakes will be glaringly obvious and disastrous in their consequences for the losing party. The victims of mistakes will usually be able to recoup their losses by subsequent arbitration or litigation, and possibly even by a subsequent adjudication. Sometimes they will not be able to do so, where, for example, there is intervening insolvency, either of the victim or of the fortunate beneficiary of the mistake.[11]

An excess of jurisdiction was recognised as a potential defence to an application for summary judgment to enforce an adjudicator's decision in these early decisions. In *Bouygues* the parties accepted that the test was the same as that for expert determination, as stated by Knox J in *Nikko Hotels (UK) Ltd v MEPC Plc*:[12] 'If he has answered the right question in the wrong way, his decision will be binding. If he has answered the wrong question, his decision will be a nullity'.[13]

Whilst the argument that the adjudicator answered the 'wrong question' has appeared from time to time, the courts have dealt with an array of other actual

---

[9] *Bouygues (UK) Limited v Dahl-Jensen (UK) Limited* [1999] EWHC 182 (TCC); [2000] BLR 49.

[10] [2000] EWCA Civ 507; [2000] BLR 522. A stay of execution was granted by the Court of Appeal on account of the fact that the subcontractor was in insolvent liquidation at the date of the adjudication. Chadwick LJ stated (at [35]) that in circumstances such as those before the Court, where there are latent claims and cross-claims between parties, one of which is in liquidation, it seemed to his Lordship that there was a compelling reason to refuse summary judgment on a claim arising out of an adjudication which is, necessarily, provisional.

[11] [2000] BLR 49, 55 at [35].

[12] *Nikko Hotels (UK) Ltd v MEPC Plc* [1991] 2 EGLR 103.

[13] [1991] 2 EGLR 103 at 108B.

or perceived jurisdictional arguments from parties seeking to avoid enforcement of adjudicator's decisions on the ground that the adjudicator did not have jurisdiction to make the decision which is the subject of enforcement proceedings in the TCC.

In *Pegram Shopfitters Limited v Tally Weijl (UK) Limited*,[14] May LJ described adjudicators' jurisdiction as a 'troublesome area'.[15] In that case the Court of Appeal allowed an appeal against an order for summary judgment enforcing an adjudicator's decision on the basis that it was arguable that there was no written construction contract. May LJ said that judges of the Technology and Construction Court had rightly been

> astute to examine technical defences to applications for summary judgment with a degree of scepticism consonant with the policy of the Act, aptly described by Ward LJ in *RJT Consulting Engineers Limited v DM Engineering (Northern Ireland) Limited* [2001] EWCA Civ 270; [2002] 1 WLR 2344 as 'pay now, argue later'.[16]

IV. The Meaning of a Dispute: *Amec Civil Engineering Limited v Secretary of State for Transport*

One line of argument that has been frequently deployed as a possible defence to enforcement of an adjudicator's decision is the argument that the dispute that was the subject of the adjudicator's decision had not crystallised as at the date on which the adjudication was commenced. Section 108 of the HGCRA permits a party to refer 'a dispute' to adjudication; if there is no dispute, there can be no referral.

The question what constitutes a dispute within the meaning of section 108 has featured in many cases. In the *Construction Adjudication and Payments Handbook*[17] the authors suggest that in the early cases some courts applied a 'high threshold' test which involved considering whether both sides had been given sufficient opportunity to consider the arguments of the other and that the dispute which crystallised included the whole package of arguments advanced and facts relied on by each side, whilst other courts adopted the 'low threshold' test in *Halki Shipping*[18] which meant that a dispute could arise whenever a claim was not admitted, even if the claim was demonstrably undeniable. The authors state that Sir Rupert 'attempted to distil the rapidly growing jungle of decisions on the meaning of "a dispute"'.[19]

---

[14] *Pegram Shopfitters Limited v Tally Weijl (UK) Limited* [2003] EWCA Civ 1750; [2004] BLR 65.
[15] [2004] BLR 65, 68 at [10].
[16] See para [1].
[17] Rawley, Williams, Martinez and Land, *Construction Adjudication and Payments Handbook* (OUP, 2013) at paras 3.31 to 3.33.
[18] *Halki Shipping Corp v Sopex Oils Ltd* [1998] 1 WLR 726 (CA).
[19] See Rawley et al (n 17 above) para 3.34.

The law in relation to the meaning of 'a dispute' was considered by Sir Rupert Jackson and later by the Court of Appeal in *Amec Civil Engineering Limited v Secretary of State for Transport*.[20] The case concerned arbitration and whether the employer was able to start arbitration proceedings before the end of the limitation period, but its significance in relation to adjudication is clear.

The facts were that Amec agreed to carry out major renovation works to the Thelwell viaduct on the M6 motorway. The works included the replacement of an existing reinforced concrete deck slab and the provision of new roller bearings permitting the slab or other elements to move. The contract was not under seal. The contract incorporated the ICE Conditions. Pell Frischmann (PF) acted as the employer's engineer and the certifying engineer under the contract.

Practical completion took place on 23 December 1996. In June 2002 some of the roller bearings appeared to have failed. Subsequent correspondence ensued:

- On 2 October 2002, the Highways Agency wrote to Amec setting out the defects and some details of likely costs. The letter made it clear that the employer would be seeking to recover the costs of the works and invited a formal response.

- Amec responded on 7 October 2002, requesting further information without which they stated they could not formally respond.

- On 6 December 2002, the Highways Agency sent a formal letter of claim to Amec which held Amec responsible for 'the situation with the Thelwell Viaduct'. It invited Amec to confirm by 10 December 2012 that they accepted liability. It was sent by post and received on 9 December 2012.

- Amec replied on 10 December 2012 in non-committal terms.

- On 11 December 2012, the Highways Agency sent two letters to PF. The first referred to their letter of 6 December 2012, stated that Amec had not accepted liability and referred the dispute to PF as engineer under clause 66 of the contract for PF's decision. This letter was not copied to Amec.

- The second letter was a letter of claim against PF holding them responsible for the defects in the viaduct.

- PF gave its decision on 18 December 2012, which concluded that Amec was in breach of contract.

- The Treasury Solicitor acting for the employer wrote to Amec on 19 December 2012, seeking immediate confirmation that Amec accepted the decision stating, that absent such confirmation, the employer would regard Amec as being dissatisfied with the decision.

- Later that day, absent a reply, the Treasury Solicitor gave Amec notice of arbitration.

---

[20] [2004] EWHC 2339 (TCC) (Jackson J); [2005] EWCA Civ 291; [2005] BLR 227 (CA).

Following the appointment of an arbitrator Amec challenged the jurisdiction on three grounds:

(a) that no dispute existed on 11 December 2012 capable of being referred to PF under clause 66, and there was therefore no valid engineer's decision. Absent this there was nothing capable of being referred to arbitration;

(b) alternatively, PF's decision was invalid because PF did not reach it by a fair process, in particular Amec was not copied in on the referral to PF, PF was not provided with a copy of Amec's letter of 10 December 2012, PF reached the decision without inviting Amec to make submissions, PF were asked to reach the decision with urgency, PF started drafting the decision before the referral of the dispute to them and finally PF were themselves in a position of direct conflict; and

(c) yet further, alternatively, if there was a valid decision, the arbitrator's jurisdiction was nevertheless limited to the matters expressly identified in the engineer's decision. The arbitrator rejected all three grounds. Amec appealed to the TCC where Mr Justice Jackson (as he then was) similarly rejected all three grounds. Amec's appeal was dismissed.

The judgment of Sir Rupert at first instance considered the relevant case law in detail.[21] The parties accepted that the following propositions should be derived from the cases:

1. The word 'dispute' which occurs in many arbitration clauses and also in section 108 of the Housing Grants Act should be given its normal meaning. It does not have some special or unusual meaning conferred upon it by lawyers.

2. Despite the simple meaning of the word 'dispute', there has been much litigation over the years as to whether or not disputes existed in particular situations. This litigation has not generated any hard-edged legal rules as to what is or is not a dispute. However, the accumulating judicial decisions have produced helpful guidance.

3. The mere fact that one party (whom I shall call 'the claimant') notifies the other party (whom I shall call 'the respondent') of a claim does not automatically and immediately give rise to a dispute. It is clear, both as a matter of language and from judicial decisions, that a dispute does not arise unless and until it emerges that the claim is not admitted.

4. The circumstances from which it may emerge that a claim is not admitted are Protean. For example, there may be an express rejection of the claim. There may be discussions between the parties from which objectively it is to be inferred that the claim is not admitted. The respondent may prevaricate, thus giving rise to the inference that he does not admit the claim. The respondent may simply remain silent for a period of time, thus giving rise to the same inference.

5. The period of time for which a respondent may remain silent before a dispute is to be inferred depends heavily upon the facts of the case and the contractual structure.

---

[21] *Amec Civil Engineering Ltd v Secretary of State for Transport* [2004] EWHC 2339 (TCC) at [42]–[67].

Where the gist of the claim is well-known and it is obviously controversial, a very short period of silence may suffice to give rise to this inference. Where the claim is notified to some agent of the respondent who has a legal duty to consider the claim independently and then give a considered response, a longer period of time may be required before it can be inferred that mere silence gives rise to a dispute.

6. If the claimant imposes upon the respondent a deadline for responding to the claim, that deadline does not have the automatic effect of curtailing what would otherwise be a reasonable time for responding. On the other hand, a stated deadline and the reasons for its imposition may be relevant factors when the court comes to consider what is a reasonable time for responding.

7. If the claim as presented by the claimant is so nebulous and ill-defined that the respondent cannot sensibly respond to it, neither silence by the respondent nor even an express non-admission is likely to give rise to a dispute for the purposes of arbitration or adjudication.[22]

In *Collins (Contractors) Limited v Baltic Quay Management (1994) Limited*,[23] Clarke LJ quoted Jackson J's seven propositions[24] and said of them:

63. For my part I would accept those propositions as broadly correct. I entirely accept that all depends on the circumstances of the particular case. I would, in particular, endorse the general approach that while the mere making of a claim does not amount to a dispute, a dispute will be held to exist once it can reasonably be inferred that a claim is not admitted. I note that Jackson J does not endorse the suggestion in some of the cases, either that a dispute may not arise until negotiation or discussion have been concluded, or that a dispute should not be likely inferred. In my opinion he was right not to do so.

64. It appears to me that negotiation and discussion are likely to be more consistent with the existence of a dispute, albeit an as yet unresolved dispute, than with an absence of a dispute. It also appears to me that the court is likely to be willing readily to infer that a claim is not admitted and that a dispute exists so that it can be referred to arbitration or adjudication. I make these observations in the hope that they may be of some assistance and not because I detect any disagreement between them and the propositions advanced by Jackson J.

In *Amec*, May LJ said that he was 'broadly content' to accept that Sir Rupert's propositions correctly stated the law, but with a number of further observations.[25] Rix LJ was also broadly content to accept the propositions set out by Sir Rupert, though he said he would be somewhat cautious about the concept of 'a reasonable time to respond' to a claim.[26] He said that the facts of the present case demonstrated the difficulty of that test. In relation to adjudication Rix LJ said this:

Thirdly, and significantly, the problem over 'dispute' has only really arisen in recent years in the context of adjudication for the purposes of Part II of the Housing Grants

---

[22] See para [68].
[23] *Collins (Contractors) Limited v Baltic Quay Management (1994) Limited* [2004] EWCA Civ 1757; [2005] BLR 63.
[24] See para [62].
[25] *Amec Civil Engineering Ltd v Secretary of State for Transport* [2005] 1 WLR 233 at [31].
[26] See para [65].

Construction and Regeneration Act 1996. Jackson J referred below to some of the burgeoning jurisprudence to which the need for a 'dispute' in order to trigger adjudication has given rise. In this new context, where adjudication is an *additional* provisional layer of dispute resolution, pending final litigation or arbitration, there is, as it seems to me, a legitimate concern to ensure that the point at which this additional complexity has been properly reached should not be too readily anticipated. Unlike the arbitration context, adjudication is likely to occur at an early stage, when in any event there is no limitation problem, but there is the different concern that parties may be plunged into an expensive contest, the timing provisions of which are tightly drawn, before they, and particularly the respondent, are ready for it. In this context there has been an understandable concern that the respondent should have a reasonable time in which to respond to any claim.[27]

Subject to the observations made by Clarke, May and Rix LJJ, the propositions suggested by Sir Rupert in *Amec* represent the law relating to the meaning of dispute for the purposes of adjudication enforcement. In *Ringway Infrastructure Services Limited v Vauxhall Motors Limited*,[28] Akenhead J provided additional guidance in which he refers to *Amec*.

(1) The existence of a dispute or difference may be inferred from what is said or not said by the party in receipt of what may be termed 'a claim'.

(2) There does not have to be an express rejection of a 'claim' by the recipient. In so far as the case of *Monmouthshire County Council v Costelloe and Kemple Ltd* suggests otherwise, the more recent cases of *AMEC* and *Collins* suggest otherwise.

(3) A 'claim' for the purpose of giving rise to a dispute or difference may not be a claim for money or for the payment of money. The variety, extent and scope of disputes are infinite. It may involve simply an assertion of a right by one party.

(4) One needs to determine whether there is 'claim' and whether or not that claim is disputed from the surrounding facts, circumstances and evidence pertaining up to the moment that the dispute, subsequently referred to adjudication (or arbitration), has crystallised.[29]

In *St Austell Printing Company Limited v Dawnus Construction Ltd*,[30] Coulson J referred to *Amec* and said that the crystallisation argument is 'almost never successful',[31] a point which he illustrated by reference to the extreme circumstances that existed in the only two recent cases in which it has been upheld namely *Enterprise Managed Services Limited v Tony McFadden Utilities Limited*[32] and *Beck Interiors Limited v UK Flooring Contractors Limited*.[33]

---

[27] See para [68].
[28] *Ringway Infrastructure Services Limited v Vauxhall Motors Limited* [2007] EWHC 2421 (TCC).
[29] See para [55].
[30] *St Austell Printing Company Limited v Dawnus Construction Ltd* [2015] EWHC 96 (TCC); [2015] BLR 224.
[31] See para [16].
[32] *Enterprise Managed Services Limited v Tony McFadden Utilities Limited* [2009] EWHC 3222 (TCC); [2010] BLR 89.
[33] *Beck Interiors Limited v UK Flooring Contractors Limited* [2012] EWHC 1808 (TCC); [2012] BLR 417.

The effect of the above guidance has been to discourage this line of defence to enforcement whilst at the same time ensuring that responding parties have had some opportunity to consider claims before they can form the subject-matter of a referral to adjudication.

V. Natural Justice: *Carillion Construction Limited v Devonport Royal Dockyard*

The other ground for seeking to resist enforcement of an adjudicator's decision is that the adjudicator failed to comply with the rules of natural justice, which are not limited to the requirement that the adjudicator be impartial but extend to the conduct of the adjudication process itself. As in the *Amec* case discussed above, Sir Rupert's judgment at first instance in *Carillion Construction Limited v Devonport Royal Dockyard*[34] provided the construction industry with guidance as to the legal principles that govern the application of the rules of natural justice in the context of adjudication.

In *Carillion* the adjudicator decided that the employer was obliged to pay the contractor in excess of £10m including £1.2m in interest. The employer challenged the decision on various grounds which included the contention that the adjudicator's decision on certain issues was reached in breach of the rules of natural justice and should not therefore be enforced. In relation to interest, the employer argued that the adjudicator had no jurisdiction to award interest. In support of its contention that the decision had been reached in breach of the rules of natural justice the employer argued that the adjudicator had disregarded certain arguments which it had advanced before him, decided an issue on a different basis from that advanced by the parties without giving the parties an opportunity to make representations, and that he had failed to give any or any adequate reasons for his decision in respect of defects.

In Part 5 of the judgment in *Carillion*, Sir Rupert analysed the case law concerning challenges based on a breach of natural justice. He detected in the first instance cases over the preceding six years some slight differences in emphasis and approach:

> In borderline cases what one judge may regard as a permissible error of law or procedure on the part of an adjudicator, another judge may characterise as excess of jurisdiction or a substantial breach of the rules of natural justice.[35]

He went on to say this:

> 80. In my view, it is helpful to state or restate four basic principles:
>
> 1.   The adjudication procedure does not involve the final determination of anybody's rights (unless all the parties so wish).

[34] [2005] EWHC 778 (TCC); [2005] BLR 310.
[35] See para [79].

2. The Court of Appeal has repeatedly emphasised that adjudicators' decisions must be enforced, even if they result from errors of procedure, fact or law: see *Bouygues, C&B Scene* and *Levolux*.

3. Where an adjudicator has acted in excess of his jurisdiction or in serious breach of the rules of natural justice, the court will not enforce his decision: see *Discain, Balfour Beatty* and *Pegram Shopfitters*.

4. Judges must be astute to examine technical defences with a degree of scepticism consonant with the policy of the 1996 Act. Errors of law, fact or procedure by an adjudicator must be examined critically before the Court accepts that such errors constitute excess of jurisdiction or serious breaches of the rules of natural justice: see *Pegram Shopfitters* and *Amec*.

Having addressed the four basic principles above, Sir Rupert advanced five propositions that he considered to be pertinent to the issue in the case before him.

1. If an adjudicator declines to consider evidence which, on his analysis of the facts or the law, is irrelevant, that is neither (a) a breach of the rules of natural justice nor (b) a failure to consider relevant material which undermines his decision on *Wednesbury* grounds or for breach of paragraph 17 of the Scheme. If the adjudicator's analysis of the facts or the law was erroneous, it may follow that he ought to have considered the evidence in question. The possibility of such error is inherent in the adjudication system. It is not a ground for refusing to enforce the adjudicator's decision. I reach this conclusion on the basis of the Court of Appeal decisions mentioned earlier. This conclusion is also supported by the reasoning of Mr Justice Steyn in the context of arbitration in *Bill Biakh v Hyundai Corporation* [1988] 1 Lloyd's Rep 187.

2. On a careful reading of His Honour Judge Thornton's judgment in *Buxton Building Contractors Limited v Governors of Durand Primary School* [2004] 1 BLR 474, I do not think that this judgment is inconsistent with proposition 1. If, however, Mr Furst is right and if *Buxton* is inconsistent with proposition 1, then I consider that Buxton was wrongly decided and I decline to follow it.

3. It is often not practicable for an adjudicator to put to the parties his provisional conclusions for comment. Very often those provisional conclusions will represent some intermediate position, for which neither party was contending. It will only be in an exceptional case such as *Balfour Beatty v the London Borough of Lambeth* that an adjudicator's failure to put his provisional conclusions to the parties will constitute such a serious breach of the rules of natural justice that the court will decline to enforce his decision.

4. During argument, my attention has been drawn to certain decisions on the duty to give reasons in a planning context. See in particular *Save Britain's Heritage v No 1 Poultry Limited*, [1991] 1 WLR 153 and *South Bucks DC and another v Porter (No 2)* [2004] 1 WLR 1953. In my view, the principles stated in these cases are only of limited relevance to adjudicators' decisions. I reach this conclusion for three reasons:

(a) Adjudicators' decisions do not finally determine the rights of the parties (unless all parties so wish).

(b) If reasons are given and they prove to be erroneous, that does not generally enable the adjudicator's decision to be challenged.

(c) Adjudicators often are not required to give reasons at all.

5. If an adjudicator is requested to give reasons pursuant to paragraph 22 of the Scheme, in my view a brief statement of those reasons will suffice. The reasons should be sufficient to show that the adjudicator has dealt with the issues remitted to him and what his conclusions are on those issues. It will only be in extreme circumstances, such as those described by Lord Justice Clerk in *Gillies Ramsay*, that the court will decline to enforce an otherwise valid adjudicator's decision because of the inadequacy of the reasons given. The complainant would need to show that the reasons were absent or unintelligible and that, as a result, he had suffered substantial prejudice.[36]

The Court of Appeal refused permission to appeal save in relation to the question of interest.[37] The Court of Appeal said that the employer had shown no prospect that it would succeed in showing that Sir Rupert was wrong to find that the adjudicator's decision was not reached in breach of the rules of natural justice. In relation to interest, the appeal was dismissed and the differences of approach between the judgments at first instance and in the Court of Appeal may be more apparent than real, as explained by the editors of the Building Law Reports in their commentary.

Chadwick LJ gave the judgment of the Court of Appeal. He referred to the general principles set out in paragraph 80 of Sir Rupert's judgment and said 'We do not understand there to be any challenge to those general principles. They are fully supported by the authorities, as the judge demonstrated in his judgment'.[38] He then set out in full the five propositions that are quoted above. Later in the judgment (in paragraphs 84 to 87), after setting out the reasons for refusing permission to appeal, Chadwick LJ addressed the general principles relating to the approach of the courts when required to address a challenge to the decision of an adjudicator. In doing so he started with Sir Rupert's general principles and the five propositions:

84. It will be apparent, from what we have said in giving our reasons for refusing permission to appeal, that we are in broad agreement with the propositions which the judge set out at para 81 of his judgment and which we have ourselves set out at para 53 in this judgment. Those propositions are indicative of the approach which courts should adopt when required to address a challenge to the decision of an adjudicator appointed under the 1996 Act. We are, perhaps, less confident than the judge that the decision in *Buxton Building Contractors Ltd* v *Governors of Durand Primary School* [2004] BLR 474 can be reconciled with the first of those propositions. We endorse that first proposition and, to the extent that *Buxton* is inconsistent with that proposition, the judge was right not to follow that decision.

85. The objective which underlies the Act and the statutory scheme requires the courts to respect and enforce the adjudicator's decision unless it is plain that the question which he has decided was not the question referred to him or the manner in which he has gone about his task is obviously unfair. It should be only in rare circumstances that

---

[36] See para [81].

[37] *Carillion Construction Ltd* v *Devonport Royal Dockyard Ltd* [2005] EWCA Civ 1358; [2006] BLR 15.

[38] See para [52].

the courts will interfere with the decision of an adjudicator. The courts should give no encouragement to the approach adopted by DML in the present case; which (contrary to DML's outline submissions, to which we have referred in para 66 of this judgment) may, indeed, aptly be described as 'simply scrabbling around to find some argument, however tenuous, to resist payment'.

86. It is only too easy in a complex case for a party who is dissatisfied with the decision of an adjudicator to comb through the adjudicator's reasons and identify points upon which to present a challenge under the labels 'excess of jurisdiction' or 'breach of natural justice'. It must be kept in mind that the majority of adjudicators are not chosen for their expertise as lawyers. Their skills are as likely (if not more likely) to lie in other disciplines. The task of the adjudicator is not to act as arbitrator or judge. The time constraints within which he is expected to operate are proof of that. The task of the adjudicator is to find an interim solution which meets the needs of the case. Parliament may be taken to have recognised that, in the absence of an interim solution, the contractor (or sub-contractor) or his sub-contractors will be driven into insolvency through a wrongful withholding of payments properly due. The statutory scheme provides a means of meeting the legitimate cash-flow requirements of contractors and their subcontractors. The need to have the 'right' answer has been subordinated to the need to have an answer quickly. The Scheme was not enacted in order to provide definitive answers to complex questions. Indeed, it may be open to doubt whether Parliament contemplated that disputes involving difficult questions of law would be referred to adjudication under the statutory scheme; or whether such disputes are suitable for adjudication under the Scheme. We have every sympathy for an adjudicator faced with the need to reach a decision in a case like the present.

87. In short, in the overwhelming majority of cases, the proper course for the party who is unsuccessful in an adjudication under the scheme must be to pay the amount that he has been ordered to pay by the adjudicator. If he does not accept the adjudicator's decision as correct (whether on the facts or in law), he can take legal or arbitration proceedings in order to establish the true position. To seek to challenge the adjudicator's decision on the ground that he has exceeded his jurisdiction or breached the rules of natural justice (save in the plainest cases) is likely to lead to a substantial waste of time and expense – as, we suspect, the costs incurred in the present case will demonstrate only too clearly.

The above passage is one of the most well known and most often cited in construction adjudication cases, including Chadwick LJ's memorable phrase describing the employer's approach in seeking to resist enforcement as 'simply scrabbling around to find some argument, however tenuous, to resist payment'.

Carillion continues to represent the law, as was recently illustrated in *Amey Wye Valley Ltd v County of Herefordshire District Council*[39] in which Fraser J stated the following, as a way of a reminder to parties generally rather than stating any innovative principle:

Adjudicator's [sic] decisions will be enforced by the courts, regardless of errors of fact or law. This has been stated many times. *Carillion v Devonport Royal Dockyard* [2005]

---

[39] *Amey Wye Valley Ltd v County of Herefordshire District Council* [2016] EWHC 2368 (TCC).

EWCA Civ 1358 is the most often quoted appellate authority, including as it does an exhortation (sometimes ignored) that dissatisfied parties should take steps finally to resolve the substantive dispute, rather than waste time and money opposing enforcement. Adjudication is a merely temporary resolution of any dispute.[40]

VI. Forum Shopping

In *Lanes Group plc v Galliford Try Infrastructure Limited*,[41] the Court of Appeal considered whether the referring party (Galliford) which had obtained the appointment of an adjudicator to whom it objected (without any legal basis for such objection) could take no further steps in the adjudication so as to prevent the adjudication from proceeding and then seek a new appointment on the same dispute. The Court held that such a course of action, although unappealing, was permissible.

Lanes argued that the second adjudicator did not have jurisdiction because Galliford's right to refer the dispute to adjudication had been exhausted by the first appointment. Whilst initially attracted to Lanes' objection, Jackson LJ concluded that it could not be accepted because an adjudication might be aborted for a number of reasons, some of which would be outside the control of the parties, and therefore it could not have been intended that the right to refer a dispute to adjudication was limited to one appointment.[42] Jackson LJ referred to the possibility that postal delay might prevent the delivery of a referral within the period permitted thus rendering the adjudication abortive. It could not be the case that the right to adjudicate would be lost once and for all in such circumstances. The entitlement of a party to withdraw a claim persists even after the referral, regardless of the motive for the withdrawal, and does not necessarily preclude that party from pursuing the claim in a later adjudication.[43]

Jackson LJ referred to his decision in *Midland Expressway Ltd v Carillion Construction Ltd*,[44] in which he decided that a party could withdraw a claim during the course of adjudication proceedings without the adjudicator's permission. It would be odd if parties could be required to continue with a claim that was bad. He added that 'both adjudicators and the courts should approach procedural issues in adjudication in a manner which accords with fairness and common sense': 'Adjudication should not become a game of chess in which the tactical skill of the players determines the outcome'.[45] In *Lanes Group plc v Galliford Try Infrastructure Limited* Jackson LJ, with whom the other Lord Justices agreed, confirmed that a party might withdraw a claim post referral and reserve it for another day.[46]

[40] [2016] EWHC 2368 (TCC) at [30].
[41] *Lanes Group plc v Galliford Try Infrastructure Limited* [2011] EWCA Civ 1617; [2012] BLR 121.
[42] See para [37].
[43] See para [38].
[44] *Midland Expressway Ltd v Carillion Construction Ltd* [2006] EWHC 1505 (TCC); [2006] BLR 325.
[45] See para [105].
[46] [2012] BLR 121 at [42].

Whilst there is no doctrine of abuse of process in adjudication,[47] it should not be assumed that 'anything goes' so far as parties' conduct is concerned. The courts' policing function is evident from the decision of O'Farrell J in *Jacobs UK Limited v Skanska Construction UK Limited*.[48]

In *Jacobs* the parties agreed a timetable for the adjudication which required service of the referral on 17 February 2017, service of the response by 24 March 2017 and service of the reply by 7 April 2017. The referral and response were served on time. Unfortunately, Skanska's counsel became unavailable and Skanska was unable to serve its reply by 7 April 2017 as agreed, and Skanska's request for an extension of time was rejected. On 11 April 2017 the adjudicator resigned. Skanska gave second notice of adjudication in June 2017 which included the same claims as the first notice.

O'Farrell J rejected Skanska's submission that it would be open to a party to start and stop serial adjudications in respect of a claim. She said that subjecting a party to serial adjudications in respect of the same claim and requiring it to incur irrecoverable costs could amount to unreasonable and oppressive behaviour.[49] It is a question of fact in each case as to whether the behaviour of the party to adjudication is found, on an objective basis, to be unreasonable and oppressive. The court has power to grant an injunction to restrain the second adjudication if it is established that it is unreasonable and oppressive. Such power will be exercised where the adjudicator does not have jurisdiction (such as where the dispute has already been decided in an earlier adjudication), where the referring party has failed to comply with the adjudication agreement (such as failures to pay awards or costs from earlier adjudications), or where the further adjudication is vexatious (such as serial adjudications in respect of the same claim).[50]

The Court considered that Skanska's withdrawal was unreasonable, but unreasonable behaviour by one party will not automatically deprive it of the right to adjudicate the dispute in question in a subsequent reference.[51] The Court will not intervene unless the further reference is both unreasonable and oppressive.[52] The required oppression did not exist because Jacobs could reuse in the second adjudication a large part the work done in respect of the first adjudication.

Whilst Jacobs did not obtain an injunction, it did establish a right to recover any additional costs incurred due to Skanska's breach of the agreed timetable. Costs incurred in adjudication proceedings are not generally recoverable, but on the facts O'Farrell J held that the parties' agreement was enforceable. The costs wasted in respect of abandoned claims were not recoverable.

---

[47] See per Dyson LJ in *Connex South Eastern Limited v MJ Building Services Group plc* [2005] EWCA Civ 193; [2005] BLR 201.
[48] *Jacobs UK Limited v Skanska Construction UK Limited* [2017] BLR 619.
[49] See para [33].
[50] See para [35].
[51] See para [36].
[52] See para [36].

VII. Possible Reforms

In addition to his judicial duties, Sir Rupert actively contributed to discussions about possible reform of the HGCRA. In March 2005 the DTI published a consultation paper entitled 'Improving payment practices in the construction industry'. Sir Rupert provided a paper in response for a DTI Conference in June 2005 in which he addressed a number of proposals.[53] Notably, Sir Rupert explained why a proposal that adjudicators should decide their own jurisdiction was, in his view, wrong. Describing the proposal as the one that caused him the greatest concern, he set out five reasons why he considered it to be wrong in principle. The suggestion that adjudicators should decide their own jurisdiction was not pursued.

Sir Rupert's paper also drew attention to the problem of the costs incurred in some adjudications, with reference to *AWG Construction Services Ltd v Rockingham Motor Speedway Ltd*[54] in which the costs were in excess of £1m, and *CIB Properties Ltd v Birse Construction Ltd*[55] in which the parties incurred around £2m in costs. Sir Rupert made the following observation:

> If the parties invest huge sums of (irrecoverable) costs in an adjudication process, which is merely the precursor to full blown arbitration or litigation, then the parties get the worst of all worlds. Although it is a matter for policy makers (not me) I really do question whether there should not be some limit on the use of adjudication in certain situations. If the parties use adjudication to fight out a major professional negligence action or a massive dispute about final accounts, they may end up devoting more costs and management time to the dispute than if they proceed straight to arbitration or litigation. The TCC can now offer much earlier hearing dates than it could in the 1990's (the time of Sir Michael Latham's seminal reports and the enactment of the Construction Act).[56]

It appears that the policymakers in the UK at least were not minded to act on this advice, with the result that 'kitchen sink' adjudications remain a generally unwelcome facet of adjudication.

VIII. Conclusion

It is respectfully suggested that Sir Rupert's judgments in the TCC, including the cases discussed above, have made a substantial contribution to the development of the law relating to the enforcement of adjudicators' decisions. The above judgments delivered clarity in areas of the law where there was some diversity of approach in the previous cases, thus enabling parties to better understand the law and providing certainty to the industry that the TCC serves.

---

[53] See n 5 above.
[54] *AWG Construction Services Ltd v Rockingham Motor Speedway Ltd* [2004] EWHC 888 (TCC).
[55] *CIB Properties Ltd v Birse Construction Ltd* [2004] EWHC 2365 (TCC).
[56] See n 5 above.

7

An Open Mind

RACHAEL O'HAGAN

I. Introduction

In *Lanes v Galliford Try Infrastructure Ltd*[1] the Court of Appeal was required to consider two issues, namely: (1) whether the appointed adjudicator had jurisdiction; and (2) whether the adjudicator's decision was tainted by apparent bias. In respect of these issues, Lord Justice Jackson delivered a detailed judgment in seven parts with which Lord Justice Richards and Lord Justice Stanley Burnton agreed entirely. The Court of Appeal's findings in respect of both of these issues (as discussed further below) has given rise to substantial legal commentary and has further shaped the legal landscape within which adjudications are considered.

This chapter focuses on the subject of adjudicator bias and the significance of Lord Justice Jackson's findings on this issue. At the time of writing, the issue of apparent bias and pre-determination in the context of adjudication and arbitration proceedings is very much a 'hot topic'.[2] Indeed, in recent years, it is an issue which the High Court has been required to decide on many occasions and which has resulted in various findings of apparent bias in the context of an adjudicator/arbitrator's conduct. In particular, the findings in *Cofley Ltd v Bingham*[3] have resulted in wide-spread debate about the circumstances in which a court is likely to make a finding of apparent bias.

It is generally accepted that although adjudicators are not judges or arbitrators, they are nevertheless professionals with their own codes of conduct.[4] In the forthcoming years, it will be interesting to see whether cases such as *Cofley* mark a high-point in findings on apparent bias and whether the industry is likely to see more challenges to adjudicators' jurisdiction based on allegations of apparent bias.

---

[1] *Lanes v Galliford Try Infrastructure Ltd (t/a Galliford Try Rail)* [2011] EWCA Civ 1617.
[2] See, for example, Mr Justice Edwards-Stuart's paper, 'Arbitrators and Adjudicators: Impartiality and an Open Mind' (2017), SCL Paper 204 (available at www.scl.org.uk).
[3] *Cofley Ltd v Bingham* [2016] EWHC 240 (Comm).
[4] *Amec Capital Projects Ltd v Whitefriars City Estates Ltd* [2004] EWCA Civ 1418 at [20].

The contents of this chapter are as follows:

(1)   What is bias?
(2)   The decision in *Lanes v Galliford Try* and the limitations identified by Lord Justice Jackson.
(3)   Bias – where are we now?

II. What is Bias?

Bias been defined by the courts as 'an attitude of mind which prevents the judge from making an objective determination of the issues he has to resolve'.[5]

Bias can take various forms. It can arise by way of actual bias, apparent bias or pre-determination. Bias may arise where (for example): a party has a pecuniary or proprietary interest in the outcome of the proceedings; if a decision-maker takes part in a determination or appeal against one of his own decisions; if the decision-maker has a close relationship with one of the parties (which may arise by way of friendship, family or in a professional context); or if there is personal animosity towards a party.[6]

In *Davidson v Scottish Ministers (No 2)*,[7] Lord Bingham considered an allegation of apparent bias concerning the Court's conduct. He commented: 'What disqualifies the judge is the presence of some factor which could prevent the bringing of an objective judgment to bear, which could distort the judge's judgment.'[8]

Pre-determination is sometimes treated as a separate branch of bias.[9] Unlike bias, which is concerned with the attitude of the mind, pre-determination is concerned with what happened as a matter of fact. Pre-determination is when a judge or other decision-maker reaches a final conclusion before he or she is in possession of all the relevant evidence and arguments. The difference between pre-determination and bias was explained by Mr Justice Beatson in *R (Persimmon Homes Limited) v Vale of Glamorgan Council*[10] as follows:

> Predetermination is the surrender by a decision-maker of its judgment by having a closed mind and failing to apply it to the task. In a case of apparent bias, the decision maker may have in fact applied its mind quite properly to the matter but a

---

[5] *Re Medicaments and Related Classes of Goods (No 2)* [2001] WLR 700 at [37].

[6] For a more detailed explanation of what may constitute bias, see: Lord Woolf, J Jowell, AP de Sueur, and CM Donnelly, *De Smith's Judicial Review of Administrative Action*, 7th edn (London, Sweet & Maxwell, 2012) at [10–19] to [10–56].

[7] *Davidson v Scottish Ministers (No 2)* [2004] UKHL 34.

[8] [2004] UKHL 34 at [6].

[9] See *Porter v Magill* [2001] UKHL 67 at [88]; *Lanes v Galliford Try* (n 1 above) at [45]; Edwards-Stuart J, 'Arbitrators and Adjudicators: Impartiality and an Open Mind' (March 2017), Society of Construction Law Paper 204, p 9.

[10] *R (Persimmon Homes Limited) v Vale of Glamorgan Council* [2010] EWHC 535 (Admin).

reasonable observer would consider that there was a real danger of bias on its part. Bias is concerned with appearances whereas predetermination is concerned with what has in fact happened.[11]

In the context of local authorities exercising their functions, the test of pre-determination is enshrined in the Localism Act 2011 (UK). Section 25 of that Act states:

Prior indications of view of a matter not to amount to predetermination etc

(1) Subsection (2) applies if—

(a) as a result of an allegation of bias or predetermination, or otherwise, there is an issue about the validity of a decision of a relevant authority, and

(b) it is relevant to that issue whether the decision-maker, or any of the decision-makers, had or appeared to have had a closed mind (to any extent) when making the decision.

(2) A decision-maker is not to be taken to have had, or to have appeared to have had, a closed mind when making the decision just because—

(a) the decision-maker had previously done anything that directly or indirectly indicated what view the decision-maker took, or would or might take, in relation to a matter, and

(b) the matter was relevant to the decision ...

It is respectfully suggested that the test set down in the Localism Act 2011 may now serve as a useful guide when considering the test for pre-determination more widely.

In practice, however, findings of actual bias or actual pre-determination are rare because they are difficult to prove on the evidence. As such, findings of apparent pre-determination or apparent bias are more common.[12]

A. Obligation to be Impartial

Procedural fairness requires that: (1) parties are afforded a proper opportunity to be heard; and (2) the decision-maker should not be biased or prejudiced in a way that does not allow fair and genuine consideration to be given to the arguments advanced by the parties.[13] The case law and, in some cases statute, prevents a decision-maker from adjudicating wherever there are circumstances which suggest that the decision-maker may be pre-determined in favour of one of the parties.[14]

---

[11] [2010] EWHC 535 (Admin) at [116].

[12] See *Lanes v Galliford Try* (n 1 above) at [46]; *Porter v Magill* [2001] UKHL 67 at [88].

[13] See per Dyson LJ (as he then was) in *Amec Capital Projects Ltd v Whitefriars City Estates Ltd* [2004] EWCA Civ 1418 at [14].

[14] *De Smith's Judicial Review*, 7th edn (n 6 above) at [10-002] and [10-003].

Insofar as adjudication is concerned, section 108(2)(a) of the Housing Grants, Construction and Regeneration Act 1996 requires a construction contract to which the Act applies to impose (amongst other things) a duty on the adjudicator to act impartially. Similarly, where the Scheme for Construction Contracts (England and Wales) Regulations 1998[15] apply, paragraph 12 of Part I of the Scheme requires the adjudicator to act impartially in carrying out his/her duties.

Indeed, an adjudicator's obligations as to impartiality largely reflect those of arbitrators.[16] For example, section 33(1) of the Arbitration Act 1996 (UK) imposes an obligation on an arbitral tribunal to 'act fairly and impartially as between the parties, giving each party a reasonable opportunity of putting his case and dealing with that of his opponent'; and 'adopt procedure suitable to the circumstances of the particular case, avoiding unnecessary delay or expense, so as to provide a fair means for the resolution of the matters falling to be determined'. Where a party is of the view that circumstances exist that may give rise to justifiable doubts as to impartiality, a party to arbitral proceedings may apply to the court to remove the arbitrator pursuant to section 24(1)(a) of the Arbitration Act 1996.

The duty of impartiality may also be set out or further defined by any rules which apply to the adjudication or arbitration. By way of example, Rule 3 of the Chartered Institute of Arbitrators (CIArb) provides: 'Both before and throughout the dispute resolution process, a member shall disclose all interests, relationships and matters likely to affect the member's independence or impartiality or which might reasonably be perceived as likely to do so.'[17]

B. Bias – The Test

As to the test which is to be applied when considering whether a tribunal's conduct amounts to bias, the starting point for the modern authorities is the authority of *Porter v Magill*.[18] In that case, the House of Lords modified the former common law test for bias in order to take into account the Strasbourg guidance on Article 6 of the European Convention on Human Rights. In that case, Lord Hope noted that:

> the concept requires not only that the tribunal must be truly independent and free from actual bias, proof of which is likely to be very difficult, but also that it must not appear in the objective sense to lack these essential qualities.[19]

The often quoted test for bias was then formulated by Lord Hope where he stated that: 'The question is whether the fair-minded and informed observer, having

---

[15] Scheme for Construction Contracts (England and Wales) Regulations 1998 (SI 1998/649).
[16] *Beumer Group UK v Vinci Construction UK Ltd* [2016] EWHC 2283 (TCC) at [29].
[17] Chartered Institute of Arbitrators, Code of Professional and Ethical Conduct for Members, October 2009 (part 2), Rule 3. See also Article 11 of the CIArb Rules.
[18] [2001] UKHL 67.
[19] [2001] UKHL 67 at [88].

considered the facts, would conclude that there was a real possibility that the tribunal was biased.'[20]

The test was further developed in *Gillies v Secretary of State for Work and Pensions*.[21] In this case Lord Hope elaborated on the 'fair-minded and informed observer test' which he had previously set out in *Porter v Magill*. He said:

> The fair-minded and informed observer can be assumed to have access to all the facts that are capable of being known by members of the public generally, bearing in mind that it is the appearance that these facts give rise to that matters, not what is in the mind of the particular judge or tribunal member who is under scrutiny. It is to be assumed ... that the observer is neither complacent nor unduly sensitive or suspicious when he examines the facts that he can look at. It is to be assumed too that he is able to distinguish between what is relevant and what is irrelevant, and that he is able when exercising his judgment to decide what weight should be given to the facts that are relevant.[22]

Following *Gillies v Secretary of State*, a fair-minded and informed observer can be assumed to have access to all the facts that are capable of being known by members of the public generally. However, in *Virdi v Law Society*[23] it was also held that the facts known to the fair-minded and informed observer are not limited to those in the public domain.

Notwithstanding the elaboration of the fair-minded observer test,[24] as detailed above, one of the leading texts on judicial review[25] notes these words of caution: 'As has been observed, assuming such extensive knowledge on the part of the objective observer may undermine the purpose of apparent bias of ensuring public confidence in the administration of justice.'[26]

The 'fair-minded observer' test as set out above applies to adjudicators.[27]

III. *Lanes v Galliford Try*

In *Lanes* the Court of Appeal considered conjoined appeals in three separate actions concerning an adjudication decision. As explained in the introduction above, the issues for the Court to consider concerned whether the adjudicator had jurisdiction and whether his decision was a nullity by reason of apparent bias.

---

[20] [2001] UKHL 67 at [103].

[21] *Gillies v Secretary of State for Work and Pensions* [2006] UKHL 2.

[22] [2006] UKHL 2 at [17].

[23] *Virdi v Law Society* [2010] EWCA Civ 100.

[24] For a more detailed analysis of the development of the 'fair-minded observer test', see: *De Smith's Judicial Review* (n 6 above) at [10-012] to [10-018].

[25] *De Smith's Judicial Review* (n 6 above).

[26] *De Smith's Judicial Review* (n 6 above) at [10-018]. See also the comments of Lord Justice Jackson in *Lanes v Galliford Try* (n 1 above) as set out further below.

[27] *Amec Capital Projects Ltd v Whitefriars City Estates Ltd* [2004] EWCA Civ 1418.

A. The Facts

The appellant in the first two appeals was Lanes, a subcontractor who had contracted to renew the roof at a traction maintenance depot. The appellant in the third appeal was Galliford, the main contractor to Network Rail Infrastructure. The sub-contract was evidenced by Galliford's sub-contract order form and incorporated the Civil Engineering Contractors Association's 'Blue Form' of sub-contract terms and conditions.

Galliford terminated Lanes' employment under the sub-contract. Lanes claimed it was entitled to extensions of time and that the sub-contract had been wrongfully terminated. Galliford alleged that Lanes had failed to proceed with the works with due diligence. The dispute was referred to arbitration. While the arbitration was proceeding, Galliford served an adjudication notice on Lanes and applied to the Institute of Civil Engineers (ICE) for an adjudicator. The ICE appointed an adjudicator. Due to previous experiences with the appointed adjudicator, Galliford chose not to send their referral documents to the appointed adjudicator but instead to serve a fresh adjudication notice and to ask the ICE to appoint a different adjudicator.

The ICE appointed a new adjudicator. Lanes argued that the new adjudicator had no jurisdiction and sought an injunction to restrain the new adjudicator from proceeding. Mr Justice Akenhead accepted that Galliford's conduct amounted to a breach of contract but refused Lanes' claim for an injunction.[28]

The adjudicator proceeded with the adjudication. Galliford served its referral documentation. Lanes was due to serve its response on 10 April 2011 but did not do so. On 11 April 2011, Lanes wrote to the adjudicator stating that it needed more time. The adjudicator invited the parties to agree an extension of time for his decision. After some to-ing and fro-ing, by an email dated 14 April 2011 (timed 10.01 am) Galliford's solicitors agreed the timetable proposed by the adjudicator, which meant that only the date for Lanes' Response remained outstanding.[29] However, on the same day the adjudicator sent to the parties a document entitled 'Preliminary Views and Findings of Fact'. The adjudicator's covering email stated:

Preliminary Views and Findings of Fact

The date for the Response specified in the ICE Adjudication Procedure has passed and lanes has made no submissions at all on the substantive issues. There has been no agreement to a revised timetable and indeed no response at all to my suggested timetable yesterday.

Accordingly, in order to assist me in my examination of the issues referred to me, in my ascertainment of the facts and the law and in order to allow the Parties the opportunity to make further submissions on the issues I enclose Preliminary views and Findings of Fact on some of the initial issues raised in the Referral.

---

[28] *Lanes Group Plc v Galliford Try Infrastructure Ltd* [2011] EWHC 1035 (TCC).
[29] *Lanes Group Plc v Galliford Try Infrastructure* [2011] EWHC 1679 (TCC) at [58] to [64].

The Preliminary View and Findings of fact are a step in making my Decision and I am not bound by them nor do I commit myself to communicate nor issue amendments or further Preliminary Views and Findings of Fact.

I direct the Parties to make any comments or submissions on the Preliminary Views and Findings of Fact by 17.00 hrs on Thursday 21st April 2011. I direct the Parties to refer to or submit any evidence, arguments, authorities etc that they consider relevant.

The Preliminary View document began with the following passage:

NOTICE

The statement 'I find', 'I find and hold' and 'Decision' and other statements are not and not intended to be decisions of the adjudicator but preliminary views and findings of fact preparatory to the decision.

The preliminary views and findings are a step in making the decision and I am not bound by them.

I do not commit myself to communicate nor issue amendments or further Preliminary Views and Findings of Fact.

Subsequently, the adjudicator considered comments and submissions submitted by both parties. The adjudicator found in favour of Galliford. Lanes commenced an action in the Technology and Construction Court challenging the validity of the adjudicator's appointment and the validity of his decision. Galliford sought to enforce the adjudicator's decision.

HHJ Waksman QC found that: (1) Galliford was entitled to serve a second notice of adjudication and therefore the adjudicator had jurisdiction; and (2) the adjudicator's decision was a nullity on the ground of apparent bias. Both parties appealed against the decision of HHJ Waksman QC. Lanes appealed against the decision of Mr Justice Akenhead.

B. First Issue: Jurisdiction

It would be wrong to set out the Court of Appeal's decision on apparent bias without setting out briefly its findings on jurisdiction. This element of the decision has also been the subject of further judicial comment and consideration.

The Court of Appeal found that the adjudicator had jurisdiction. The upshot of this finding was that the Court of Appeal concluded that where a party serves an adjudication notice but fails to serve its referral documentation a party does not lose its right to adjudicate. Instead, a party has a right to serve a fresh adjudication notice. Lord Justice Jackson explained the reasoning for this decision in his judgment.[30] In particular, the Court took into account that: (1) sometimes an adjudication is not pursued past the preliminary steps but there was no authority

---

[30] [2011] EWCA Civ 1617 at [37]–[42].

to suggest that as a consequence the claimant lost its right to adjudicate the dispute for all time; (2) the Scheme for Construction Contracts (England and Wales) Regulations 1998 and (in this case) the ICE Adjudication Procedure recognised a right to restart an adjudication in various circumstances and, as such, it could not be right that the claimant's entitlement to adjudicate the dispute in question was 'irretrievably lost'.

During its oral and written submissions, Lanes argued that Galliford's conduct was tantamount to forum shopping, where referring parties could effectively shop for their adjudicators until a preferred adjudicator was nominated. As to this, Lord Justice Jackson gave the following guidance:

> Forum shopping is never attractive. My first view of this case was that Galliford could not be permitted simply to drop the first adjudication and then adjudicate before a different adjudicator whom it preferred. Mr Marrin's submissions have persuaded me, however, that Galliford's conduct was permissible under the contract and the second adjudicator did indeed have jurisdiction.[31]

Lastly, the Court of Appeal considered whether Galliford's conduct could amount to an abuse of process. However, applying the reasoning of Lord Justice Dyson (as he then was) in *Connex South Eastern Ltd v MJ Building Services Group Plc*,[32] it was noted by Lord Justice Jackson that 'abuse of process has no place in adjudication'.[33]

C. Second Issue: Apparent Bias

The Court of Appeal found that the adjudicator's provision of the Preliminary Views document did not amount to a pre-determination and therefore the adjudicator's decision was not a nullity.

Lord Justice Jackson's findings on this issue were as follows:

> There is nothing objectionable in a judge setting out his or her provisional view at an early stage of proceedings, so that the parties have an opportunity to correct any errors in the judge's thinking or to concentrate on matters which appear to be influencing the judge. Of course, it is unacceptable if the judge reaches a final decision before he is in possession of all the relevant evidence and arguments which the parties wish to put before him. There is, however, a clear distinction between (a) reaching a final decision prematurely and (b) reaching a provisional view which is disclosed for the assistance of the parties.

---

[31] [2011] EWCA Civ 1617 at [42]. See *Jacobs UK Ltd v Skanska Construction UK Ltd* [2017] EWHC 2395 (TCC), where Mrs Justice O'Farrell found that: a party to adjudication was entitled to unilaterally withdraw a dispute referred to adjudication and to start a further adjudication in respect of the same, or substantially the same, dispute; however, the court had the power to grant an injunction restraining pursuit of the further adjudication if it was both unreasonable and oppressive.

[32] *Connex South Eastern Ltd v MJ Building Services Group Plc* [2005] EWCA Civ 193.

[33] [2011] EWCA Civ 1617 at [41].

In my view the fair minded observer, with all the admirable qualities identified above, would have no difficulty in deciding this case. He would characterise the Preliminary View as a provisional view, disclosed for the assistance of the parties, not as a final determination reached before [the adjudicator] had considered Lanes' submissions and evidence.[34]

Lord Justice Jackson then went on to explain that he was reinforced in his conclusion set out above because the Court of Appeal was dealing with an adjudication, and not an arbitration award or a judicial decision. He went on to explain that:

Adjudication is a rough and ready process carried out at great speed. Vast masses of submissions and evidence have to be assimilated by the adjudicator in a short space of time. The adjudicator will fashion his procedure in whatever way enables him to discharge his onerous duties most swiftly, effectively and fairly. See clause 5.5 of the ICE Adjudication Procedure and paragraph 13 of the Scheme. An adjudication decision is not final. It is only binding until such time as the parties have concluded their litigation or their arbitration or their settlement negotiations or some other form of ADR.

Because adjudication has all of these features, courts are reluctant to strike down adjudication decisions for breach of natural justice or on similar grounds, unless the complainant's case is clearly made out: see the judgment of the Court of Appeal in *Carillion Construction Ltd v Devonport Royal Dockyard Ltd* [2005] EWCA Civ 1358; [2006] BLR 15 at paras 52–53 and 84–87.[35]

In reaching his decision, Lord Justice Jackson helpfully commented on the definition of pre-determination as being:

Pre-determination is sometimes treated as a species of bias, though it is conceptually somewhat different. Pre-determination arises when a judge or other decision maker reaches a final conclusion before he or she is in possession of all the relevant evidence and arguments.[36]

(i) Limitations Identified with the Current Test

Lord Justice Jackson identified some of the practical problems and limitations with the 'fair-minded observer' test as set out by the House of Lords. He commented:

One complication in recent years is the elaboration of the 'fair minded observer' test. In view of the authorities mentioned above, the fair minded observer must be

---

[34] [2011] EWCA Civ 1617 at [56]–[57].

[35] [2011] EWCA Civ 1617 at [60]–[61].

[36] [2011] EWCA Civ 1617 at [45]. Note that *Miller v Parliamentary and Health Service Ombudsman* [2015] EWHC 2981 (Admin) considered the law applicable to pre-determination in the context of a decision of an ombudsman decision. At [79] of the judgment, it was stated that: 'The precise scope of the principles governing pre-determination, and the extent to which it differs from the principles of bias, are not yet settled. For present purposes it is not necessary to explore those issues. It is sufficient to refer to the following paragraphs in the judgment of Jackson L.J. (with whom Stanley Burnton and Richards L.JJ. agreed) in *Lanes Group plc v Galliford Try Infrastructure plc* [2012] Bus L R 1184.' At the time of writing, an appeal is currently outstanding in this case.

assumed to know all relevant publically available facts. He or she must be assumed to be neither complacent nor unduly sensitive or suspicious. He or she must be assumed to be fairly perspicacious, because he or she is able 'to distinguish between what is relevant and what is irrelevant, and when exercising his judgment to decide what weight should be given to the facts that are relevant': see *Gillies* at paragraph 17.

There are conceptual difficulties in creating a fictional character, investing that character with an ever growing list of qualities and then speculating about how such a person would answer the question before the court. The obvious danger is that the judge will simply project onto that fictional character his or her personal opinions. Nevertheless, this approach is established by high authority. I must follow it and do my best to avoid the pitfall just mentioned.[37]

If I may respectfully say so, these paragraphs very clearly identify the difficult task when considering allegations of bias. It is both difficult for the person against whom it is alleged and also the person who is judging the allegation. It highlights the risk of different tribunals coming to different conclusions about similar fact cases.

D. Scope of the Decision in *Lanes v Galliford Try*

In light of the comments made in *Lanes v Galliford Try*, it is interesting to step back from the facts in that case and to ask whether the outcome on predetermination might have been different on slightly altered facts. For example, would the position have been different if: the Preliminary Views document had been provided in the context of an arbitration; the Preliminary Views document had only been sent to one of the parties; the adjudicator had failed to take into account the parties' further submissions.

IV. Where Are We Now?

As indicated in the introduction to this chapter, in the past few years bias has very much been a 'hot topic'. This section considers some of the key cases on bias from the past few years.

---

[37] [2011] EWCA Civ 1617 at [51]–[52]. In *Belize Bank Ltd v Attorney General of Belize* [2011] UKPC 36, Lord Kerr made a similar comment at [38]. He stated that here was a danger of characterising the observer as 'someone who, by dint of his agreement in the system that has generated the challenge, has acquired something of an insider's status'. See also: M Elliott, 'The appearance of bias, the fair-minded and informed observer, and the "ordinary person on Queen Square market"' (2012) 71 *Cambridge Law Journal* 247, which observed at p 250 that: 'if legal doctrine in this sphere is to reflect that policy that underpins it [being to preserve public confidence] ... reviewing judges should certainly make greater efforts to avoid ... "holding up a mirror" to themselves'.

A. Adjudication

In *Paice v Harding*,[38] the Technology and Construction Court considered one of the many disputes which had arisen between the parties to this case. On the facts, Mr Justice Coulson refused to enforce an adjudicator's decision because the defendant had established an appearance of bias on the part of the adjudicator.

In this instance, prior to the adjudicator's appointment Mr Paice's former partner (Ms Springall) telephoned the adjudicator's office on a number of occasions and spoke with the adjudicator's office manager. The adjudicator's office manager was also the adjudicator's wife. On one occasion, the conversation lasted for nearly an hour. It was thought that the purpose of the calls was to seek advice as to how to proceed with the dispute between the claimants and MJ Harding Contractors. MJ Harding Contractors discovered the existence of these calls and requested the adjudicator's telephone records. Subsequently, the adjudicator responded to MJ Harding's allegations of bias by denying that he had spoken to Ms Springall. The adjudicator found in favour of Mr Paice and Mr Paice commenced enforcement proceedings. MJ Harding challenged enforcement on the grounds of bias.

Mr Justice Coulson considered whether these facts gave rise to bias or a potential for apparent bias. He found that the facts did give rise to the real possibility of bias. Notwithstanding the fact that the adjudicator was not a party to the conversations, he had actual knowledge about their content and it was 'self-evident'[39] that the adjudicator should have disclosed them to MJ Harding Contractors. Further, the adjudicator's emails denying that the verbal conversations occurred would, in any event, alter the view that there was no real possibility of bias. In reaching his decision, Mr Justice Coulson stated:

> First, I agree with Mr Stansfield QC that Mr Sliwinski's witness statements are aggressive and unapologetic. Their tone is unfortunate, given what I have found to be Mr Sliwinski's errors of judgment. The terms in which he expresses himself would, I think, give a fair-minded observer the impression that he had concluded that something had gone wrong, and that accordingly attack was the best form of defence.
>
> I note in particular his use of words 'misconceived' (paragraph 24 of his first statement); 'false' (paragraph 38 of his first statement); and 'totally unsupported allegation' (paragraph 37 of his first statement) to describe the defendant's assumption that the conversation on 12 August 2014 had been with Mr Sliwinski himself.[40]

And, further, Mr Justice Coulson observed:

> [A] fair-minded observer would conclude that it was inappropriate for a decision-maker who knows about, and fails to disclose, a material but unilateral conversation,

---

[38] *Paice v Harding (trading as MJ Harding Contractors)* [2015] EWHC 661 (TCC).
[39] [2015] EWHC 661 (TCC) at [32].
[40] [2015] EWHC 661 (TCC) at [47]–[48].

subsequently to say that it was not disclosable because it has taken place with his practice manager/wife, not him personally.[41]

Shortly after the decision above, Mr Paice and MJ Harding Contractors were back in the Technology and Construction Court in relation to yet another adjudication.[42] Once again, the Court was required to consider the question of apparent bias. However, on the particular facts of this further adjudication Mrs Justice O'Farrell found that there was no apparent bias on the part of the adjudicator.

In this instance, in January 2015 MJ Harding Contractors made a formal complaint to the Royal Institute of Chartered Surveyors (RICS) about Mr Sliwinski's conduct (as described above). The RICS investigated his conduct and held a disciplinary hearing. In March 2016, MJ Harding Contractors commenced another adjudication on the same subject-matter as that which is considered in the case summary above. Mr Linnett was appointed as adjudicator. Mr Linnett found in favour of MJ Harding Contractors. Mr Paice resisted enforcement on a number of grounds, including on the ground that there had been apparent bias.

In her judgment, Mrs Justice O'Farrell described the issue as being:

> There is no suggestion by either party of any actual bias on the part of Mr Linnett that prevented him from making an objective determination of the dispute before him. The issue is whether the defendant has a real prospect of establishing apparent bias, namely that a fair minded observer would conclude that there was a real possibility that the tribunal was biased. The facts relied on are that Mr Linnett provided a reference for Mr Sliwinski in connection with the disciplinary investigation by the RICS, he failed to disclose that the reference had been provided until asked directly by the defendant and the manner of Mr Linnett's response to the defendant's questions was unsatisfactory.[43]

In reaching her decision, Mrs Justice O'Farrell summarised the applicable legal principles, including the fair-minded observer test summarised by Lord Justice Jackson in *Lanes v Galliford Try*. Further, she drew together various other threads to state at paragraphs 40 to 42:

> The test is an objective one and not dependent upon the characteristics of the parties: A v B [2011] EWHC 2345 (Comm. Ct.) per Flaux J at paragraph 23.

> The court must look at all the circumstances as they appear from the material before it, not just the facts known to the objectors or available to the hypothetical observer at the time of the decision: A v B (above) at paragraph 27.

> The material circumstances will include any explanation given by the decision-maker under review as to his knowledge or appreciation of those circumstances: In re Medicaments (above) per Lord Phillips at paragraph 86; Paice v Harding [2015]

EWHC 661 per Coulson J at paragraphs 46–61; <u>Cofely v Anthony Bingham and Knowles</u> [2016] EWHC 240 (Comm Ct.) per Hamblen J at paragraph 75.[44]

After applying the principles above, Mrs Justice O'Farrell found that Mr Linnett did not have an obligation to disclose the fact that he had provided a general character reference for Mr Sliwinski to the RICS. Although Mr Linnett was required to determine the same dispute that had been determined by Mr Sliwinski he was not required to consider or assess the abortive adjudication decision produced by Mr Sliwinski. As such, on an objective basis, Mr Linnett's view of Mr Sliwinski could not impact on the exercise he was undertaking in the adjudication. MJ Harding Contractors had been aware before the appointment of Mr Linnett that he had been approached to provide a reference for Mr Sliwinski. If MJ Harding Contractors had thought this was a matter of significance, MJ Harding Contractors would have raised it when Mr Linnett accepted the appointment. But MJ Harding Contractors did not. As such, in this instance the challenge failed.

Beumer Group UK v Vinci Construction UK Limited[45] was a case which considered natural justice and, in particular, the impartiality of adjudicators. In *Beumer v Vinci*, Vinci was employed by Gatwick Airport to carry out construction works at the airport. Vinci sub-contracted a works package to Beumer. Beumer sub-subcontracted some of its works to Logan. Disputes arose between the entities. The sub-contract data identified three individuals as possible adjudicators. Dr Chern was one of them. Beumer ended up being appointed in two different adjudications: one with Vinci and one with Logan. Beumer proceeded on the basis of different factual assumptions in the two adjudications. Dr Chern was appointed adjudicator in both of them. In its adjudication with Vinci, the adjudicator found in favour of Beumer. Vinci resisted enforcement on the basis that the adjudicator's conduct amounted to a material breach of natural justice.

Mr Justice Fraser found that: (1) Beumer had advanced factually inconsistent cases in the two adjudications; (2) Vinci was entitled to disclosure of the information; and (3) Vinci's inability to make submissions about the factually inconsistent material constituted a breach of natural justice.[46] In reaching his decision, Mr Justice Fraser helpfully commented as follows:

> The rules of natural justice have two limbs, and these are firstly, that a party must have an opportunity to present his own case and meet the case against him, and secondly, that the matter is decided by an impartial tribunal. It is the second of those two limbs that concerns bias, both actual and apparent.[47]

---

[44] [2016] EWHC 2945 (TCC) at [40]–[42].

[45] *Beumer v Vinci* [2016] EWHC 2283 (TCC).

[46] But also see *H v L* [2017] EWHC 137 (Comm), where the Commercial Court heard an application for removal of an arbitrator for apparent bias where the arbitrator was acting in more than one case with overlapping facts and parties. The Court found that the extent of overlap was minor and was not such as to give rise to any difficulty in the arbitrator acting independently and impartially. The arbitrator had dealt with the challenge in a courteous and fair way, demonstrating even-handedness.

[47] [2016] EWHC 2283 (TCC) at [13].

And later:

> It is therefore clear that for breaches of natural justice to be sufficient to justify the court declining to order summary judgment enforcing an adjudicator's decision, they must be the plainest of cases; the adjudication proceedings must have been obviously unfair. Combing through what has occurred, or concentrating on the fine detail of the material before the adjudicator, to allege a breach of natural justice, will neither be encouraged nor permitted by the court. Adjudications are conducted very quickly, and this speed is part of the process imposed by Parliament on those who enter into construction contracts. The framework within which adjudicators have to reach decisions has to be taken into account when complaints are made by losing parties.[48]

And subsequently:

> Some appointing bodies, if asked to make an appointment of an adjudicator, will enquire of the potential appointee what contact, or other matters, that person has had with either party. For example, the RICS form to Request appointment of an adjudicator states:
>
> > 'Adjudicators are required **to disclose involvement** or potential conflicts of interest to RICS prior to nomination'. [emphasis added]
>
> The Chartered Institute of Arbitrators Code of Professional and Ethical Conduct for Members at Rule 3 states:
>
> > 'Both before and throughout the dispute resolution process, a member shall disclose all interests, relationships and matters likely to affect the member's independence or impartiality or which might reasonably be perceived as likely to do so'.
>
> This rule is quoted by Hamblen J (as he then was) in *Cofley Ltd v (1) Anthony Bingham (2) Knowles Ltd* [2016] EWHC 240 (Comm)[49] … That case was put before me by Mr Curtis QC and concerned a successfully application to remove an arbitrator. Adjudicators are not arbitrators, but in my judgment are governed by the same principles so far as disclosure is concerned. Indeed, paragraph [33] of *Cofley* refers to the case of *Eurocom Ltd v Seimens plc* [2014] EWHC 3710 (TCC) … which was a case concerning adjudication. Adjudicators are acting as impartial tribunals and though involvement in other adjudications does not of itself constitute a conflict of interest, that involvement should be disclosed.
>
> It is important that adjudicators should not only act, but be seen to act, fairly. It is for this reason, as an example, that unilateral conversations should be avoided.[50]

In light of the overlapping of the material facts in the two set of proceedings, *Beumer* seems to be a clear case where disclosure was required.

In *Rydon Maintenance Ltd v Affinity Sutton Housing Limited*,[51] the Court was required to consider (amongst other things) whether the adjudicator had

---

[48] [2016] EWHC 2283 (TCC) at [16].
[49] *Cofley* is discussed in more detail below (see text to nn 57–61).
[50] [2016] EWHC 2283 (TCC) at [28]–[30].
[51] *Rydon Maintenance Ltd v Affinity Sutton Housing Limited* [2015] EWHC 1306 (TCC).

over-stepped the mark by pre-judging matters before him. HHJ Judge Raeside QC held that the starting point when considering this question was the decision of Lord Justice Jackson in *Lanes v Galliford Try*.[52] In applying the applicable principles, the judge found that there was no basis to find that the adjudicator had given the impression of apparent bias. Both parties had been given an equal and reasonable opportunity to present their case and to deal with each other's cases and each party was fully appraised of the arguments against it. As to whether the adjudicator had pre-judged matters, the judge held:

> I am satisfied on the facts … that the adjudicator did no more than comment on the dispute as the procedure progressed and he did not reach any final conclusions as to the outcome prior to the close of all material put before him … I am satisfied, in my judgment, there was no apparent pre-determination on his part as to the decision that he had to make.[53]

In the circumstances, *Rydon Maintenance v Affinity* is a good example of the direct application of the Court of Appeal's findings on pre-determination being applied to the facts of that case.

However, in *John Sisk & Son Ltd v Duro Felguera UK Ltd*,[54] Mr Justice Edwards-Stuart further considered the law concerning pre-determination. In that case, the judge had to consider an allegation of pre-determination where an adjudicator had expressed some preliminary views in the form of a non-binding conclusion on jurisdiction. The principal issue before the Court was the point in time at which the question of pre-determination was to be considered: was it when the adjudicator provided his initial view, his final view or when the matter came before the Court? In making its submissions, Duro sought to rely on the decision in *Lanes v Galliford Try* to argue that the question had to be considered at the time that the adjudicator's initial view was reached. Mr Justice Edwards-Stuart disagreed. He found that the matter was to be judged at the time when the matter came before the Court, so that all the circumstances could be taken into account. When taking into account the facts, the judge found that this was not a case where pre-determination was made out. The adjudicator had provided the parties with his initial view but had subsequently allowed the parties to make submissions and had considered the same in reaching his decision. In reaching his decision, the judge commented as follows:

> As will be evident from the discussion in the next section of this judgment, the point which in my view is at the heart of this part of the case is the question of the stage at which the issue of Bias or predetermination has to be addressed. There was no discussion about that in *Lanes v Galliford Try*. It is right to note that the Court of Appeal appears to have decided the case primarily on the contents of the Preliminary View, which might go some way to supporting Duro's case (as summarised in

---

[52] [2015] EWHC 1306 (TCC) at [91].
[53] [2015] EWHC 1306 (TCC) at [106(2)].
[54] *John Sisk & Son Ltd v Duro Felguera UK Ltd* [2016] EWHC 81 (TCC).

paragraph 37 below), but it is clear from the facts of the case that the court did not need to go any further. The question could be and was answered on the basis of the Preliminary View alone. In my judgment, that decision provides very limited assistance on the question of the stage at which the question of bias or predetermination has to be decided. Certainly it says nothing to contradict or undermine the earlier decisions which I have cited.[55]

As to when the Court was to consider the position, Mr Justice Edwards-Stuart held:

> [I]t is clear from the authorities that the circumstances have to be considered at the time when the matter comes before the court, so that all the circumstances which by then would be known to a properly informed and fair-minded observer fall to be taken into account. But, as a matter of common sense, it would in my view be quite artificial not to consider the manner in which the Adjudicator went about reaching his Decision when deciding whether or not there was a real danger that he had approached the issues with a closed mind.[56]

The findings in *John Sisk v Duro* appear to be a sensible development of the position on pre-determination, as set out by the Court of Appeal in *Lanes v Galliford Try.*

B. Arbitration

A recent case which has caused much commentary within the industry is that of *Cofley Limited v Bingham.*[57] In that case, Mr Justice Hamblen considered whether an arbitrator should be removed on the ground of apparent bias. Mr Bingham had been appointed as arbitrator by the Chartered Institute of Arbitrators at the request of Knowles. Cofley had disagreed about the technical skills of the appointed arbitrator. Subsequently, Cofley became aware of a decision in *Eurocom Ltd v Siemens Plc*[58] where the Court had found that Knowles had wrongly influenced the RICS scheme for appointing adjudicators. As a result, Cofley requested information about the nature and extent of the professional relationship between the arbitrator and Knowles (including, for example, the number of cases involving them both and the proportion of the former's income that these represented). The arbitrator did not respond to the questions and instead called a hearing. But at the hearing, the arbitrator still refused to answer the questions and instead requested to know why the claimant had asked the questions of him. The arbitrator issued a decision that he had no conflict of interest and declined to recuse himself. The claimant commenced proceedings in the Commercial Court seeking the removal of the arbitrator pursuant to section 24 of the Arbitration Act 1996.

---

[55] [2016] EWHC 81 (TCC) at [34].
[56] [2016] EWHC 81 (TCC) at [37].
[57] [2016] EWHC 240 (Comm).
[58] *Eurocom Ltd v Siemens Plc* [2014] EWHC 3710 (TCC).

The claimant relied on the following grounds as cumulatively giving rise to the real possibility of bias:

(1) Ground 1: As a result of the *Eurocom Case* it was clear that the arbitrator acted regularly for Knowles.[59]

(2) Grounds 2 and 3: The arbitrator's responses to Cofley's requests for information and, also his hostile conduct at the hearing, would have led the fair-minded observer to have increased concerns about the possibility that he was biased.

(3) Ground 4: Against that background, the arbitrator's relationship with Knowles is to be considered (including the number of times he has acted as arbitrator or adjudicator for them and the income which he has derived from them).

(4) Ground 5: The tone of the arbitrator's witness statement makes the possibility of apparent bias more, rather than less, likely.

(5) Ground 6: The arbitrator appears to have been engaging in inappropriate communications with Knowles.

(6) Ground 7: The arbitrator's general conduct of the Referral.

The judge found that Grounds (1) to (5) raised concerns of apparent bias.[60] On the evidence before the Court, in the previous three years, 18 per cent of the arbitrator's appointments and 25 per cent of his income had been from cases involving Knowles. In reaching his decision, the judge stated that:

> The fact that an arbitrator is regularly appointed or nominated by the same party/legal representative may be relevant to the issue of apparent bias, particularly if it raises questions of material financial dependence – see *A v B* [2011] 2 Lloyd's Rep 591 per Flaux J at [62]; *Fileturn Ltd v Royal Garden Hotel* [2010] TCC 1736; [2010] BLR per Edwards-Stuart J at [20(7)].

> The tribunal's explanation as to his/her knowledge or appreciation of the relevant circumstances are also a factor which the fair minded observer may need to consider when reaching a view as to apparent bias – see, for example, *In re Medicaments and Related Classes of Goods (No 2)* … and *Woods Hardwick Ltd v Chiltern Air Conditioning Ltd* [2001] BLR 23. In this regard Cofley relied in particular on *Paice v Harding* [2015] EWHC 661, [2015] BLR 345, per Coulson J at [46]–[51] in which it was held that explanations given by the adjudicator made apparent bias more rather than less likely having regard in particular to the 'aggressive' and 'unapologetic' terms in which they were expressed which suggested that he had concluded that something had gone wrong and that 'attack was the best form of defence'.[61]

---

[59] For a different approach to the question of pecuniary interest, see *W Ltd v M Sdn Bhd* [2016] EWHC 422 (Comm) where Mr Justice Knowles CBE considered that there was neither bias nor a real possibility of bias where the arbitrator was a partner in a firm which regularly advised a company which had the same corporate parent as the respondent, and earned substantial remuneration from doing so.

[60] *Cofley Limited v Bingham* [2016] EWHC 240 (Comm) at [103]. See also paragraph 115 of the judgment.

[61] [2016] EWHC 240 (Comm) at [74]–[75].

If the facts of *Cofley* had been slightly different, the Court's conclusions may have differed. For example, had the tone of the arbitrator's responses been less aggressive and defensive, the Court may not have reached the same conclusion.

V. Conclusions

At this juncture it is time to pause and remember the words of Lord Justice Jackson in *Lanes v Galliford Try* where he considered whether the adjudicator's provision of the Preliminary Views document amounted to apparent bias and he stated that:

> Adjudication is a rough and ready process carried out at great speed. Vast masses of submissions and evidence have to be assimilated by the adjudicator in a short space of time ... An adjudication decision is not final. It is only binding until such time as the parties have concluded their litigation or their arbitration or their settlement negotiations or some other form of ADR.[62]

Indeed, there is some concern within the industry that decisions such as *Cofley* will lead to adjudicators and arbitrators recusing themselves at the very suggestion of bias in order to avoid any public scrutiny over their conduct.[63] Furthermore, the fact that Mr Justice Hamblen gave so much weight to Mr Bingham's familiarity with Knowles may not have been fully balanced against the fact that in the construction industry there is only a limited number of people who act as adjudicators in large construction disputes.

In light of *Cofley*, and due to the pool of adjudicators being relatively small, it is likely that the industry would welcome further guidance from the courts on how to apply the 'fair-minded observer' test in the context of adjudication cases. These are matters which appear to have been foreshadowed by Lord Justice Jackson in *Lanes v Galliford Try*, where he acknowledged the difficulties in creating a 'fictional character' and

> investing that character with an ever growing list of qualities and then speculating about how such a person would answer the question before the court. The obvious danger is that the judge will simply project onto that fictional character his or her personal opinions.[64]

---

[62] [2011] EWCA Civ 1617 at [60].
[63] See, for example: Bailey, 'Tribunal Bias – Familiarity Breeds Concern' [2016] *International Construction Law Review* 233.
[64] [2011] EWCA Civ 1617 at [52].

PART V

Construction Contracts

8

Fitness for Purpose Obligations

MICHAEL CURTIS QC

I. Introduction

All but the simplest construction contracts incorporate a large number of documents. These will usually include a set of terms and conditions – standard or bespoke – along with drawings, specifications, employer's requirements, contractor's proposals and the like. The different documents will often be drafted by different people at different times. This creates the risk of one part of the contract being inconsistent with another part. To deal with the risk, the parties often include a term which establishes a hierarchy between the documents in the event of any inconsistency between them. However, contracts do not always include a term like this. Even when they do, the term does not help where one part of a document is inconsistent with another part of the same document. Further the term will not apply at all if a court decides that the apparently inconsistent provisions in the different documents are in fact consistent with each other.

A. Design

Contracts which require the contractor to design part or all of the finished works (the Works) typically include a term which requires the contractor to use reasonable skill and care when it produces the design. However, it has become increasingly common for design and build contracts to include an additional term or terms which say that the Works or part of them are to have a design life of a certain number of years or are to fulfil a particular purpose. Where a contract does so, the requirement to take reasonable skill and care is typically found in the contract conditions, and the requirement that the Works or part of them will have a specified design life or achieve a particular purpose is more often found in a drawing or in a specification. Where the contract contains terms like this alongside each other, what does the contract mean? More generally, what happens when a contract says that the contractor has to take reasonable skill and care when designing the Works and also says that the Works or part of them have to achieve a particular purpose, for example that they are to perform a specific function or to perform it for a specific period of time? Are the two terms inconsistent? What standard does the contractor have to achieve?

When trying to answer these questions, a possible starting point is the difference between the standard a contractor typically has to meet in respect of its design of the Works and the standard it has to meet in respect of the materials which it uses to construct the Works.

So far as the design of the Works is concerned, the standard which a designer typically has to meet is the exercise of reasonable skill and care.

This is because under the traditional form of building procurement, the employer engages an architect, an engineer or another professional to design the Works and, in the absence of an express term to the contrary, the law implies a term that the architect or engineer or other professional will exercise reasonable skill and care when providing his services. In most cases the terms of the architect's or engineer's appointment will contain an express term to the same effect.

In the same way, where the employer engages a contractor to design and build the Works, the express terms of the design and build contract typically include an express provision saying the contractor has to exercise reasonable skill and care when designing the Works. It is true that *in the absence of an express term to this effect*, the law will usually imply a term that the Works will be fit for their purpose. This is because the law treats a design and build contractor in the same way that it treats people who supply goods. Where the design and build contract contains the implied term as to fitness for purpose and where the contractor designs the Works so that they are not fit for their purpose, it is no defence for the contractor to prove that he took reasonable skill and care in the design of the Works.

It is precisely in order to avoid this result that design and build contracts typically contain an express term providing that the contractor has to exercise the same skill and care as a professional designer, in other words reasonable skill and care. Putting it another way, the fact that the parties include an express term providing that the contractor has to exercise reasonable care and skill shows that the parties did not intend the contractor to have to meet the more onerous 'fitness for purpose' standard.

It is suggested that it is logical for a design and build contract to provide that the design and build contractor owes the same standard of duty in respect of the design as an independent professional who is retained by the employer. There is no reason why the standard which the designer has to meet should depend on the procurement route which the employer selects.

B. Materials

So far as the materials which the contractor uses to build the Works are concerned, all but the simplest contracts contain express terms (in the specification or elsewhere) setting out the specific standards that the materials have to meet.

The contract will also contain the usual implied terms as to the quality of the materials, including fitness for purpose. In the absence of a term expressly excluding the implied terms, the inclusion in the contract of express terms as to quality does not usually have the effect of excluding the implied terms. Where the contractor fails to use materials which comply with the express or implied terms, the contractor will be liable. It will not be a defence for him to show that he took reasonable skill and care to use materials that complied with those terms.

C. In Summary

In summary, the standard a design and build contractor typically has to meet in respect of the design of the Works is reasonable care and skill, and the standard it has to meet in respect of the materials which it uses to construct the Works is compliance with the warranties in the contract, including any warranty of fitness for purpose. If one takes this difference as one's starting point when trying to answer the questions at the start of this chapter, it might lead one to conclude that so far as the design of the Works is concerned, the usual position should be that any warranties that the Works as designed will be fit for purpose and/or have a particular design life are likely to be intended to be subject to the overriding obligation to take reasonable care and skill in the design of the Works. This is because the whole point of including an express term that the contractor is to exercise reasonable skill and care in respect of the design of the Works is to prevent the implication of the stricter standard that the Works will be fit for purpose and to limit the contractor's design obligation to the lesser standard of reasonable skill and care.

II. The Cases

Is this the starting point which the courts have taken and is it the conclusion which they have reached? The short answer is that it is not.

Instead the courts have taken as their starting point a series of cases where the terms of the contract required the contractor to construct the Works to the employer's design but also included a promise by the contractor that the Works would achieve a particular result.

Thorn v The Mayor and Commonalty of London[1] was a case about the replacement of the existing Blackfriars Bridge. The contract stated that the work was to be carried out pursuant to a specification, which included wrought iron caissons. These were intended to form the foundations of the piers 'as shewn on [certain] drawings'. The contractor designed the caissons in accordance with the specification. However, the caissons so designed turned out to be not fit to form the

---

[1] *Thorn v The Mayor and Commonalty of London* (1876) 1 App Cas 120.

foundations of the piers as shown on the drawings. As a result the contractor incurred expense and delay. The contractor sought to recover the expense from the employer on the basis that the employer had impliedly warranted that the bridge could be built according to the specification. The House of Lords rejected that argument. Lord Chelmsford and Lord O'Hagan said that a contractor who bids on the basis of a defective specification provided by the employer bears responsibility if he does not check that the specification is practical and if it turns out to be defective.

In *Hydraulic Engineering Co Ltd v Spencer and Sons*,[2] the defendant contractor agreed to make and deliver to the plaintiff employer 15 cast-iron cylinders according to specifications and plans provided by the plaintiff. The contract also provided that the cylinders would be able to stand a pressure of 25 cwt per square inch. The cylinders failed as a result of flaws in the plaintiff's plans. The defendant was nonetheless held to be liable. Lindley LJ said that it was that clear the defendant thought that it could cast the cylinders on the pattern sent by the plaintiff without defects. Although he accepted that the defect was unavoidable, he said that there was clearly a defect and that the defendant was therefore liable. The other two judges agreed.

In the Scots case *AM Gillespie & Co v John Howden & Co*[3] the contract required the ship 'to carry 1,800 tons deadweight' and to be built according to a model approved by the claimant customer. The ship as built was unable to carry 1,800 tons deadweight. The defendant shipbuilders argued that they should not be liable to the claimant for damages because it would have been impossible to construct a ship capable of carrying 1,800 tons according to the model approved by the customer. Rejecting this argument, Lord Rutherford-Clark (with whom Lord Craighill and Lord Young agreed) said that 'this [was] no defence', as '[t]he fact remains that the [shipbuilders] undertook a contract which they could not fulfil and they are consequently liable in damages for the breach'.

In the Canadian case *Steel Company of Canada Ltd v Willand Management Ltd*,[4] the contractor claimed the cost of repair work to three defective roofs on buildings which it had constructed for the employer. The contractor argued that the defects were not its fault, as it had constructed the buildings under a contract requiring it to comply with the requirements of the employer. The contractor said that the defects resulted from defects in those requirements. The Supreme Court of Canada rejected this argument. This was because the contract also contained a guarantee by the contractor that all work would remain weather-tight and that all material and workmanship would be first class and without defect. Ritchie J rejected the contractor's contention that it 'guaranteed only that, as to the work done by it, the roof would be weather-tight *in so far as the plans and*

---

[2] *Hydraulic Engineering Co Ltd v Spencer and Sons* (1886) 2 TLR 554.
[3] *AM Gillespie & Co v John Howden & Co* (1885) 22 SLR 527.
[4] *Steel Company of Canada Ltd v Willand Management Ltd* [1966] S.C.R. 746.

specifications with which it had to comply would allow' and approved a statement in the then current (8th) edition of *Hudson's Building and Engineering Contracts*, p 147 that

> generally the express obligation to construct a work capable of carrying out the duty in question overrides the obligation to comply with the plans and specifications, and the contractor will be liable for the failure of the work notwithstanding that it is carried out in accordance with the plans and specification. Nor will he be entitled to extra payment for amending the work so that it will perform the stipulated duty.

The reasoning of the Canadian Supreme Court was applied by the Court of Appeal for British Columbia in *Greater Vancouver Water District v North American Pipe & Steel Ltd*,[5] where a 'clear and unambiguous' provision whereby a supplier 'warrant[ed] and guarantee[d]' that the supplied goods were 'free from all defects … arising from faulty design' was held to apply in full, notwithstanding the immediately preceding warranty by the supplier that the goods would 'conform to all applicable specifications', and despite the fact that those specifications were unsatisfactory and led to the defect complained of.

Ultimately these are all cases about the proper interpretation of the terms of the relevant contracts. However, they suggest that where the contract, on its proper construction, contains a promise by the contractor that the completed works will achieve a particular result and where they do not do so, then it is no defence for the contractor to say that he constructed the works, as he was required to do, in accordance with a plan or specification provided by the employer. The proper conclusion will usually be that there is no inconsistency between the promise to achieve the particular result and the requirement to construct the works in accordance with the employer's plans or specification, because the latter promise is impliedly subject to the former.

This interpretation of the authorities is consistent with the speech of Lord Wright in *Cammell Laird and Co Ltd v Manganese Bronze and Brass Co Ltd*.[6] Lord Wright referred to *Thorn* and *Gillespie* and said that

> [i]t has been laid down that where a manufacturer or builder undertakes to produce a finished result according to a design or plan, he may be still bound by his bargain even though he can show an unanticipated difficulty or even impossibility in achieving the result desired with the plans or specification.

Lord Wright said that *Thorn* was such a case. He then said that *Gillespie* was a case where

> the Court of Session held it was no defence to a shipbuilder who had contracted to build a ship of a certain design and of a certain carrying capacity, that it was impossible with the approved design to achieve the agreed capacity: the shipbuilder had to answer in damages.

---

[5] *Greater Vancouver Water District v North American Pipe & Steel Ltd* 2012 BCCA 337.
[6] *Cammell Laird and Co Ltd v Manganese Bronze and Brass Co Ltd* [1934] AC 402 at 425.

Lord Wright explained, however, that although this was the general principle of law, its application in respect of any particular contract must vary with the terms and circumstances of that contract.

In one sense the cases above do not directly concern the questions posed at the start of this chapter. This is because they were all cases where the contract required the contractor to build the Works to the employer's design and also required the contractor to achieve a particular result. They were not cases where the contract required the contractor itself to design the Works with reasonable skill and care and where the contract also included a provision to the effect that the Works as designed by the contractor were to meet a particular standard or to achieve a particular result. However, in another sense they do tackle those questions. This is because they are cases where the contractor agreed to do what was specified (albeit to comply with a particular specification as opposed to exercising reasonable skill and care when designing the works) and to achieve a particular result.

The cases were reviewed by the Supreme Court in *MT Højgaard a/s v E.ON Climate and Renewables UK Robin Rigg East Ltd.*[7] The case arose out of the failure, shortly after the completion of the project, of the foundation structures of two offshore wind-farms at Robin Rigg in the Solway Firth, which were designed, fabricated and installed by MT Højgaard (MTH). The question whether MTH was liable turned on how the Court should construe the documents which constituted, or were incorporated into, the design and build contract in the case.

Part C of the Contract contained a List of Definitions. 'Fit for Purpose' was defined as 'fitness for purpose in accordance with, and as can properly be inferred from, the Employer's Requirements'. 'Employer's Requirements' was stated to include the Technical Requirements (TR), which were themselves attached as Part I of the Contract. 'Good Industry Practice' meant

> those standards, practices, methods and procedures conforming to all Legal Requirements to be performed with the exercise of skill, diligence, prudence and foresight that can ordinarily and reasonably be expected from a fully skilled contractor who is engaged in a similar type of undertaking or task in similar circumstances in a manner consistent with recognised international standards.

Section 3 of the TR was concerned with the 'Design Basis (Wind Turbine Foundations)'. Part 3.2 of the TR was headed 'Design Principles'. Paragraph 3.2.2.2(i) required MTH to prepare the detailed design of the foundations in accordance with a document known as J101, using the 'integrated analysis' method (which was one of the four methods addressed in J101). Paragraph 3.2.2.2(ii) went on to state that: 'The design of the foundations shall ensure a lifetime of 20 years in every aspect without planned replacement. The choice of structure, materials, corrosion protection, system operation and inspection programme shall be made accordingly.'

---

[7] *MT Højgaard a/s v E.ON Climate and Renewables UK Robin Rigg East Ltd* [2017] UKSC 59, 173 Con LR 1.

J101 was a reference to an international standard for the design of offshore wind turbines published by Det Norske Veritas (DNV), an independent classification and certification agency based in Norway. J101 contained design principles which were, among other things, aimed at limiting the annual probability of failure to somewhere in the range of one in 10,000 to one in 100,000. Section 7 of J101 dealt with the design of steel structures, and paragraph K104 provided: 'The design fatigue life for structural components should be based on the specified service life of the structure. If a service life is not specified, 20 years should be used.' Section 9 of J101 dealt with the design and construction of grouted connections. Part A included reference to shear keys, which, it was explained, 'can reduce the fatigue strength of the tubular members and of the grout'. Part B of section 9 set out a number of equations applicable to such a design, including one (the Equation) which showed how the interface shear strength due to friction was to be calculated.

Clause 8.1 of Part D of the Contract required MTH 'in accordance with this Agreement, [to] design, manufacture, test, deliver and install and complete the Works' in accordance with a number of requirements, including:

(iv) in a professional manner in accordance with modern commercial and engineering, design, project management and supervisory principles and practices and in accordance with internationally recognised standards and Good Industry Practice

[as defined in the List of Definitions – ie with reasonable skill and care: see above];

...

(viii) so that the Works, when completed, comply with the requirements of this Agreement ...;

(ix) so that [MTH] shall comply at all times with all Legal Requirements and the standards of Good Industry Practice;

(x) so that each item of Plant and the Works as a whole shall be free from defective workmanship and materials and fit for its purpose as determined in accordance with the Specification using Good Industry Practice;

...

(xv) so that the design of the Works and the Works when Completed by [MTH] shall be wholly in accordance with this Agreement and shall satisfy any performance specifications or requirements of the Employer as set out in this Agreement.

MTH's design provided for (i) monopiles with a diameter of just over four metres, (ii) transition pieces about eight metres long, weighing approximately 120 tonnes, and (iii) grouted connections without shear keys. No shear keys were specified because the Equation in J101 indicated that the grouted connections, as designed, had more than sufficient axial capacity to take the axial load.

At first instance[8] and in the Court of Appeal,[9] MTH contended that it had exercised reasonable skill and care, and had complied with all its contractual

---

[8] *MT Højgaard a/s v E.ON Climate and Renewables UK Robin Rigg East Ltd* [2014] EWHC 1088 (TCC).
[9] *MT Højgaard a/s v E.ON Climate and Renewables UK Robin Rigg East Ltd* [2015] EWCA Civ 407.

obligations, and so should have no liability for the cost of the remedial works, whereas E.ON contended that MTH had been negligent and also had been responsible for numerous breaches of contract. E.ON claimed declarations to the effect that MTH was liable for the defective grouted connections. As Jackson LJ put it in the Court of Appeal, the issue that had to be resolved was as follows:

> 79. It is not unknown for construction contracts to require the contractor (a) to comply with particular specifications and standards and (b) to achieve a particular result. Such a contract, if worded with sufficient clarity, may impose a double obligation upon the contractor. He must as a minimum comply with the relevant specifications and standards. He must also take such further steps as are necessary to ensure that he achieves the specified result. In other words, he must ensure that the finished structure conforms with that which he has warranted ...
>
> 80. The question which I must address is whether the agreement negotiated between [the parties] is a contract of that character.

At first instance Edwards-Stuart J, rejected the suggestion that MTH had been negligent, and he also rejected a number of allegations of breach of contract made by E.ON. However, he found for E.ON primarily on the ground that (i) clause 8.1(x) of the Contract required the foundations to be fit for purpose, (ii) fitness for purpose was to be determined by reference to the TR, and (iii) paragraph 3.2.2.2(ii) (and also paragraph 3b.5.1) of the TR required the foundations to be designed so that they would have a lifetime of 20 years.

The Court of Appeal allowed MTH's appeal for the reasons given by Jackson LJ, with whom Patten and Underhill LJJ agreed. Jackson LJ accepted that, if one was confined to the TR, paragraph 3.2.2.2(ii) appeared to be 'a warranty [on the part of MTH] that the foundations will function for 20 years'.[10] However, in the light of the provisions of the contract, he said that there was 'an inconsistency between [paragraphs 3.2.2.2(ii) and 3b.5.1 of the TR] on the one hand and all the other contractual provisions on the other hand',[11] and that the other contractual provisions should prevail. He went on to describe paragraphs 3.2.2.2(ii) and 3b.5.1 of the TR as 'too slender a thread upon which to hang a finding that MTH gave a warranty of 20 years life for the foundations'.[12]

Hopefully it is not reading too much into the reasoning underlying Jackson LJ's 'too slender a thread' argument to suggest that it is similar to what this chapter suggests above that the starting point should be when considering what such a contract means: namely, that where the parties expressly include a term limiting the contractor's design duty to a duty to take reasonable care, it would be surprising if the parties intended other terms in the contract to impose a strict design obligation; and that where it is the parties' intention to impose such an obligation, one would expect that intention to be clearly expressed.

---

[10] [2015] EWCA Civ 407 at [90].
[11] [2015] EWCA Civ 407 at [104].
[12] [2015] EWCA Civ 407 at [106].

In the Supreme Court the central question was whether, in the light of paragraph 3.2.2.2(ii) (and paragraph 3b.5.1) of the TR, which referred to ensuring a life for the foundations (and the Works) of 20 years, MTH was in breach of contract, despite the fact that it used due care and professional skill, adhered to good industry practice, and complied with J101.

E.ON's case was that paragraph 3.2.2.2(ii) of the TR was incorporated into the Contract, because (i) clause 8.1(x) of the Contract required the Works to be fit for purpose, (ii) Part C of the Contract equated fitness for purpose with compliance with the Employer's Requirements, (iii) Part C also defined the Employer's Requirements as including the contents of the TR, and (iv) the TR included paragraph 3.2.2.2(ii), which specifically refers to the foundations having a life of 20 years.

On that basis, E.ON argued that paragraph 3.2.2.2(ii) had clearly been infringed, and, as it was a term of the Contract, it must follow that MTH was liable for breach of contract. MTH on the other hand supported the reasoning of Jackson LJ. It contended that it was clear that the Contract stipulated that the Works must be constructed in accordance with the requirements of J101 (and with appropriate care), and it was unconvincing to suggest that a provision such as paragraph 3.2.2.2(ii) of the TR rendered MTH liable for faulty construction, given that the Works were constructed fully in accordance with J101 (and with appropriate care).

MTH contended that the references to a 20-year life in various provisions of the TR, including paragraph 3.2.2.2(ii), ultimately did no more than reflect the fact that, as envisaged by J101, Part 1.6 of the TR specified a 'design life' for the Works. MTH also adopted Jackson LJ's description of the contractual documentation as being of multiple authorship and containing much loose wording and that it included many 'ambiguities, infelicities and inconsistencies' (quoting Lord Collins in *In re Sigma Finance Corp (in administrative receivership)*[13]). MTH said that the TR were 'in their nature technical rather than legal', and that if the parties had intended MTH to warrant that the foundations would have a 20-year lifetime, or that they would be designed to have a 20-year life, a term to that effect would have been included in plain terms, probably as a Key Functional Requirement in paragraph 1.6 of the TR.

The Supreme Court found in favour of E.ON. Lord Neuberger PSC was of the view that if one considered the natural meaning of paragraph 3.2.2.2(ii) of the TR, it involved MTH warranting either that the foundations would have a lifetime of 20 years or agreeing that the design of the foundations would be such as to give them a lifetime of 20 years. Given that the combination of clause 8.1(x) of the Contract and the definitions of 'Employer's Requirements' and 'Fit for Purpose' resulted in the provisions of the TR being incorporated into the Contract, Lord Neuberger said that there were only two arguments open to MTH as to why

---

[13] *In re Sigma Finance Corp (in administrative receivership)* [2010] 1 All ER 571, para 35.

paragraph 3.2.2.2(ii) should not be given its natural effect. The first argument was that such an interpretation resulted in an obligation which was inconsistent with MTH's obligation to construct the Works in accordance with J101. The second argument was that paragraph 3.2.2.2(ii) was simply too slender a thread on which to hang such an important and potentially onerous obligation.

So far as the first argument was concerned, after reviewing the authorities referred to above, Lord Neuberger said this:

> 44. Where a contract contains terms which require an item (i) which is to be produced in accordance with a prescribed design, and (ii) which, when provided, will comply with prescribed criteria, and literal conformity with the prescribed design will inevitably result in the product falling short of one or more of the prescribed criteria, it by no means follows that the two terms are mutually inconsistent. That may be the right analysis in some cases (and it appears pretty clear that it was the view of the Inner House in relation to the contract in *AM Gillespie*). However, in many contracts, the proper analysis may well be that the contractor has to improve on any aspects of the prescribed design which would otherwise lead to the product falling short of the prescribed criteria, and in other contracts, the correct view could be that the requirements of the prescribed criteria only apply to aspects of the design which are not prescribed. While each case must turn on its own facts, the message from decisions and observations of judges in the United Kingdom and Canada is that the courts are generally inclined to give full effect to the requirement that the item as produced complies with the prescribed criteria, on the basis that, even if the customer or employer has specified or approved the design, it is the contractor who can be expected to take the risk if he agreed to work to a design which would render the item incapable of meeting the criteria to which he has agreed.

> 45. Turning to the centrally relevant contractual provisions in the instant case, it seems to me that MTH's case, namely that the obligation which appears to be imposed by para 3.2.2.2(ii) is inconsistent with the obligation imposed by para 3.2.2.2(i) to comply with J101, faces an insurmountable difficulty. The opening provision of Section 3, para 3.1, (i) 'stresse[s]' that 'the requirements contained in this section ... are the MINIMUM requirements of [E.ON] to be taken into account in the design', and (ii) goes on to provide that it is 'the responsibility of [MTH] to identify any areas where the works need to be designed to any additional or more rigorous requirements or parameters'. In those circumstances, in my judgment, where two provisions of Section 3 impose different or inconsistent standards or requirements, rather than concluding that they are inconsistent, the correct analysis by virtue of para 3.1(i) is that the more rigorous or demanding of the two standards or requirements must prevail, as the less rigorous can properly be treated as a minimum requirement. Further, if there is an inconsistency between a design requirement and the required criteria, it appears to me that the effect of para 3.1(ii) would be to make it clear that, although it may have complied with the design requirement, MTH would be liable for the failure to comply with the required criteria, as it was MTH's duty to identify the need to improve on the design accordingly.

> 46. As to the facts of the present case, para 3.2.2.2(i) could indeed be said to require that (as recorded in the note to the Equation in J101) 6 should 'be taken as 0.00037 Rp for rolled steel surfaces', and, as explained above, this was a mistake,

in that it substantially over-estimated the connection strength. However, given the terms of para 3.1(i), this figure for 6 was a 'MINIMUM requirement', and, if para 3.2.2.2(ii) was to be complied with, the value of 6 stipulated by J101 had to be decreased (as it happens by a factor of around ten). Furthermore, para 3.1(ii) makes it clear that MTH should have identified that there was a need for a 'more rigorous' requirement than 6 being 'taken as 0.00037 Rp' to ensure that the design was satisfactory, or at least complied with para 3.2.2.2(ii).

47. It is right to add that, even without para 3.1(i) and (ii), I would have reached the same conclusion. Even in the absence of those paragraphs, it cannot have been envisaged that MTH would be in breach of its obligations under para 3.2.2.2(i) if it designed the foundations on the basis of 6 being less than 0.00037 Rp for rolled steel surfaces. Accordingly, at least in relation to the Equation, it represented a minimum standard even in the absence of paras 3.1(i) and (ii), and therefore there would have been no inconsistency between para 3.2.2.2(i) and 3.2.2.2(ii). I also draw assistance in reaching that conclusion from the cases discussed in paras 38 to 43 above. The notion that the Contractor might be expected to depart from the stipulations of J101, where appropriate, is also supported by para 3.1.2 of the TR, which specifically envisages that the Contractor's Foundation Design Basis document may include 'departures from … standards', and J101 is expressly treated as a 'standard' in para 3.2.3.2. In addition, given that satisfaction of the Equation is required to justify the absence of shear keys, E.ON's contention is assisted by the terms of para 10.5.1, which starts by stating that MTH 'shall determine whether to employ shear keys within the grouted connection'; had shear keys been provided, the problems which arose would, it appears, have been averted.

Lord Neuberger went on to reject the 'too slender a thread' argument. Applying the usual principles of contractual interpretation, he decided that there was no reason not to give effect to the clear meaning of paragraph 3.2.2.2(ii).[14]

Pausing there, it appears that the Supreme Court was uninfluenced by considerations such as those outlined at the start of this chapter. They were not part of the background which informed the interpretation of the Contract. The Supreme Court's focus was on the words the parties had used to express their intentions.

Similar issues arose in two other recent cases.

In *125 OBS (Nominees) v Lend Lease Construction (Europe) Ltd*[15] (decided prior to the Supreme Court decision in *MT Højgaard*) the contractor carried out development works to the former London Stock Exchange under a design and build contract comprising a collection of documents but containing no term establishing a hierarchy of precedence.[16] The Works included the supply and installation of toughened glass panels, 17 of which spontaneously broke in the four years after practical completion. The employer sought damages for breach of contract. It was common ground that toughened glass was susceptible to spontaneous breakages

---

[14] [2017] UKSC 59 at [48]–[51].
[15] *125 OBS (Nominees) v Lend Lease Construction (Europe) Ltd* [2017] EWHC 25 (TCC).
[16] [2017] EWHC 25 (TCC) at [88]–[89].

caused by nickel sulphide inclusions. A process known as 'heat soaking' minimised the incidence of such breakages and the contract expressly provided that the glass panels should be heat soaked in accordance with European Standard EN 14178 2005.

The contractor argued that it had complied with its obligation to heat soak the glass and had no other contractual obligations in relation to nickel-sulphide-induced breakages; that one of the technical clarifications in the panel specification meant that the employer was responsible for the risk posed to third parties by nickel-sulphide-induced breakages after practical completion; and that by opting for heat soaked glass knowing that there was a residual risk of nickel-sulphide-induced breakages, the employer was responsible for that risk after completion.[17] The employer argued that the contractor was in breach of its obligation to heat soak the glass and that even if it was not, it was in breach of separate contractual obligations to provide glass panels with a service life of 30 years and a design life of at least 30 years; to complete the works in accordance with the employer's requirements and the contractor's proposals; and to use materials that were of good quality and appropriate for their purpose.[18]

Stuart-Smith J applied the principles of contractual interpretation in *Arnold v Britton*[19] to what he described as 'the interpretative question for the Court in this case' namely

> whether the obligation upon the Defendants to heat soak the toughened glass in accordance with the 2005 Standard ... is additional to the other obligations that appear to be imposed by the contract or whether it qualifies or supersedes those other obligations.[20]

The judge held that on its natural and ordinary meaning the contract imposed several discrete obligations in addition to the obligation to heat soak.[21] There was no intrinsic inconsistency between the obligation to heat soak and the obligations concerning the service and design life of the glass panels and the quality of the materials. On the contrary, the residual risk of spontaneous breakage after heat soaking arguably reinforced the commercial sense of imposing additional obligations on the contractor in order to provide a satisfactory outcome.[22] Although the technical clarification stipulated that responsibility for third-party risks rested with the employer after practical completion, it was vague about what was meant by third party risks. If the intention was to exclude all liability that would otherwise be incurred as a consequence of nickel-sulphide-induced breakages, much

---

[17] [2017] EWHC 25 (TCC) at [94]–[95].
[18] [2017] EWHC 25 (TCC) at [92]–[93].
[19] *Arnold v Britton* [2015] UKSC 36, as summarised by Stuart-Smith J: [2017] EWHC 25 (TCC) at [96]–[99].
[20] [2017] EWHC 25 (TCC) at [100].
[21] [2017] EWHC 25 (TCC) at [117].
[22] [2017] EWHC 25 (TCC) at [103]–[110].

clearer language was required.[23] Further there was no basis for the suggestion that the employer knowingly accepted the risk of breakages at anything like the rate that occurred.[24]

In the earlier case of *MW High Tech Projects UK Ltd v Haase Environmental Consulting GmbH*,[25] Coulson J concluded that the obligation to exercise reasonable skill and care was not overridden by the more specific terms to be found elsewhere in the Contract. The claimant contractor was contracted to design a waste treatment plant for a waste firm. The claimant engaged the defendant consultant to design the waste treatment plant in advance of the claimant agreeing the price, delivery plan and design specification with the waste firm. The claimant subsequently finalised the contract with the waste firm in reliance on the defendant's design proposal. The claimant then appointed the defendant to develop and complete the design under a separate appointment, which incorporated the design proposal, delivery plan and specification. The waste company subsequently terminated its contract with the claimant. The claimant sought to blame the defendant for this, alleging that the defendant had breached the terms of the appointment by modifying the design such that the overall cost of the works was much higher and did not comply with the design specification or delivery plan. In the course of adjudication proceedings, various issues arose between the parties as to which the claimant sought declarations from the Technology and Construction Court.

The issues included how the obligation of reasonable skill and care operated with the more specific obligations under the contract and whether by changing the design so that it did not comply with the specification and delivery plan, the defendant had prima facie breached the contract between it and the claimant. Coulson J held that the defendant's overriding obligation was to design exercising reasonable skill and care. This was because he held that on a proper interpretation of the contract the other obligations under it were made expressly or impliedly subject to that obligation. As a result all other obligations were overridden by the obligation to exercise reasonable skill and care.[26] However, he held that the adjudicator had been wrong to conclude that provided the design was non-negligent, the consultant would not be in breach of contract. Coulson J held that the consultant had additional specific obligations to comply with – for example, the specification and delivery plan; that as a matter of contractual construction those obligations could be read alongside the overriding obligation to take reasonable skill and care; that if compliance with the specification or delivery plan was not possible without the consultant being negligent, then it would not be obliged to comply with the specification or delivery plan; but that

---

[23] [2017] EWHC 25 (TCC) at [111]–[113].
[24] [2017] EWHC 25 (TCC) at [114]–[116].
[25] *MW High Tech Projects UK Ltd v Haase Environmental Consulting GmbH* [2015] EWHC 70 (TCC).
[26] [2015] EWHC 70 (TCC) at [44]–[46].

if it was possible to comply with the specification and delivery plan by way of a non-negligent design, then in the first instance it was contractually obliged to take reasonable skill and care to do so.[27]

In addition to the two cases above, there is a 2006 Australian case where similar issues arose. In *Baulderstone Hornibrook Engineering Pty Ltd v Gordian Runoff Ltd & Others*[28] the contract between the employer and the contractor contained apparently inconsistent express terms: one imposed a duty to take reasonable skill and care in respect of the design of the works; others appeared to impose a stricter design life or fitness for purpose obligation. The insurer defendant argued that the insured claimant contractor owed the employer a strict design life obligation and that it would be inconsistent with that strict obligation to find that the insured claimant contractor owed the employer a duty of care in tort to take reasonable care in respect of the design of the works.[29] The importance of this was that the insurance policy would only respond if the claimant contractor did owe a duty of care of this sort. It was in this context that the Supreme Court of New South Wales had to decide what the design and build contract meant. In the event, the judge found that on a proper interpretation of the contract, the insured contractor owed the employer a contractual duty to take reasonable skill and care and that the apparently strict design life obligations were subject to that duty.[30]. In reaching this conclusion the NSW Supreme Court's approach appears to have been more in line with Jackson LJ's in *MT Hojgaard* than with Lord Neuberger's.

III. Conclusion

So far as the question posed at the start of this chapter is concerned, what lessons can be drawn from these cases?

First, construction contracts invariably include express terms about the quality of the materials which the contractor has to provide. Where one of the terms is a warranty that the materials will have a particular life in service – whether this is expressed as a design life or in some other way – or will perform a particular function, the inclusion of such a term in the contract should occasion no surprise. It would be unsurprising to find such a term sitting alongside other, more general express and/or implied terms that appeared to set a lower standard. There would no reason not to give that term its obvious meaning.

Second, where a design and build contractor agrees to use reasonable skill and care in the design of the Works but also warrants that the Works will produce a particular result, it seems likely that the court will resolve the tension between the

---

[27] [2015] EWHC 70 (TCC) at [47]–[50] and the summary at [70].
[28] *Baulderstone Hornibrook Engineering Pty Ltd v Gordian Runoff Ltd & Others* [2006] NSWSC 223.
[29] [2006] NSWSC 223 at [1066(ii)].
[30] [2006] NSWSC 223 at [1048]–[1079] and in particular [1079(ii)].

two provisions by considering whether, on a proper interpretation of the contract, the warranty is expressly or impliedly subject to the obligation to exercise reasonable skill and care. If it is, the contractor will only be liable if he is negligent: *MW High Tech*. If it is not, the contractor will be taken to have accepted the risk and to be liable if the warranty is broken: *MT Højgaard*.

Third, when the court has to decide on which side of the line a particular case falls, it seems that the court will focus on the words the parties have used. It seems that it is unlikely that the court will be persuaded that parties who include a 'reasonable skill and care' term in their contract should be presumed not to have intended other terms in the contract to impose a stricter standard in respect of the design of part or all of the works.

Fourth, the decision in *125 (OBS) Nominees* takes, it seems, the same approach as the Supreme Court later took in *MT Højgaard*. Although the decision in *MW High Tech* might be said to echo Jackson LJ's 'too slender a thread' approach in *MT Højgaard*, Coulson J was able to reach the conclusion he did on the basis that all the other terms of the contract were expressly or impliedly subject to the obligation to exercise reasonable care and skill. In *Baulderstone* the Supreme Court of New South Wales reached a similar conclusion on a similar basis.

Fifth, it follows that if the parties include in their contract terms which apparently impose a stricter design standard on the contractor, and if they intend those terms to be subject to an overriding obligation on the part of the contractor to use reasonable skill and care when designing the works, they should say so clearly.

Sixth, if they fail to do so, the contractor may find to his surprise that he has undertaken a 'fitness for purpose' design obligation notwithstanding the inclusion in the contract conditions of a term requiring him to exercise reasonable skill and care in the design of the Works.

9

The Legacy of *Williams v Roffey*: Death Knell for Consideration or Infusion of New Blood?

MINDY CHEN-WISHART*

I. Introduction

In the late 1980s 'a small case about carpentry in the Kingston-upon-Thames County Court, which the grandee there passed down to the new assistant recorder,'[1] was decided. Mr Rupert Jackson QC entered judgment for the plaintiff for £3,500 damages plus interest and costs. His decision has disappeared. No copy of it can be located. Yet, that decision was not only unanimously upheld in the Court of Appeal,[2] but its contents, mediated through the Court of Appeal judgment, were included by Sir Guenter Treitel as one of the *Landmarks of Twentieth Century Contract Law*.[3] Its study is familiar to all law students in the common law world (and for at least some, a source of despair). The High Court has applied it on nine occasions[4] (although in two of these, the judge made clear

---

*With thanks to Emma Hughes for stellar research assistance.

[1] Description of the case by Jackson LJ in email correspondence with Julian Bailey, 26 June 2017.

[2] *Williams v Roffey Brothers & Nicholls (Contractors) Ltd* [1989] EWCA Civ 5, [1990] 1 QB 1; Glidewell LJ, at 16 'the judge was, as a matter of law, entitled to hold'; Russell LJ, at 19, 'I think that the assistant recorder came to a correct conclusion'; and Purchas LJ, at 23 'he was entitled to reach the conclusion'.

[3] *Some Landmarks of the Twentieth Century*, Clarendon Law Lectures (Oxford, Clarendon Press, 2002), 18–23.

[4] *Stevensdrake Limited v Stephen Hunt* [2016] EWHC 1111 (Ch); *Pickwell v Pro Cam CP Ltd* [2016] EWHC 1304 (QB); *Birmingham CC v Forde* [2009] EWHC 12 (QB), [2009] 1 WLR 2732; *Adam Opel Gmbh v Mitras Automotive (UK) Ltd* [2008] EWHC 3205 (QB); *South Caribbean Trading Ltd v Trafigura Beheer BV* [2004] EWHC 2676 (Comm), [2005] 1 Lloyd's Rep 128; *Davis v Giladi* [2000] WL 976085; *Simon Container Machinery Ltd v Emba Machinery AB* [1998] 2 Lloyd's Rep 429; *Lee v GEC Plessey Telecommunications* [1993] IRLR 383; *Anangel Atlas Compania Naviera SA v Ishikawajima-Harima Heavy Industries Co Ltd (No 2)* [1990] 2 Lloyd's Rep 526.

his distaste for doing so),[5] and distinguished it on two.[6] The Court of Appeal has applied it on four occasions[7] and distinguished it in one.[8] The Privy Council has applied it once.[9] It has been the subject of numerous articles[10] and is referred to in many more.[11] I myself have made a small career of writing about it,[12] and evidently continue to do so.

The case has been described, not only as 'controversial'[13] and 'a bold step',[14] but also as a 'landmark'[15] and as placing the consideration doctrine 'under siege'.[16] It concerns no less than the existential question of the identity of an enforceable contract. In particular, it spotlights the quintessential common law requirement of consideration for the enforceability of otherwise seriously intended promises. Does consideration perform a useful function or are its days numbered?

Abolitionists regard *Williams v Roffey* as 'an important staging post in the transformation of our conception of consideration' that releases contract law 'from

---

[5] In *South Caribbean Trading Ltd v Trafigura Beheer BV* [2005] 1 Lloyd's Rep 128, 150 Colman J said: 'But for the fact that *Williams v Roffey* ... was a decision of the Court of Appeal, I would not have followed it'. In *Adam Opel Gmbh v Mitras Automotive (UK) Ltd* [2008] EWHC 3205 (QB) [42] David Donaldson QC states that he was 'bound to apply the decision accordingly, whatever view I might take of its logical coherence'.

[6] *Corbern v Whatmusic Holdings Ltd* [2003] EWHC 2134 (Ch); *Mahmoud Assi v Dina Foods Limited* [2005] EWHC 1099 (QB).

[7] *Gribbon v Lutton* [2001] EWCA Civ 1956, [2002] QB 902; *Compagnie Noga D'Importation et D'Exportation SA v Abacha (No 4)* [2003] EWCA Civ 1100, [2003] 2 All ER (Comm) 915; *Attrill v Dresdner Kleinwort Ltd* [2011] EWCA Civ 229; *MWB Business Exchange Centres Ltd v Rock Advertising Ltd* [2016] EWCA Civ 553, [2017] QB 604, [2018] UKSC 24.

[8] *Re Selectmove* [1995] 1 WLR 474 (CA).

[9] *Attorney-General for England and Wales v R* [2003] UKPC 22. This relied on the concept of practical benefit to find consideration, although no reference was made to *Williams v Roffey*.

[10] For example, J Adams and R Brownsword, 'Contract, Consideration and the Critical Path' (1990) 53 *MLR* 536; R Halson, 'Sailors, sub-contractors and consideration' (1990) *LQR* 183; D Fleming, 'Contract – consideration – promise to perform existing duty owed to promisee' (1990) 49 *Cambridge Law Journal* 204; B Coote, 'Consideration and Benefit in Fact and in Law' (1990–91) 3 *JCL* 21; D Halyk, 'Consideration, Practical Benefits and Promissory Estoppel: Enforcement of Contract Modification Promises in Light of *Williams v Roffey Brothers*' (1991) 55 *Saskatchewan Law Review* 393; ABL Phang, 'Consideration at the crossroads' (1991) *LQR* 21–24; J O'Sullivan, 'In Defence of *Foakes v Beer*' (1996) 55 *Cambridge Law Journal* 219; B Coote, 'Consideration and the Variation of Contracts' (2003) *New Zealand Law Review* 361; B Coote, 'Variations Sans Consideration' (2011) 27 *JCL* 185; M Giancaspro, 'Practical Benefit: An English Anomaly or a Growing Force in Contract Law' (2013) 30 *JCL* 12.

[11] A westlaw search for '*Williams v Roffey*' on 2 November 2017 yielded 93 journal references.

[12] See eg, M Chen-Wishart, 'Consideration: Practical Benefit and the Emperor's New Clothes' in J Beatson and D Friedmann, *Good Faith and Fault in Contract Law* (Oxford, Clarendon Press, 1995), 123; 'A Bird in the Hand: Consideration and Promissory Estoppel' in A Burrows and E Peel (eds), *Contract Formation and Parties* (Oxford, OUP, 2010) 89–113; 'Reform of Consideration: No Grass' in S Degeling, J Edelman and J Goudkamp (eds), *Contract in Commercial Law* (Sydney, Thomson, 2017), 77.

[13] M Lobban, '*Foakes v Beer*' in C Mitchell and P Mitchell (eds), *Landmark Cases in the Law of Contract* (Oxford, Hart Publishing, 2008), 265.

[14] J Adams and R Brownsword, 'Contract, Consideration and the Critical Path' (1990) 53 *MLR* 536, 540.

[15] *Some Landmarks of the Twentieth Century*, Clarendon Law Lectures (Oxford, Clarendon Press, 2002), 18–23.

[16] *Chitty on Contracts*, vol 1, 32nd edn (London, Sweet & Maxwell, 2015), p 14 [1-015].

the shackles of the nineteenth century'.[17] In it, the Court is described as 'squarely facing up to the doctrine of consideration and its place in the commercial world'.[18] In characteristically more dramatic fashion, Professor Birks described it as a 'great development' that 'drives a fatal nail into the doctrine of consideration'.[19]

Traditionalists have adopted two responses. The first is to criticise the reasoning in the case. Thus, the novel concept of 'practical benefit' at the heart of *Williams v Roffey* has been described as illusory, like the emperor's new clothes.[20] Indeed, Professor Coote remarks that 'no court of final resort' could approve its reasoning 'without hopelessly compromising the doctrine of consideration'.[21] Alternatively, I have offered an interpretation of *Williams v Roffey* that is consistent with the core idea of contract as exchange.[22]

The Court of Appeal recently extended the application of *Williams v Roffey* and its core concept of 'practical benefit' to a new situation in *MWB v Rock*.[23] On appeal, the Supreme Court decided the case on a different point, but recognised the controversies generated by concept of 'practical benefit' as warranting re-examination by an enlarged panel.[24]

How has this 'small case about carpentry in the Kingston-upon-Thames County Court' decided by 'the new assistant recorder' precipitated all of this? Why is the decision controversial? Which interpretation is warranted and which should be adopted? What are its ramifications for the consideration doctrine?

II. *Williams v Roffey*

A. Facts and Result

Roffey Brothers contracted with a Housing Association to refurbish a block of 27 flats. They subcontracted the carpentry work to Williams for £20,000. Williams finished the work on nine flats but was at risk of non-completion of the rest due to financial difficulties arising partly from the underpricing of the subcontract (a reasonable price would have been £23,783) and partly from deficiencies in Williams' supervision of his workers. Realising this, Roffey Brothers called a meeting at which they agreed to pay Williams an additional sum of £575 on the

---

[17] J Adams and R Brownsword, 'Contract, consideration and the Critical Path' (1990) 53 *MLR* 536, 541–42.

[18] ibid 541.

[19] P Birks, 'The Travails of Duress' [1990] *LMCLQ* 342, 344.

[20] M Chen-Wishart, 'Consideration: Practical Benefit and the Emperor's New Clothes' in J Beatson and D Friedmann, *Good Faith and Fault in Contract Law* (Oxford, Clarendon Press, 1995), 123.

[21] B Coote, 'Consideration and Benefit in Fact and in Law' (1990–91) 3 *JCL* 23, 29.

[22] M Chen-Wishart, 'A Bird in the Hand: Consideration and Promissory Estoppel' in A Burrows and E Peel (eds), *Contract Formation and Parties* (Oxford, OUP, 2010) 89–113.

[23] *MWB Business Exchange Centres Ltd v Rock Advertising Ltd* (n 7 above).

[24] *MWB Business Exchange Centres Ltd v Rock Advertising Ltd* [2018] UKSC 24 at [18].

completion of each of the remaining 18 flats (a total of £10,350). Eight further flats were substantially completed, but Roffey made only one further payment of £1,500, whereupon, Williams discontinued work and brought an action claiming £10,847. Roffey denied this claim on the basis that Williams had given no consideration for it. Roffey also counterclaimed for damages of £18,121.46 arising from Williams' non-completion.

Rupert Jackson QC gave judgment for Williams, awarding £3,500 plus interest and costs. The Court of Appeal unanimously upheld this award on the basis that Roffey's promise to pay an additional price at the rate of £575 per completed flat was enforceable because the defendants secured 'practical benefits' by promising to pay the carpenters an extra £10,350.

B. The Novelty of *Williams v Roffey*

Far from signalling the death knell for consideration, as Professor Birks claimed,[25] *Williams v Roffey* was decided squarely within the conventional framework of requiring consideration for the enforcement of a promise. The Court of Appeal:

- affirmed the necessity of consideration,[26] and
- affirmed *Stilk v Myrick* as the applicable law to 'more-for-the-same' variations (henceforth 'increasing pacts').[27]

In the words of Glidewell LJ, the propositions in *Williams v Roffey* 'refine, and limit the application of that principle [in *Stilk v Myrick*], but they leave the principle unscathed';[28] words that Arden LJ later repeats in the context of promises of 'the-same-for-less' (henceforth 'decreasing pacts').[29]

The novelty of *Williams v Roffey* is that it expands the scope of valuable consideration to include 'practical benefit' in the context of increasing pacts; that is, where X's promise to pay more is enforceable if she receives additional 'practical benefit' from Y's pre-existing contractual duty owed to X. *Stilk v Myrick*[30] had held that such variations are only enforceable if they are supported by additional 'legal benefit'. I must give you some additional enforceable *right* (over and

---

[25] See (n 19 above).

[26] *Williams v Roffey* (n 2 above) Russell LJ, at 18 'consideration remains a fundamental requirement before a contract not under seal can be enforced'; at 19 'A gratuitous promise, pure and simple, remains unenforceable unless given under seal.'

[27] ibid, Glidewell LJ, at 16: 'If it be objected that the propositions above contravene the principle in *Stilk v Myrick* ... I answer that in my view they do not'; Russell LJ, at 19: 'I do not base my judgment upon any reservation as to the correctness of the law long ago enunciated in *Stilk v. Myrick*'; Purchas LJ, at 21: [It] form[s] a pillar stone of the law of contract which has been observed over the years and is still recognised in principle in recent authority' 'the rule in *Stilk v. Myrick* ... remains valid as a matter of principle.'

[28] ibid 16.

[29] See text to n 93 below.

[30] *Stilk v Myrick* (1809) 2 Campbell 317.

above your existing entitlement) in order to enforce your promise of additional payment. After *Williams v Roffey*, I can enforce that promise if you obtain 'practical benefit' from my pre-existing contractual duty owed to you.

The questions are normative and descriptive: 'why should this be so?' and 'what does practical benefit actually mean?'

III. Why Should Increasing Pacts be Enforceable?

The main policies against the enforcement of increasing pacts are the related ones of security of contracts and the prevention of exploitation. The *Stilk v Myrick* rule protects the party willing to pay more for performance to which she is already entitled from two vulnerabilities. The first is exploitation by the other party. This is recognised by the Court of Appeal in *Williams v Roffey* as adequately addressed by the doctrine of economic duress,[31] thus relieving the consideration doctrine of any anti-coercion role.[32]

The second source of vulnerability is the inadequacy of contract remedies to ensure that a promisee actually obtains the performance to which she is entitled or its monetary equivalent. This is the result of the many bars to specific performance, the inevitable delay even if specific performance is ordered, the limits on legally recognisable losses, the way loss is measured, and the deductions to which it is subject.[33] Ironically, this vulnerability weighs in favour of the enforceability of increasing pacts, rather than against it. Purchas LJ recognised that it is open to a party in difficulty 'to be in deliberate breach of the contract in order to "cut his losses" commercially.'[34] Such a party would have no incentive to continue performance if the law refused to enforce increasing pacts. The other party could not pay more to ensure her receipt of the performance even if that performance was desperately wanted, could not be readily obtained elsewhere, and non-receipt would cause losses that would be inadequately compensated by the law.

Although it is controversial to say so, another reason favouring the enforceability of increasing pacts can broadly be described as that of good faith (in the sense of restraint of self-interest and some minimal regard for the other party's interests). Significant change of circumstances subsequent to contract formation, although insufficient to amount to frustration, may make performance so

---

[31] *Williams v Roffey* (n 2 above) 13 (Glidewell LJ).

[32] ibid, Glidewell LJ, at 13–14: duress 'may provide another answer in law to the question of policy which has troubled the courts since before *Stilk v. Myrick* 2 Camp. 317, and no doubt led at the date of that decision to a rigid adherence to the doctrine of consideration.' See also Purchas LJ, at 21: 'the court is more ready in the presence of this defence being available in the commercial context to look for mutual advantages which would amount to sufficient consideration to support the second agreement under which the extra money is paid'.

[33] See section IV.B(ii) below.

[34] *Williams v Roffey* (n 2 above) 23.

difficult for one party that it must realistically renegotiate the contract in order to complete its performance. The values of co-operation and mutual accommodation support contract renegotiations when one party gets into difficulty. Rupert Jackson QC observed that, 'the original contract price was too low to enable the plaintiff to operate satisfactorily and at a profit by something a little over £3,780'; Roffey Brothers knew of this[35] and of Williams' failure to adequately supervise his workers which aggravated Williams' financial difficulties. Rupert Jackson QC's reasoning and conclusion bear setting out here:[36]

> The judge quoted and accepted the evidence of Mr. Cottrell [Williams' surveyor] to the effect that a main contractor who agrees too low a price with a subcontractor is acting contrary to his own interests. He will never get the job finished without paying more money. The judge therefore concluded:
>
> > 'In my view where the original subcontract price is too low, and if the parties subsequently agree that additional moneys shall be paid to the subcontractor, this agreement is in the interests of both parties. This is what happened in the present case, and in my opinion [it] … does not fail for lack of consideration.'

A final support for the enforceability of increasing pacts is the avoidance of waste. Reasonable renegotiations that render contractual performance possible may be economically efficient since they may 'minimize the waste and inconvenience between parties already embarked on a project, and to bring projects safely to a conclusion without interruptions and unnecessary ill-will.'[37] It may be cheaper overall to throw in a few more resources to get the job done than to have the whole thing unravel with its consequential waste and hassle.

IV. What does 'Practical Benefit' Mean?

A. Bilateral or Unilateral Contract Analysis?

The 'practical benefit' to the party promising more for the same can be conceived in two ways:

- On a bilateral contract analysis, the practical benefit consists of the other party's re-promise of the same performance. The original contract morphs into the varied one and is immediately binding. This is a one-contract analysis.
- Alternatively, on the two-contracts analysis, the original contract is supplemented by a unilateral collateral offer to pay an additional sum *if and only if* the stipulated performance in the original contract is actually received. The latter only becomes binding on the promisee's actual performance.

---

[35] ibid 19. See also 6.
[36] ibid 10.
[37] P Birks, 'The Travails of Duress' [1990] *LMCLQ* 342, 346.

This ambiguity is latent in the subsequent case law;[38] it is brought into the light in *MWB v Rock*[39] and was not resolved by the Supreme Court.[40] My thesis here is that the unilateral collateral contract analysis is explicitly and implicitly contained within the Court of Appeal judgment, based on the findings and reasoning of Rupert Jackson QC, and that this is the correct approach.

B. Arguments in Favour of the Unilateral Contract Analysis

(i) The Judgments in Williams v Roffey

(a) Words and Meaning

The issue is the interpretation of (iii) and (iv) in Glidewell LJ's often-cited statement that:[41]

> the present state of the law on this subject can be expressed in the following proposition:
>
> (i)   if A has entered into a contract with B to do work for, or to supply goods or services to, B in return for payment by B; and
>
> (ii)   at some stage before A has completely performed his obligations under the contract B has reason to doubt whether A will, or will be able to, complete his side of the bargain; and
>
> (iii) B thereupon promises A an additional payment in return for A's *promise* to perform his contractual obligations on time; and
>
> (iv) as a result of giving his promise, B obtains in *practice a benefit*, or obviates a disbenefit; and
>
> (v)   B's promise is not given as a result of economic duress or fraud on the part of A; then
>
> (vi) the benefit to B is capable of being consideration for B's promise, so that the promise will be legally binding (emphasis added).

Factor (iii) appears to support the bilateral contract analysis. Yet (iv) shows that the re-promise per se is not enough. The other party must actually *obtain* a practical benefit or obviate a disbenefit *as a result of* the re-promise. What will count?

On the bilateral contract analysis, it has been suggested that the practical benefit conferred on Williams by Roffey's re-promise is the *comfort* derived 'from their

---

[38] See, eg *Ashley v Blue* [2017] EWHC 1928 (Comm) Leggatt J states at para [59] that 'The decision of the Court of Appeal in *Williams v Roffey* effectively … accept[ed] that performance or a promise to perform an existing duty can satisfy the requirement of consideration'. See also *South Caribbean Trading Ltd v Trafigura Beheer BV* [2005] 1 Lloyd's Rep 128. Colman J at para [107] considers that *Williams v Roffey* ameliorated the rule in *Stilk v Myrick* that 'a promise to perform an enforceable obligation under a pre-existing contract … is incapable of amounting to sufficient consideration' but goes on to say that, for *Williams v Roffey* to apply, the promisor must 'derive a practical benefit from such performance'.

[39] *MWB v Rock* (n 7 above).

[40] *MWB Business Exchange Centres Ltd v Rock Advertising Ltd* [2018] UKSC 24 at [18].

[41] *Williams v Roffey* (n 2 above) 15–16.

own perception of a greater chance of completion of the project on time.[42] Given that Roffey was already entitled to timely completion, this comfort has no more than sentimental value and should be rejected as (additional) consideration.[43] To regard it as relevant practical benefit for valuable consideration would collapse the doctrine of consideration from within. All promises confer reassurance on the promisee (unless the promise is known not to be seriously intended). Indeed, even altruistic/gratuitous promises can confer reassurance and satisfaction on the promisor. Benefit is then merged with motive, and consideration becomes meaningless as a criterion of enforceability.

A promisor of additional payment is not intending to buy the same promise of reciprocal performance twice. She agrees to do so in the expectation of obtaining *actual performance*. Professor Coote objects to this characterisation on the basis that consideration 'is required for the formation of a contract. Performance, ex hypothesi, comes too late to qualify.'[44] Of course, this criticism only attaches to a bilateral contract analysis of the increasing pact. The criticism disappears on a unilateral contract analysis; the performance is simultaneously the consideration and the acceptance of the unilateral collateral offer; its timing fixes the formation of the collateral contract; it cannot be 'too late'.

The unilateral collateral contract analysis is also borne out by the practical benefits identified by Rupert Jackson QC, and accepted by the Court of Appeal.[45] Purchas LJ concluded that 'As a result of the agreement [Roffey Brothers] secured their position commercially.'[46] The practical benefits were stated as: (i) to ensure that Williams continued work and did not stop, in breach of the subcontract; (ii) to avoid the penalty for delay under the main contract; and (iii) to avoid the trouble and expense of engaging other people to complete the carpentry work. The point is obvious; these benefits do not accrue to Roffey Brothers, and the latter's position is not 'secured', unless Williams *actually performs* his pre-existing contractual obligations. It is the actual performance of the pre-existing contractual duty, not its re-promise, which constitutes the practical benefit sufficient to earn the reciprocal promise to pay more.

Recognition that the gist of practical benefit is actual performance makes sense of the Court of Appeal's preoccupation with promissory estoppel, which emphasises the promisee's 'reliance'. Glidewell LJ recognised that promissory estoppel did not be apply to increasing pacts[47] since it can only function as a 'shield and not a sword'. However, Russell LJ said that he

> would have welcomed the development of argument, if it could have been properly raised in this court, on the basis that there was here an estoppel and that [Roffey Brothers],

---

[42] R Hooley, 'Consideration and the Existing Duty' [1991] *JBL* 19, 28.
[43] *White v Bluett* (1853) 23 LJ Ex 36; *Thomas v Thomas* (1842) 2 QB 851.
[44] B Coote, 'Consideration and Benefit in Fact and in Law' (1990–91) 3 *JCL* 23, 26.
[45] *Williams v Roffey* (n 2 above) 3, 11, 19, 20, 21, 23.
[46] ibid 23.
[47] ibid 13.

in the circumstances prevailing [ie performance by Williams], were precluded from raising the defence that their undertaking to pay the extra £10,300 was not binding.[48]

Purchas LJ approved the following from a case[49] decided on estoppel to the effect that if an offer was

> accepted *and acted upon* ... I imagine that a modern court would have found no difficulty in discovering consideration for such a promise. Business men know their own business best even when they appear to grant an indulgence (emphasis added).[50]

(b) The Terms of the Contract Variation

Rupert Jackson QC's statement of the terms of the variation in *Williams v Roffey* is very clearly that of a unilateral collateral contract. As the Court of Appeal accepted:

> The agreement which the judge found was made between the parties ... provided for payment as follows: 'The [additional] sum of £10,300 was to be paid at the rate of £575 per flat to *be paid on the completion of each flat.*' (emphasis added).[51]

Indeed, this was the basis of Roffey Brothers' defence that no payment was due, since Williams had not wholly completed any of the flats before he left the site.[52] The judge's response, upheld by the Court of Appeal, was that Williams had *substantially* completed eight of the flats and this entitled Williams to be paid the sum promised, with a deduction for the cost of making good the defects or omissions.[53]

(c) The Calculation of Damages

The calculation of damages due to Williams by Rupert Jackson QC, upheld by the Court of Appeal, also bears out the unilateral collateral contract analysis:[54]

> The judge calculated that this entitled the plaintiff to receive £4,600 (8 × £575) 'less some small deduction for defective and incomplete items.' He held that the plaintiff was also entitled to a reasonable proportion of the £2,200 which was outstanding from the original contract sum ... Adding these two amounts, he decided that the plaintiff was entitled to further payments totalling £5,000 against which he had only received £1,500, and that the defendants were therefore in breach of contract, entitling the plaintiff to cease work.

---

[48] ibid 17.
[49] *Woodhouse AC Israel Cocoa Ltd SA v Nigerian Produce Marketing Co Ltd* [1972] AC 741, 757–58.
[50] *Williams v Roffey* (n 2 above) 21.
[51] ibid 4, 7. See also 6, 7.
[52] ibid 4, 7, 8, 17.
[53] ibid 8–10 on the authority of *Hoenig v Isaacs* [1952] 2 All ER 176 (CA).
[54] ibid 7. See also 23.

That is, the court added two sums:

[£2,200 (the portion of the payment under the original contract that is due)

+ £4,600 (being 8 × £575 for substantial performance of eight unilateral collateral contracts)]

– [£1,500 (amount already received) – £y (deductions for defective performance on the flats substantially completed)]

= £5,300 – £y.

Rupert Jackson QC awarded £3,500 plus interest and costs.

The calculation should have been very different on a bilateral contract analysis of the variation. It is often overlooked that it was Roffey Brothers' breach by failing to make due payment that entitled Williams to terminate his performance. On a bilateral contract analysis of the variation, Williams should, prima facie, have been entitled to the full expectation on the additional promise, calculated as:

[£20,000 (original promise) + £10,300 (additional promise)]

– [£16,200 (amount paid before variation) + £1,500 (amount paid after variation)]

– [£x (cost avoided by not having to complete on termination) – £y (deductions for defective performance on the flats substantially completed)]

= £12,600 – £x – £y.

Williams claimed £10,847. Yet, as we saw, only £3,500 was awarded. On a bilateral contract analysis, the question is not 'why was the plaintiff's claim treated so generously',[55] but rather, 'why so mean?'

(ii) Identifying the Additional Benefit

The unilateral collateral contract analysis is also supported by the maxim: 'A bird *in the hand* is worth two in the bush' (emphasis added).[56] The corollary is that, a bird in the hand (actual performance) must logically be worth more than *one* in the bush (the mere right to sue on it). This is recognised by those who deny that

---

[55] J Adams and R Brownsword, 'Contracts, Consideration and the Critical Path' (1990) 53 *MLR* 536, 538. The assumption here seems to be that the non-completion was due to the promisee's default. They refer, at fn 11, to the 'promise of additional payment having failed to keep the plaintiff working'.

[56] *Foakes v Beer* (1884) 9 App Cas 607 (HL) 622, Lord Blackburn noted his 'conviction that all men of business, whether merchants or tradesmen, do every day recognise and act on the ground that prompt payment of a part of their demand may be more beneficial to them than it would be to insist on their rights and enforce payment of the whole. Even where the debtor is perfectly solvent, and sure to pay at last, this is often so. Where the credit of the debtor is doubtful it must be more so.' And see *Collier v Wright* [2007] EWCA Civ 1329, [2008] 1 WLR 643 [3], Arden LJ notes that *Pinnel's Case* (1602) 5 Co Rep 117a [77 ER. 237] frustrates the parties' expectations and makes it difficult to make modifications when this may 'be commercially beneficial for both parties to do.'

one-sided modifications are gratuitous.[57] But precisely in what sense does actual performance give the recipient who is already entitled to the performance 'more' than she had before? I have previously answered this question:[58]

[W]e need to fix the baseline against which the 'more' consideration should be measured. Two are possible. First, the baseline can be fixed by reference to the 'eye of the law'. *Stilk v Myrick* and *Foakes v Beer* take this approach. The 'eye of the law' sees a 'contract right' as the 'right to contractual performance' and this, in turn, is equated with the '*receipt* of performance'. On this view, the promisor gets nothing more (when she gets her hands on the stipulated bird) than she originally had (the right to the bird in the bush). The problem is that if you start with a legal fiction, you are bound to end up with some odd results. Here, you prevent the promisor from bargaining for actual performance or part performance because the promisee knows that the law will not enforce it.

We should be wary of tracking logical deductions beyond common sense ... Equating a *right to* performance with the *receipt of* performance creates a baseline against which the value of actual performance (over the right to performance) simply disappears. As Dawson observes, 'within the limits of the obligation their agreement had created, the parties had destroyed their own power to contract.'[59] We need an alternative baseline that is intellectually coherent, yet sufficiently accounts for human and legal realities.

The second, and preferable, baseline is fixed by reference to the 'eyes of the parties'. We bargain for performance, but what we get is a more fragile right in remedial terms. The unpalatable truth is that there is no straightforward equivalence between the two. In recognising the possibility of gain-based damages for breach of contract in *Attorney-General v Blake*, Lord Nicholls[60] noted Lionel Smith's argument[61] that contract rights should be protected as strongly from expropriation by the defendant's breach as property rights (which traditionally yield gains-based remedies). However, it is trite law that many features of contract law are inconsistent with the protection of an innocent party's performance interest.[62] Unless contractual performance comprises the payment

---

[57] B Coote, 'Consideration and Benefit in Fact and in Law' (1990) 2 *JCL* 23; F MB Reynolds and G Treitel, 'Consideration for the Modification of Contract' (1965) 7 *Malaysian Law Review* 1; J Beatson, *Anson's Law of Contract*, 28th edn (Oxford, OUP, 2002) 125–26; Kotz and Flessner, *European Contract Law*, vol 1 (Oxford, OUP, 1977) 68–71. In *Antons Trawling Co Ltd v Smith* [2003] 2 NZLR 23 at [92]: 'insofar as consideration serves to exclude gratuitous promise, it is of little assistance in the context of on-going, arms-length, commercial transactions where it is utterly fictional to describe what has been conceded as a gift, and in which there ought to be a strong presumption that good commercial "considerations" underlie any seemingly detrimental modification.' See also B Reiter, 'Courts, Consideration and Common Sense' (1977) 27 *University of Toronto Law Journal* 439, 507; and MA Eisenberg, 'The Principles of Consideration' (1982) 67 *Cornell Law Review* 640, 644: 'The proposition that bargains involving the performance of a pre-existing contractual duty are often gratuitous is empirically far-fetched.'

[58] M Chen-Wishart, 'A Bird in the Hand: Consideration and Promissory Estoppel' in A Burrows and E Peel (eds) *Contract Formation and Parties* (Oxford, OUP, 2010) 89, 92–96.

[59] J Dawson, *Gifts and Promises: Continental and American Law Compared* (Yale, Yale University Press, 1980), 210.

[60] *Attorney-General v Blake* [2001] 1 AC 268, 283.

[61] L Smith, 'Disgorgement of Profits of Contract: Property, Contract and "Efficient Breach"' (1995) 24 *Canadian Business Law Journal* 121.

[62] For example, the rarity of gain-based damages itself; the limited availability of specific performance; agreed damages clauses are unenforceable if they amount to penalties or indirect specific performance; agreed specific performance will generally be unenforceable; rules such as remoteness

of money, an innocent party's right to performance will not normally translate into actual performance or its moneys-worth in remedial terms. Against *this* baseline, the receipt of actual performance or part performance may well give the promisor *more* than she had before. Likewise, it may be a detriment for the promisee to perform a pre-existing duty. This is clear where a promisee would otherwise risk bankruptcy. But even when solvent, the promisee's performance might be more advantageously applied elsewhere and her liability for breach will generally bear no relationship to the extent of this advantage.[63] The potential availability of gain-based damages[64] does not substantially undermine this argument given its very exceptional nature, and the uncertainties surrounding its basis,[65] availability[66] and measure.[67]

Professor Coote objects to this line of reasoning because it would necessitate 'some break in the link between a contract and its performance which is inherent in the concept of an enforceable legal obligation'.[68] It is true that it appears to contradict the idea of contract as creating binding obligations and to support the Holmesian heresy that the contractual obligation is only to perform or pay damages for non-performance.[69] Purchas LJ recognised in *Williams v Roffey* that it was 'open to the plaintiff to be in deliberate breach of the contract in order to "cut his losses" commercially'.[70] His Lordship conceded that 'the suggestion that a contracting party can rely on his own breach to establish consideration is distinctly unattractive'[71] and it is certainly arguable that exploitation of the inadequacies of contract remedies should not be recognised as valid consideration to support one-sided modifications.[72]

However, recognition that the contractual right will not always be vindicated by an order for specific performance or the cost of cure need not contradict the idea that contract law recognises a duty to perform or mean that the remedy determines the right.[73] It is simply that the law on contractual remedies is not solely concerned with vindicating

---

and mitigation cut back the expectation damages to leave the claimant's pecuniary losses inadequately compensated, meanwhile her non-pecuniary losses from the breach (anxiety, annoyance and so on) and from seeking legal redress (typically delay, hassle, time and effort) are not normally compensable at all; punitive damages are generally rejected; and the innocent party may even be prevented from affirming and performing the contract on the other's breach if it would be wholly unreasonable to do so.

[63] P Atiyah, *Essays on Contract* (Oxford, Clarendon Press, 1986) 190 quoting *Corbin on Contracts*, revised edn (St Paul MN, West Publishing Co, 1963), vol 1, para 172.

[64] *Attorney-General v Blake* [2001] 1 AC 268.

[65] ibid at 920. The remedy is available when (i) contract remedies would be inadequate; (ii) the claimant has a 'legitimate interest' in preventing the defendant from making or retaining his profits, and (iii) it is required by 'all the circumstances of the case'.

[66] Contrast *Esso Petroleum Co Ltd v Niad Ltd* [2001] EWHC 458 (Ch) with *AB Corp v CD Co* (*The Sine Nomine*) [2002] 1 Lloyd's Rep 805.

[67] For example, 5% was awarded in *Wrotham Park v Parkside Homes* [1974] 1 WLR 798, 100% in *Attorney-General v Blake*; 30–50% in *Lane v O'Brien Homes Ltd* [2004] EWHC 303; the case was sent back for quantification of the reasonable user in *Experience Hendrix LLC v PPX Enterprises* [2003] EWCA Civ 323 and for damage to the innocent party's reputation in *WWF World Wide Fund for Nature v World Wrestling Federation Entertainment Inc* [2007] EWCA Civ 286.

[68] B Coote, 'Consideration and Benefit in Fact and in Law' (1990) 2 *Journal of Contract Law* 23, 28.

[69] Holmes, *The Common Law* (1881) 298. See P Atiyah, 'Holmes and the Theory of Contract' in Atiyah (ed), *Essays on Contract* (Oxford, Clarendon Press, 1986) 59ff.

[70] *Williams v Roffey* (n 2 above) 23.

[71] ibid.

[72] S Williston, 'Successive Promises of the Same Performance' (1894–95) 8 *Harvard Law Review* 27, 30–31.

[73] Holmes, *The Common Law* (1881) 298. See P Atiyah, 'Holmes and the Theory of Contract' in Atiyah (ed), *Essays on Contract* (Oxford, Clarendon Press, 1986) 59ff.

performance. This must be weighed against contract law's *other* concerns, for example, to avoid waste and unnecessary harshness to the contract-breaker; encourage mitigation; promote finality in dispute resolution and terminate hostile relationships. If we accept these concerns as important and legitimate, then 'inadequacy of remedies', to that extent, is inevitable. We can agree with Professor Friedmann that 'the essence of contract is performance. Contracts are made in order to be performed.'[74] But, this just fixes the starting point from which deviation is not only possible, but likely, in recognition of the other interests in play ...

To press the point, unless contract law is prepared to make specific performance the primary remedy, backed up by the cost of cure or account of profits from breach, then, ironically, in order to protect the promisor's performance interest, contract law should concede that obtaining actual performance will often be more valuable than simply the right to sue for non-performance. The 'eye of the law' should defer to the 'eyes of the parties' so long as contract law does not fully protect the performance interest, particularly when the concern to prevent opportunistic exploitation can be controlled directly at stage two by the doctrine of economic duress.[75]

This explains the rightness of *Williams v Roffey* in going beyond 'legal benefit' to recognising 'practical benefit'. I concluded that:[76]

A bird in the hand is better than one in the bush. The Emperor who is merely given a repromise of new clothes gets nothing more than he had before; he may still end up naked. But the Emperor who actually gets his new clothes receives something more than he had before. The 'eye of the law' may not see it, but the Emperor, facing a state occasion, will have no doubt.

(iii) Consistency with the Parties' Intentions

The unilateral collateral contract analysis better reflects the parties' intentions when entering the variation. It is nonsense to say that a rational party intends to buy the same promise of reciprocal performance twice; she is not paying more for the same right to sue. She only agrees to pay more in order to get actual performance, as the judges implicitly recognise. Russell LJ said:[77]

What was the true intention of the parties when they arrived at the [new] agreement ...? The plaintiff had got into financial difficulties. The defendants, through their employee Mr. Cottrell, recognised the price that had been agreed originally with the plaintiff was less than what Mr. Cottrell himself regarded as a reasonable price. There was a desire on Mr. Cottrell's part to *retain the services of the plaintiff so that the work could be completed without the need to employ another subcontractor.* There was further a need to replace what had hitherto been a haphazard method of payment by a more formalised scheme

---

[74] D Friedmann, 'The Performance Interest in Contract Damages' (1995) 111 *Law Quarterly Review* 628, at 629; C Webb, 'Performance and Compensation: An Analysis of Contract Damages and Contractual Obligation' (2006) 26 *Oxford Journal of Legal Studies* 41.

[75] TE Robinson, 'Enforcing Extorted Contract Modifications' (1983) 68 *Iowa Law Review* 699, 751.

[76] M Chen-Wishart, 'A Bird in the Hand: Consideration and Promissory Estoppel' in A Burrows and E Peel (eds), *Contract Formation and Parties* (Oxford, OUP, 2010) 89, 113.

[77] *Williams v Roffey* (n 2 above) 19.

involving the payment of a specified sum on the *completion* of each flat. These were all advantages accruing to the defendants which can fairly be said to have been in consideration of their undertaking to pay the additional £10,300 (emphasis added).

Russell LJ also noted that:[78] 'As the judge found, the plaintiff must have continued work in the belief that he would be paid £575 as he finished each of the 18 uncompleted flats.'

Purchas LJ concluded that:[79]

> there were clearly incentives to both parties to make a further arrangement in order to relieve the plaintiff of his financial difficulties and also *to ensure that the plaintiff was in a position, or alternatively was willing, to continue with the subcontract works to a reasonable and timely completion* … This arrangement was beneficial to both sides (emphasis added).

(iv) Avoiding a Perverse Result if the Promisee Fails to Perform

The unilateral collateral contract analysis preserves the position of the party promising to pay more if the promisee ultimately fails to perform. For, in that case, the unilateral contract does not eventuate, and the original contract retains full force. In contrast, a bilateral contract analysis produces an absurd and unjust result which would leave a promisor of additional payment worse off than before because her damages would be reduced by the original *and additional* sums she undertook to, but now need not, pay.

Let's say that X promises to pay Y £60,000 for a job; later X promises another £30,000 (total £90,000), but Y still does not perform. X has yet to pay and it would cost X £100,000 for substitute performance:

- On a unilateral collateral contract analysis, X can sue Y for:

  £100,000 (expected value) – £60,000 (being costs saved from termination) = £50,000.

- On the bilateral contract analysis, X can sue Y for much less:

  £100,000 (expected value) – £90,000 (being costs saved from termination) = £10,000.

The Ontario Law Reform states that where the promisee of additional payment fails to perform, the appropriate deduction is the *original sum* promised, and not the greater modified sum: 'it would be an implicit understanding between the parties that failure to comply with the terms of the new agreement would revive the old one.'[80]

---

[78] ibid 17.

[79] ibid 19–20.

[80] Ontario Law Reform Commission 'Report on the Amendment of the Law of Contract' (No 82, 1987) 12–13, discussing the promise to accept part performance.

(v) Avoiding the Void if the Variation is Rescinded for Duress

A unilateral contract analysis avoids another potentially anomalous result, instanced by *Pao On v Lau Yiu Long*.[81] A bilateral contract analysis of an increasing pact means that if it is set aside for the promisee's duress, the promisor is left without any contract to sue on. Say that X promises to pay more for Y's performance, but this is rescinded for Y's duress, X's claim against Y for breach of the original contract can be met by Y's argument that the original contract has been varied and the variation has been set aside – the contract has disappeared. In contrast, a unilateral collateral contract analysis would restrict the vitiating effect of any duress to the unilateral contract (assuming Y actually performed). X would not have to pay more, but the original contract would remain in place to regulate the parties' rights and obligations.

(vi) Applications of Williams v Roffey

Although a full survey of the decisions applying *Williams v Roffey* must await a separate paper, suffice it to say that the majority of these support a unilateral collateral contract analysis, in substance if not in name. For example:

- In *Newman Tours Ltd v Ranier Investment Ltd*,[82] Fisher J said 'the agreement to perform [its] existing contractual obligations, followed by actual performance in reliance upon that subsequent agreement, can constitute fresh consideration'.

- In *Anangel Atlas Compania Naviera SA v Ishikawajima-Harima Heavy Industries Co Ltd (No 2)*,[83] Hirst J regards *Williams* as reversing the ruling in *Stilk v Myrick* that 'the *performance* of an existing contractual duty cannot constitute consideration.' (emphasis added).[84] His understanding of 'the ratio of *Williams*' is that 'whoever provides the services, where there is a practical conferment of benefit or a practical avoidance of disbenefit for the promisee, there is good consideration'.[85]

- In a group of employment contracts (such as *Attrill v Dresdner Kleinwort Ltd*),[86] the court has held that there is consideration for an employer's modification of the terms of an employment contract where the employee continues to work.

---

[81] *Pao On v Lau Yiu Long* [1980] AC 614 (PC).

[82] *Newman Tours Ltd v Ranier Investment Ltd* [1992] 2 NZLR 68, 80. See also *Birmingham City Council v Forde* [2009] EWHC 12 QB, [2009] 1 WLR 2732.

[83] *Anangel Atlas Compania Naviera SA v Ishikawajima-Harima Heavy Industries Co Ltd (No 2)* [1990] 2 Lloyd's Rep 526.

[84] ibid 544.

[85] ibid 545.

[86] *Attrill v Dresdner Kleinwort Ltd* [2011] EWCA Civ 229 [35]. See also *Pickwell v Pro Cam CP Ltd* [2016] EWHC 1304 (QB); *Lee v GEC Plessey Telecommunications* [1993] IRLR 383.

- In *Attorney-General for England and Wales v R*,[87] the Privy Council held that the confidentiality agreement signed by an SAS soldier was supported by consideration because the Ministry of Defence had not exercised its power to return him from the elite regiment to his regular regiment. It was this act of forbearance, rather than a mere promise to forbear (which it could not have made for public policy reasons), which was 'sufficient consideration to support the contract'.

V. *MWB v Rock*

I conclude with the most recent judicial pronouncement on 'practical benefit' in the Court of Appeal. In *MWB Business Exchange Centres Ltd v Rock Advertising Ltd*[88] Rock was a licensee in office space operated and managed by MWB. Rock incurred arrears of licence fees and other charges, whereupon the parties agreed an oral variation to reschedule the debt. Rock paid £3,500 on the same day in accordance with the revised payment schedule. A month later, MWB locked Rock out of the premises and purported to terminate the agreement, claiming damages against Rock. Rock counterclaimed for wrongful exclusion based on the enforceability of the rescheduling agreement. MWB's defences: (a) that there was no agreement, (b) that, anyway, it would lack consideration, and (c) that the oral variation would contradict the express no oral variation clause, were all rejected by the Court of Appeal.

The Court of Appeal rightly held that *Williams v Roffey*'s acceptance of 'practical benefit' as good consideration for increasing pacts must *logically* apply to reducing pacts, as in this case.[89] In doing so, the Court of Appeal claimed to be 'refining and limiting the common law but leaving the principle (the actual rule in *Pinnel's case*) unscathed'.[90] This was held not to contradict *Foakes v Beer*[91] and *In re Selectmove*[92] (which refused to enforce decreasing pacts) by describing the benefit to the creditor in those previous cases in the narrowest terms – as merely 'payment of part of a sum which is owed',[93] a reciprocal promise 'to pay an existing debt by instalment',[94] or a promise of part payment of debt[95] – these are not good consideration for decreasing pacts.

---

[87] *Attorney-General for England and Wales v R* [2003] UKPC 22.
[88] *MWB v Rock* (n 7 above).
[89] ibid [79]. The Supreme Court of New South Wales had already accepted as much in *Musumeci v Winadell Pty Ltd* (1994) 34 NSWLR 723.
[90] *MWB v Rock* (n 7) [85].
[91] *Foakes v Beer* (1884) 9 App Cas 605 (HL).
[92] *In re Selectmove* [1995] 1 WLR 474 (CA).
[93] *MWB v Rock* (n 7) [38].
[94] *MWB v Rock* (n 7) [84].
[95] ibid [85].

Nevertheless, the Court of Appeal in *MWB v Rock* went on to identify *additional* practical benefits to the creditor in the very forms rejected by *Foakes v Beer* and *In re Selectmove*, namely:[96]

(i)   an immediate payment of some of the arrears, and

(ii) the recovery of the whole debt in due course.

In both *Foakes v Beer* and *In re Selectmove*, (i) was present,[97] and (ii) must be implicit, so that no distinction can be drawn on these bases; Julia Beer and the Inland Revenue must have also hoped to recover some (if not all) of their debts on the reasoning that 'a bird in the hand is worth two in the bush'. Indeed, the Judge in *MWB v Rock* concedes that:

> it is fair to say [MWB, the creditor] is doing no more than accepting payments of monies that [Rock] was contractually obliged to pay in any event (whether as licence fees for the future or payment of arrears in the past).[98]

The third benefit to MWB identified by the Court of Appeal may appear different. Arden LJ refers to 'avoiding the void' in the sense of avoiding 'unoccupied and therefore unproductive property, which may cause loss in the form of loss of rent and in other ways'.[99] Her Ladyship relies on the judge's finding of a benefit to MWB in:

> retaining an existing tenant, even if a questionable payer, in the hope of perhaps recovering its arrears rather than getting rid of them, probably saying goodbye to the arrears and allowing the property to stand empty for some time at further loss to themselves.[100]

Kitchin LJ also found practical benefit on the basis that 'Rock would remain a licensee and continue to occupy the property with the result that it would not be left standing empty for some time at further loss to MWB'.[101] Is this third benefit something additional to what was already due to MWB?

Can a positive answer be advanced on the basis that Rock's payment of rental is distinguishable from its *actual occupation* of the premises? It is true that *if* Rock remains in physical occupation as a licensee, MWB obtains the very real *practical* benefit of 'obviating the disbenefits' of an empty property.[102] These would, moreover, be *additional* to that expressly stipulated in the original contract (being merely to pay rent). The same can be said of one of the additional benefits the Court of Appeal identified in *Williams v Roffey* itself, namely a scheme of making the additional payments that incentivised Williams to perform in a more orderly way.

---

[96] ibid [47]–[49], [67], [74]–[76], [87].

[97] In both, payments had been made pursuant to the new agreement.

[98] ibid [10], [73].

[99] ibid [72].

[100] ibid [73], [75].

[101] ibid [47]–[48].

[102] For example, squatters, vandalism, theft, water damage from leaks, fly tipping, occupier's liability and the general depressing effect on other lettings of a vacant set of premises.

It was not promised by Williams, but *if* adopted by Williams, would allow Roffey to direct their other subcontractors towards more efficient and timely completion of the main contract.[103] In neither case was the promisee obliged to confer the additional benefit (remaining in occupation or performing sequentially). So, the benefit to the promisors boils down to the *increased chance* of obtaining this additional benefit, the realisation of which depends entirely on the other party (the promisee) and which yields nothing to the promisors at the remedial end.

The additional benefit recognised in *Anangel Atlas Compania Naviera SA v Ishikawajima-Harima Heavy Industries Co Ltd (No 2)*[104] is even more tangential – being the increased chance of obtaining a benefit from third parties. There, a ship builder was suffering a serious slump in the shipping industry. Many buyers were threatening cancellation, seeking delays in delivery and seeking price reductions. The ship builder responded by promising various concessions to the claimants if they would accept the delivery of the hull as originally agreed. Hirst J held that the defendant's promise was supported by consideration in the form of a practical benefit. It was 'conclusively demonstrated' that the defendants' 'main objective' 'was to make sure that the plaintiffs, who they described as their "core customers", did indeed take delivery ... in order to encourage their other reluctant customers to follow suit'.[105]

The thesis of this chapter is that, in all these cases, it is only *actual performance*, rather than the mere re-promise to perform, or the consequential perception of an increased chance of obtaining performance, that confers an additional practical benefit on the party promising to pay more or to accept less, and so renders that promise binding. This requires the collateral unilateral contract analysis, which Arden LJ explicitly supports.[106] Her 'provisional view (in the absence of argument)':[107]

> is that Rock's acceptance of MWB's promise gave rise to a 'collateral unilateral contract', meaning that, collaterally to the licence, for *so long as Rock was entitled to and did occupy the unit and paid the licence fee as renegotiated*, MWB would be bound on payment of the initial £3,500 to accept the deferral of the arrears in accordance with the variation agreement ... [I]t was not suggested by either party that Rock could take the benefit of the variation agreement without performing its side of the bargain, or that MWB could withdraw[108] from the variation agreement *so long as Rock was complying with it* (emphasis added).

---

[103] *Williams v Roffey Brothers* (n 2 above), 19, 20.

[104] [1990] 2 Lloyd's Rep 526.

[105] ibid, 544.

[106] *MWB v Rock* (n 7 above) [89]–[90].

[107] But citing M Chen-Wishart, 'Reforming Consideration – No Greener Pastures' in S Degeling, J Edelman and J Goudkamp (eds), *Contract in Commercial Law* (Sydney, Thomson, 2017) 77, and 'A Bird in the Hand: Consideration and Contract Modifications' in A Burrows and E Peel (eds), *Contract Formation and parties* (Oxford, OUP, 2010) 89–113).

[108] See discussion on the revocation of such unilateral offers in M Chen-Wishart, 'A Bird in the Hand: Consideration and Promissory Estoppel' in A Burrows and E Peel (eds), *Contract Formation and Parties* (Oxford, OUP, 2010) 89, 99–102.

Extra-judicially,[109] Arden LJ describes this as an 'additional (provisional) analysis':

> The importance of the unilateral contract analysis is that it facilitates the result which is likely to have been what the parties intended, namely, that the creditor should only be bound to accept the reduced debt in discharge of the payment of the whole debt when he had actually received the appropriate part payment. If the debtor wants to bind a creditor to his promise he has to deliver on his promise, and the creditor must allow him to set about doing so within the agreed timetable.

Kitchin LJ's judgment is less clear. At times he seems to adopt a bilateral contract analysis, stating that: 'the payment by Rock of the £3,500 and its *promise* to make further payments in accordance with the revised payment schedule' were adequate consideration (emphasis added).[110] While agreeing with Arden LJ in all other respects, Kitchin LJ preferred 'to express no view as to whether the oral variation agreement can properly be characterised as a collateral unilateral contract',[111] since no submissions were heard on this. But, critically, he adds an implied term into the bilateral variation to the effect that it would only bind MWB, the promisor 'for so long as Rock continued to make payments in accordance with the revised payment schedule.' This is, in substance, a unilateral collateral contract analysis.[112]

The Supreme Court's judgment hearing on 1 February 2018 was notable in the following respects:

- Lady Hale PSC asked why the Supreme Court had not been asked to convene a seven-judge court given the argument that extending practical benefit to the part payment situation would abolish consideration by the backdoor.

- Lords Wilson, Sumption and Briggs JJSC all seem to agree that there are practical benefits beyond the greater expectation of performance. Crucially, though it was not expressly acknowledged, these would only accrue if actual performance were rendered according to the variation.

- Lord Briggs JSC made the point that it is important for the law to allow contracting parties to renegotiate in response to the otherwise disabling effects of commercial realities.

In the end, the Supreme Court[113] held that the contract variation was unenforceable because the original contract contained an enforceable 'no oral variation' clause. Since this disposed of the appeal, it was unnecessary to decide whether practical benefit amounts to good consideration in part payment cases. Lord Sumption, who delivered the leading judgment, can be read as: (i) recognising

---

[109] M Arden, 'Should Consideration Be Required for the Consensual Discharge of an Agreement by Part Payment?' in A Dyson, J Goudkamp and F Wilmot-Smith (eds), *Defences in Contract* (Oxford, Hart Publishing, 2017) 121.

[110] *MWB v Rock* (n 7 above) [49].

[111] ibid.

[112] McCombe LJ agreed with Kitchin and Arden LJJ but expressed a preference 'not to base my own decision upon the issue of "collateral unilateral contract" with which Arden LJ deals', ibid [67].

[113] *MWB Business Exchange Centres Ltd v Rock Advertising Ltd* [2018] UKSC 24 at [18].

the difficulty of reconciling the notion of practical benefit with *Foakes v Beer*, (ii) clearly opposing practical benefit as a mere repromise of performance, but (iii) accepting the need to re-examine *Foakes v Beer*. He said:

> That makes it unnecessary to deal with consideration. It is also, I think, undesirable to do so. The issue is a difficult one. The only consideration which MWB can be said to have been given for accepting a less advantageous schedule of payments was (i) the prospect that the payments were more likely to be made if they were loaded onto the back end of the contract term, and (ii) the fact that MWB would be less likely to have the premises left vacant on its hands while it sought a new licensee. These were both expectations of practical value, but neither was a contractual entitlement. In *Williams v Roffey Bros & Nicholls (Contractors) Ltd* [1991] 1 QB 1, the Court of Appeal held that an expectation of commercial advantage was good consideration. The problem about this was that practical expectation of benefit was the very thing which the House of Lords held not to be adequate consideration in *Foakes v Beer* (1884) 9 App Cas 605: see in particular p 622 per Lord Blackburn. There are arguable points of distinction, although the arguments are somewhat forced. A differently constituted Court of Appeal made these points in *In re Selectmove Ltd* [1995] 1 WLR 474, and declined to follow *Williams v Roffey*. The reality is that any decision on this point is likely to involve a re-examination of the decision in *Foakes v Beer*. It is probably ripe for re-examination. But if it is to be overruled or its effect substantially modified, it should be before an enlarged panel of the court and in a case where the decision would be more than obiter dictum.

In *Williams v Roffey* Rupert Jackson QC deployed the unilateral collateral contract analysis to the contract variation in all but name. There is ample basis for interpreting the Court of Appeal's judgment in like manner, applicable generally to increasing pacts. *MWB v Rock* rightly extends the analysis to decreasing pacts; accordingly, the promisor makes a unilateral offer to permit delayed or part payment *if and only if* the promisee renders the stipulated performance. The 'practical benefit' to the promisor is the 'bird in the hand' over the 'two in the bush' to which she is entitled. Again, this accurately reflects the motivation of the party accepting less. Again, it would protect her position if the promisee failed to make the scheduled payment/s – the decreasing pact would not be binding and the full amount would remain due. This fully accords with the recommendation of the 1937 Law Revision Committee (LRC).[114] For, despite the LRC's view that it is 'more logical and more convenient to recommend that the greater obligation can be discharged either by a promise to pay a lesser sum or by actual payment of it',[115] the critical qualification is that 'if the new agreement is not performed then the original obligation shall revive.'[116]

---

[114] Law Revision Committee, *Sixth Interim Report (Statute of Frauds and the Doctrine of Consideration)* (1937, Cmd 5449) [26]–[40], [50]; see also Ontario Law Reform Committee, *Report on Amendment of the Law of Contract* (Ministry of the Attorney General, 1987) ch 2.
[115] ibid [35].
[116] ibid.

Far from dealing a fatal blow to the venerable doctrine of consideration, *Williams v Roffey* has 'refined and limited' the principle in *Stilk v Myrick* for increasing pacts, and so realign the doctrine with modern commercial and legal realities. Likewise, the Court of Appeal in *MWB v Rock* has 'refined and limited' the principle in *Foakes v Beer* for decreasing pacts. The consideration doctrine is infused with new blood, making it fit for purpose in the twenty-first century. The Supreme Court recognised *Foakes v Beer* as 'ripe for re-examination' by an enlarged panel of judges. Watch this space.

10

Of Chocolate Mousse and Good Faith

SHY JACKSON

I. Introduction

Good faith is not a concept that should generate controversy. In the English legal world, however, good faith is a term fraught with ambiguity with the result that lawyers often advise against including any obligation to act in good faith. That seems counter-intuitive to a layman, but lawyers have good reasons to be cautious about good faith obligations.

Certainty is a key issue, and a term which some see as vague or amorphous creates uncertainty, in particular where the interpretation of such an obligation is dependent on subjective notions as to what may be a fair or commercially reasonable outcome. The other objection to good faith as a principle is that it is simply unnecessary. English commercial law is well developed and a popular choice of law for international contracts, which suggests that the absence of a general principle of good faith is not seen as a hindrance.

There is therefore an understandable reluctance by the courts to recognise an overarching principle of good faith. This has not stopped what appears to be an increased use of good faith clauses in bespoke contracts, as well as in standard forms of construction contracts, as part of a wider drive for more collaborative contracts.

The use of such clauses has resulted in the courts having to consider how they are enforced. Often, a party seeking to rely on good faith will do so as an additional or alternative cause of action, or when it recognises that it has no other contractual remedies, but seeks to argue that the other party's conduct is nonetheless prohibited under the contract. In addition to relying on express clauses, there have been attempts to argue that such an obligation should be implied. One recent case in particular has sought to put forward a compelling case for implying a duty of good faith for certain types of contract.[1]

---

[1] *Yam Seng Pte Ltd v International Trade Corp* Ltd [2013] EWHC 111 (QB).

That is the background to the judgment in the Court of Appeal in *Mid Essex Hospital Services NHS Trust v Compass Group UK and Ireland Ltd.*[2] As the title of this chapter suggests, this was a case where a party was seeking to make what, on their face, appeared to be absurd deductions, such as £85,000 for a one-day-expired chocolate mousse. The other party sought to rely on an express good faith clause to argue that such absurd deductions were in breach of an express good faith obligation. That case therefore provided Jackson LJ with the opportunity to test how such good faith clauses operate in practice. The *Mid Essex* decision is one of the key judgments dealing with good faith clauses and obligations in the last few years, but the rising number of such decisions shows that this is a growing trend. Parties are increasingly using such clauses and it is the courts that then need to enforce these obligations. More interestingly, it appears to have raised the question as to whether, and to what extent, ethics and commercial morality should play a role in the enforcement of contractual obligations related to good faith.

It is therefore not a surprise that good faith has generated a large volume of commentary in recent years, including by Arden LJ in 2013,[3] Mr Justice Leggatt (as he then was) in 2016,[4] and more recently by Jackson LJ in 2017.[5] In order to understand why good faith is such a controversial topic it is necessary to consider how it has traditionally been treated under English law and how that may have changed in recent years.

II. Background to Good Faith

Good faith may not be a general principle of English law, but it is not unknown to the English legal system. In a commercial context, it forms part of the law of insurance and also part of the law of partnerships. These are, however, specific areas of law which have their own special circumstances. That has not stopped the courts from revisiting the general position. Bingham LJ, in *Interfoto Picture Library Ltd v Stiletto Visual Programs Ltd*,[6] stated as follows:

> In many civil law systems, and perhaps in most legal systems outside the common law world, the law of obligations recognises and enforces an overriding principle that in making and carrying out contracts parties should act in good faith. This does not simply mean that they should not deceive each other, a principle which any legal system must recognise; its effect is perhaps most aptly conveyed by such metaphorical colloquialisms as 'playing fair', 'coming clean' or 'putting one's cards face upwards on the table'. It is in

---

[2] *Mid Essex Hospital Services NHS Trust v Compass Group UK and Ireland Ltd (t/a Medirest)* [2013] EWCA Civ 200.

[3] 'Coming to Terms with Good Faith', Singapore Academy of Law, 26 April 2013.

[4] 'Contractual duties of good faith', Lecture to the Commercial Bar Association, 18 October 2016.

[5] 'Does Good Faith have any Role in Construction Contracts?' The Pinsent Masons Lecture, Hong Kong, 22 November 2017, now an SCL paper downloadable at: www.scl.org.uk.

[6] *Interfoto Picture Library Ltd v Stiletto Visual Programs Ltd* [1989] QB 433.

essence a principle of fair and open dealing. In such a forum it might, I think, be held on the facts of this case that the plaintiffs were under a duty in all fairness to draw the defendants' attention specifically to the high price payable if the transparencies were not returned in time and, when the 14 days had expired, to point out to the defendants the high cost of continued failure to return them.

English law has, characteristically, committed itself to no such overriding principle but has developed piecemeal solutions in response to demonstrated problems of unfairness. Many examples could be given. Thus equity has intervened to strike down unconscionable bargains. Parliament has stepped in to regulate the imposition of exemption clauses and the form of certain hire purchase agreements. The common law also has made its contribution, by holding that certain classes of contract require the utmost good faith, by treating as irrecoverable what purport to be agreed estimates of damage but are in truth a disguised penalty for breach, and in many other ways.[7]

The key point coming out of this statement is not that English law has a difficulty with good faith, but that good faith is not needed, as the law has developed alternative ways of dealing with unfairness. Similar statements were made by Bingham LJ in subsequent cases[8] and this view is central to many of the subsequent decisions that reject arguments based on good faith.

The traditional approach was confirmed in the House of Lords' decision in *Walford v Miles*,[9] which concerned the pre-contractual position. Lord Ackner stated that:

the concept of a duty to carry on negotiations in good faith is inherently repugnant to the adversarial position of the parties when involved in negotiations. Each party to the negotiations is entitled to pursue his (or her) own interest, so long as he avoids making misrepresentations ... A duty to negotiate in good faith is unworkable in practice as it is inherently inconsistent with the position of a negotiating party.[10]

Jackson J (as he then was) followed *Walford v Miles* in his judgment in *Multiplex Constructions (UK) Ltd v Cleveland Bridge UK Ltd*,[11] discussing an obligation to use reasonable endeavours to agree to re-programme the completion of the sub-contract works and to agree a fixed lump sum. He held that such an obligation was a statement of aspirations but too uncertain to impose a contractual obligation

---

[7] [1989] QB 433 at 439.

[8] See for example *Timeload Limited v British Communications Plc* [1995] EMLR 459 at 468 and *Balfour Beatty Civil Engineering Limited v Docklands Light Railway Limited* (1996) 78 BLR 42 at 46 and 47.

[9] *Walford v Miles* [1992] 2 AC 128. The same approach was followed in *Ultraframe (UK) Limited v Tailored Roofing Systems* [2004] EWCA Civ 585 at [17], where Waller LJ agreed with Bingham MR's observation in *Philips Electronique Grand Public SA v British Sky Broadcasting Ltd* [1995] EMLR 472 at 484 that the implication of terms is so potentially intrusive that the law enforces strict constraints on the exercise of this extraordinary power, all the more so when parties enter into lengthy and carefully drafted contracts.

[10] [1992] 2 AC 128 at 138.

[11] *Multiplex Constructions (UK) Ltd v Cleveland Bridge UK Ltd* [2006] EWHC 1341 (TCC) at [634–638].

and was therefore unenforceable. In *Costain Ltd v Bechtel Ltd*[12] it was argued that there should be an implied term of good faith, and while Jackson J did not consider it necessary to decide this point, he observed that 'a semantic debate about the precise meaning of the phrase "in good faith" in the context of certification seems to me to serve no useful purpose'.[13]

Where the parties choose to use good faith obligations, the courts have been willing to consider whether such obligations could be enforced. In *Petromec Inc v Petroleo Brasileiro SA Petrobas (No 3)*[14] the court did not find it difficult to enforce an obligation to negotiate in good faith, by ascertaining what reasonable costs would have been agreed if good faith negotiations had been carried out.

In other cases the courts have sought to identify the nature of the good faith obligation. In *Berkeley Community Villages Ltd v Pullen*[15] the judge suggested that good faith meant an obligation to observe reasonable commercial standards of fair dealings in relation to contractual obligations. This also required faithfulness to the agreed common purpose and consistency with the justifiable expectations of the claimant. In *Gold Group Properties Ltd v BDW Trading Ltd*[16] the judge observed that good faith 'does not require either party to give up a freely negotiated financial advantage clearly embedded in the contract'.[17] In *CPC Group Ltd v Qatari Diar Real Estate Investment Co*[18] the judge observed:

> Thus, it seems to me that the content of the obligation of utmost good faith in the SPA was to adhere to the spirit of the contract … to observe reasonable commercial standards of fair dealing, and to be faithful to the agreed common purpose, and to act consistently with the justified expectations of the parties.[19]

The question of whether a term requiring good faith can be implied into a contract raises very different questions from the interpretation of an express good faith provision. Shortly before the Court of Appeal decision in *Mid Essex* (but after the first instance decision), the strongest case for recognising a general duty of good faith in English law was made in *Yam Seng Pte Ltd v International Trade Corp Ltd*.[20] This case concerned an agreement providing exclusive rights to distribute fragrances under the Manchester United brand in the Far East. It was a brief agreement, which was drafted by the individuals concerned without the benefit of legal advice. The relationship between the parties deteriorated and there were allegations of competitive pricing and a failure to disclose information. Ultimately, the agreement was terminated.

---

[12] *Costain Ltd v Bechtel Ltd* [2005] EWHC 1018 (TCC).
[13] [2005] EWHC 1018 (TCC) at [69].
[14] *Petromec Inc v Petroleo Brasileiro SA Petrobas (No 3)* [2005] EWCA Civ 891.
[15] *Berkeley Community Villages Ltd v Pullen* [2007] EWHC 1330 (Ch).
[16] *Gold Group Properties Ltd v BDW Trading Ltd* [2010] EWHC 1632 (TCC).
[17] [2010] EWHC 1632 (TCC) at [91].
[18] *CPC Group Ltd v Qatari Diar Real Estate Investment Co* [2010] EWHC 1535 (Ch).
[19] [2010] EWHC 1535 (Ch) at [246].
[20] *Yam Seng Pte Ltd v International Trade Corp Ltd* [2013] EWHC 111 (QB).

Part of Yam Seng's case was that it was an implied term of the agreement that the parties were to deal with each other in good faith. This led to Leggatt J (as he then was) undertaking an extensive review of the cases relating to good faith both in England and internationally. He observed that the refusal to recognise, if there was such refusal, a general obligation of good faith in England would appear to be swimming against the tide, pointing out that the concept of good faith has been gaining ground in other common law jurisdictions, including the Canadian, Australian and American courts.

Having demonstrated his willingness to consider a good faith obligation, he began by looking at the test for implying terms as set out in *Attorney-General of Belize v Belize Telecom Ltd*[21] and the emphasis in case law dealing with the interpretation of contracts on looking at the background of unstated shared understandings which informed their meaning.

Leggatt J then applied these principles to the facts. He began by observing that the relevant background contained not only matters of fact, but also shared values and norms of behaviour. The paradigm example was an expectation of honesty, which was essential to commerce, but was seldom made the subject of an express contractual obligation.[22] In his view, good faith was not simply limited to acting honestly, but there were other aspects which could be described as fidelity to the parties' bargain. He also thought that, in order to apply a contract to circumstances not specifically provided for, the language had to be given a reasonable construction which promoted the values and purposes expressed, or implicit, in the contract.

Leggatt J suggested that it was unlikely that a wider good faith duty would be implied where the contract involved a simple exchange. However, it could be relevant to contracts which involve longer-term relationships between the parties, in which they make a substantial commitment. He described such contracts as 'relational contracts' and provided examples of such relational contracts as joint venture agreements, franchise agreements and long-term distributorship agreements. Applying those principles to the facts, the judge distilled the good faith principle into specific obligations, which were a duty not to give false information and a duty not to undercut duty free prices.

The review of the state of good faith under English law also included Leggatt J's responses to what he identified as the reasons for the traditional reluctance to recognise an implied duty of good faith under English law. Overall, his view was that the concept of good faith was not inconsistent with English law; that there was no real risk of uncertainty, and in fact such a clause could be established on the basis of accepted principles such as the parties' intentions with regard to the agreed bargain.

---

[21] *Attorney-General of Belize v Belize Telecom Ltd* [2009] UKPC 10.
[22] See in that regard JW Carter, 'Good Faith in Contracts: Is There an Implied Promise to Act Honestly?' (2016) 75 *Cambridge Law Journal* 608–19, challenging the reliance on honesty as an underlying contractual principle.

III. The Facts in *Mid Essex*
and the First Instance Decision

Good faith arguments are sensitive to context. Claims will often be based on an allegation that certain actions are so unexpected that they go against the parties' expectations of the contract. It is for that reason that it is necessary to look closely at the facts behind any decision dealing with good faith.

Mid Essex concerned a contract made in April 2008, for facilities management and catering services between Medirest and the Mid Essex Hospitals NHS Trust. The contract had a seven-year term and was based on a standard NHS contract coupled with a mechanism for service failure points and deductions, taken from a standard form for Private Finance Initiative contracts. The mechanism dealt with performance failures, and service failure points were awarded on the occurrence of performance failures. There was a reference to rectification periods but no rectification times were included in the contract. Deductions were £5 (minor), £15 (medium) and £30 (major) and once a performance failure had occurred, Medirest had to demonstrate to the Trust's reasonable satisfaction that the failure was remedied, or a further deduction would occur.

Under clause 3 of the contract, headed 'Performance of the Services', clause 3.5 imposed an obligation in the following terms:

> The Trust and the Contractor will co-operate with each other in good faith and will take all reasonable action as is necessary for the efficient transmission of information and instructions and to enable the Trust or, as the case may be, any Beneficiary to derive the full benefit of the Contract.

The contract did not start well. Within a week, the Trust's commercial director asked for a copy of the contract, noting that the relationship 'could get contractual' and a few weeks later he asked his colleague to 'read the riot act' to Medirest, highlighting the payment mechanism provisions. This appeared to be a response to the poor performance Medirest had demonstrated at that time. In particular, Medirest failed to self-monitor as it was required to under the contract.

This led to the Trust undertaking its own performance monitoring in mid to late 2008. In late 2008 Medirest accepted that it was in breach of the 1,400 service failure points which would justify termination. In 2009, however, matters were improving in terms of performance but the Trust's acceptance of Medirest's action plan in January 2009 included a list of deductions for the July to December 2008 period, amounting to £587,207.67. A more detailed breakdown was provided in March 2009, including out-of-date ketchup, £46,320; undated butter sachets, £94,830; out-of-date bagels, £96,060; spoons, £43,612 and a one-day-expired chocolate mousse, £84,450. Following discussions between the parties, a revised schedule was produced in June whereby some items increased (spoons at £91,740) and some reduced (butter sachets at £540).

In later discussions the Trust stated that the deductions came to £716,197, providing a revised spreadsheet reinstating some of the original deductions

(£94,830 for butter sachets). Medirest issued a notice of termination on 10 September 2009 and the Trust issued a notice of termination expiring on 23 October 2009, followed by Medirest extending its termination date to 27 October 2009. On 21 September, apparently following legal advice, the Trust issued a revised deductions schedule changing the previous deductions to ketchup, £30; butter sachets, £990; bagels, £12,990; spoons, £690 and mousse, £30. Both parties then sought to terminate the contract, claiming their post-termination costs.

The trial judge,[23] Cranston J, began by considering the interpretation of clause 3.5. Medirest argued for a wide interpretation so that the parties had a general obligation to cooperate in good faith, coupled with a narrower obligation to take all reasonable action for the two stated purposes of efficient transmission of information and to enable the Trust and Beneficiaries to obtain the benefit of the contract. The Trust argued for a narrower interpretation, saying the good faith obligation was limited to the two stated purposes.

The judge noted that the parties had entered into a long-term contract, the performance of which required continuous and detailed cooperation between the parties at a number of levels. In the circumstances, his view was that it was highly likely that the parties intended that there should be a general obligation that they should cooperate in good faith with each other. He relied on the fact that even looking at the two stated purposes, the Trust was obliged to secure the benefits of the contract for Beneficiaries (a defined term under the contract) and could not simply act in its own self-interest.

Cranston J also emphasised the Trust's character as a public body, which must be devoted to high standards of behaviour and to the public good, and held that the objective standard of conduct demanded under the contract primarily encompassed faithfulness to the common purpose, with fair dealing and acting consistently with justified expectations being corollaries of that.

Having identified a wide duty of good faith, he went on to consider the Trust's argument that the calculation of service failure points was a mechanical exercise that did not require discretion. The judge considered that the main flaw in that argument was that it ignored the obligations in clause 3.5. The judge considered this a question of interpretation, finding that reasonable commercial parties would not have contracted on the basis that calculations could be made on an absurd basis and he was also of the view that the contractual language conferred discretion, as this was a long-term, complex contract and there was no obligation to make the deductions. On that basis, reasonable people with the background knowledge the parties had would interpret the clause as giving a power to act in line with the purpose of the mechanism, which he regarded as curbing performance failure, not generating discounts on payments due to Medirest.

In effect, the judge relied on his interpretation of clause 3.5 as the context for interpreting the service failure points mechanism (as well as referring

[23] *Compass Group UK and Ireland Ltd (t/a Medirest) v Mid Essex Hospital Services NHS Trust* [2012] EWHC 781 (QB).

to the long-term, complex nature of the contract) and whether this was a discretionary power.

Not surprisingly, when looking at the Trust's actual conduct he held that the Trust was in breach of contract in calculating the deductions and that there was no sign that the Trust did not intend to carry on with excessive and unjustifiable calculations. The Trust was also in breach of an implied term that it would not exercise its powers in an arbitrary, capricious and irrational manner.

The judge held that the Trust's breaches in failing to cooperate in good faith and the abuse of its contractual powers entitled Medirest to terminate the contract. He also held, however, that the Trust was also entitled to terminate the contract as Medirest had accumulated the requisite number of service failure points. As a result, both parties failed in their claims.

IV. The Court of Appeal Decision

In the Court of Appeal,[24] Jackson LJ took a different approach. He began by considering a more established principle of law; whether there was an implied term that meant the Trust could not exercise any discretion, when making deductions, in an arbitrary, irrational or capricious manner. He found that such a term could only be implied where the discretion involved an assessment or choosing from a range of options, taking into account the interests of both parties. In his view, this was not the case where the only discretion was whether or not to exercise an absolute contractual right. In that regard, he relied on the fact the Trust was a public body delivering a vital service, which rightly could demand high standards of service. There was therefore no implied term that the Trust would not act arbitrarily, irrationally or capriciously and the Trust was not in breach of such an obligation.

Jackson J then turned to clause 3.5. Like Cranston J, he noted the poor drafting of the clause which he described as 'having possible meanings, depending upon where one places the caesuras and what imaginary punctuation one inserts'. He then pointed out that there was no general doctrine of good faith under English law, although it was implied into certain categories of contracts (referring to *Yam Seng* in that regard). Having made that point, he went on to consider the interpretation of the clause and agreed with the Trust's narrow interpretation of the good faith obligation.

The next step was to consider the extent of the narrower duty of good faith. In his view, the reference to Beneficiaries did not add anything, as the defined term did not include patients. Looking at the context of the clause he found that the obligation was to work together honestly, endeavouring to achieve the two stated purposes. Having identified the extent of the obligation, he then held that there

---

[24] [2013] EWCA Civ 200 (n 2 above).

was no breach of the obligation under clause 3.5. This was for two reasons: first, the lack of any finding that the Trust acted dishonestly; and second, the deductions being irrelevant to the two stated purposes. The Trust was in breach of other provisions in making the deductions but that did not provide grounds for Medirest's termination.

Lewison LJ agreed that any discretion that the Trust had was limited to whether or not to make a deduction. As to clause 3.5, he found that it could be no more than a duty to cooperate in good faith and that cooperation was irrelevant to the Trust's deductions. Beatson LJ referred to the *Yam Seng* decision, relied upon by Medirest's counsel, to point out that the scope of the obligation to cooperate in good faith had to be considered in light of the rest of the contract and the overall context. In his view, as awarding excessive service failure points and making excessive deductions was a breach of contract under other provisions, it was unnecessary to give clause 3.5 a wide meaning. He then warned against construing a good faith clause in a general and open-ended manner, as that may cut across the more specific express terms of the contract.

V. The Position Post *Mid Essex*

Mid Essex was a case about the interpretation of a good faith clause, not about whether a good faith obligation should be implied into the contract, which was the issue in *Yam Seng*. In practice, it seems that notwithstanding any reservations from the courts, long-term contracts that require cooperation are being drafted to include good faith clauses. Indeed, a similar situation then came up in the *Portsmouth City Council v Ensign Highways Ltd*.[25]

That case concerned a long-term PFI contract for the maintenance and operation of the Council's highway network. In the usual way, the agreement provided for the award of service points against breaches of the agreement and the council would award a number of service points against defined default events. This included a range and maximum event values. After a few years, cuts were made to the Council's funding and it realised the contract would become unaffordable. It appears that the Council then engaged in a strategy of awarding a high number of service points, refusing to communicate, finding breaches which were difficult to remedy and storing points so Ensign could be ambushed with a large number of service points at once. Ensign referred the dispute about the service points to expert determination and it was found that the Council had acted in bad faith, without mutual cooperation and unfairly, but that Ensign's performance had not always been as it should have been.

In the court proceedings, Edward-Stuart J reviewed clause 44 of the contract which was concerned with best value and stated that the parties 'shall deal fairly,

[25] *Portsmouth City Council v Ensign Highways Ltd* [2015] EWHC 1969 (TCC).

in good faith and in mutual co-operation with one another and with Interested Parties'. Not surprisingly, the Council relied extensively on the decision in *Mid Essex* but the judge found that the position here was different, because there was an element of judgement as to the number of service points that each breach warranted. He also held that it made no commercial sense to have a system that resulted in the same number of points awarded regardless of the gravity of the breach, and that the parties intended for there to be some flexibility rather than a fixed tariff.

The judge then went on to consider whether the good faith duty in clause 44 applied to the service points mechanism under clause 24. Ensign relied on the *Yam Seng* decision and argued that the good faith duty in clause 44 filled gaps in clause 24 and that the clauses were linked. Looking at the language of the contract and the separate provisions it contained, the judge held that the good faith duty in clause 44 did not apply to the rest of the agreement or to clause 24. He also agreed with the statements by Lewison LJ in *Mid Essex* to the effect that the imposition of the service points was not a matter that required any cooperation by the parties.

Both parties, however, agreed that if clause 44 did not apply to the award of service points, there had to be some implied term that governed its operation. The council argued for a formulation based on 'proper grounds and for proper purposes, and without dishonesty or deceit'. Ensign relied on a decision by Jackson J (as he then was) concerning decision-making under a building contract[26] and argued for wording requiring the Council's representative to 'hold the balance fairly as between [the parties] and in a manner which is independent, impartial, fair and honest'.

The judge, however, stated that he had some difficulty with a term that required fairness or impartiality and observed that a duty to act fairly when awarding service points might be taken as introducing wider considerations beyond the circumstances of the breach. He also thought such words created some uncertainty or could provide scope for a dispute. His formulation of the term was based on the authorities cited in *Mid Essex* in connection with discretion, leading to the wording: 'act honestly and on proper grounds and not in a manner that is arbitrary, irrational or capricious'.

This decision, like *Mid Essex*, deals with the tension between what is argued to be a wide duty of good faith and what is a narrower application of a duty to exercise discretion. Even where contracts contain express good faith obligations, the courts are reluctant to regard them as imposing an overarching obligation.

A similar issue was addressed by Akenhead J in *TSG Building Services Plc v South Anglia Housing Ltd*,[27] in the context of exercising a right of termination. The contract was based on the ACA standard form of contract for term partnering

---

[26] *Scheldebouw BV v St James Homes (Grosvenor Dock) Ltd* [2006] BLR 113.
[27] *TSG Building Services Plc v South Anglia Housing Ltd* [2013] EWHC 1151 (TCC).

(TPC 2005, amended 2008) and one of the issues was whether the right to terminate under the contract needed to have been effected in good faith, or at least
reasonably.

Akenhead J held that, properly construed, clause 1.1, which required the partnering team to 'work together and individually in the spirit of trust, fairness and
mutual co-operation for the benefit of the Term Programme', did not require South
Anglia to act reasonably in terminating under clause 13.3. In his view, this clause
entitled termination for any, or even no reason.[28] In addition, by including this
clause, there was no basis for implying a separate good faith duty.

The nature of partnering agreements was also considered in *Fujitsu Services Ltd
v IBM United Kingdom Ltd*,[29] where the contractual definition of the term 'Good
Industry Practice' included 'seeking in good faith to comply with its contractual
obligations'. It was held that clear words were necessary for an express duty of
good faith to arise and that the contractual partnering principles lacked contractual certainty and, objectively construed, were not intended to be the subject of
direct contractual effect.

The preference for a narrow interpretation of good faith clauses was also
demonstrated in *Hamsard 3147 Ltd v Boots UK Ltd*,[30] where the original agreement had a clause stating that

> both parties agree at all times to act in good faith towards one another in relation to the
> operation of the Agreement to approach their dealings with one another on an open
> and collaborative basis so as to ensure that they maximise the Net Profit generated
> under the Agreement.

The claimant relied on the *Yam Seng* decision and argued that this was a relational contract and that a good faith obligation should be implied into the ad hoc
arrangement which followed the original agreement. Norris J accepted that such
an obligation may give rise to an obligation to deal with one another on an open
and collaborative basis, but it did not extend to a party subordinating its own
commercial interest, or qualify the other terms of the contract.

This principle was also highlighted in *Chelsfield Advisers LLP v Qatari Diar
Real Estate Investment Co*,[31] where a party argued that it could terminate an agreement since the nature of the relationship was such that the parties cannot have
intended for it to continue if their mutual trust and confidence no longer existed.

---

[28] This is the same rationale as in the Australian decision in *Leighton Contractors Pty Ltd v Arogen
Pty Ltd* [2012] NSWSC 1370 at paragraph 22, putting the emphasis on specific express rights. See
also *Monde Petroleum SA v Westernzargos Limited* [2016] EWHC 1472 (Comm), where *Yam Seng* was
considered but it was held there was no relational contract and the right to terminate could be exercised
irrespective of reasons and no justification had to be given. See also *Ilkerler Otomotiv Sanayai Ticaret
Anonim Sirketi v Perkins Engines Company* [2017] EWCA Civ 183.

[29] *Fujitsu Services Ltd v IBM United Kingdom Ltd* [2014] EWHC 752 (TCC).

[30] *Hamsard 3147 Ltd v Boots UK Ltd* [2013] EWHC 3251 (Pat).

[31] *Chelsfield Advisers LLP v Qatari Diar Real Estate Investment Co* [2015] EWHC 1322 (Ch).

The judge rejected this argument and expressed his scepticism about the basis for implying such a term, noting its similarity to implying a good faith term. Referring to Jackson LJ's judgment in *Mid Essex*, he held that the general rule in commercial contracts is that 'if the parties wish to impose such a duty they must do so expressly'.[32]

In practice, the courts will prefer to rely on more established legal principles; and as noted by Bingham LJ in *Interfoto*,[33] English law already provides remedies.[34] This was the case in *Mears Ltd v Shoreline Housing Partnership Ltd*,[35] which concerned the NEC3 Term Service Contract. Having agreed and executed an Option C version (target cost with price list), both parties proceeded to operate the contract on a different basis (an agreed schedule of rates). The employer then sought to revert to the terms of the executed contract and ignore the way the parties had conducted themselves. The contractor argued that there was a cause of action based on the trust and partnership language used in the NEC form of contract and clause 10.1 (in NEC3). The contractor claimed that this resulted in an implied term that a party would not take advantage of the other party due to a departure from the strict terms of the contract, when that party was aware of the departure, and without warning the other party and giving it an opportunity to act differently.

The judge rejected the employer's claim, but on the basis of estoppel by convention. With reference to clause 10.1, the judge stated:

> [H]owever, I am, further, not satisfied that there would be any such implied term or that the obligation to act in a spirit of mutual trust and cooperation or even in a 'partnering way' would prevent either party from relying on any express terms of the contract freely entered into by each party.[36]

In *Sainsbury's Supermarkets Ltd v Bristol Rovers (1883) Ltd*[37] the court confirmed the principle that an obligation of good faith in relation to the fulfilment of a specific obligation contained in a contract cannot be used to require the parties to do things not specified by the agreement.

Mid Essex established the trend for a narrow interpretation of good faith provisions and emphasised their subordination to other contractual provisions. Some decisions, however, have shown that the courts are more willing to accept

---

[32] ibid at paragraph 80.

[33] [1989] QB 433.

[34] See in that context S Jackson, 'Good Faith in Construction – Will it Make a Difference and is it Worth the Trouble?' (2007) 23 *Construction Law Journal* 420.

[35] *Mears Ltd v Shoreline Housing Partnership Ltd* [2015] EWHC 1396 (TCC) at [70].

[36] Similarly, an argument based on good faith was rejected in *ING v Ros Roca* [2011] EWCA Civ 353 at paragraph 92 where the Court of Appeal relied on estoppel to sanction a failure to disclose significant information but observed: 'Nor is there any general notion, as there is in the civil law, of a duty of good faith in commercial affairs, however much individual concepts of English common law, such as that of the reasonable man, and of waiver and estoppel itself, may be said to reflect such a notion'.

[37] *Sainsbury's Supermarkets Ltd v Bristol Rovers (1883) Ltd* [2016] EWCA Civ 160.

good faith duties where they are consistent with and support other contractual provisions.

The *Willmott Dixon Housing Ltd v Newlon Housing Trust*[38] decision concerned an ACA Standard Form of Contract for Project Partnering (PPC 2000). In rejecting an attempt to resist enforcement of adjudications, Ramsey J pointed out that the parties had agreed to use the standard form of project partnering contract, including the agreement to work in mutual cooperation, and that this obligation also included performing the problem-solving and dispute-avoidance or -resolution provisions, including the adjudication process. The party that failed to contact the other to confirm the position with regard to the referral document was in breach of its obligation to work in mutual cooperation and could not rely on a failure to receive the referral document. This decision is interesting, as it applies the general partnering obligation not only to the performance of the contractual obligations relating directly to the construction project, but also to the obligations relating to the dispute resolution process.

In *Northern Ireland Housing Executive v Healthy Buildings (Ireland) Ltd*[39] the Northern Ireland Court of Appeal considered the interpretation of clause 61.1 of the NEC3 Professional Services Contract and suggested that interpreting that clause had to be done in the context of clause 10.1. In a subsequent decision in the same case,[40] the Court looked at a party's refusal to provide relevant documents and commented that:

> it seems to me that a refusal by the consultant to hand over his actual time sheets and records for work he did during the contract is entirely antipathetic to a spirit of mutual trust and co-operation. Further clauses in the contract such as Clause 15 reinforce that spirit.

These decisions are more consistent with what new standard forms of construction contract seek to achieve. They recognise that parties are expected to be pro-active, to cooperate and exchange relevant information when working together. A failure to do so cannot be simply dismissed on the basis that there is no express contractual obligation to that effect, but only as long as there is no inconsistency with any express contractual provisions.

VI. *Yam Seng* and the Implication of Good Faith Terms

The decision in *Yam Seng* featured in a number of subsequent cases but, to date, has not resulted in a wider acceptance of good faith as an implied term.

---

[38] *Willmott Dixon Housing Ltd v Newlon Housing Trust* [2013] EWHC 798 (TCC).
[39] *Northern Ireland Housing Executive v Healthy Buildings (Ireland) Ltd* [2014] NICA 27 at [29].
[40] *Northern Ireland Housing Executive v Healthy Buildings (Ireland) Limited* [2017] NIQB 43 at [43].

It did highlight the term 'relational contract' but perhaps a marketing agreement for Manchester United branded toiletries was not the best example of such contracts.

Nonetheless, there has been some acceptance of arguments based on relational contracts. In *Bristol Groundschool Ltd v Intelligent Data Capture Ltd*[41] Richard Spearman QC considered both the *Yam Seng* and *Mid Essex* decisions in detail and held that the agreement (relating to training materials for the UK Civil Aviation Authority and the EU Joint Aviation Authority) was a 'relational contract' of the kind referred to in *Yam Seng* and that there was an implied duty of good faith. The judge noted[42] that although the Court of Appeal in *Mid Essex* made only a passing reference to the *Yam Seng* decision and did not consider implied terms, he detected no element of disapproval of the *Yam Seng* judgment in the judgments of the Court of Appeal. He held that good faith includes at the very least the requirement for honesty, which he observed was the same test used by Beatson LJ in *Mid Essex*.

Similarly, in *D&G Cars v Essex Police Authority*,[43] which concerned a contract for the recovery of vehicles for the Essex Police Authority, Mr Justice Dove held this was 'a "relational" contract par excellence' and that there was an implied term that the parties would act with honesty and integrity in operating the contract.

The decision in *Yam Seng* relied on Lord Hoffmann's formulation of the test for implied terms in *Attorney-General of Belize v Belize Telecom Ltd*.[44] The later formulation of the test in *Marks and Spencer Plc v BNP Paribas Securities Service Trust Co (Jersey) Ltd*,[45] however, makes a clearer distinction between contract interpretation, which was the issue in *Mid Essex*, and the implication of terms, which was the issue in *Yam Seng*. To the extent business necessity plays a more important role, this is likely to make it harder to imply a good faith term on the basis that the contract cannot operate without such a term. If the earlier test is used, it seems clear that a reasonable person being asked whether the parties would have regarded it as obvious that they will act in good faith would say yes. But the better test may be to ask whether a reasonable person, having read the commentary and judgments dealing with good faith and being familiar with the English law approach to good faith, would still say that the parties would regard an obligation to act in good faith as an obvious term that goes without saying.

Significantly, *Yam Seng* was also decided before the series of cases on contract interpretation shifting the emphasis from the underlying commercial rationale to the literal meaning, such as *Arnold v Britton*.[46] The courts now appear more

---

[41] *Bristol Groundschool Ltd v Intelligent Data Capture Ltd* [2014] EWHC 2145 (Ch).
[42] ibid, at paragraph 196.
[43] *D&G Cars v Essex Police Authority* [2015] EWHC 226 (QB) at paragraph 176.
[44] [2009] UKPC 10.
[45] [2015] UKSC 72.
[46] *Arnold v Britton* [2015] UKSC 36.

willing to consider the concept of 'relational contracts', albeit that they have yet to find that such contracts automatically give rise to an implied duty of good faith.[47] Beatson LJ commented on *Yam Seng* in *Globe Motors Inc v TRW Lucas Verity Electric Steering Ltd*[48] and observed that the implication of a duty of good faith will only be possible where the language of the contract, viewed against its context, permitted it, but it was not a special rule of the interpretation for that type of contract.

The position seems to be that there is no conceptual difficulty in implying a duty of good faith. A 'relational contract' may provide a better basis for such implication, but that will still be based on the test recently formulated in *Marks and Spencer*[49] and in practice it will not be easy to satisfy a court that such a term should be implied.

VII. Good Faith in Other Jurisdictions

It is not possible to set out fully in this chapter the position in other jurisdictions, but that has been covered extensively by other commentators.[50] It is, however, worth noting that while civil law systems are often mentioned in any comparison, such a comparison has limited value. As Mr Justice Leggatt pointed out, good faith in civil law systems is an overarching, policy-based principle that applies even before the contract comes into existence, while under English law it is a duty anchored in the contract and reflecting the parties' intentions.[51]

Common Law legal systems are therefore more pertinent to the development of the law on good faith. As is the case with the English courts, good faith arguments are on the increase and there is a variety of approaches. In Singapore, the decision in *HSBC Institutional Trust Services (Singapore) Ltd v Toshin Development Singapore Pte Ltd*[52] provides some interesting commentary on the rationale for good faith in a local context. In that case, the Singaporean Court of Appeal held that there was no good reason why an express agreement between contracting parties that they must negotiate in good faith should not be upheld. It was further

---

[47] In *General Nutrition Investment Company v Holland and Barrett* [2017] EWHC 746 (Ch) Mr Justice Warren refused to find an implied duty of good faith because the contract had no need for communications to operate effectively, so it was not a relational contract.

[48] *Globe Motors Inc v TRW Lucas Verity Electric Steering Ltd* [2016] EWCA Civ 396 at [68].

[49] [2015] UKSC 72.

[50] See for example Jackson LJ's annual lecture which covers the position in numerous jurisdictions including China (see above, n 5).

[51] But see Fuchs's suggestion that a German court would enforce clause 3.5 in *Mid Essex* and would consider such deductions to be excessive by looking at the underlying value (Dr Jur Sebastian Fuchs and S Jackson, 'Good faith: An Anglo-German comparison' [2015] *International Construction Law Review* 404).

[52] *HSBC Institutional Trust Services (Singapore) Ltd v Toshin Development Singapore Pte Ltd* [2012] SGCA 48.

observed that obligations to negotiate in good faith were in the public interest, as they promote the consensual disposal of any potential disputes. VK Rajah JA suggested that it was fairly common practice for Asian businesses to include similar clauses in their commercial contracts, and rejected any suggestion that uncertainty should affect the enforcement of such a clause. In a more recent decision,[53] the Singaporean Court of Appeal rejected the suggestion that good faith should be implied into commercial contracts but recognised that such terms might be implied where there was a high degree of reliance and partnership. The Court referred to the decisions in *Yam Seng* and *Mid Essex*, noting that the law was in a state of flux.

In Canada, the Supreme Court in *Bhasin v Hrynew*[54] decided to recognise good faith contractual performance as a general organising principle, holding that 'finding that there is a duty to perform contracts honestly will make the law more certain, more just and more in tune with reasonable commercial expectations'. The Supreme Court referred to what it described as 'enhanced attention to the notion of good faith, mitigated by reluctance to embrace it as a stand-alone doctrine' and referred to the decision in *Yam Seng* as well as the *Mid Essex* decision, the latter as endorsing the proposition that good faith terms can be implied.[55]

Mr Justice Leggatt referred to this decision in *MSC Mediterranean Shipping Co SA v Cottonex Anstalt*,[56] when he repeated his observations from *Yam Seng* that good faith is increasingly recognised in the common law. In the Court of Appeal, however, Lord Justice Moore-Bick noted that the decision in *Bhasin v Hyrnew* also acknowledged that in *Mid Essex* the Court confirmed that English law did not recognise a general duty of good faith, and warned of the danger that a general principle of good faith would often be invoked to undermine the terms in which the parties have reached agreement.[57]

In Australia there have been a number of cases dealing with good faith, but a clear consensus is yet to emerge. In *Masters Home Improvement Pty Ltd v North East Solutions Pty Ltd*[58] the Supreme Court of Victoria overturned the trial judge's findings that an express duty of good faith clause was breached, and rejected his findings as to what a reasonable person would have done, finding that this would take the good faith obligation too far and cautioning against applying the wisdom of hindsight to determine whether a party acted in good

---

[53] *One Suites Pte Ltd v Pacific Motor Credit (Pte) Ltd* [2015] SGCA 21 at paragraph 44. See also *PH Hydraulics & Engineering Pte Ltd v Airtrust (Hong Kong) Ltd* [2017] SGCA 26 where it was held it was possible to argue for an implied duty of good faith but the court rejected an argument such a duty allows recovery of punitive damages.

[54] *Bhasin v Hrynew*, 2014 SCC 71 at [57].

[55] Although the paragraphs cited refer to the implication of good faith in certain categories, rather than as a more general proposition, overall the Court seemed to rely more on the *Yam Seng* decision than *Mid Essex*.

[56] *MSC Mediterranean Shipping Company SA v Cottonex Anstalt* [2015] EWHC 283 (Comm).

[57] *MSC Mediterranean Shipping Company SA v Cottonex Anstalt* [2016] EWCA Civ 789 at [45].

[58] *Masters Home Improvement Pty Ltd v North East Solutions Pty Ltd* [2017] VSCA 88.

faith. This seems consistent with the tendency to interpret express clauses on a narrow basis. In another decision two weeks earlier, however, when considering whether to grant an anti-suit injunction, the Supreme Court of Western Australia noted that:

> the courts have been willing to imply such a duty in contracts for joint ventures or part-nerships where there is a need for a high degree of co-operation and reliance by all the parties on the good faith of each other party, particularly in the context of their working together to achieve a common objective.[59]

In Ireland, *Yam Seng* was considered in detail in the decision in *Flynn v Breccia*[60] in the context of a shareholders' agreement and it was held by Haughton J that the shareholders' agreement and the context in which it was executed demonstrated elements of a relational contract. In making that finding, he relied on the context of the agreement, including the fact that the shareholders' agreement restricted the alteration of the ethical principles of the company, being not to engage with any procedure or practice that was inconsistent with the teachings of the Roman Catholic Church. In his view, an implied term of good faith and fair dealings was necessary to give business efficacy to the contract.

The above discussion demonstrates that the debate as to good faith extends beyond England. While some of the cases concern the implication of terms, they show that, despite any scepticism by lawyers, parties generally feel that there is a benefit to including express good faith clauses in their contracts.

VIII. Conclusions on Good Faith

The *Mid Essex* decision did not consider implying good faith obligations. While *Yam Seng* has presented a strong case for such arguments, the reliance on the concept of relational contracts might have been more persuasive if the case was not about a contract for distributing Manchester United toiletries. Further, it seems clear that parties now use express good faith clauses in contracts which they consider are relational in the sense that they require long-term cooperation, and there will therefore be a reduced need for implying such terms.[61]

That means that, as was the case in *Mid Essex*, it is more relevant to consider how the courts approach a contract where the parties made a choice to include an express good faith clause. The principle of freedom of contract means that parties are free to include obligations which are general in nature and give rise to uncer-tainty in the same way they are free to enter into a bad bargain. Both Arden LJ and

---

[59] *Insurance Commission of Western Australia v The Bell Group Ltd (In Liq)* [2017] WASC 122 at [57].
[60] *Flynn v Breccia* [2015] IEHC 547.
[61] See Robert Scrivener, 'Good Faith and Construction Contracts', *Construction Law*, 2 December 2015, p 20.

Jackson LJ referred to the NEC standard form of contract as including a good faith clause, and Arden LJ referred also to the ISDA Master Agreement as containing a number of good faith duties.

The present approach seems to be to interpret such clauses on a narrow basis and as subordinate to the other terms. This seems sensible when dealing with a poorly drafted clause, as was the case in *Mid Essex*, but will present more of a challenge where the words used by the parties make it clear that they wish to have good faith as an underlying principle; for example, by drafting a term to say that the parties' performance of their obligations shall be the subject of an overarching duty of good faith and all obligations must be interpreted in accordance with such a principle.

In that regard, McMeel observed the relationship between the recent trend for literalism in contract interpretation and the approach to contracting on the basis of good faith and fair dealing.[62] He compared the strict approach in *Arnold v Britton* and *Marks and Spencer* against the advocacy of good faith in *Yam Seng*, noting the swing of the pendulum towards literalism. McMeel is correct to highlight the relationship between these two strands, as part of the driver for the more literal approach is the courts' reluctance to determine issues based on what they perceive as subjective notions as to commercial reasonableness or fairness. In *Skanska Rashleigh Weatherfoil Ltd v Somerfield Stored Ltd*,[63] it was stated that: 'judges are not always the most commercially-minded, let alone the most commercially experienced, of people, and should, I think, avoid arrogating to themselves overconfidently the role of arbiter of commercial reasonableness or likelihood'.[64]

Similarly, in *BMA Special Opportunity Hub Fund Ltd v African Minerals Ltd*[65] it was stated that: 'parties should not be subjected to "… the individual judge's own notions of what might have been the sensible solution to the parties' conundrum"'.[66] This is similar to the sentiment expressed more recently in *Costain Ltd v Tarmac Holdings Ltd*,[67] where, in considering an argument for good faith under an NEC form of contract, the judge stated that:

> it is a form of contractual duty which requires the obliger to have regard to the interests of the obligee, while also being entitled to have regard to its own self-interest when acting … I respectfully agree with that summary … although I am a little uneasy about a more general obligation to act 'fairly'; that is a difficult obligation to police because it is so subjective.[68]

---

[62] Gerald McMeel, 'Foucault's Pendulum: Text, Context and Good faith in Contract Law' (2017) *Current Legal Problems* 1.
[63] *Skanska Rashleigh Weatherfoil Ltd v Somerfield Stored Ltd* [2006] EWCA Civ 1732.
[64] [2006] EWCA Civ 1732 at [22].
[65] *BMA Special Opportunity Hub Fund Ltd v African Minerals Ltd* [2013] EWCA Civ 416.
[66] [2013] EWCA Civ 416 at paragraph 24, referring to *Jackson v Dear* [2012] EWHC 2060 (Ch).
[67] *Costain Ltd v Tarmac Holdings Ltd* [2017] EWHC 319 (TCC).
[68] [2017] EWHC 319 (TCC) at [122]–[123].

It is true that seeking to determine what good faith means is likely to involve a subjective view as to the extent of such duties in the context of expected norms of behaviour. That is difficult for lawyers, who regard contracts as documents intended to provide a clear mechanism based on rights, obligations and remedies and nothing else. In practice, good faith is sensitive to context and, as the cases above show, it is a principle that cannot be considered in a vacuum. Where terms provide for discretion, it seems clear that such discretion must be exercised in a manner which is not arbitrary, irrational or capricious and in a manner that is in effect the same as good faith. As highlighted in *Mid Essex*, this is not the same for other contractual terms and it seems all commentators agree good faith does not require a party to go against its own commercial interest.

One way of testing such a proposition is to put it in a practical context, for example by examining the common mechanism for the deduction of liquidated and ascertained damages in the event of delay. This is a common feature of all construction contracts, which simply involves multiplying an agreed amount by the period of delay. If a contractor became liable to pay such damages due to an event which was his risk, but for which he had no culpability – say, the unexpected insolvency of a sub-contractor – would the position be different if such a contractual provision was subject to an overarching good faith obligation? It is difficult to see how the employer would be expected to give up the agreed compensation in such a situation, especially where it reflected the employer's actual loss caused by such delay.

Another example is a time-bar and notification provision, where a party loses its entitlement unless it issues a notice within a fixed period; also a common feature of commercial contracts. This can lead to a situation where a party may lose its entitlement to be paid due to a lack of the requisite notice, for example because it was served one day late due to an error or at the wrong address. This will be the case even if the other party is the cause of the additional cost or delay or suffers no real prejudice. Jackson J (as he then was) considered the commercial rationale for such provisions in *Multiplex v Honeywell*[69] and explained that such contractual terms serve a valuable purpose, enabling matters to be investigated while they are still current and providing the employer with the opportunity to withdraw instructions. In that case, however, the nature of the employer's commercial interest may be less clear than in the case of the liquidated delay damages. There is a short-term commercial benefit to the employer in avoiding payment but the long-term effect may be open to debate. Proponents of collaborative contracting would argue that in the long term the employer would benefit from not enforcing the black letter of the contract, but traditional lawyers would say the underlying bargain remains the same and is based on the contractual terms and nothing else.

---

[69] *Multiplex Constructions (UK) Ltd v Honeywell Control Systems Ltd (No 2)* [2007] EWHC 447 (TCC) at [103].

As noted above, courts are sometimes reluctant to make judgments based on what is a reasonable or fair commercial outcome. Yet this may be necessary if a court has to decide in what situations a party will be regarded as giving up its commercial interest to the extent that it is required to comply with a contractual good faith obligation. Indeed, it may require the courts to decide what have been described as 'prevailing notions of commercial morality'.[70] In *Mid Essex* that resulted in the trial judge relying on the Trust's being a public body and committed to high standards, to find it should not have made the deductions, while in the Court of Appeal it was held that the Trust as a public body had a duty to demand high standards of service.

There is, however, a deeper underlying issue. In addition to certainty, when looking at what is commercially reasonable, some lawyers hold the view that, in modern commerce, a party is entitled to take any steps it wishes unless there is an express prohibition against such conduct. In an earlier decision, Jackson J described a party's conduct, based on a strategy of certifying the lowest values it believed it could defend, as being ruthless but lawful.[71] A similar sentiment was expressed by Lord Rodger in a case concerning the disclosure of information in *Hamilton v Allied Domecq PLC*, when he stated that 'a failure on the part of Mr Beatty to speak might be regarded as morally questionable. But that is different from saying that he was under a legal duty to speak'.[72] This was expressed in stronger terms by Warren CJ in *Esso Australia Resources Pty Ltd v Southern Pacific Petroleum NRL*,[73] where she observed that:

> Therefore, the current reticence attending the application and recognition of a duty of good faith probably lies as much with the vagueness and imprecision inherent in defining commercial morality. The modern law of contract has developed on the premise of achieving certainty in commerce ... Where commercial leviathans are contractually engaged, it is difficult to see that a duty of good faith will arise, leaving aside duties that might arise in a fiduciary relationship. If one party to a contract is more shrewd, more cunning and out-manoeuvres the other contracting company who did not suffer a disadvantage and who was not vulnerable, it is difficult to see why the latter should have greater protection than that provided by the law of contract.

This approach was described by Mr Justice Leggatt in his 2016 talk[74] as lawyers' tendency to see commerce as a Darwinian struggle where each party tries to gain at the expense of the other; an adversarial activity and a 'zero sum game'.

---

[70] See Michael Levenstein, 'Where Angels Fear to Tread: The Limits of Good Faith in Commercial Contracts' (2017) 32 *Journal of International Banking & Finance Law* 569 for a review of the legal and policy considerations.

[71] *Multiplex Constructions (UK) Ltd v Cleveland Bridge UK Ltd* [2006] EWHC 1341 (TCC) at [628].

[72] *Hamilton and others v Allied Domecq Plc* [2007] UKHL 33, 2007 SC (HL) 142, 2007 SLT 697 at paragraph 20. See also S Jackson, 'The Duty to Disclose: A Clash of Laws and Morality' (2008) 24 *Construction Law Journal* 675.

[73] *Esso Australia Resources Pty Ltd v Southern Pacific Petroleum NRL* [2005] VSCA 228 at [2].

[74] Contractual duties of good faith, Lecture to the Commercial Bar Association, 18 October 2016.

Bridge has referred to good faith as being presented as a measure of the ethical content of a legal system, so that its absence in legal systems belonging to the common law tradition could be seen as a measure of its materialistic character (recognising that this was a crude dichotomy).[75] Some parts of commerce may well be adversarial in that manner but there is an increasing call for modern contracts that embrace notions of collaboration and do more than just set out rights and obligations.[76]

In construction, the practical impact of good faith clauses is exemplified by the NEC form of contract (used by the UK Government for major projects such as the 2012 Olympics and Crossrail) and the partnering contracts referred to above, but also in the recent move to alliancing structures. In 2018, NEC published a new standard form alliancing contract and a new Framework Alliancing Contract (FAC-1) was published in 2017. Professor Mosey described the latter as providing collaborative machinery and governance that goes beyond a relational contract and has highlighted the government's support for collaborative contracting, aimed at delivering efficiencies and cost savings.[77]

This was recognised by Arden LJ in her 2013 paper,[78] which set out some of the traditional objections to good faith clauses but noted Lord Scott's statement in *Golden Strait Corp v Nippon Yusen Kubishika Kaisha*[79] that 'certainty is a desideratum and a very important one, particularly in commercial contracts. But it is not a principle and must give way to principle'. She was of the view that English law was developing in a way that could accommodate the concept of good faith[80] and saw economic advantages in providing a more appropriate structure for cooperative arrangements that will give English law more flexibility and make it more attractive in the global market for commercial law. In her view, it was for judges to develop the law in line with evolving commercial and social need. At the same time it is necessary to recognise the limits of a good faith principle and that it must be based on a clear underlying principle as opposed to a more vague concept of 'fairness'. This was highlighted by Chief Justice Allsop, who stated as follows:[81]

> The proper balance of values and norms in the fabric of the law and the creation of certainty in the law must also recognise the requirement that principle and rule conform

---

[75] Michael Bridge, 'Good Faith, the Common Law, and the CISG' (2017) 22(1) *Uniform Law Review* 98–115.

[76] See also the Society of Construction Law, *Statement of Ethical Principles* (2006) and other information from the Ethics Working Group at www.scl.org.uk.

[77] 'Improving Value Through the FAC-1 Framework Alliance Contract', SCL paper D209, November 2017.

[78] 'Coming to Terms with Good Faith', Singapore Academy of Law, 26 April 2013.

[79] *Golden Strait Corp v Nippon Yusen Kubishika Kaisha* [2007] 2 AC 353.

[80] Albeit she relied in that regard on European law and earlier decisions on contract interpretation, both of which may be seen as less relevant following the UK's departure from the EU and the *Arnold v Britton* line of cases.

[81] Justice James Allsop, 'Conscience, Fair Dealing and Commerce – Parliaments and the Courts' [2015] *Federal Judicial Scholarship* 17.

to moral standards as the gauge of the law's flexibility and as its avenue for growth, but without confounding law with the suspension of principle and rule by the drift into a void of sentiment and personal intuitive benevolence, being the antithesis of law as the exercise of personal will.

In his lecture on good faith,[82] Jackson LJ has pointed out that parties to a contract need to know what the contract requires and what the contract permits. This is undoubtedly true and while there is clearly a wider discussion to be had about collaborative contracting and the law may evolve, that is of limited assistance to the parties who operate contracts which include good faith obligations and may need to understand what such an obligation means precisely in a given set of facts.

As noted by Bridge, supporters of good faith may be content to see the flag being flown, though if they have ambitions for a more ethical contract law, there is little evidence to show that good faith is taking the law further in that direction.[83] In other words, an express contractual obligation is unlikely, on its own, to result in changes in behaviours.

One can see from the *Mid Essex* decision the importance of identifying what the issues are and applying established legal principles, and in such a context the relevance of the apparent absurdity of certain actions may well be very limited. All the more so if it is necessary to demonstrate dishonesty in order to prove a breach of a good faith obligation, as suggested in *Mid Essex*. As noted above, it is one thing to say a general duty of good faith should apply and another to then apply such a principle when enforcing a contractual mechanism to do with notices or liquidated damages. Describing good faith using terms such as 'adhering to the spirit of the contract', 'observing reasonable commercial standards' or 'being faithful to the agreed common purpose' does not lead to clarity. As Bingham LJ stated in *Interfoto*, English law has developed piecemeal solutions to problems of unfairness and it is difficult to see the Supreme Court following the Canadian example of recognising good faith as a general principle.

Nevertheless, the users in construction and other sectors seem to favour good faith clauses, lacking the lawyers' suspicion of vague uncertain terms. It is also the case that lawyers, and especially the courts, only observe the very small minority of contracts that end up in dispute and legal proceedings. Where does that leave the lawyers being asked to advise on such clauses? This may well depend on how a party sees its contractual relationship and whether it believes that including such a clause represents the intentions and aspirations of the parties. If that is the case, such a clause can be included but it must be drafted carefully with consideration as to which parts of the contract it would apply to. The parties will need to recognise that how such a clause may be enforced is uncertain and that while English courts recognise parties can enter into contracts containing good faith clauses, these tend

---

[82] 'Does Good Faith have any Role in Construction Contracts?' The Pinsent Masons Lecture, Hong Kong, 22 November 2017, now SCL paper no 207, downloadable at: www.scl.org.uk.

[83] Michael Bridge, 'Good Faith, the Common Law, and the CISG' (n 75 above) p 98.

to be interpreted narrowly and there is a preference to rely on more established principles.

Whatever views one holds on good faith, it is clear from the extensive and international nature of the commentary on this topic, including by senior judges, and the number of judgments in different jurisdictions dealing with this topic, that it is more than a purely academic debate. The law will no doubt keep developing and one can only hope that future cases will deal with items which are as memorable as chocolate mousses and Manchester United toiletries.

PART VI

Negligence & Nuisance

11

Rectifying the Defects in Builders' Concurrent Liability

FIONA SINCLAIR QC

I. Introduction

The construction industry has made an art form of contract. The sector is amply supplied with standard form contract terms which express the obligations of building contractors in detailed formulations. In comparison, contractors' obligations in tort have received relatively sparse attention.

'Concurrent liability' typically means liability both in contract and in tort. Two species of concurrent liability may be distinguished. The first is where A owes to C a duty of care in respect of the subject-matter of a contract between A and B; this situation is commonly discussed under the heading 'liability in tort to third parties'. The second is where A owes a duty of care to B and there is a contract between A and B which addresses the same subject-matter. Lord Justice Jackson's judgment in *Robinson v PE Jones (Contractors) Ltd*[1] and his later article in the Australian *Tort Law Review*[2] were concerned with the second situation, in which a party owes duties of care in both contract and tort to its contractual counterparty. The parallel obligations are not only concurrent but also coextensive in scope: the requirement is to exercise reasonable care in performing a skilled task. It is this kind of concurrent liability which is discussed below.

In *Robinson*, Jackson LJ responded to calls for appellate guidance on building contractors' concurrent liability by restricting the ambit of such liability. He made clear that, but for binding authority on the point, he would have decided that English law did not recognise concurrent liability at all. Jackson LJ's wider reasoning appears from his later article. He argued that the common law 'took a wrong turning' when in *Henderson v Merrett*[3] the House of Lords allowed that

---

[1] *Robinson v PE Jones (Contractors) Ltd* [2012] QB 44.
[2] An article based on Jackson LJ's lecture to the Technology and Construction Court Bar Association and the Society of Construction Law on 30 October 2014. Rupert Jackson LJ, 'Concurrent Liability: Where have things gone wrong?' (2015) 23(1) *Tort Law Review* 3.
[3] *Henderson v Merrett Syndicates Ltd* [1995] 2 AC 45.

a contractual obligation to perform services might of itself generate a concurrent and coextensive tortious duty of care to the other contracting party. In Jackson LJ's view, the principle of freedom of contract – due respect for the contracting parties' consensus on their mutual obligations and risk allocation – requires that the parties' mutual obligations in contract and tort should not overlap.

Commentators have used the term 'ConTorts'[4] to describe the results of 'mission creep' from the law of tort into the territory of contract law. Concurrent liability is a kind of ConTort. Jackson LJ might be expected to appreciate the irony: the ordinary meaning of 'contort' in English is to twist, bend, or draw out of shape.

II. The Controversy

The starting point for any consideration of *Robinson* in context is the seminal decision of the House of Lords in *Murphy v Brentwood*.[5] In the days of negligence under *Anns v Merton LBC*,[6] the requirements for the imposition of a duty of care in tort were merely a 'proximate relationship' and an absence of policy factors weighing against a duty of care. In *Murphy*, that approach was substituted by a return to the broad exclusionary rule established in *Donoghue v Stevenson*.[7] The careless provision of a defective article which causes injury to person or damage to property creates a liability for damages in the tort of negligence. But damages are not recoverable for the loss represented by the defect itself, such as the cost of repairing or replacing the article, or the difference between its value and the price paid for it. Such losses amount to 'pure economic loss' and are recoverable only in contract. *Murphy* confirmed that this rule applies as much to defective buildings as it does to ginger beer made with snails. A building contractor owes to a later purchaser of a building he has constructed no duty of care to see that the building is free of defects. Lord Oliver said:[8]

> I am able to see no circumstances from which there can be deduced a relationship of proximity such as to render the builder liable in tort for pure pecuniary damage sustained by a derivative owner with whom he has no contractual or other relationship.

For the House of Lords in *Murphy*, the absence of a contractual relationship between the builder and the purchaser mattered for the reasons explained in *Donoghue v Stevenson*: the recovery of economic loss which is unrelated to personal injury or property damage is the province of the law of contract.

---

[4] A term thought to have been coined by Professor Gilmore in *The Death of Contract*, 2nd edn (Columbus OH, Ohio State University Press, 1995).

[5] *Murphy v Brentwood District Council* [1991] 1 AC 398.

[6] *Anns v Merton London Borough Council* [1978] AC 728.

[7] *Donoghue v Stevenson* [1932] AC 562.

[8] *Murphy* (n 5 above) at 489.

Lord Oliver's reference to the absence of some 'other relationship' between the parties was a reference to what later expanded to become the major inroad upon the exclusionary rule: *Hedley Byrne v Heller*[9] liability for negligent misstatement between non-contracting parties in a 'special relationship'. In *Henderson v Merrett*,[10] the House of Lords extended *Hedley Byrne* liability from statements to services. It explained that where one party assumes a responsibility to another to perform skilled services with care and that other relies upon the assumption of responsibility, the service provider will normally be liable in tort for economic loss which flows from his failure to perform those services with care. A contract between the parties for the provision of the services would prevent such a duty of care from arising only if the contract terms were inconsistent with concurrent liability in tort. Indeed, a contract for professional services was identified as a paradigmatic assumption of responsibility for the purposes of a concurrent tortious duty of care. A contractual obligation to perform professional services with due care would be mirrored by a corresponding duty of care at common law.

Lord Goff gave the leading speech in *Henderson*. He adopted reasoning which Lord Oliver had deployed to hold, in *Midland Bank v Hett Stubbs & Kemp*,[11] that a solicitor owed concurrent duties in contract and in tort to the client with whose affairs he had been entrusted. Lord Goff put it this way:[12]

> [T]he law of tort is the general law, out of which the parties can, if they wish, contract; and … the same assumption of responsibility may, and frequently does, occur in a contractual context. Approached as a matter of principle, therefore, it is right to attribute to that assumption of responsibility, together with its concomitant reliance, a tortious liability, and then to inquire whether or not that liability is excluded by the contract because the latter is inconsistent with it. This is the reasoning which Oliver J, as I understand it, found implicit, where not explicit, in the speeches in *Hedley Byrne*. With his conclusion I respectfully agree. But even if I am wrong in this, I am of the opinion that this House should now, if necessary, develop the principle of assumption of responsibility as stated in *Hedley Byrne* to its logical conclusion so as to make it clear that a tortious duty of care may arise not only in cases where the relevant services are rendered gratuitously, but also where they are rendered under a contract.

Thus professionals working in the construction industry found that *Murphy* offered no refuge for them. In fact, it had been established before *Murphy* that a professional building designer owed concurrent duties in contract and tort to his client. That was the decision on the liability of designing engineers in *Pirelli v Oscar Faber*,[13] which in *Murphy* Lord Keith explained on *Hedley Byrne* principles.[14] It became generally accepted that construction professionals, like

---

[9] *Hedley Byrne & Co Ltd v Heller & Partners Ltd* [1964] AC 465.

[10] [1995] 2 AC 145.

[11] *Midland Bank v Hett Stubbs & Kemp* [1979] Ch 384 at 415.

[12] [1995] 2 AC 145 at 193.

[13] *Pirelli General Cable Works Ltd v Oscar Faber & Partners* [1983] 2 AC 1.

[14] *Murphy v Brentwood District Council* [1991] 1 AC 398 at 466: 'It would seem that in a case such as *Pirelli*, where the tortious liability arose out of a contractual relationship with professional people,

other professionals, owed concurrent duties of care in tort to protect their clients against pure economic loss.[15]

But what of building contractors, including those who contract not only to construct a building but also to design it?

Murphy did not settle the question whether a building contractor owes a duty of care in tort to its employer under the building contract, because there was no contract between the parties in that case. In the pre-*Henderson* case of *Nitrigin v Inco Alloys Ltd*,[16] May J held that a specialist manufacturer did not owe a concurrent duty of care when supplying pipes for a chemical plant because the relationship between the parties was 'neither a professional relationship in the sense in which the law treats professional negligence nor a [*Hedley Byrne v Heller*] relationship'.[17] But in the years between 1995 (when *Henderson v Merrett* was decided) and 2011 (when the question came squarely before the Court of Appeal in *Robinson*) the effect of *Henderson* was a general consensus among the judges of the Technology and Construction Court that contractors owed concurrent duties in tort.

A design and build contractor was held to owe a concurrent duty of care in *Storey v Charles Church Developments*[18] and in *Tesco v Costain*,[19] albeit in respect of its design work only. The rationale was that there is no reason to distinguish a professional designer from a contractor which carries out design, especially when many design and build contractors employ design professionals. Moreover, in three cases, a contractor was held to owe a concurrent duty of care in respect of services which did not correspond with those offered by the traditional professions. *Barclays Bank v Fairclough (No 2)*[20] concerned a subcontractor engaged to clean a roof using a power-hose; *How Engineering v Southern Insulation*[21] concerned a specialist subcontractor which installed mechanical and electrical services; and the third case was *Robinson* at first instance.[22]

The claim in *Robinson* was for pure economic loss: the cost of repairing defects in a house which the defendant building contractor had built pursuant to its contract with the claimant. It was alleged that flues for gas fires had not been constructed in accordance with good building practice or the applicable building regulations. The claim in contract was statute-barred, so the claimant alleged

---

the duty extended to take reasonable care not to cause economic loss to the client by the advice given. The plaintiffs built the chimney as they did in reliance on that advice. The case would accordingly fall within the principle of *Hedley Byrne & Co Ltd v Heller & Partners Ltd*.'

[15] See, for example, *Ove Arup v Mirant Asia-Pacific Construction (No 2)* [2004] EWHC 1750 (TCC); this part of the decision was not challenged on appeal [2005] EWCA Civ 1585.

[16] *Nitrigin Eireann Teoranta v Inco Alloys Ltd* [1992] 1 WLR 498.

[17] ibid at 503–04.

[18] *Storey v Charles Church Developments Ltd* (1995) 73 Con LR 1.

[19] *Tesco Stores Ltd v Costain Construction Ltd* [2003] EWHC 1487 (TCC).

[20] *Barclays Bank Plc v Fairclough Building Ltd (No 2)* (1995) 76 BLR 1 (CA).

[21] *How Engineering Services v Southern Insulation (Medway) Ltd* [2010] EWHC 1878 (TCC).

[22] *Robinson v PE Jones (Contractors) Ltd* [2010] EWHC 102 (TCC). Cf *Payne v John Setchell Ltd* [2002] BLR 489, where HHJ LLoyd QC considered that although a professional or a contractor might owe a concurrent duty of care in tort, that duty would not extend to preventing economic loss.

breach of a concurrent duty of care in tort. The existence or not of that duty was tried as a preliminary issue.

At first instance, the judge[23] recognised that *Henderson* allowed the possibility that a contractual undertaking to exercise reasonable skill and care would be sufficient to constitute an assumption of responsibility by a building contractor to its employer. Mr Robinson's contract imposed an express obligation upon the contractor to build 'in an efficient and workmanlike manner', which was tantamount to an obligation of reasonable skill and care.[24] The judge concluded that, so far as concurrent liability was concerned, there was no sustainable distinction between the design services provided by a builder and the building work which he carried out. He observed that building contractors possessed special skills which their clients relied upon them to exercise carefully, whether in carrying out their design work or their construction work. There was no sensible reason for a different outcome to be achieved depending upon whether, on the facts in *Robinson*, the flues were defective due to the builder's negligent design as opposed to its negligent construction. The concurrent duty of care in tort 'extends just as much to the physical workmanship itself'.[25]

Thus, without more, the judge would have held that the building contractor in *Robinson* owed a concurrent duty of care in tort to safeguard against economic loss. However, the contract expressly limited the contractor's liability for breach to that described in the then-current NHBC Agreement. That limitation was inconsistent with liability in negligence: accordingly, a concurrent duty of care could not arise.

III. The Court of Appeal in *Robinson*

Worse was to come for Mr Robinson in the Court of Appeal. The Court agreed that the exclusion clause in the parties' contract would preclude a concurrent tortious duty of care. But this was moot, because in the Court's view the building contractor had no concurrent duty of care to exclude. Jackson LJ delivered the leading judgment. He quoted a leading textbook's call[26] for guidance at appellate level on the question whether, and if so when, the making of a building contract will itself constitute a *Henderson* assumption of responsibility.

Jackson LJ identified the two streams of authority which, before *Henderson*, had imposed concurrent liability in tort on professionals (eg, *Pirelli*,[27] *Nitrigin*[28])

---

[23] His Honour Judge Stephen Davies, sitting as a Judge of the High Court (Technology and Construction Court).

[24] Even if an undertaking to exercise reasonable skill and care is not an express term of the contract, such an obligation is implied into any contract for services by section 13 of the Supply of Goods and Services Act 1982.

[25] *Robinson v PE Jones (Contractors) Ltd* [2010] EWHC 102 (TCC) at para 60.

[26] *Keating on Construction Contracts*, 8th edn (London, Sweet & Maxwell, 2006), para 7-018.

[27] *Pirelli General Cable Works Ltd v Oscar Faber & Partners* [1983] 2 AC 1.

[28] *Nitrigin Eireann Teoranta v Inco Alloys Ltd* [1992] 1 WLR 498.

but not on the manufacturer of a product (*Nitrigin*) or the builder of a building (*Murphy*[29]). As to the latter group, he concluded that:[30]

> the relationship between (a) the manufacturer of a product or the builder of a build-ing and (b) the immediate client is primarily governed by the contract between those two parties. Long established principles of freedom of contract enable those parties to allocate risk between themselves as they see fit ... Absent any assumption of responsi-bility, there do not spring up between the parties duties of care co-extensive with their contractual obligations. The law of tort imposes a different and more limited duty upon the manufacturer or builder. That more limited duty is to take reasonable care to protect the client against suffering personal injury or damage to other property. The law of tort imposes this duty, not only towards the first person to acquire the chattel or the build-ing, but also towards others who foreseeably own or use it.

Jackson LJ made plain that, in the absence of authority, he would hold that a build-ing contractor's concurrent duty of care was limited to this '*Donoghue v Stevenson*' duty to avoid causing personal injury and damage to other property.[31] In the light of *Henderson*, however, he accepted that this conclusion was not open to him. It remained necessary in each case to consider the relationship and the dealings between the parties so as to decide whether the contractor had assumed respon-sibility to its client in respect of economic loss caused by the contractor's careless performance of its contractual obligations.

Jackson LJ's starting point was the recognition that, following *Henderson*, a professional agreeing to provide services for reward would normally be regarded as thereby making an assumption of responsibility. He said:[32]

> It is perhaps understandable that professional persons are taken to assume responsi-bility for economic loss to their clients. Typically, they give advice, prepare reports, draw up accounts, produce plans and so forth. They expect their clients and possibly others to act in reliance upon their work product, often with financial or economic consequences.

However, he described as 'nonsensical' any conclusion that, beyond the profes-sional realm, every contracting party assumes a responsibility to its counterparty in respect of negligently-caused economic loss. That would be nonsensical, in Jackson LJ's view, because the tort and contract are jurisprudentially distinct sources of obligation:[33]

> Contractual and tortious duties have different origins and different functions. Contractual obligations spring from the consent of the parties and the common law principle that contracts should be enforced. Tortious duties are imposed by law, as a matter of policy, in specific situations.

---

[29] *Murphy v Brentwood District Council* [1991] 1 AC 398.
[30] *Robinson v PE Jones (Contractors) Ltd* [2012] QB 44 (CA) at paras 67–68.
[31] ibid, at para 75.
[32] ibid.
[33] ibid, at para 76.

On the facts of *Robinson*, the Court of Appeal found no assumption of responsibility in the *Hedley Byrne* sense. Jackson LJ observed that the parties entered a 'normal contract whereby the defendant would complete the construction of a house for the claimant to an agreed specification'.[34] The contract set out the builder's warranties of quality and the client's remedies for breach of warranty. The parties were not in a professional relationship. A duty of care at common law would also be inconsistent with the narrow remedies under the NHBC Agreement to which the contract limited the builder's liability; but Jackson LJ made clear that he would not have found a concurrent duty of care even in the absence of the contractual limitation clause. The builder's express contractual undertaking to carry out works in accordance with a design and in an 'efficient and workmanlike manner' (tantamount to an obligation to exercise reasonable care and skill) was not sufficient to amount to an assumption of responsibility.

The other members of the Court agreed with Jackson LJ's judgment. Stanley Burton LJ was categorical:[35]

> In my judgment, it must now be regarded as settled law that the builder/vendor of a building does not by reason of his contract to construct or to complete the building assume any liability in the tort of negligence in relation to defects in the building giving rise to purely economic loss. The same applies to a builder who is not the vendor, and to the seller or manufacturer of a chattel.

However for Stanley Burton LJ the important distinction was between the product, for defects in which there could be no liability outside contract, and damage to other property caused by defects in the product, for which *Donoghue v Stevenson* liability in tort would attach:[36]

> Thus the crucial distinction is between a person who supplies something which is defective and a person who supplies something (whether a building, goods or a service) which, because of its defects, causes loss or damage to something else. An architect owes a duty of care not in respect of the value of his drawings or specification, but in respect of the building that is to be constructed with them ... The managing agents in *Henderson v Merrett Syndicates Ltd* owed a duty of care to their Names because they were managing the Names' assets.

On Stanley Burnton LJ's analysis, the professional's concurrent duty of care is not a duty of care to avoid causing economic loss which arises because of a *Hedley Byrne* assumption of responsibility. It is, rather, a traditional *Donoghue v Stevenson* duty of care to avoid causing damage to other property.[37] Although it is difficult to reconcile this analysis with *Hedley Byrne* and *Henderson*, it serves to highlight the profound unease with which all members of the Court in *Robinson* regarded concurrent liability under *Henderson*.

---

[34] ibid, at para 83.
[35] ibid at para 92.
[36] ibid at paras 93–94.
[37] For further discussion, see J Carrington, 'A crucial distinction' (2014) 4 *Professional Negligence* 185.

IV. The Wider Problem

In his 2015 article, Jackson LJ identified fundamental objections to concurrent liability as an extension of tort liability into the realm of contract. His starting point was a comparative study of concurrent liability in Roman law and under the French and German civil codes. In *Henderson*, Lord Goff had briefly considered the same systems of law and appeared fortified in his views by his conclusion that 'no perceptible harm has come to the German system from admitting concurrent claims'.[38]

Jackson LJ argued that for the study of comparative law to be fruitful in the context of law reform, it must be detailed and sensitive to context. Roman law, from which the French and German jurisprudence developed, had no truck with concurrent liability: the law of contract and the law of delict were separate domains. While the respect accorded to freedom of contract under French law means that a contracting party cannot bring a tort claim in respect of the same subject-matter (the '*non cumul*' rule), another justification is that the French law of tort is so wide that if concurrency were permitted, contracting parties could resort to a tort claim in respect of all contractual obligations. Moreover, while a claimant generally has a choice of remedies in contract and tort under German law, it is inappropriate to conclude that German law has concurrent liability in the sense allowed by *Henderson*: German tort law only exceptionally permits recovery of pure economic loss caused by defects. (Jackson LJ had had the detailed comparative law analysis firmly in mind when deciding *Robinson*. He pointed out there that concurrent liability under German law did not involve the replication in tort of contractual obligations.[39]) Evidently, in Jackson LJ's view, the consideration of comparative law suggested by Lord Goff's speech in *Henderson* was too superficial to support the radical incursion of tort law into the domain of contract law which that decision sanctioned.

What then remained of the grounds for the *Henderson* extension of concurrent liability? For Jackson LJ, it represented the sacrifice of principle to purely pragmatic considerations. Under *Henderson*, the law of contract is wholly subordinated to the law of tort. Even although the making of the contract can itself be the assumption of responsibility which causes the *Henderson* duty of care to arise, thereafter the contract is relevant only to the extent that its terms are inconsistent with such a duty of care. This is deliberately to subjugate the law of contract to the law of tort in a way which both ignores the fundamental differences between those two systems of obligations and profoundly offends the principle of freedom of contract which is at the heart of English commercial law. Lord Scarman expressed a similar view in *Tai Hing Cotton Mill v Liu Chong Hing Bank*:[40]

> Their Lordships do not believe that there is anything to the advantage of the law's development in searching for a liability in tort where the parties are in a contractual

---

[38] *Henderson v Merrett Syndicates Ltd* [1995] 2 AC 145 at 184.
[39] *Robinson v PE Jones (Contractors) Ltd* [2012] QB 44 at para 78.
[40] *Tai Hing Cotton Mill Ltd v Liu Chong Hing Bank Ltd* [1986] AC 80 at 107.

relationship. This is particularly so in a commercial relationship. Though it is possible as a matter of legal semantics to conduct an analysis of the rights and duties inherent in some contractual relationships including that of banker and customer either as a matter of contract law when the question will be what, if any, terms are to be implied or as a matter of tort law when the task will be to identify a duty arising from the proximity and character of the relationship between the parties, their Lordships believe it to be correct in principle and necessary for the avoidance of confusion in the law to adhere to the contractual analysis: on principle because it is a relationship in which the parties have, subject to a few exceptions, the right to determine their obligations to each other, and for the avoidance of confusion because different consequences do follow according to whether liability arises from contract or tort, e.g. in the limitation of action.

In *Henderson*, Lord Goff dismissed Lord Scarman's appeal to principle as 'the temptation of elegance'.[41] His concern was avowedly practical: the point of concurrent liability was precisely to avoid the different consequences of liability in contract and tort to which Lord Scarman had referred. Foremost among those was the different treatment of claims in contract and tort by the law of limitation. In the tort of negligence, the occurrence of damage triggers the running of the limitation period, and an extended limitation period, based on the date of knowledge of damage, is available.[42] In contract, time runs from the date of breach.[43] Lord Goff's concern was that, without the option of a claim in tort, a claimant's cause of action could become statute-barred before he even knew about it, and the recipient of gratuitous advice would therefore be in a better position than the client who contracted and paid for it.[44]

For Jackson LJ, the appropriate response to problems caused by procedural law is to change the procedural law. It is not to subject the law of contract – the law of strict obligations voluntarily undertaken in order to confer mutual benefit – to the law of tort – the law of fault-based remedies imposed by the general law to allow compensation for harm caused. His article made a renewed call for implementation of the proposals made in the Law Commission's 2001 report, 'Limitation of Actions'.[45] The Law Commission recommended a single, core limitation regime which would apply to contractual and to tortious claims. There would be a primary limitation period of three years from the date of actual or constructive knowledge, supplemented by a long-stop period of 10 years from the date of breach. The institution of a uniform limitation period for claims in contract and tort, Jackson LJ pointed out, would mean that 'judges will no longer need to stretch the common law in order to circumvent the statute'.

In *Henderson*, Lord Goff had acknowledged that reform of the law of limitation would remove the discrepant positions of claimants in tort and contract which concerned him, but he regarded that as 'crying for the moon'.[46] The Law

---

[41] *Henderson v Merrett Syndicates Ltd* [1995] 2 AC 145 at 186.
[42] See Limitation Act 1980, ss 2 and 14A.
[43] Limitation Act 1980, ss 5 and 8.
[44] *Henderson v Merrett Syndicates Ltd* [1995] 2 AC 145 at 187.
[45] Law Com No 270.
[46] *Henderson v Merrett Syndicates Ltd* [1995] 2 AC 145 at 187.

Commission's subsequent proposals for a uniform regime belied Lord Goff's pessimism, but unfortunately those proposals were rejected by the UK Government in 2009.[47] To date they have not been revived.

Jackson LJ argued with conviction that the rights and liabilities of contracting parties should be regulated by the contracts which they have made and not by an 'amorphous and ever-expanding law of tort'. He did not spell out an interim solution, pending legislative reform, to the practical difficulties perceived by Lord Goff. Perhaps it is not difficult to imagine what one of his answers might be. The law of tort should not operate as some kind of financial safety net for contracting parties. If the law of limitation is a difficulty for contracting parties, they are at liberty to contract out of that law. The recipient of services who has agreed to pay for them can stipulate warranties of quality, remedies and limitation periods which are at least as advantageous as those which are provided by the common law to the recipient of gratuitous advice. Contractual limitation periods are a common feature of commercial relationships in the construction and other sectors; if clearly worded, they are effective to oust the Limitation Act.[48]

V. Where We Are Now

The Court of Appeal in *Robinson* accepted, in the light of *Henderson*, that the making of a contract for professional services will normally be sufficient to activate a concurrent duty of care in tort. The Court did not regard the building contract in *Robinson* as falling into that category. The decision has been understood as authority for the proposition that a contractual obligation to carry out building works using reasonable skill and care will not normally be attended by a corresponding duty of care in tort. Thus in *Broster v Galliard*[49] Akenhead J took *Robinson* to mean that a design and build contractor could be liable in tort for its poor design (professional services) but not for its poor workmanship (non-professional services).

Arguably, the correct position is not so straightforward. In *Robinson*, Jackson LJ explained that the contract between the parties did not constitute a *Hedley Byrne/Henderson* assumption of responsibility because, even ignoring the exclusion clause, it was

> a normal contract whereby the defendant would complete the construction of a house for the claimant to an agreed specification ... The parties were not in a professional

---

[47] Hansard, 9 November 2009. The Parliamentary Under-Secretary of State for Justice asserted that the reforms recommended by the Law Commission offered 'insufficient benefits and potentially large-scale costs'.

[48] See, for an example, *Inframatrix Investments Ltd v Dean Construction Ltd* [2012] EWCA Civ 64; and for further discussion see *Chitty on Contracts*, 32nd edn (London, Thomson Reuters, 2015), ch 28, paras 28-107–28-112.

[49] *Broster v Galliard Docklands Ltd* [2011] EWHC 1722 (TCC) at para 21.

relationship whereby, for example, the claimant was paying the defendant to give advice or to prepare reports or plans upon which the claimant would act.[50]

This suggests it was a contract for materials and labour only, not a design and build contract. The reference to an 'agreed specification' suggests the traditional arrangement where the employer obtains a design from a professional designer and the building contractor agrees to build that design, but does not accept responsibility for it. However the builder's primary obligation under the contract in *Robinson* was to 'complete the work shown on the drawings and specification relative thereto already produced to and made available for inspection by the purchaser at the offices of the vendor'. Therefore this was not a case where the client procured the design and the builder agreed to construct that design. Rather, in a manner typical of small builder-developers, the builder provided the design as well as the construction of a new-build house which was sold off-plan. The agreed purchase price paid for design services as well as for building work.

If this interpretation of the facts is correct, then arguably *Robinson* is authority for the proposition that a *design and build* contractor does not normally owe a concurrent duty of care in respect of its design or its construction services. If so, then the decision conforms fully with Jackson LJ's views on the proper scope for concurrent liability.

However tempting this analysis, it is probably unrealistic. Both at first instance and on appeal, the case appears to have been argued as if the contract were a traditional building contract, under which the builder accepted no responsibility for the design of the building. The preliminary issue for determination was whether 'a builder who contracts with his client to undertake building works' would owe a concurrent duty of care in respect of those works. The issue may have been limited in this way because only workmanship defects, rather than design defects, were pleaded. In any event, the Court of Appeal was asked to address the effect in tort of a contract for *building works only*.

Even understood in this narrow sense, the decision in *Robinson* serves to highlight several difficulties with the *Henderson* approach to concurrent liability. It is unclear how the decision is to be reconciled with prior Court of Appeal authority that a building contractor owed a concurrent duty of care in tort to prevent pure economic loss. In *Barclays v Fairclough (No 2)*[51] it was held that a roof-cleaning sub-subcontractor owed a concurrent duty of care to the maintenance subcontractor which sat above it in the contractual chain. Beldam LJ (with whom the other members of the Court agreed) cited *Henderson* and reasoned that:[52]

> A skilled contractor undertaking maintenance work to a building assumes a responsibility which invites reliance no less than the financial or other professional adviser does in undertaking his work. The nature of the responsibility is the same though it will differ in extent.

[50] ibid at para 83.
[51] *Barclays Bank Plc v Fairclough Building Ltd (No 2)* (1995) 76 BLR 1.
[52] ibid at 24.

Barclays cannot be distinguished on the basis that the contract there was purely to provide (roof-cleaning) services, whereas a building contractor under the kind of 'normal contract' referred to in *Robinson* typically agrees to provide materials as well as services. It is the contractual obligation to perform skilled services with reasonable skill and care which amounts to a *Hedley Byrne/Henderson* assumption of responsibility. The builder's obligation to provide materials of satisfactory quality is a strict obligation, a creature of contract, which would not on any view give rise to a concurrent duty of care: strict obligations do not exist in the law of negligence.

It is more likely that the decisions in *Barclays* and *Robinson* simply reflect different responses to the treatment of professional engagements as paradigms of concurrent liability in *Henderson*. The court in *Barclays* recognised that building services also require the exercise of special skills, on which clients rely. The court in *Robinson* instead used the clear but largely unexplained distinction drawn in *Henderson* between professional engagements and other contracts, to limit the scope of concurrent liability. The two decisions draw attention, in diametrically opposite ways, to the fundamental difficulty of the *Henderson* professional/non-professional distinction.

Plainly, the existence or not of concurrent liability depends on the nature of the services provided rather than on whether or not the service provider is a member of one of the traditional professions. But the *Hedley Byrne/Henderson* assumption of responsibility merely requires an agreement to provide services requiring 'special skill' and concomitant reliance by the client upon the provision of those services with skill and care. Beyond pointing out that a professional expects his client to rely upon his work product, Jackson LJ did not attempt to supplement the reasoning in *Henderson* with an explanation of why professional services give rise to concurrent liability. The difficulty is that neither the possession of special skills nor an expectation of client reliance serves to distinguish professionals from building contractors. When a client moves its employees into a building designed for it by an architect and constructed for it by a building contractor, the client expects that the 'work product' of each will be free of defects caused by want of skill and care.

Moreover, the modern construction industry increasingly frustrates attempts to draw clear distinctions between 'professional' and 'non-professional' services. The category of services which might reasonably be regarded as 'professional' is ever-expanding. Contractors with specialist expertise beyond the reach of the traditional professions proliferate. From the point of view of the client's interest in the successful completion of its project, it is difficult to see any principled distinction between, for example, the work of the generalist building services engineer (a traditional professional) and that of the specialist refrigeration contractor. Indeed, generalist construction professionals commonly defer to specialist contractors. Typically, the generalist engineer prepares a specification which identifies the outcomes which a suitable system must deliver, while the specialist contractor provides the detailed characteristics of a system which will meet those performance requirements. Both the engineer and the specialist contractor are providing design services. To complicate matters further, detailed design is commonly carried out by specialist contractors and manufacturers who employ individuals with traditional professional qualifications. To take another example, a management contractor enters into a building contract but subcontracts the entirety of the works. It is paid the actual cost of the works as determined by the subcontract prices, plus a management fee. The management contractor's own function is really project management, which these days is recognised as a professional service.[53] It remains unclear whether a management contractor which contracts to build to a design supplied by the client would be regarded as owing a concurrent duty of care (because it is providing a professional service) or as not owing a duty of care (because it contracts to provide completed building works).

Far more common than management contracts are design and build contracts; currently the most common form of procurement in the UK. The majority in *Robinson* did not overrule the earlier decisions in *Storey v Charles Church*[54] and *Tesco v Costain*[55] that a design and build contractor owes a concurrent duty of care in respect of its design work. There is no satisfactory basis for treating differently a professional designer and a designer who also builds, so far as the obligations attaching to their design services are concerned. The design 'work product' of a design and build contractor is not sold separately to the client before the design is built; but it is unreal to suggest that the employer places any less reliance upon those designs having been prepared with due care and skill than he would if he had procured the design under a separate contract. It seems entirely reasonable to conclude, notwithstanding *Robinson*, that a design and build contractor does have concurrent liability in respect of its design work.

The court in *Storey v Charles Church*[56] distinguished between the 'professional' elements and the 'ordinary' construction elements of a design and build contractor's contractual obligations. This suggests a workable basis for distinguishing those obligations in respect of which there is a concurrent duty of care, and those in respect of which there is not. Although the factual line between design (for example) and construction is not always easy to draw, the distinction is one with which construction lawyers are familiar. Thus, for example, many standard form design and build contracts include an express 'professional' warranty of skill and care in respect of the design element of the contractor's work, and require the contractor to take out professional indemnity insurance in respect of it. To regard

---

[53] See eg, *Ampleforth Abbey Trust v Turner & Townsend Project Management Ltd* [2012] EWHC 2137 (TCC). In *Great Eastern Hotel Co Ltd v John Laing Construction Ltd* [2005] EWHC 181 (TCC) at para 35, the obligations of a building contractor under a construction management contract (an arrangement where the employer contracts directly with the trade contractors) were regarded as equivalent to those of a professional project manager.

[54] *Storey v Charles Church Developments Ltd* (1995) 73 Con LR 1.

[55] *Tesco Stores Ltd v Costain Construction Ltd* [2003] EWHC 1487 (TCC).

[56] *Storey v Charles Church Developments Ltd* (1995) 73 Con LR 1.

such obligations as creating an assumption of responsibility would be consistent with the majority line in *Robinson*. It remains unclear why the contractor's warranty to exercise reasonable skill and care in workmanship should not likewise amount to an assumption of responsibility; but, on Jackson LJ's thinking, that difficulty only exists because *Henderson* wrongly extended concurrent liability to contracted-for 'professional' services.

VI. The Way Ahead

The decision in *Robinson* turned ultimately on the express terms of the particular building contract, but most standard form contracts in common use do not exclude common law remedies available to the employer. Given his antipathy towards concurrent liability, it is not surprising that Jackson LJ in *Robinson* offered no examples of factual circumstances in which a building contractor might assume responsibility in respect of his construction obligations. It might be thought surprising that there have not been subsequent decisions which address such circumstances, or which directly address the liability in tort of design and build contractors. There are several probable reasons for this. Building contracts for substantial projects are typically made under seal, so that the limitation periods in contract and tort are of comparable generosity; such contracts anyway often stipulate a single limitation period for any proceedings, regardless of the cause of action. Then there is the practice of subcontracting. Few main contractors nowadays use their own employees to perform the services which they contract to provide. Since liability in negligence is fault-based, a main contractor is not normally liable for the negligence of its subcontractors.[57] In consequence, allegations of breach of a concurrent duty of care will not 'bite' except between the parties at the end of the contractual chain. Such parties are likely to be smaller contractors which lack the appetite or means to fight claims to judgment, especially since insurance in respect of liability for workmanship defects is not generally available. Finally, it is the practice on major projects to require those of the main contractor's subcontractors which have design obligations to provide collateral warranties in favour of the employer. Parties which owe contractual obligations to the same claimant are more likely to claim against each other for statutory contribution[58] than for breach of a concurrent duty in tort, since the limitation period for a contribution claim is even more generous than for a tort claim.[59]

---

[57] *Woodland v Swimming Teachers' Association* [2013] UKSC 66, [2014] AC 537 at para 5. An exception to the rule exists only where the activity in question is exceptionally dangerous even when conducted with reasonable care and skill or where a non-delegable obligation has been accepted: *Biffa Waste Services Ltd v Maschinenfabrik Ernst Hese GmbH* [2009] QB 725 (CA).

[58] Under the Civil Liability (Contribution) Act 1978.

[59] Time for a contribution claim does not run until the liability of the contribution claimant has been ascertained by judgment, settlement or an award: Limitation Act 1980, s 10.

Ironically, there is reason to believe that the significance of post-*Henderson* concurrent liability will be eroded not by future decisions concerning building contractors but by developments in the law of professional liability. Recent events in three disparate areas suggest this. The first is the law of remoteness of damages. One of the practical reasons for extending concurrent liability which Lord Goff identified in *Henderson* was that the rules governing the remoteness of damages are generally more generous (from a claimant's point of view) in tort than in contract.[60] In *Wellesley Partners v Withers*[61] the Court of Appeal's unanimous view was that in cases of concurrent liability only the contractual test for remoteness should apply. A strong thread in the Court's reasoning was that, since the parallel duty of care in tort arises only because of the parties' contract, it should not be permitted to subvert the rules of the contractual setting in which they have chosen to place their relationship.[62] Jackson LJ was not a member of the Court in *Wellesley*, but might be expected to approve.

Secondly, one of the most important ways in which professionals are accorded special status in law is distinctly under attack. A distinctive feature of the law of professional liability is that breach of a professional's duty of care is measured using the *Bolam*[63] test: did the professional act in accordance with respected professional opinion? In effect, the profession sets the standard by which its members are judged, whereas the court determines what constitutes reasonable skill and care for other defendants. Recent decisions suggest a reduced scope of application for the *Bolam* test. In *Montgomery v Lanarkshire Health Board*[64] the Supreme Court held that *Bolam* did not apply to a doctor's duty to advise a patient on the risks of treatment. Subsequently, *Bolam* was held not to apply to an investment adviser's duty to advise on investments.[65] Although *Bolam* is not yet vanquished,[66] there is a clear impetus towards permitting the court to set the standards for professionals' duties of skill and care, just as it does for other defendants.[67]

Finally, if the Supreme Court ever comes to reconsider the question of building contractors' concurrent liability, the reason may well be the proliferation of new forms of technical expertise in the construction sector. New technologies emerge at an accelerating pace, accompanied by ever-increasing specialisation of expertise. The digital revolution has seen the sector embrace building information modelling (software which allows contributors to a project to work interactively in

---

[60] *Henderson v Merrett Syndicates Ltd* [1995] 2 AC 145 at 187.

[61] *Wellesley Partners LLP v Withers LLP* [2016] Ch 529.

[62] ibid, see paras 60–80 (Floyd LJ), 145–63 (Roth LJ) and 181–88 (Longmore LJ).

[63] *Bolam v Friern Hospital Management Committee* [1957] 1 WLR 582.

[64] *Montgomery v Lanarkshire Health Board* [2015] UKSC 11.

[65] *O'Hare v Coutts & Co* [2016] EWHC 2224 (QB). See also *Baird v Hastings (t/a Hastings & Co Solicitors)* [2015] NICA 22; *Thomas v Triodos Bank NV* [2017] EWHC 314 (QB).

[66] See *Barker v Baxendale Walker Solicitors* [2017] EWCA Civ 2056 (*Montgomery* not applied to allegedly negligent legal advice by solicitors).

[67] See R Jackson, 'The professions: power, privilege and legal liability' (2015) 31(3) *Journal of Professional Negligence* 122.

real time) as well as artificial intelligence in areas as disparate as brick-laying and project cost management. Those who have the skills to develop or operate such technologies often do not come from the traditional construction professions. It is increasingly difficult to discern whether or not contracts for their services are professional engagements, so as to effect the de facto assumption of responsibility which generates *Henderson* concurrent liability in tort. It may be the erosion in practice of the distinction between professionals and contractors which, ultimately, allows the Supreme Court to retrace its steps and achieve the principled separation of contract and tort for which Jackson LJ argued.

12

Complex Structure Theory: Testing the Limits of a Builder's Liability for Economic Loss

KARIM GHALY QC

I. Introduction

In July 1994, Mr Recorder Jackson QC was tasked with reading the obiter runes scattered across four of the speeches in *Murphy v Brentwood*[1] and deciphering whether their Lordships had intended the survival of the 'complex structure' theory. Depending on one's perspective, this was either an exciting or an unenviable endeavour – stepping into the end-game of a 20-year controversy that had seen the House of Lords overrule itself.

As Mr Recorder Jackson QC observed in *Jacobs v Morton*,[2] the 'complex structure theory' is better described as the 'complex structure exception': an exception to the principle that damage to property, caused by an inherent defect in that same property, is to be categorised as economic loss[3] and therefore excluded from the scope of protection offered by the tort of negligence.

This chapter will consider the case for a 'complex structure exception'. Before doing so, it is necessary to say a little about the merits of the rule that denies negligence protection to most, but not all, categories of economic loss.

II. Background

In the decades prior to *Donoghue v Stevenson*,[4] the development of the tort of negligence had been uneven. In addition to a general concern as to the effect of

---

[1] *Murphy v Brentwood District Council* [1991] 1 AC 398.
[2] *Jacobs v Morton & Partners* (1994) 72 BLR 92.
[3] In this chapter: (i) 'economic loss' means pure economic loss, rather than economic loss consequent upon personal injury or damage to property; (ii) the 'economic torts' are not considered.
[4] *Donoghue v Stevenson* [1932] AC 562.

opening the 'floodgates' and exposing defendants to unpredictable liability, there was a particular concern that the creation of an independent tortious duty to take care would undermine the ability of commercial parties to allocate risk through contract. This concern made the courts more willing to recognise a duty where the act in issue had not been carried out pursuant to contractual obligation (eg, a road collision between strangers).

The pre-*Donoghue* concerns are illustrated by Lord Tomlin's dissenting speech, where he warns against the 'Babylonian' consequences of disregarding the contractual chain and extending the tort so that even a builder might be liable for injury caused to strangers by defective works:

> The principle contended for must be this: that the manufacturer, or indeed the repairer, of any article, apart entirely from contract, owes a duty to any person by whom the article is lawfully used to see that it has been carefully constructed. All rights in contract must be excluded from consideration of this principle; such contractual rights as may exist in successive steps from the original manufacturer down to the ultimate purchaser are ex hypothesi immaterial ...

> The principle of tort lies completely outside the region where such considerations apply, and the duty, if it exists, must extend to every person who, in lawful circumstances, uses the article made ... If such a duty exists, it seems to me it must cover the construction of every article, and I cannot see any reason why it should not apply to the construction of a house. If one step, why not fifty? Yet if a house be, as it sometimes is, negligently built, and in consequence of that negligence the ceiling falls and injures the occupier or any one else, no action against the builder exists according to the English law, although I believe such a right did exist according to the laws of Babylon.[5]

The majority did not find that the 'risks of contractual circumvention', or the opening of the 'floodgates',[6] outweighed the appellant's right to be protected from reasonably foreseeable injury or damage to property caused by a lack of reasonable care. However, Lord Atkin's 'neighbour principle' did not extend to taking reasonable care to prevent reasonably foreseeable economic loss.

The limits of *Donoghue v Stevenson*, and the 'floodgates' justification for those limits, were explained by Lord Pearce in *Hedley Byrne v Heller*:

> [T]hey were certainly not purporting to deal with such issues as, for instance, how far economic loss alone, without some physical or material damage to support it, can afford a cause of action in negligence by act ... The House in Donoghue v. Stevenson was, in fact, dealing with negligent acts causing physical damage, and the opinions cannot be read as if they were dealing with negligence in word causing economic damage. Had it been otherwise some consideration would have been given to problems peculiar to

---

[5] [1932] AC 562 at 567 to 578.

[6] [1932] AC 562 at 567 at 578, where Lord Tomlin cites the following passage of *Mullen v Barr* [1929] SC 461, 479 with approval: 'In a case like the present, where the goods of the defenders are widely distributed throughout Scotland, it would seem little short of outrageous to make them responsible to members of the public for the condition of the contents of every bottle which issues from their works. It is obvious that, if such responsibility attached to the defenders, they might be called on to meet claims of damages which they could not possibly investigate or answer.'

negligence in words. That case, therefore, can give no more help in this sphere than by affording some analogy from the broad outlook which it imposed on the law relating to physical negligence.

How wide the sphere of the duty of care in negligence is to be laid depends ultimately upon the courts' assessment of the demands of society for protection from the carelessness of others. Economic protection has lagged behind protection in physical matters where there is injury to person and property. It may be that the size and the width of the range of possible claims has acted as a deterrent to extension of economic protection.[7]

Hedley Byrne has been criticised[8] for conflating the issue of how the loss was caused (whether negligent words gave rise to liability) and the problems presented by permitting the recovery of economic loss. However, later cases[9] made clear that the principle to be taken from *Hedley Byrne* – a duty of care to avoid economic loss where there is a 'special relationship' arising from the assumption of responsibility – is as applicable to a case of negligent acts as it is to negligent words.

For the purposes of the present discussion, the importance of the *Hedley Byrne* species of negligence liability is that:

- whilst the 'floodgates' problem is clearly identified, it is not an insurmountable obstacle to liability for economic loss: the floodgates do not need to be fully opened, they can be left ajar. The classic description of the problem, in *Ultramares Corporation v Touche*,[10] is of a potential liability 'in an indeterminate amount for an indefinite time to an indeterminate class.' Of these three concerns, it is indeterminacy of amount and class that are particularly relevant to the recovery of negligently caused economic loss.[11] The requirement for an assumption of responsibility addresses indeterminacy of class and, to some extent, indeterminacy of amount.

- in contrast to the pre-*Donoghue* concern to maintain a space between the domains of tort and contract, in *Hedley Byrne* their Lordships looked to control the floodgates risk by requiring, as a pre-condition of liability for economic loss, 'a relationship equivalent to contract'.[12]

It is against this, relatively stable, background – a general duty to take care to avoid reasonably foreseeable injury or damage to property and a duty to avoid economic loss which arose only in relationships equivalent to contract – that one considers the cases that gave us the complex structure theory: the charge forward in *Dutton v Bognor Regis UDC*[13] and *Anns v Merton LBC*;[14] the retreat in

---

[7] [1964] AC 465 at 536–37.

[8] See J Stapleton, 'Duty of Care and Economic Loss: A Wider Agenda' (1991) 107 *LQR* 249.

[9] *Henderson v Merrett Syndicates Ltd* [1995] 2 AC 145; *White v Jones* [1995] 2 AC 207.

[10] *Ultramares Corporation v Touche, Niven & Co* (1931) 255 NY 170.

[11] Indeterminacy of time being equally relevant to all forms of damage that are not coincident with the breach.

[12] Per Lord Devlin at 530.

[13] *Dutton v Bognor Regis Urban District Council* [1972] 1 QB 373.

[14] *Anns v Merton London Borough Council* [1978] AC 728.

D&F Estates v The Church Commissioners[15] and *Murphy v Brentwood.*[16] The complex structure theory is a product of the inappropriate recognition of duty relationships[17] in the former cases, followed by a refusal to recognise a more appropriate set of duty relationships in the latter cases.[18]

III. *Dutton* and *Anns* – Liability Extended to the Wrong Defendant

In *Dutton*, the purchaser of a dwelling with defective foundations brought claims for diminution in value and the cost of repairs against the builder and the local authority that had, pursuant to a statutory duty, inspected and certified the property. The claim against the builder[19] was compromised prior to trial and the case proceeded against the local authority only. The Court of Appeal held:

- the local authority was liable in negligence on the *Donoghue* principle.
- the builder would also have been liable in negligence on the *Donoghue* principle.
- the loss was to be characterised as damage to property rather than economic loss (per Lord Denning MR):

    The damage done here was not solely economic loss. It was physical damage to the house. If [the council]'s submission were right, it would mean that if the inspector negligently passes the house as properly built and it collapses and injures a person, the council are liable: but if the owner discovers the defect in time to repair it – and he does repair it – the council are not liable. That is an impossible distinction. They are liable in either case.[20]

- in relation to the class of individuals to whom a duty is owed (per Lord Denning MR):

    Applying the test laid down by Lord Atkin in Donoghue v. Stevenson, I should have thought that the inspector ought to have had subsequent purchasers in mind when he was inspecting the foundations. He ought to have realised that, if he was negligent, they might suffer damage.[21]

- in relation to 'floodgates' generally (per Lord Denning MR):

    If we permit this new action, are we opening the door too much? Will it lead to a flood of cases which neither the council nor the courts will be able to handle? Such considerations have sometimes in the past led the courts to reject novel claims. But I see no need to reject this claim on this ground. The injured person will always have

---

[15] *D&F Estates v The Church Commissioners* [1989] AC 177.
[16] [1991] 1 AC 398.
[17] A point advanced with force by Ian Duncan Wallace, 'Anns Beyond Repair' (1991) 107 *LQR* 228.
[18] Above, n 17, a point advanced on a qualified basis.
[19] With whom there was no contractual relationship.
[20] [1972] 1 QB 373 at 396.
[21] At 396.

his claim against the builder. He will rarely allege – and still less be able to prove – a case against the council.[22]

Even Lord Denning acknowledged, in his later extra-judicial writing,[23] that the loss in *Dutton* had been mischaracterised as physical damage.[24] Putting characterisation of loss to one side for the moment, Lord Denning's question is powerful: why should there be a bright line between liability for personal injury, or damage to neighbouring property, caused by the collapse of a building, and liability for the economic loss involved in correcting a defect that might in time cause such injury or damage? 'Floodgates'[25] does not provide a satisfactory answer to this narrow question: not all forms of economic loss give rise to serious issues of indeterminacy of class and amount, and this narrowly-defined form of economic loss[26] is not difficult to anticipate. However, this does not automatically lead to the conclusion that it was appropriate for the Court to recognise *an inspecting authority's* duty to protect against this form of economic loss.

The error in *Dutton* was perhaps the result of poor prognostication.[27] Lord Denning's reasoning was predicated on the assumption that the case before him – a claimant proceeding against the local authority – was an anomaly. The important new class of liability that is foreseen in Lord Denning's judgment is that of the builder, to subsequent purchaser, in respect of the cost of pre-emptive repairs; claims against the inspecting authority were expected to be a rarely-used auxiliary route to the remedy. In fact, after *Dutton*, claims against local authorities became common-place – the authority was a convenient target with deep pockets. This led to a situation where the 'poacher' responsible for the defective state of a building might find that he was not pursued or, if he was, could see his liability reduced through a contribution from the 'gamekeeper'.

The problem was compounded in *Anns*, another claim against the builder and local authority in respect of defective foundations which had caused movement and cracking to walls. Again, the builder exited the proceedings early, leaving the local authority to face allegations of negligent failure to carry out an inspection or, if the inspection was made, a failure to take reasonable care to see that the relevant byelaws were observed. It is noteworthy that the local authority had a right (but no statutory duty) to inspect the foundations before they were covered up. The House of Lords held:

- that a duty was owed by the local authority:

    They are under a duty to give proper consideration to the question whether they should inspect or not …

---

[22] At 398.

[23] Lord Denning, *The Discipline of Law* (Oxford, OUP, 1979).

[24] It is difficult to believe that this was an inadvertent error.

[25] In the *Ultramares* sense (indeterminacy) rather than the sense in which Lord Denning uses the term (a high number of claims).

[26] Compare, for example, with the issues of indeterminacy that would be raised by a loss of profits claim in respect of a commercial building.

[27] Or, it might be said, interference in a complex market without the benefit of the information and consultation that would feed into an Act of Parliament.

Passing then to the duty as regards inspection, if made. On principle there must surely be a duty to exercise reasonable care. The standard of care must be related to the duty to be performed – namely to ensure compliance with the byelaws. It must be related to the fact that the person responsible for construction in accordance with the byelaws is the builder, and that the inspector's function is supervisory.[28]

- that a *Donoghue* claim could have been brought against the builder.

- in relation to economic loss, that this could not be recovered in negligence or, at least, was 'limited'.[29]

- the damage was not economic loss (per Lord Wilberforce):

  If classification is required, the relevant damage is in my opinion material, physical damage, and what is recoverable is the amount of expenditure necessary to restore the dwelling to a condition in which it is no longer a danger to the health or safety of persons occupying and possibly (depending on the circumstances) expenses arising from necessary displacement.[30]

- In relation to the class of individuals to whom a duty may be owed and 'indeterminacy' (per Lord Wilberforce):

  A right of action can only be conferred upon an owner or occupier, who is such when the damage occurs. This disposes of the possible objection that an endless, indeterminate class of potential plaintiffs may be called into existence.[31]

In addition to endorsing the *Dutton* characterisation of the cost of remedying an inherent defect *that created a danger to health or safety*, the House of Lords suggested a possible expansion of the category of recoverable loss – to include the expenses arising from the cost of vacating the dangerous building. Following the logic of *Dutton* – that the cost of remedying the defect is the cost of repairing *physical damage* – then why should the property owner not also recover the consequential economic loss caused by vacating the building?

In the period that followed *Anns*, another reason emerged for distinguishing between the liability of the builder and that of the local authority: the stretching of the principle controlling and restricting liability for remedying an inherent defect – danger to health and safety. In *Ketteman v Hansel Properties*,[32] the Court of Appeal reversed the first instance judge's ruling that a local authority was not liable for the cost of remedying defective foundations that had resulted in cracks to the walls of five houses. The judge had found that there was no imminent danger to the health or safety of the claimants. The Court of Appeal held that although there was no present danger, 'the likelihood of danger arising soon' was sufficient to

---

[28] *Anns v Merton London Borough Council* [1978] AC 728 at 755.
[29] See Lord Wilberforce's references to *SCM Ltd v WJ Whittall & Son Ltd* [1971] 1 QB 337 and *Spartan Steel & Alloys Ltd v Martin & Co Ltd* [1973] QB 727 at 752 and implicit in his discussion of the 'nature of the damages recoverable' [1978] AC 728 at 760–61.
[30] At 759.
[31] At 758.
[32] *Ketteman v Hansel Properties* [1984] 1 WLR 1274.

found liability.[33] In other cases, defects that permitted damp penetration or caused 'occasional flooding or drainage problems'[34] were sufficient to trigger liability in negligence for the cost of remedial works.

The more elastic the concept of 'danger to health and safety', the closer one comes to a transmissible non-contractual warranty of the duties created by the original building contract. The burden created by that non-contractual duty lies heavier on the shoulders of the local authority – which did not negotiate the duty, has little or no knowledge of its content and was not paid to discharge it – than on those of the builder, who, in this context, is asked to undertake a lesser responsibility (reasonable care), in respect of the same subject property, to a limited class of subsequent purchasers.

IV. 'Complex Structure Theory' or 'A Forlorn Attempt to Justify *Anns*'[35]

It is at this point that 'complex structure theory' – the wrong solution to the wrong problem – emerged in English law.[36] In *D&F Estates*,[37] the subsequent lessees of a flat constructed in the mid-1960s brought proceedings against the main contractor for the cost of repairing plasterwork that had, by 1980, begun to fall from the ceiling. The House of Lords held that the builder was not liable in negligence for the cost of repairing the plasterwork.

As Lord Bridge later noted in *Murphy*,[38] the House of Lords could not depart from the decision in *Anns* unless directly invited to do so. In *D&F Estates*, there was no inspecting local authority before the Appellate Committee, only the builder, and to the extent that Lord Wilberforce's speech in *Anns* had dealt with the common law negligence of the builder, it was obiter. Their Lordships therefore:

- addressed the *Dutton/Anns* mischaracterisation of the anticipatory cost of remedying a dangerous inherent defect as 'damage to other property'; this was now understood to be economic loss;

- being bound by *Anns*, were unable address the problem of the liability of local authorities for the anticipatory cost of remedying a defect that posed an 'imminent danger';

---

[33] Although the Court of Appeal's decision in *Ketteman* on limitation issues was later affirmed on different grounds by the House of Lords, there was no appeal on this particular point – [1987] AC 189 at 197.

[34] See Ian Duncan Wallace, 'Anns Beyond Repair' (1991) 107 *LQR* 228 at 231.

[35] Mr Recorder Jackson QC's description in *Jacobs v Morton* (1994) 72 BLR 92 at 102.

[36] It had been deployed by the German courts in the 1970s and 1980s, in answer to a slightly different problem, see further below.

[37] *D&F Estates v The Church Commissioners* [1989] AC 177.

[38] [1991] 1 AC 398 at 474.

- attempted to reconcile the finding of non-liability in the case before them with the finding of liability in *Anns* by distinguishing between 'defective foundations that caused cracking in the walls' (as in *Anns*) and 'defective plaster that had not damaged any other part of the building' (per Lord Bridge):

> Thus, if I acquire a property with a dangerously defective garden wall which is attributable to the bad workmanship of the original builder, it is difficult to see any basis in principle on which I can sustain an action in tort against the builder for the cost of either repairing or demolishing the wall. No physical damage has been caused. All that has happened is that the defect in the wall has been discovered in time to prevent damage occurring ...

> My example of the garden wall, however, is that of a very simple structure. I can see that more difficult questions may arise in relation to a more complex structure like a dwelling-house. One view would be that such a structure should be treated in law as a single indivisible unit. On this basis, if the unit becomes a potential source of danger when a hitherto hidden defect in construction manifests itself, the builder, as in the case of the garden wall, should not in principle be liable for the cost of remedying the defect ...

> However, I can see that it may well be arguable that in the case of complex structures, as indeed possibly in the case of complex chattels, one element of the structure should be regarded for the purpose of the application of the principles under discussion as distinct from another element, so that damage to one part of the structure caused by a hidden defect in another part may qualify to be treated as damage to 'other property,' and whether the argument should prevail may depend on the circumstances of the case.[39]

Per Lord Oliver:

> [T]he builder of a house or other structure is liable at common law for negligence only where actual damage, either to person or to property, results from carelessness on his part in the course of construction. That the liability should embrace damage to the defective article itself is, of course, an anomaly which distinguishes it from liability for the manufacture of a defective chattel but it can, I think, be accounted for on the basis which my noble and learned friend, Lord Bridge of Harwich, suggested, namely that, in the case of a complex structure such as a building, individual parts of the building fall to be treated as separate and distinct items of property. On that footing, damage caused to other parts of the building from, for instance, defective foundations or defective steel-work would ground an action but not damage to the defective part itself except in so far as that part caused other damage, when the damages would include the cost of repair to that part so far as necessary to remedy damage caused to other parts. Thus, to remedy cracking in walls and ceilings caused by defective foundations necessarily involves repairing or replacing the foundations themselves. But, as in the instant case, damage to plaster caused simply by defective fixing of the plaster itself would ground no cause of action apart from contract or under the Defective Premises Act 1972.[40]

---

[39] [1991] 1 AC 398 at 206.
[40] [1991] 1 AC 398 at 214.

Why shouldn't the builder be liable in this case? And if he is to be liable in certain circumstances, how does the complex structure theory assist the ascertainment of those circumstances? It is difficult to see how the attempt to reconcile the outcomes in *D&F Estates* and *Anns* was anything more than 'kicking the can down the road'. To what end is the notion that an inherent defect may, if it poses a danger, constitute physical damage replaced with the notion that a single building is to be divided into 'defective property' and 'other property'? What is the underlying legal principle or policy aim that points to this distinction?

As to the reasons why the builder should not be liable – it is noteworthy that 'floodgates', a regular feature in the cases discussed above, received no consideration in *D&F Estates*; they were not raised in argument or in their Lordships' speeches. There is no indeterminacy issue when the class of potential claimants is subsequent owners of the property and the amount is as predictable as the sums that would have been claimed by the original employer. The three justifications for denying a duty were:

- it was inappropriate for the courts to create this area of liability, which went 'much farther than the legislature were prepared to go in [the Defective Premises Act] 1972'.[41]

- consumer protection is an area of law best left to the legislators, who are better able to limit the scope of the protection.[42]

- such a duty would equate to a 'transmissible warranty of fitness'.[43]

These justifications are not very convincing:[44]

- the Law Commission report[45] annexing the draft bill that was to later become the 1972 Act, makes clear that the purpose is to provide a basic protection against the background of a developing body of common law. The Act was not intended to be definitive.

- the need to leave consumer protection to the legislature was not a bar to the creation of *Hedley Byrne* liability for economic loss or the extension of that liability in *Smith v Bush*[46] to protect purchasers of a structurally unsound house who had relied on a survey commissioned by the building society.

- *as between the builder and the subsequent purchaser*, what is the serious objection to the builder owing a lesser duty (to take reasonable care) than that specifically undertaken to the employer to a limited class of subsequent

---

[41] Per Lord Bridge at 207–08.
[42] Per Lord Bridge at 208.
[43] Per Lord Oliver at 214–15.
[44] See further the discussion in Stapleton, 'Duty of Care and Economic Loss: A Wider Agenda' (1991) 107 *LQR* 249.
[45] *Civil Liability of Vendors and Lessors for Defective Premises* (Law Com No 40) dated 15 December 1970.
[46] *Smith v Bush* [1990] AC 831.

purchasers? If the objection is the absence of contractual privity, then that argument was disposed of in *Donoghue*.

Even if one starts from the position that liability for negligence should lie against the builder for some, but not all, inherent defects, how does the complex structure theory assist in determining which builders should be liable to compensate and which building owners should be eligible for protection? Why is the builder of a complex structure more likely to be liable to compensate? Why is the owner of the freestanding wall less eligible for protection than the owner of a complex structure?

The German courts had already grappled with the concept of complex structures,[47] in the context of both product liability and real property claims. The concept proved difficult to apply and increased litigation.[48] However, the German courts persisted because it afforded a means to side-step the German Civil Code's strict prohibition on tortious liability for pure economic loss. This artifice was unnecessary in English law, there being no comparable prohibition, and particularly unnecessary in *D&F Estates*, where the concept was not required in order to decide the case. The most convincing explanation for the deployment of the concept in *D&F Estates* is as an exercise in diplomatic semantics – rationalising how a series of distinguished judges had come to describe damage to the thing itself as physical damage to property. Per Lord Oliver in *Murphy*:

> I confess that I thought that both my noble and learned friend and I had made it clear that it was a theory which was not embraced with any enthusiasm but was advanced as the only logically possible explanation of the categorisation of the damage in Anns as 'material, physical damage'.[49]

In *Murphy*, the House of Lords was given the opportunity to overrule *Anns*. The claimant had purchased a house from the builder in 1970. By 1981, cracking had appeared in the walls as a consequence of defectively designed foundations. The design of the foundations had been approved by the local authority acting pursuant to a statutory duty and in reliance on the negligent advice and calculations of independent consulting engineers. The House of Lords:

- held that the local authority was not liable in respect of the damage suffered, that damage being pure economic loss – in the process departing from *Anns*, *Dutton* and the 'imminent danger' basis for the liability of a local authority.

- distinguished the position of the local authority from that of a builder, holding that the local authority may not even owe a *Donoghue* duty to guard against personal injury.[50]

---

[47] Beginning, in the Federal Court, with *Schwimmerschelter-Fall* (1976) BGHZ 67, 359.

[48] See Fleming, 'Property Damage-Economic Loss: A Comparative View' (1989) 105 *LQR* 508 and Markesinis and Deakin (1992) 55 *MLR* 619.

[49] [1991] 1 AC 398 at 484.

[50] Per Lord Bridge at 479, Lord Oliver at 490, Lord Keith at 463.

However, the decoupling of the builder's liability from that of the local authority did not lead their Lordships to question whether the builder's duty had been needlessly constrained in *D&F Estates*; instead they took the opportunity to qualify further the circumstances in which the complex structure theory *might* provide a route to liability in negligence. Given the tone of *Murphy*, it is unsurprising that when, three years later, in *St Martins Property Corporation v Sir Robert McAlpine*,[51] the House of Lords was again required to consider the issue of builder's liability for loss caused to a subsequent purchaser by an inherent defect, they heard no argument that this loss might be recoverable in negligence, whether through the application of the complex structure theory or otherwise.

In *St Martins*, the original lessees of a mixed-use development site, together with the assignees of that leasehold interest, brought proceedings against the main contractor for the cost of remedying a defectively constructed (leaking) podium deck. The building contract had been between the original lessees and the main contractor only and had contained a prohibition on assignment of 'the contract' without written consent. The transfer of the leasehold interest took place before practical completion of the building works and was for full value; as part of the transaction, the original lessee purported to transfer the benefit of the building contract, without having obtained the consent of the contractor. The House of Lords held:

- the assignment of the benefit of the building contract had not been effective.

- it followed that the original lessees had a cause of action under the contract but had sustained no loss of their own (having transferred ownership before the relevant breach), whilst the subsequent owners had suffered damage (being the cost of remedying the defective works) but had no cause of action under the contracts.

- the original lessee was entitled to recover substantive damages on the 'narrower ground' set out in the speech of Lord Browne-Wilkinson:

> The contract was for a large development of property which, to the knowledge of both [the Employer] and McAlpine, was going to be occupied, and possibly purchased, by third parties and not by [the Employer] itself. Therefore it could be foreseen that damage caused by a breach would cause loss to a later owner and not merely to the original contracting party ... McAlpine had specifically contracted that the rights of action under the building contract could not without McAlpine's consent be transferred to third parties who became owners or occupiers and might suffer loss. In such a case, it seems to me proper, as in the case of the carriage of goods[52] by land, to treat

---

[51] *St Martins Property Corporation v Sir Robert McAlpine* [1994] 1 AC 85.

[52] Note the elusive rationale that governs when recherché carriage of goods cases are deployed in support of a general principle and when they are limited to their specific context – in this case *Dunlop v Lambert* (1839) 6 Cl & F 600, but see also the way in which *The Greystoke Castle* [1947] AC 265 is relied upon in *Hedley Byrne* (at 509 and 536) as establishing that pure economic loss was recoverable in negligence but regarded by Lord Keith in *Murphy* (at 468) as 'turning on specialties of maritime law concerned in the relationship of joint adventurers at sea.'

the parties as having entered into the contract on the footing that [the Employer] would be entitled to enforce contractual rights for the benefit of those who suffered from defective performance but who, under the terms of the contract, could not acquire any right to hold McAlpine liable for breach. It is truly a case in which the rule provides 'a remedy where no other would be available to a person sustaining loss which under a rational legal system ought to be compensated by the person who has caused it'.[53]

Setting aside the counter-intuitive conclusion that a contractual prohibition on assignment indicates a readiness to bear the burden of losses sustained by the subsequent purchaser, the facts of *St Martins* offered a weaker basis for recovery from the builder than those in *D&F Estates*, whilst the route to recovery was unnecessarily tortuous:

- The employer and subsequent purchaser were subsidiaries of the same holding company. At the point at which the property interests were transferred, there had been no breach of the building contract (practical completion being four years away). It seems inconceivable that the builder would not, at this point, have granted an assignment or collateral warranty, but it was not asked to do so. In *The Aliakmon*,[54] Lord Brandon had dismissed a 'black-hole' argument in support of a negligence claim for economic loss on the basis that the buyer could have secured alternative protection through a contractual variation. This reasoning did not feature in *D&F Estates* or *St Martins* but the availability, or otherwise, of alternative protection provides a principled basis for distinguishing between the loss sustained by a commercial party that could have obtained contractual protection but did not and a householder who had no direct relationship with the builder and could not have discovered the defect through inspection.

- A party that had suffered no loss was permitted to recover substantial damages in order to afford a remedy to the subsequent purchaser where no other remedy would be available. Although it was not discussed in *St Martins*, in *Panatown v Alfred McAlpine*,[55] the House of Lords confirmed that the damages recovered would be held on trust for the subsequent purchaser. What then, if the original contracting party does not wish to bring a claim or is no longer in existence? Why should recovery depend on this?

- Furthermore, how is a court applying the 'narrower ground' in *St Martins* to determine when a builder contracts on the footing that the Employer is entitled to enforce contractual rights for the benefit of a third party? How is the court to discern the 'black holes' that exist despite the possibility of alternative protection and to interpret the principle that a contractual prohibition on assignment points towards, not away from, third-party protection? It is difficult to see why

---

[53] [1994] 1 AC 85 at 114–15.

[54] *The Aliakmon, Leigh and Sillavan Ltd v Aliakmon Shipping Co Ltd* [1986] AC 785 at 819.

[55] *Panatown Ltd v Alfred McAlpine Construction Ltd* [2001] 1 AC 518.

this is to be preferred to the recognition of a duty, owed by the builder, to take reasonable care in the performance of its contractual duties, so as to guard against economic loss on the part of such subsequent purchasers as are unable to protect themselves by other means.

One wonders whether, if the issues of local authority liability and builder liability had come before the House of Lords in reverse order, there might now be a wider and more principled basis to hold a builder liable for economic loss resulting from an inherent defect. Having first disposed of the false analogy between the liability of the builder and the inspecting local authority (and recognised the more compelling case for builder's liability), unburdened of the need to explain how an inherent defect might be 'other property', their Lordships would have had a clear run at the right question – whether there were circumstances[56] in which a *builder* should be liable to a limited class of subsequent purchasers for pure economic loss. As it was, it is not surprising that there was little appetite in *Murphy* for a root-and-branch reconsideration of both *Anns* and *D&F Estates*. The direction of travel having been set in *D&F Estates*, there was no enthusiasm for any widening of the circumstances in which a builder might be liable, in negligence, for the cost of remedying an inherent defect.

V. What Remains of the Complex Structure Theory?

The extent to which the complex structure theory survived *Murphy* is a matter of continuing debate. In the immediate aftermath of the decision, some commentators speculated that it had not survived;[57] others took the view that, despite the scorn poured on the concept in the speeches that considered it, complex structure theory was still capable of giving rise to liability in certain cases.[58]

The relevant passages in *Murphy* were:

• Per Lord Keith:

> In *D. & F. Estates Ltd* ... Lord Bridge of Harwich and Lord Oliver of Aylmerton expressed themselves as having difficulty in reconciling the decision in *Anns* with pre-existing principle and as being uncertain as to the nature and scope of such new principle as it introduced. Lord Bridge ... suggested that in the case of a complex structure such as a building one element of the structure might be regarded for *Donoghue v. Stevenson* purposes as distinct from another element, so that damage to one part of the structure caused by a hidden defect in another part might qualify to be treated as damage to 'other property'. I think that it would be unrealistic to take

---

[56] Other than the *Hedley Byrne* type case.

[57] See the commentary by the editors of the Building Law Reports on *Jacobs v Morton* (1994) 72 BLR 92 at 94.

[58] See Ian Duncan Wallace, 'Anns Beyond Repair' (1991) 107 *LQR* 228 at 235–37; B Markesinis and S Deakin, 'The Random Element of their Lordships' Infallible Judgment: An Economic and Comparative Analysis of the Tort of Negligence from *Anns* to *Murphy*' (1992) 55 *MLR* 619 at 635–36.

this view as regards a building the whole of which had been erected and equipped by the same contractor. In that situation the whole package provided by the contractor would, in my opinion, fall to be regarded as one unit rendered unsound as such by a defect in the particular part. On the other hand where, for example, the electric wiring had been installed by a subcontractor and due to a defect caused by lack of care a fire occurred which destroyed the building, it might not be stretching ordinary principles too far to hold the electrical subcontractor liable for the damage.[59]

- Per Lord Bridge:

  The reality is that the structural elements in any building form a single indivisible unit of which the different parts are essentially interdependent. To the extent that there is any defect in one part of the structure it must to a greater or lesser degree necessarily affect all other parts of the structure. Therefore any defect in the structure is a defect in the quality of the whole and it is quite artificial, in order to impose a legal liability which the law would not otherwise impose, to treat a defect in an integral structure, so far as it weakens the structure, as a dangerous defect liable to cause damage to 'other property.'

  A critical distinction must be drawn here between some part of a complex structure which is said to be a 'danger' only because it does not perform its proper function in sustaining the other parts and some distinct item incorporated in the structure which positively malfunctions so as to inflict positive damage on the structure in which it is incorporated. Thus, if a defective central heating boiler explodes and damages a house or a defective electrical installation malfunctions and sets the house on fire, I see no reason to doubt that the owner of the house, if he can prove that the damage was due to the negligence of the boiler manufacturer in the one case or the electrical contractor on the other, can recover damages in tort on *Donoghue v. Stevenson* principles. But the position in law is entirely different where, by reason of the inadequacy of the foundations of the building to support the weight of the superstructure, differential settlement and consequent cracking occurs.[60]

- Per Lord Jauncey:

  [T]o apply the complex structure theory to a house so that each part of the entire structure is treated as a separate piece of property is quite unrealistic. A builder who builds a house from foundations upwards is creating a single integrated unit of which the individual components are interdependent. To treat the foundations as a piece of property separate from the walls or the floors is a wholly artificial exercise. If the foundations are inadequate the whole house is affected. Furthermore, if the complex structure theory is tenable there is no reason in principle why it should not also be applied to chattels consisting of integrated parts such as a ship or a piece of machinery. The consequences of such an application would be far-reaching. It seems to me that the only context for the complex structure theory in the case of a building would be where one integral component of the structure was built by a separate contractor and where a defect in such a component had caused damage to other parts of the structure, e.g. a steel frame erected by a specialist contractor which

---

[59] [1991] 1 AC 398 at 470.
[60] [1991] 1 AC 398 at 478–79.

failed to give adequate support to floors or walls. Defects in such ancillary equipment as central heating boilers or electrical installations would be subject to the normal *Donoghue v. Stevenson* principle if such defects gave rise to damage to other parts of the building.[61]

In *Jacobs v Morton*,[62] the first reported case after *Murphy* which deals with the complex structure theory, it fell to Mr Recorder Jackson QC, to distil and apply the principles to be found in the speeches cited above. The claimants in *Jacobs* had purchased a house in 1988. The year before, the defendant firm of consulting engineers had designed and supervised a scheme of foundation works to rectify and prevent cracking in the property. The remedial works were negligently designed. They failed to stop further cracking and also made the situation worse – whereas the property was previously capable of being repaired through foundation works, the insertion of a defective foundation system precluded repair through further foundation works and the property would have to be demolished.

Mr Recorder Jackson QC concluded that the consulting engineers did owe a duty to guard against the damage suffered by the claimants. In doing so, he determined that

> the complex structure theory is indeed part of English law. However, the scope of the complex structure theory is strictly limited. It is a modest exception to the general principle laid down in *Murphy* that defects in a building should generally be characterised as economic loss suffered by the building owner. This exception must not be allowed to outflank or to dwarf the general principle.[63]

As to the scope of the complex structure exception, three factors – relevant to the assessment of whether one part of a building was to be treated as 'other property', damaged by a defect – were drawn from the speeches in *Murphy*: (i) whether the defective part of the building was constructed by someone other than the main contractor; (ii) whether the defective part had retained a separate identity; and (iii) whether the defective part had positively inflicted damage or whether it had simply failed to perform its function and therefore permitted damage to occur. A fourth consideration, which had not arisen on the facts in *Murphy*, was added: whether the defective part had been constructed at a different time from the rest of the building.

Mr Recorder Jackson QC reached the commercially sensible result by the only route available after *D&F Estates*. For the reasons set out above, there was a more compelling case for the protection of the claimant here than in *St Martins*. However, below the House of Lords, the only way of achieving that result, on the facts in *Jacobs*, was through the application of complex structure exception.

---

[61] [1991] 1 AC 398 at 497.
[62] *Jacobs v Morton* (1994) 72 BLR 92.
[63] (1994) 72 BLR 92 at 102.

Even in its pared-back *Murphy* form, the complex structure theory remained problematic:

- Why should liability turn on whether the defective part was constructed by the main contractor or subcontracted out? HHJ Humphrey LLoyd QC called this distinction 'absurd' in *Samuel Payne v John Setchell*.[64] Why should recovery turn on something as arbitrary as this? Why is a subcontractor better placed to avoid the loss or make provision for it to be made good than a main contractor performing the same work?

- As to the retention of a defective part's separate identity and positive infliction of damage – how do these factors assist in distinguishing between cases when protection is justified and cases when it is not? Or between those who should bear the burden of providing compensation and those that are not required to do so?

Because these post-*Murphy* complex structure considerations lack an underlying policy rationale, they are apt to be applied inconsistently. How many of them must be present or absent for the exception to prevail? What is the relative weight to be accorded to each? The cases that followed *Jacobs* provide no answers to these questions. Similarly, the German courts' experience of trying to distinguish – based on whether the nature of the loss was identical with the defect itself[65] – between the defective accelerator pedal which causes a car crash (property damage),[66] the hydraulic jack which collapses due to a defective part (economic loss)[67] and the compressor that is damaged by reason of the lack of a supporting bracket (property damage),[68] illustrates the difficulty in finding a controlling principle that can be applied consistently.

In *Bellefield Computer Services Ltd v Turner*,[69] the complex structure was a dairy and storage area, constructed at the same time by one contractor. The compartment wall between the storage area and the dairy was defectively constructed such that it did not prevent, but should have prevented, the spread of a fire from the storage area to the rest of the dairy. At first instance, and in the Court of Appeal, the (subsequent) owner at the time of the fire, recovered damages from the builder in respect of the contents of the dairy but not the cost of remedial work to the dairy itself. Schiemann LJ's judgment is noteworthy for its attempt to find an underlying policy rationale:

> I confess that my instinctive reaction to that finding was one of unease and a desire to discover what policy considerations could lead to such a result. It seemed odd to exempt a builder for damage to the building which he had seen but fix him with liability

---

[64] *Samuel Payne v John Setchell* [2002] BLR 489.
[65] See Fleming, 'Property Damage-Economic Loss: A Comparative View' (1989) 105 *LQR* 508.
[66] *Gaszug-Fall* (1983) BGHZ 86, 256.
[67] *Hebebuhne-Fall* (1983) NJW 358.
[68] *Kompressor-Fall* (1985) NJW 2420.
[69] *Bellefield Computer Services Ltd v Turner* [2000] EWHC Admin 284, [2000] BLR 97.

for damage for the contents which he had not seen … [Counsel for the builder] was not in a position to indicate any considerations of policy which argued in favour of the judge's conclusion but submitted that that conclusion was one to which the judge rightly recognised that he was compelled to come by reason of the speeches in *Murphy v Brentwood*.[70]

There follows a mostly vain search for the policy considerations that support the decision in *Murphy*[71] and the complex structure theory, before the defeated Lord Justice offers this:

> One may wonder whether if, for instance, the present case had preceded *Murphy* the principled parts of the speeches would have been expressed differently. However, the fact is that they were not. Whilst it would perhaps be possible, without disloyalty to the principle of *stare decisis*, to hold that on facts such as the present the claimants should have a remedy, I consider that the judge was right not to depart from the guidance given in *Murphy* and the cases cited in it to the effect that where the damage is to the very building itself there should be no liability. I do not say that I would necessarily have reached that conclusion absent authority but there is no denying that, after the fullest argument, the speeches clearly point to that conclusion. In those circumstances I do not think it would be right for us to depart from the guidance there given.[72]

In *Payne v John Setchell Ltd*,[73] HHJ Humphrey LLoyd QC held that two cottages built on the same foundation slab, by the same contractor at the same time were a single indivisible unit for the purposes of the complex structure theory. The judge was unconvinced that the *Murphy* complex structure considerations were, by themselves, sufficient to support a finding that the adjoining cottage was 'other property', preferring the view that 'catastrophic damage' was also required.

In *Linklaters Business Services v Sir Robert McAlpine*,[74] the issue was whether an insulation sub-subcontractor owed a duty to the lessees of an office block to guard against pipework corrosion caused by carelessly installed insulation. Akenhead J concluded that 'the insulated chilled water pipework was essentially one "thing" for the purposes of tort. One would simply never have chilled water pipework without insulation because the chilled water would not remain chilled and it would corrode.'[75] This single factor – absence of separate identity – was sufficient to resolve the issue of whether the complex structure exception applied. But given that one would not have an office block without a water boiler – the repeatedly cited example of a component that might retain a separate identity or cause active damage – it is difficult to see the hard edges of this criterion. Little weight attached to the fact that the sub-subcontractor had not installed the pipework, and

---

[70] [2000] BLR 97 at 102.
[71] There is passing reference to their Lordships' desire not to go beyond the protection afforded by Parliament in the Defective Premises Act 1972 – considered above.
[72] [2000] BLR 97 at 104.
[73] *Payne v John Setchell Ltd* [2002] BLR 489.
[74] *Linklaters Business Services v Sir Robert McAlpine* (2010) 133 Con LR 211.
[75] (2010) 133 Con LR 211 at [119].

there was no consideration of the absence of positive damage or the relative timing of the pipe installation and insulation works. It is noteworthy that Akenhead J fortified his conclusion that the insulation contractor was not liable with a better reason than anything offered up by the complex structure theory – the availability of alternative protection. There was a network of collateral warranties going up the contractual chain but no collateral warranty had been sought from the insulation contractor.

In *Broster v Galliard Docklands*,[76] it was argued that the roof to a terrace of six townhouses, which had lifted off and then fallen back on to the top of the walls during high winds, was to be regarded as having caused property damage to the remainder of the terrace. Akenhead J was unwilling to reach a conclusion as to 'whether or not the "complex structure" theory still has a material part to play in the law of negligence relating to buildings and structures'; however, it was clear to him that it could not extend to this case. Again, the absence of separate identity – the roof being an integral component of the structure – appears to have been the decisive consideration, although it was also noted that the entire terrace had been built by one contractor. The judge further noted that this was not an 'exploding boiler'-type scenario but, in so far as that observation was a reference to the 'active damage' consideration, one might ask why the damage done to walls when a roof lifts off and then lands on them is 'passive' but the damage caused by an exploding boiler is 'active'.

Most recently, in *Robinson v PE Jones*,[77] Jackson LJ pointed to the passages in *Murphy* that discuss the complex structure theory and, noting that it had not been invoked in the case before him, resolved to 'pass over those passages in silence and not discuss whether the complex structure theory survives'. For the construction lawyer, it is to be regretted that *Robinson* did not afford an opportunity for Jackson LJ to add his insights to those of Mr Recorder Jackson QC. To the extent that the complex structure theory survives, it survives because the courts do not wish to forever part with an imperfect tool of last resort, a tool which might prove useful in the right case – as it did in *Jacobs v Morton*.

---

[76] *Broster v Galliard Docklands Ltd* [2011] BLR 569.
[77] *JA Robinson v PE Jones (Contractors) Ltd* [2011] EWCA Civ 9, [2011] 3 WLR 815 at [45].

13

All Care, No Responsibility – Limiting Liability for Negligence

MANUS McMULLAN QC

I. *Persimmon Homes Ltd v Ove Arup & Partners Ltd*[1]

It should not have been a surprise when I learnt on the first morning of the appeal in *Persimmon Homes Ltd v Ove Arup & Partners Ltd* that Lord Justice Jackson knew more about land contaminated by asbestos than any other lawyer in the courtroom. It had begun by him asking my opponent, Marcus Taverner QC, some detailed and precise questions about the history of the site and continued when he himself rattled off different contaminants that might be found in land that had had a history as a breakers yard for old railway stock. A lake had been filled in. Fuel and coal had been stored there, as well as coal tar. Dock waste, including methane and radon were present. Because locomotives had been scrapped, there were heavy metals, not just asbestos. Lord Justice Jackson's questions showed that he was clearly familiar with all the practical issues which arose from dealing with such a site and what might be expected.

When I had appeared in front of him on other cases he had often shown a keen interest in the location where projects where based. I vividly remember explaining the orientation of a photograph which showed the Mourne Mountains in the background when doing a case about a harbour in Ireland. He wanted to understand, in detail, what he was seeing in context. The mountains had formed the backdrop of my teenage years and in those days I could never have imagined explaining them to a High Court judge in London.

But this was different. He clearly had a knowledge of asbestos and land contamination that was deeper than could be gleaned from the papers before the Court of Appeal. Sensing that those appearing before him were a little surprised by the depth of his questions and knowledge, he explained that he had spent many months fighting a case about contaminated land and remembered the issues well and was still interested.

---

[1] *Persimmon Homes Ltd v Ove Arup & Partners Ltd* [2017] EWCA Civ 373.

These episodes captured two of the qualities in Lord Justice Jackson for which he is so well regarded – a genuine interest in matters and a formidable memory.

The claim in *Persimmon* arose out of the redevelopment of a site in Barry, South Wales, known as Barry Waterfront. From the early 1990s until 2007, Arup was from time to time involved with the site, acting as a consultant for Associated British Ports (ABP), which was the owner at that time. Arup had acted pursuant to an agreement with ABP entered into in 1996. Arup's advice to ABP concerned the regeneration of the site and included clearance, reclamation, decontamination, earthworks and the provision of infrastructure. It was a large site with a long history. Over that period of time, and beyond, the authorities' understanding of environmental issues had changed, and the regulation of such issues had changed with it.

In late 2006, ABP invited bids for purchase of the site. The claimants, all house building companies, decided to join together to acquire the site and, in January 2007, engaged a different team within Arup to provide consultancy services. A consortium of house builders purchased the site in September 2007 for over £50 million.

For a while Arup continued to provide consultancy services for the consortium following the purchase and on 22 September 2009, following negotiations, the parties entered into a detailed written consultancy appointment, referred to in the proceedings as 'the Agreement'. The Agreement was retrospective in nature but one of the questions in the case had been whether the Agreement covered Arup's work for the consortium pre-purchase of the site. It was held at first instance that it did not.

Having negotiated the Agreement with Arup to cover the work that it had done on the Development, in December 2009 the consortium advised Arup that the detailed remediation design for the site was to be put out to tender. The tender was awarded to Healers and its sub-consultant, ESP. Arup did not, therefore, provide any detailed design services to the consortium.

In 2010, Arup entered into a collateral warranty with each of the three consortium members (the Warranties). In essence, these warranted to the consortium that Arup had exercised reasonable care and skill in relation to the services that Arup had historically provided for ABP regarding the site and contained the same relevant wording in terms of its liabilities.

On 10 July 2012 the consortium's ground works contractor, Cuddy, encountered asbestos on site. It was this discovery that led to the claim. The consortium made a case alleging that Arup had failed to advise it correctly in relation to this asbestos.

When proceedings commenced Arup felt strongly that they had done nothing wrong. They had engineers who had done fine work and were happy to discuss it in detail. But given the long history of the site and the many issues raised (the Particulars of Claim were 87 pages long) they knew that proceedings would be long and expensive. They therefore suggested preliminary issues in order to resolve matters quickly and cost effectively. The preliminary issues were to be based on assumed facts, with no acceptance of responsibility. The consortium agreed and the Technology and Construction Court approved of this approach.

At the heart of the preliminary issues was the question of whether all of the claims made by the consortium against Arup could be made at all. The claims all centred on the fact that asbestos had been found on the site. There was an exclusion clause in the Agreement (with similar wording in the Warranties):

> The Consultant's aggregate liability under this Agreement whether in contract, tort (including negligence), for breach of statutory duty or otherwise (other than for death or personal injury caused by the Consultant's negligence) shall be limited to £12,000,000 (twelve million pounds) with liability for pollution and contamination limited to £5,000,000 (five million pounds) in aggregate. Liability for any claim in relation to asbestos is excluded.

After a first instance preliminary issues trial, Mr Justice Stuart-Smith held that none of the claims made by the consortium which alleged a failure under the Agreement could be progressed.[2] It was on this issue that the consortium appealed.

Marcus Taverner QC, for the consortium leading Tom Owen, had come up with an ingenious argument – set out at paragraph 44 of the Court of Appeal judgment:

> I turn now to the second limb. The claimants' case is neatly distilled in paragraphs 47 and 48 of their skeleton argument as follows:
>
> '47 … the word "for" has a causative connotation such that it means "for" in the sense of meaning "for causing". It is not a matter of adding words, it is simply a matter of construing the meaning of the word "for" in its context.
>
> 48. In contrast, a liability consequent upon a failure properly to advise about a pre-existing, in-situ state of contamination or pollution is not a liability "for" pollution, or contamination but for failing to advise about a state of affairs.'

Mr Taverner's argument was that the exclusion clause was effective in preventing Arup from being liable if it spread asbestos, but was not effective in preventing liability if Arup failed to advise properly. This argument had been good enough for the consortium to be successful in its written application for permission to appeal, by no one less than Lord Justice Jackson himself. So when we found ourselves before the same Lord Justice Jackson, I was unsure which way the wind was blowing.

The way in which his argument had sought to find something for the exclusion clause to exclude, while at the same time making sure the consortium's claims would survive, was typical of the astute approach Mr Taverner is known for.

An important part of Arup's case was to put exclusion clauses in the context of modern professional services contracts. Paragraphs 56 to 58 of the judgment set out some of that argument. Whereas historically there has been hostility toward

---

[2] *Persimmon Homes Ltd v Ove Arup & Partners Ltd* [2015] EWHC 3573 (TCC).

exclusion clauses, not least because in some cases they were manifestly unreasonable, a number of cases record that the passing of the Unfair Contract Terms Act in 1977 was a watershed moment. It meant that unreasonable clauses could be struck down in certain circumstances. It also meant that reasonable exclusion clauses might be left alone.

There can be no doubt that commercial contracts, including professional appointments, have become much more sophisticated than they were in 1977. Whereas traditional procurement saw the employer engaging a designer then going out to tender on that design for a fixed price, there are now multifarious methods of procurement used. There are even standard forms for all these different procurement methods. Management contracting, construction management, design and build are all methods of procurement that have moved on hugely in the last 40 years. There are many different forms of contracting which the industry has become used to.

With the growth of the different types of procurement and contracting a more sophisticated approach has also been taken to the allocation of risk, limitation of liability and exclusion of liability. This allows innovation and permits deals to be done on mutually acceptable terms that might not have been possible if the allocation of risk, limitation of liability or exclusion of liability were not possible. A number of recent cases have said that the courts should not upset the allocation of risk agreed between parties. A contract might be seen as a package of rights and responsibilities, intrinsic to which is the allocation of risk, limitation of liability and exclusion of liability. If one looks at the limitations of liability only, or the exclusions of liability only, one upsets the balance of the agreement which the parties have freely reached. Rather than being regarded with hostility, this type of approach is now regarded as good or even best practice, as with it the parties know where they stand.

The greater context is that English law places a very high value on freedom to contract and certainty in its list of priorities. Indeed, English law is regarded as extremely suitable for commerce because of these characteristics. It is therefore popular as a choice of law internationally.

More generally, the interpretation of contracts has been the subject of great judicial interest in the same period. There has been a modernisation of approach and a number of older authorities on interpretation are regarded as guidance rather than rules and must be seen in their time and context. Courts no longer approach exclusion clauses strictly. There is no longer a policy reason, or indeed any other reason, to do so. The courts interpret contracts as they are written. So, today the law reports provide ample examples of courts enforcing exclusion clauses which have been agreed between the parties. The cases suggest that one should not begin with a pre-conceived destination and work backwards. Instead one interprets the clauses by seeking to find the common intention of the parties at the time, as reflected in their written agreement. As noted in *Arnold v Britton*,[3] context and

---

[3] *Arnold v Britton* [2015] UKSC 36.

common sense are important principles in the interpretation of contractual provisions, but the starting point, and often the finishing point, is the ordinary meaning of the words used.

Arup argued that the courts should not strain to find distinctions or nuances where they do not exist. Where the language used is clear, as it was in their agreement, it is not necessary to try to contextualise or interpret it other than by its language. The latin maxim *'in claris non fit interpretatio'* is apposite: Where it is clear, no interpretation is needed. Extra-textual or interpretative criteria need not be employed. This was Arup's argument on the correct approach, which ultimately was preferred.

To deal with the consortium's case, Arup had to then show how this approach worked in practice, by dealing with the argument that 'liability for asbestos' meant 'liability for causing asbestos'. There were six main arguments.

(1) Neither the clause in the Agreement nor in the Warranties make the distinction that the consortium were arguing for. The clause says: 'Liability for any claim in relation to asbestos is excluded'. The clause does not talk about spreading asbestos or not spreading asbestos. It is much wider. In fact, the whole concept of 'causing' asbestos on a site which has asbestos on it already is a difficult one.

(2) The consortium's argument that the word 'for' means 'causing' did not fit in the sentence. Furthermore, the consortium were then morphing 'causing' into 'spreading'.

(3) The consortium's argument made a distinction between negligence which leads to the spreading of asbestos and negligence which does not involve spreading asbestos. But if an engineer fails to deal with a problem on site that his design should take into account, isn't that causing contamination by asbestos? Couldn't the claim simply be reframed in that way?

(4) The distinction being sought was contrary to business common sense. It led to a false and arbitrary distinction. Negligence that leaves asbestos in place may be much worse than negligence that spreads the asbestos to another part of the site where it is unlikely to be a problem. Why would the consortium (or anyone else) regard one as worthy of exclusion and one not worthy of exclusion?

(5) The distinction sought by the consortium was impractical in practice and ignored Arup's scope of work. Rather than being straightforward and clear, as the clause is, it was likely to lead to further arguments as to whether the situation was in fact covered by the exclusion. If there were asbestos on a site, does an engineer 'cause asbestos' by moving it from one location to another? If there is a housing development and the asbestos is moved from one end to the other does this 'cause' asbestos? If there is a larger development, a retail store and a residential part, and asbestos is moved from one part (retail) to the other (residential), is this 'causing' asbestos? It was difficult to see how this would work in practice.

(6)   The approach by the consortium ignored how professional indemnity insurance works. A professional does not obtain insurance with coverage depending upon whether its advice involves omission or commission. It is difficult to see how a professional would be in a better position having agreed this exclusion given the various issues with how it would in fact work.

The judgment ultimately accepted many of these arguments. It dealt with it in this way:

> 48. Having reviewed the skeleton arguments and oral submissions of counsel, I am satisfied that Arup's interpretation of limbs 2 and 3 is correct. I reach this conclusion for four reasons:
>
> (i)   Arup's interpretation accords with the natural meaning of the words used.
> (ii) If 'for' means 'for causing' as Mr Taverner submits, the last sentence of the exemption clauses becomes bizarre, if not ungrammatical. One cannot sensibly read that sentence as saying: 'Liability for causing any claim in relation to asbestos is excluded'.
> (iii) As Mr McMullan submits, it would be nonsensical for the parties to agree that Arup are not liable if asbestos is moved from one part of the site to another, but are liable if it is left in place.
> (iv) Clause 6 of the 2009 agreement and clause 4 of the individual warranties set out the professional indemnity insurance which Arup were required to obtain for the Barry Quays project. Clause 6.3 of the 2009 agreement and clause 4.3 of the warranties were clearly intended to limit Arup's liability to the extent of the insurance cover. In that context it is absurd to read limbs 2 and 3 of the exemption clauses as confined to claims for moving contamination from one place to another.

In dealing with the case Lord Justice Jackson was at all times courteous and kind (which had been my experience every time I appeared before him). He asked questions but when he was satisfied he understood what was being said he patiently listened without interrupting. It is a great boon for parties, and their advocates, to have a judge who will act in this way, making sure he has understood the case but at the same time allowing the argument to develop.

One argument which Lord Justice Jackson was obviously interested in was the consortium's argument that the exclusion clause did not exclude negligence, because it did not specifically say that it excluded negligence. The *Canada Steamship* case[4] was relied upon as authority for this proposition. The consortium's skeleton argument put the case this way:

(1)   The judge at first instance had failed to apply *Canada Steamship* guidelines properly or at all.

(2)   The words 'Liability for any claim in relation to asbestos is excluded' were not wide enough, in their ordinary meaning, to cover negligence. There is no reference, for example, to liability 'howsoever arising'.

---

[4] *Canada Steamship Lines v The King* [1952] AC 192.

(3) Even if there were a doubt as to whether the words were wide enough to cover negligence, it must be resolved against the *proferens* (Arup).

(4) If liability for negligence is sought to be excluded, the clause must do so in the clearest of terms or by necessary implication – *Canada Steamship* and other authorities since then.

(5) The rationale for the guidelines is that clear words are needed to exclude liability for negligence as it is inherently improbable that one party one agreed to assume responsibility for the consequences of the other's negligence.

When this argument was raised, Lord Justice Jackson asked both sides whether they were of the view that the *Canada Steamship* guidelines were more suited to indemnity clauses than to exemption clauses, and indeed, this found its way into the judgment.

> 55. Over the last 66 years there has been a long-running debate about the effect of that passage [the *Canada Steamship* guidelines] and the extent to which it is still good law. In hindsight we can see that it is not satisfactory to deal with exemption clauses and indemnity clauses in one single compendious passage. It is one thing to agree that A is not liable to B for the consequences of A's negligence. It is quite another thing to agree that B must compensate A for the consequences of A's own negligence.

Ultimately the Court was of the view that the *Canada Steamship* guidelines were of little relevance in interpreting the particular clauses in question, but held that even if they applied, the words were clear enough to cover negligence.[5]

II. *Greenwich Millennium Village Ltd v Essex Services Group Plc*[6]

The same guidelines were rather more central in the case of *Greenwich Millennium Village Ltd v Essex Services Group Plc*. The principal issue in the appeal was whether the respondent's negligent failure to detect workmanship defects precluded recovery under an indemnity clause. Did the guidelines mean the indemnity would not bite where the claimant had been negligent?

The claimant employed a contractor to construct a block of flats. The contractor engaged a subcontractor to do the mechanical works. The subcontractor engaged a sub-subcontractor, which in turn engaged a sub-sub-subcontractor, to do those works. As a result of workmanship defects which the sub-sub-subcontractor negligently failed to notice, the claimant suffered significant losses.

This contractual chain is not unusual in construction projects, and was relevant to how the Court of Appeal approached matters. Putting it in context, the sub-sub-subcontractor (the party at the end of the contractual chain) had

---

[5] [2017] EWCA Civ 373 at [59]–[60].
[6] *Greenwich Millennium Village Ltd v Essex Services Group Plc* [2014] EWCA Civ 960.

installed anti-surge arrestors at the top of major risers in blocks of residential flats. Unfortunately, below that it had installed a non-return valve and an isolation valve which it left in a closed position. This had the effect of nullifying the arrestor so that when a surge did occur in the riser the arrestor did not work and there was a serious 'water hammer' event which caused a flood. The party claiming against it had negligently failed to notice its defective workmanship.

The indemnity clause in question was worded thus:

> The Subcontractor hereby agrees to indemnify HS Environmental Services Ltd against each and every liability which HS Environmental Services Ltd may incur to any other person or persons and further to indemnify HS Environmental Services Ltd in respect of any liability, loss, claim or proceedings of whatsoever nature such as shall arise by virtue of the breach or breaches of this Subcontract Agreement by, or act, default or negligence of the Subcontractor.

The appellant in *Greenwich* had reason to believe that it had good prospects on appeal. A number of authorities supported its proposition that where a party was negligent it could not have the benefit of an indemnity clause, unless that clause expressly said that it applied even in situations of negligence. At paragraphs 67 and 68 of the judgment, Lord Justice Jackson set out the *Canada Steamship* guidelines.

> 67. Lord Morton of Henryton cited with approval the guidance on the interpretation of exemption clauses, which Lord Greene MR gave in *Alderslade v Hendon Laundry Ltd* [1945] KB 189 at 192. He then stated the principles as follows at [1952] AC 192 at 208:
>
>> '(1) If the clause contains language which expressly exempts the person in whose favour it is made (hereafter called "the *proferens*") from the consequence of the negligence of his own servants, effect must be given to that provision … (2) If there is no express reference to negligence, the court must consider whether the words used are wide enough, in their ordinary meaning, to cover negligence on the part of the servants of the *proferens*. If a doubt arises at this point, it must be resolved against the *proferens* … (3) If the words used are wide enough for the above purpose, the court must then consider whether "the head of damage may be based on some ground other than that of negligence" to quote again Lord Greene MR in the *Alderslade* case. The "other ground" must not be so fanciful or remote that the *proferens* cannot be supposed to have desired protection against it, but, subject to this qualification, which is, no doubt, to be implied from Lord Greene's words, the existence of a possible head of damage other than that of negligence is fatal to the *proferens* even if the words used are, *prima facie*, wide enough to cover negligence on the part of his servants.'
>
> 68. I shall refer to this formulation as 'the *Canada Steamship* principle'. The Privy Council applied this principle to the construction of clause 7, which was an exemption clause. The Privy Council adopted a broadly similar approach to clause 17, which was an indemnity clause. In a number of subsequent cases concerned with the operation of indemnity clauses the courts have held that the *Canada Steamship* principle applies to indemnity clauses as well as exemption clauses. Lord Fraser confirmed this

in *Smith v South Wales Switchgear Co Ltd* [1978] 1 WLR 165 at 172. Lord Wilberforce and Lord Salmon agreed with Lord Fraser.

Lord Justice Jackson then considered a number of authorities and agreed with counsel for the appellant that the *Canada Steamship* guidelines were of general application and had been applied in a number of cases involving shipping contracts. But the Court was more interested in how the specific clause in question worked in the particular industry. As noted at paragraphs 86 and 87 of the judgment, most building projects involve chains of contracts in which entitlement to be paid and liability for non-performance pass up or down the line. The basic intention is that each party in the chain should be paid for the work it does and should be responsible for the shortcomings in its own work. If a subcontractor is responsible for defective workmanship, contractors higher up the chain can often be criticised for failing to notice the mistakes. But it would largely defeat the commercial purpose of the contractual chain if a failure to notice something prevented indemnity clauses from operating. The participants in building projects arrange their affairs and take out insurance on the basis that they will be held liable for shortcomings in their own work.

The judge went on to cite *Hudson's Building and Engineering Contracts*, which noted that there were no English cases which had attempted to distinguish between categories of indemnitee negligence which, on a basis of presumed intention, might be regarded as not invalidating an indemnity. The Court then noted that while in most situations it is so unlikely that one man would agree to indemnify another man for the consequences of that other's own negligence, that was not the case here. In a chain of building contracts, it was held, it is not inherently unlikely that each party will agree to be liable for shortcomings in its own work, even if superior parties in the chain fail to detect those shortcomings.

In his inimitable style, the judgment stated:

> 94. Let me now draw the threads together. In my view the rule of construction stated in *Canada Steamship* and *Walters v Whessoe* is of general application. Nevertheless it is based upon the presumed intention of the parties. In applying that rule the court must have regard to the commercial context of the contract under consideration. In the case of a construction contract a failure by the indemnitee to spot defects perpetrated by its contractor or sub-contractor should not ordinarily defeat the operation of an indemnity clause, even if that clause fails expressly to encompass damage caused by the negligence of the indemnitee.

Lord Justice Jackson also said that it could not be presumed that the parties intended to confine the indemnity to workmanship breaches which were invisible upon reasonable inspection: 'The clause does not say that. No-one other than an enthusiastic reader of the law reports would think of construing it in that way.'

This was a departure from how the *Canada Steamship* principles had been thought to apply. But in this particular case there was a breach of contract by the sub-sub-contractor and it is not clear that the indemnity clause was adding much. In other words, if the sub-subcontractor had simply been sued for breach it would have been liable for the same result.

For both the *Greenwich* and *Persimmon* cases one can see that while in the past the courts have laid down certain principles of general application, whether an exclusion clause covers negligence or whether an indemnity clause is undermined by the negligence of the party relying upon it ultimately turns on the interpretation of the contract in question, in its proper context, rather than a general rule. The criticism of this would be that it introduces uncertainty. But the benefit is that for each case the appropriate result is found. The reasoning in each case is impeccable.

It might be argued that both *Greenwich* and *Persimmon* allow professionals who have made mistakes and fallen below an acceptable standard of care to wrongly escape liability. But that is not what should be taken from the cases. The sanctity of contract is a cornerstone of English law, and indeed of almost all common law and civil law systems. The doctrine of *pacta sunt servanda* was important in Roman law and is recognised today as a principle of international law. What both cases show is that the parties are able to agree what should happen when something goes wrong. Such agreements can even include provision that a party making a mistake does not bear the cost of any such mistake. Provided the parties understand this and what they are doing, in English law there is no public policy to prevent it.

The cases point out that there is much to recommend this approach. Construction and engineering projects are often technically complex. There are many risks. Some are known but others are unknown (and known to be unknown). In appropriate cases, it can make good sense for the parties to agree in advance what is going to happen if things go wrong, and to agree where losses should lie. Indeed, some would argue that this is not only acceptable but also desirable, as the parties can plan when they know what the position is, but otherwise are in a state of uncertainty. Parties can then make arrangements for insurance or seek assistance from other parties who will bear the responsibility. Even with written contracts there will of course often be arguments about precisely what an agreement means and it is important to interpret each contract in its own context. But one possibility can be that particular losses, even if contributed to by one party, are not to its account.

14

Good Neighbours?

PHILIP BRITTON[1]

I. Introduction

When a 'neighbour dispute' erupts into litigation, the trigger is often construction activity – the area with which a key part of Jackson LJ's career as advocate and judge is specially associated. Many of the landmark cases concerning claimants' rights in (or deriving from) land and the protection the law offers for those rights have come out of situations where a neighbour has attempted to stop construction activity, or to get after-the-event compensation for disruption caused by a project close by.[2] When this occurs, two specific aspects of the law of tort which focus directly on land are potentially in the frame: protection for the physical integrity of land (trespass); and for the amenity (enjoyment) of occupation of land (private nuisance). Both have evolved over centuries within the common law, with almost no intervention from statute.[3] Of the three recent 'trouble with the neighbours' cases where these torts were involved and in which Jackson LJ gave judgment in the Court of Appeal (Civil Division) – in each case, the leading or only judgment – two directly concerned construction; but none started in construction cases' natural home, the Technology and Construction Court.

The earliest of the three, *Coventry v Lawrence* from 2012, concerned an attempt by householders to impose controls on noisy operations at a car racing,

---

[1] Philip Britton LLB BCL is a former Visiting Professor and Director, Centre of Construction Law & Dispute Resolution, Dickson Poon School of Law, King's College London; also Senior Fellow, Melbourne Law School; e-mail *philip@linden60.co.uk*.

[2] Attempting to stop crane jibs from oversailing (trespassing into the claimant's airspace): *Anchor Brewhouse Developments Ltd v Berkley House (Docklands Developments) Ltd* (1987) 38 BLR 82 (Ch); and damages for noise and dust while a project was underway (private nuisance): *Hunter v Canary Wharf Ltd, Hunter v London Docklands Development Corporation* [1997] AC 655, [1997] 2 WLR 684, [1997] 2 All ER 426 (HL).

[3] For the competing views about the evolution of the law of private nuisance in the Industrial Revolution and its remedies, see Ben Pontin, 'Nuisance Law and the Industrial Revolution: A Reinterpretation of Doctrine and Institutional Competence' (2012) 75 *MLR* 1010. Private nuisance has, at least in English law, a special sub-category of liability under *Rylands v Fletcher* for 'escapes' from the defendant's land which cause damage to or on the claimant's land. Since none of the cases in this chapter included such a claim, or one founded in negligence, neither is discussed further here.

speedway and motocross facility close to their home.[4] It is the only one where judgment was reserved, as well as the only one published more widely than online. It eventually gave the Supreme Court the opportunity to reshape many aspects of the law of private nuisance, so the debates have clear relevance to relations between a construction project, its parties and those living or working in the locality.

The second and third cases were more narrowly domestic: in *Yeung v Potel*, the dispute was between the long leaseholders of two flats, one above the other, about remodelling work which one lessee wanted to do and its impact on the other;[5] in *Rashid v Sharif*, two neighbouring families were at loggerheads over the positioning of the new shed which one of them had built at the far end of their garden.[6] In each case, there were issues of legal rights, powers and duties (in *Yeung v Potel*, this meant a close look at the terms of the relevant leases). Questions of the appropriate remedy loomed equally large, with issues of the proper exercise of judicial discretion and (if damages were to be awarded) on what basis.

As would be expected of any Jackson judgment, the three cases in this chapter show his clearly structured and meticulous approach, pithily summarising the background to the litigation and its earlier stages, going on to state and analyse the issues at stake and finally laying out steps towards the outcome on the merits. This trio of judgments also demonstrates his willingness to engage both with the detail of 'authority' and with broader questions of principle or policy.

II. Motor Sports, Noise and Nuisance:
Coventry v Lawrence

A. Background

In 2006, the two claimants in this tort action (a fireman and a management consultant) bought and moved into 'Fenland', an aptly named bungalow on Cook's Drove, in the low-lying flat, open land in the northwest corner of Suffolk, in the river system of the Great Ouse, which empties north into The Wash. Less than a kilometre southeast of 'Fenland' is Mildenhall Stadium, a venue first established in 1975 for speedway racing. Stock-car and 'banger' racing were added in 1984; motocross started in 1992 on a new track south of the stadium.[7] Soon after the two claimants arrived, they put pressure on the local Council to enforce existing

---

[4] *Coventry (t/a RDC Promotions) v Lawrence* [2012] EWCA Civ 26, [2012] 1 WLR 2127, [2012] Env LR 28, [2012] 3 All ER 168, 141 Con LR 79.

[5] *Yeung v Potel* [2014] EWCA Civ 481.

[6] *Rashid v Sharif* [2014] EWCA Civ 377.

[7] Estimates of the distance between the house and stadium vary, though all sources agree that it is more than 500m and less than 1km, the track being further away from 'Fenland' than the stadium.

noise restrictions on the stadium and track; abatement notices followed. Still finding the situation unacceptable, in 2009 they started civil legal action.

The basis of their case was simple: noise created by events at the stadium and track constituted an actionable nuisance, for which the appropriate remedies would be an award of damages (for the past) and an injunction (for the future).[8] They had six original target defendants, all owners or operators in different capacities of the stadium or adjoining motocross track. However, the relevant law – derived from centuries of case law, but now overlaid with the public law of planning and environmental protection – turned out to be far from straightforward. Nor was it obvious how to apply it to the facts, or what remedies could (or should) be available.

B. At First Instance

The case originated in the Queen's Bench Division, where Richard Seymour QC, formerly a TCC judge, heard the case as a High Court judge.[9] After an 11-day hearing, he concluded at the end of a long reserved judgment – 300+ paragraphs – that the noise impact on the claimants' occupation of their home made the activities at the stadium and track tortious; and that to have regularly generated noise over many years (in line with planning conditions, but occasionally in conflict with environmental regulation) could, in law, give the defendants no prescriptive right to continue with these operations. Nor was the defendants' planning position – which included Certificates of Lawful Use from the local planning authority and precise conditions on the number and timing of motocross events, with a limit on the perceived noise at the boundary of the track – relevant to the claimants' rights.

By way of remedy, Judge Seymour refused the claimants' request for aggravated and exemplary damages, instead awarding 'ordinary' (compensatory) damages of £20,850 for the past injury to the amenity of living at 'Fenland', assessed in the light of expert valuation evidence and apportioned between three of the defendants. After further representations, he imposed an injunction with effect from 1 January 2012. This would (a) limit the frequency of activities at the stadium and track; and (b) impose a maximum perceived noise level at 'Fenland' for those activities.[10]

---

[8] Since 1992 the stadium has also housed greyhound racing and occasional exhibitions and circuses. Unsurprisingly, these relatively quiet activities played no part in the litigation.

[9] *Lawrence v Fen Tigers Ltd* [2011] EWHC 360 (QB), [2011] 4 All ER 1191 (Note); for a pre-trial application before Edwards-Stuart J on the exemplary damages claims, see *Lawrence v Fen Tigers Ltd* [2010] EWHC 2449 (QB).

[10] For the details of the injunction, see the Court of Appeal judgment (n 4 above) [42]. The defendants in the Queen's Bench Division did not argue that damages should have been the proper remedy for the future, but were permitted to make the case for this after the first Supreme Court judgment: see text to nn 35–36 below.

The house had in fact become uninhabitable in 2010 following criminal damage to an oil storage tank, which flooded the building with heating oil, and then an arson attack, for which the claimants originally sought to pin responsibility on some of the defendants in court. The house remained a derelict shell while litigation was underway. As a result, the injunction imposed by Judge Seymour did not take effect as intended, though in the light of the claimants' ultimate success in the Supreme Court, they could ask the court to revive it once living in the house again.

C. In the Court of Appeal

Two of the three defendants against whom Judge Seymour gave judgment (the Coventry brothers, who owned the stadium, and Moto-Land, the company which had a lease of the track) then appealed to the Court of Appeal, challenging his findings on liability.[11] The key issues raised by the appellants were three:

1   Did the planning position mean that activities at the stadium and track which might otherwise have constituted a nuisance at common law were no longer so?

2   If these activities were potentially actionable as a nuisance, could the two respondents still complain, having arrived at 'Fenland' with the nuisance already in existence?; and

3   Could the appellants acquire a prescriptive right to commit such a nuisance? And if they could, had they done so?

The claimants (now respondents) sought to uphold Judge Seymour's findings, as well as to overturn his dismissal of their action against two other defendants who were merely landlords of the stadium or track.[12] Alongside Jackson LJ at the three-day hearing sat Lewison and Mummery LJJ. Both concurred with Jackson LJ's eight-part judgment, which occupied the lion's share of the law report, Lewison LJ adding a few paragraphs on Issue 3.

Explaining his approach, Jackson LJ noted that, if the planning position meant that there was no nuisance at common law (Issue 1), the appellants' other two issues would fall away. No surprise, then, that a summary of the planning history of the stadium and track formed Part 1 of his judgment; Part 5 looked at existing case law on the interaction between the public law of planning and

---

[11] The case changed its name on appeal, as the original lead defendant, Fen Tigers Ltd, dropped out upon going into liquidation in 2010.

[12] A landlord's liability for nuisance committed by a tenant is discussed in the second Supreme Court judgment (n 17 below); see also Ian Loveland, 'Landowner and Landlord Liability for the Nuisance-Causing Actions of Third Parties on the Landowner/Landlord's Land: an analysis of *Brumby v Octavia Housing*' [2013] *Journal of Planning and Environment Law* 5.

the private law protections for land occupation offered by the tort of private nuisance.[13] Opening this discussion, he said:

> The first point to note is that the planning system exists to protect the public interest, not to protect private interests … Nevertheless both grants and refusals of planning permission impact upon private interests, sometimes to a substantial extent. Grants of planning permission, when implemented, may result in the character of an area being changed, with consequential effects upon private rights.[14]

Such a change would vary the baseline against which negative impacts on individuals' amenity were to be tested for their actionability in tort. Here is his further summary:

> i) A planning authority by the grant of planning permission cannot authorise the commission of a nuisance.

> ii) Nevertheless the grant of planning permission followed by the implementation of such permission may change the character of a locality.

> iii) It is a question of fact in every case whether the grant of planning permission followed by steps to implement such permission do have the effect of changing the character of the locality.

> (iv) If the character of a locality is changed as a consequence of planning permission having been granted and implemented, then:

> a) the question whether particular activities in that locality constitute a nuisance must be decided against the background of its changed character;

> b) one consequence may be that otherwise offensive activities in that locality cease to constitute a nuisance.[15]

But how should these principles apply in this case? In Part 6 of his judgment, Jackson LJ differed from Judge Seymour, holding that the pattern of activities at the stadium and track, consistent with the planning conditions in force, had in fact changed the character of the locality. This raised the threshold above which noise would become actionable, so the first-instance judge was in error in finding a nuisance at common law:

> In January 2006, when the claimants purchased Fenland, the position was this. For the last thirteen years various forms of motor sports had been taking place at the Stadium and the Track on numerous occasions throughout the year. These noisy activities,

---

[13] Notably *Gillingham Borough Council v Medway (Chatham) Dock Co Ltd* [1993] QB 343 (QB); *Hirose Electrical UK Ltd v Peak Ingredients Ltd* [2011] EWCA Civ 987, [2011] Env LR 34; *Wheeler v JJ Saunders Ltd* [1996] Ch 19 (CA); and *Watson v Croft Promosport Ltd* [2009] EWCA Civ 15, [2009] 3 All ER 249. All are also discussed at length in Lord Carnwath's judgment in *Coventry v Lawrence (No 1)* (n 17 below) [191]–[216]. For a critical analysis of this aspect of the Court of Appeal judgment, see Maria Lee, 'Nuisance and Regulation in the Court of Appeal' [2013] *Journal of Planning and Environment Law* 277.

[14] *Coventry v Lawrence* (n 4 above) [26].

[15] *Coventry v Lawrence* (n 4 above) [65].

regarded by some as recreation and by others as an unwelcome disturbance, were an established feature, indeed a dominant feature, of the locality.[16]

But for an argument from the respondents' counsel that the case should be remitted back to the trial judge, elegantly and persuasively rejected in Part 7 of the judgment, the outcome of the appeal was then clear: the appellants were to succeed on the merits and the respondents' cross-appeal must fail.

That was, however, not the end of the story. It might have been possible to imagine a negotiated solution acceptable to both sides (for example, the stadium and track owners or operators buying out the two respondents, or agreeing levels of activity and/or emitted noise lower than those already in force); evidently, no such 'deal' emerged. The owners of 'Fenland' therefore appealed to the Supreme Court, where all three issues in the first appeal resurfaced, Issues 2 and 3 not being substantively discussed in Jackson LJ's judgment in the court below.[17]

D. In the Supreme Court

In the light of the approach the Supreme Court judges took to these three issues, the shape of the whole dispute changed significantly. Lord Neuberger, second President of the Court and with a Chancery background, gave the leading and longest judgment (150+ paragraphs), the key conclusions of which the four other judges agreed with. In summary, the two claimants won in the end, the judges together re-affirming the widely held understanding that for claimants to 'come to a nuisance' does not exclude them from taking legal action.[18] This acquired the qualification from Lord Neuberger that the use the claimant(s) have made of their land must be in effect unchanged from that of their predecessors (in *Coventry v Lawrence* the Reltons, from whom the two claimants bought 'Fenland', the vendors having lived there since 1984). This use must pre-date the

---

[16] *Coventry v Lawrence* (n 4 above) [69].

[17] *Coventry v Lawrence (No 1)* [2014] UKSC 13, [2014] 1 AC 822, [2014] 2 WLR 433, [2014] 2 All ER 622, 152 Con LR 1, [2014] 2 P & CR 2, [2014] BLR 271. The Supreme Court's judgment on additional issues is reported as *Coventry v Lawrence (No 2)* [2014] UKSC 46, [2015] 1 AC 106, [2014] 3 WLR 555; and the further hearing on costs issues, as *Coventry v Lawrence (No 3)* [2015] UKSC 50, [2015] 1 WLR 3485, with the Supreme Court justices split 5:2 on the compatibility with the First Protocol to the European Convention on Human Rights of the rules then applicable where the legal representation of a successful party was structured via a conditional fee arrangement and ATE insurance. It seems that the losing Coventry brothers did not pursue a possible application against the UK in the European Court of Human Rights; instead, their costs liability and the resulting financial weakness of RDC Promotions led them to look for a buyer for the stadium and track, whose sale to Spedeworth Ltd was announced in August 2016.

[18] This was assumed to be the rule by the Court of Appeal in the famous 'Belgrave Square versus Bermondsey' case, *Sturges v Bridgman* (1879) LR 11 Ch D 852; also in *Miller v Jackson* [1977] 1 QB 986 (Lord Denning MR dissenting). On *Sturges v Bridgman*, see AW Brian Simpson in Gerald Korngold and Andrew Morriss (eds), *Property Stories*, 2nd edn (New York, Foundation Press, 2009), ch 1 ('The Story of *Sturges v Bridgman*: the Resolution of Land Use Disputes between Neighbors').

start of the activities alleged to constitute a nuisance: a test the claimants here easily passed.[19]

The claimants themselves asserted (Judge Seymour making no clear finding on the state of their knowledge) that they bought the house without being aware of the potential impact on their amenity of noise on event days. As Jackson LJ said in the Court of Appeal:

> The relevant planning permissions and certificate of lawful use were all available for inspection on the register maintained by the local planning authority. It is a matter of prudence, indeed basic common sense, to inspect that register before purchasing a property in a rural location.[20]

But such unawareness or incuriousness (if that is what it was) did not in the end diminish their legal protection. At least in this specific tort law context, *caveat emptor* ('let the buyer beware') seems not to apply – a doctrine which would almost certainly have deprived the buyers of 'Fenland' of any breach of contract claim against the Reltons, had the sellers failed to disclose the existence of noise from the stadium and track.[21] Lord Neuberger made two further points in favour of the Supreme Court's traditional approach to 'coming to a nuisance':

> [T]he notion that coming to the nuisance is no defence is consistent with the fact that nuisance is a property-based tort, so that the right to allege a nuisance should, as it were, run with the land. It would also seem odd if a defendant was no longer liable for nuisance owing to the fact that the identity of his neighbour had changed, even though the use of his neighbour's property remained unchanged.[22]

It was this part of the Supreme Court judgment which stadium operators, motor sports fans and *Autocar* magazine found least acceptable. The Coventry brothers at Mildenhall Stadium sponsored a petition to Parliament, signed by 14,000+ people, claiming that the law should protect existing operations at all noisy venues against nuisance claims, as long as these complied with existing planning and other public law restrictions. The Ministry of Justice responded by defending the existing law.[23]

In a different part of the judgment – and in a direction less favourable to claimants – the judges in Parliament Square diverged from what many assumed to be the English law position on nuisance and how a landowner might lose the

---

[19] *Coventry v Lawrence (No 1)* (n 17 above) [51]–[58] (Lord Neuberger).

[20] *Coventry v Lawrence* (n 4 above) [26].

[21] Contrast *Farley v Skinner* [2002] 2 AC 732, [2001] 3 WLR 899 (HL), where the buyers of a house close to air traffic from Gatwick Airport could claim damages – though only £10,000 – for loss of amenity against the surveyor whom they had instructed specifically to find them a country property not affected by aircraft noise and whose report suggested that the house was not so affected.

[22] *Coventry v Lawrence (No 1)* (n 17 above) [52].

[23] See: www.petition.parliament.uk/archived/petitions/62894. For an Australian example of statute protecting a specific public entertainment venue against nuisance clams, see the Luna Park Site Act 1990 (NSW) s 19A.

right to complain about it.[24] Emanations from the defendant's land which amount in law to a nuisance in relation to one or more neighbours (eg noise, vibration, smoke or smell) and have continued 'as of right' for 20 years may now, via the law of prescription, acquire immunity from legal action. Such an activity can therefore lead, over time, to a form of implied positive easement, benefitting the defendant's plot of land (giving a right to transmit sound, etc, over the claimant's land) and burdening the claimant's (taking away the right to complain of the activity as a nuisance), potentially forever.[25]

So there was a risk that the claimants had bought 'Fenland' with the right to complain about the noise (assuming it would in theory have been actionable) already definitively lost, if the Reltons as their predecessors-in-title had tacitly acquiesced in the noise for long enough. But Lord Neuberger suggested that it would not be easy for a defendant to discharge the burden of showing that its activities were an actionable nuisance for a 20-year period, ahead of the start of litigation.[26] So it proved in *Coventry v Lawrence*, the court finding that the defendants had failed to show that they had been committing a nuisance for this period, so this 'new' principle did not block legal action by the two claimants.[27] In similar fashion, in *Peires v Bickerton's Aerodromes Ltd*, a nuisance claim directly following *Coventry v Lawrence* and based on long-standing helicopter noise from an airport, the defendants' claim of prescription also failed. Peter Smith J pointed out the evidential difficulties involved and held that the claimant's repeated objections over decades to the defendants' noisy operations prevented these being carried out 'as of right'.[28] As will be obvious, this prescription aspect of the law of nuisance will seldom limit the rights of neighbours unhappy about the impact on their amenity of construction close by, unless the project is of an exceptionally long-lasting character.

---

[24] See eg Michael A Jones (General Editor), *Clerk & Lindsell on Torts*, 21st edn (London, Sweet & Maxwell, 2014) para 20-85; also AWB Simpson, *A History of the Land Law*, 2nd edn (Oxford, Clarendon Press, 1986) 264: 'the repeated emission of foul smells … can never found a prescription claim'.

[25] *Coventry v Lawrence (No 1)* (n 17 above) Lord Neuberger [28]–[46], with whom on this point all other judges concurred. The landowners of the two properties could of course agree to modify the effect of such a 'right to commit a nuisance'; but in contrast with restrictive covenants English law does not at present give the courts power to modify or discharge an easement on a prescribed list of grounds, though the Law Commission has recommended adding such a power: *Making Land Work: Easements, Covenants and Profits à Prendre* (Law Com No 327, 2011).

[26] The 20-year requirement for easements comes from the much criticised Prescription Act 1832: (2 & 3 Will IV c 71), s 2: 'a model of obscure drafting' suggests Martin Dixon in 'Easements and the Law Commission' (2012) 76 *Conveyancer and Property Lawyer* 1.

[27] *Coventry v Lawrence (No 1)* (n 17 above) [140]–[146] (Lord Neuberger). Had the noise been a nuisance for the necessary 20-year period, Lord Neuberger suggests at [37] that it would not have to have been continuously so, time continuing to run in periods when there was in fact no racing, as had happened at Mildenhall. However the Law Commission's proposed statutory restatement of the law on prescription for implied easements (n 25 above) includes 'continuous' as one of the tests.

[28] *Peires v Bickerton's Aerodromes Ltd* [2016] EWHC 560 (Ch) [83]–[87]. The judge also rejected the defendants' claim of statutory immunity under the Civil Aviation Act 1982, though their success on this point on appeal led his judgment on liability to be overturned: *Peires v Bickerton's Aerodromes Ltd* [2017] EWCA Civ 273, [2017] 1 WLR 2865, [2017] 2 Lloyd's Rep 330, [2017] Env LR 32.

Following well-established case law, the Supreme Court judges all acknowledged that the character of an area at the key time is highly relevant in determining what uses of land by a defendant are unreasonable – or, put the other way round, determining what interferences with a claimant's amenity are so unreasonable that they should be actionable.[29] But they differed from existing case law and from Jackson LJ, being reluctant to find any automatic causal link between the planning position and a change in the character of an area – in this case, the locality which included the stadium, track and 'Fenland'.

The judges were in effect asserting that the private law of nuisance is historically (and logically) prior to the public law of land use planning (and any other relevant system of public law regulation). So the fact that an activity is consistent with planning permission does not give it immunity from being actionable, if carried on in such a way that it becomes a nuisance. To that extent, the Supreme Court agreed with Jackson LJ's first point in his summary in the Court of Appeal.[30] This reflected the claimants' approach in the case: they were not objecting to the activities at the stadium and track as such; but rather to the way in which they were carried on and the impact of this on 'Fenland'. Lord Neuberger put the point this way:

> [T]he mere fact that the activity which is said to give rise to the nuisance has the benefit of planning permission is normally of no assistance to the defendant in a claim brought by a neighbour who contends that that activity caused a nuisance to her land in the form of noise or other loss of amenity.[31]

The Supreme Court judges therefore shared Judge Seymour's view that the noise from the stadium and track could and did constitute a nuisance, reinstating the first-instance judge's damages award and injunction (suspended while the house was unoccupied). The judges also differed explicitly from the Court of Appeal in holding that a defendant cannot rely on the very activities which in fact constituted a nuisance (though consistent with the planning or other regulatory regimes in force) as having changed the character of an area. If this were not so, Lord Neuberger pointed out, a defendant could profit from his/her own wrongdoing; and few nuisance actions would ever be successful.[32]

---

[29] As exemplified by *Sturges v Bridgman* (n 18 above).

[30] Text to n 15 above.

[31] *Coventry v Lawrence (No 1)* (n 17 above) [94]: here Lord Neuberger held that much of the reasoning of Buckley J in *Gillingham* (n 13 above) could not now stand, though the result may have been correct; and accepted that the Court of Appeal had less freedom of manoeuvre in relation to the existing case law on planning and nuisance than the Supreme Court. He also explained what 'normally' in the quotation above meant, differentiating the impact of a simple grant of planning permission from express or implied statutory authority to commit a nuisance, the same point also being discussed by Lord Carnwath [192]–[195]. 'True' authorisation is illustrated by *Allen v Gulf Oil Refining Ltd* [1981] AC 1001 (HL), where Parliament specifically and directly permitted the construction and operation of an oil refinery via the (private) Gulf Oil Refining Act 1965.

[32] *Coventry v Lawrence (No 1)* (n 17 above) [65]–[76] (Lord Neuberger). On this aspect of the Supreme Court judgment, see Sandy Steel, 'The Locality Principle in Private Nuisance' (2017) 76 *Cambridge Law Journal* 145.

In the situation which is the reverse of *Coventry v Lawrence* – housing newly built or converted close to an existing noisy operation, like a motocross stadium, music venue or sports club (or even a church with regular bell-ringing) – the planning system may now help operators like the Coventry brothers, protecting them against conflict with neighbours. In early 2018 the then Secretary of State for Housing, Communities and Local Government (Rt Hon Sajid Javid MP) said that developers of housing close to such an operation would be required, as part of a new National Planning Policy Framework, to add extra noise-proofing to their new homes (beyond what Building Regulations would otherwise require). This would protect the stadium, venue, club or church against its new neighbours, whose potential to sue in nuisance might otherwise limit its activities or shut these down entirely: 'I have always thought it unfair that the burden is on long-standing music venues to solve noise issues when property developers choose to build nearby', the Minister said.[33] This is known as the *Agent of Change Principle*, already adopted in the Australian State of Victoria in 2014 via amendments to the planning and liquor licensing rules.[34] Under the principle, the person implementing development in an area must accommodate the area's existing characteristics (including its noise patterns), rather than expecting or requiring these to change to suit the new development. It does not, however, affect the rights of *existing* homeowners in relation to noise nearby and leaves the law of nuisance intact.

The Supreme Court judgments also included a discussion (unnecessary in the Court of Appeal, given its views on liability) about remedies for property torts: notably on the factors which might argue for a one-off award of damages for a continuing nuisance, rather than an injunction, by the application of Lord Cairns' Act.[35] This led to a fresh look at the well-known passage on this issue from AL Smith LJ in *Shelfer v City of London Electric Lighting Co*:

(1) If the injury to the plaintiff's legal rights is small,

(2) And is one which is capable of being estimated in money,

(3) And is one which can be adequately compensated by a small money payment,

(4) And the case is one in which it would be oppressive to the defendant to grant an injunction:—

then damages in substitution for an injunction may be given.

There may also be cases in which, though the four above-mentioned requirements exist, the defendant by his conduct, as, for instance, hurrying up his buildings so as if possible

---

[33] Rowena Mason, 'Ministers back call to save small gig venues from noise complaints', *The Guardian* (19 January 2018); see also: www.gov.uk/government/news/strengthened-planning-rules-to-protect-music-venues-and-their-neighbours.

[34] See: www.apraamcos.com.au/news/2014/september/music-industry-celebrates-implementation-of-agent-of-change-principle.

[35] Lord Cairns' Act, the Chancery Amendment Act 1858 (21 & 22 Vict c 27), is named after Sir Hugh, later Lord, Cairns (1819–1885), who as Solicitor-General in the second Lord Derby Government piloted these changes through Parliament. For England & Wales its relevant provisions (in s 2) now form the Senior Courts Act 1981, s 50. Many cases which discuss the choice between an injunction and damages do so without referring expressly to Lord Cairns' Act.

to avoid an injunction, or otherwise acting with a reckless disregard to the plaintiff's rights, has disentitled himself from asking that damages may be assessed in substitution for an injunction.[36]

The significance of this as a set of hard-and-fast rules now appears downplayed in English law, at least in relation to private nuisance (probably in relation to property torts generally). However, little clear guidance has yet replaced it, save for the Supreme Court's views that judges' discretion on remedy should not be unduly fettered and that such decisions are necessarily highly fact-sensitive.[37] But in *Coventry v Lawrence* itself the first-instance injunction was restored, though the losing side could now in fresh proceedings pursue the argument that Judge Seymour should have, in effect, expropriated the two claimants' rights for the future by making a one-off award of damages instead.[38]

Additionally, Lord Sumption suggested that the court could take account of the planning position and of the benefit to the public of what were otherwise actionable activities (in the case of a stadium, pleasurable leisure-time activities for the community, plus local employment) by choosing to award damages rather than impose an injunction.[39] Further, Lord Clarke reminded the court that damages in substitution for an injunction can be 'gain-based': transferring from defendant to claimant some of the profit the defendant has made or will make from tortious conduct.[40] But these views were technically *obiter* and were not clearly shared by the other judges, though it would be easy to imagine the issues re-surfacing in future. As for the damages in fact awarded in noise nuisance cases, one observer suggests that there are no hard and fast formulae: 'The reported decisions tend to suggest that an award of between £825 and £5,500 (per year of past nuisance) will be the likely outcome in most cases.'[41]

---

[36] *Shelfer v City of London Electric Lighting Co* [1895] 1 Ch 287 (CA) 322–23. For a dramatic example of *Shelfer* in action before *Coventry v Lawrence*, see *HKRUK II (CHC) Ltd v Heaney* [2010] EWHC 2245 (Ch), [2010] 3 EGLR 15, discussed by the Law Commission in *Rights to Light* (Law Com no 356, 2014) (not yet accepted by the Government): www.lawcom.gov.uk/report.

[37] See *Coventry v Lawrence (No 1)* (n 17 above) [100]–[132] (Lord Neuberger). This revised approach has not yet been followed in Australia: see eg *Janney v Steller Works Pty Ltd* [2017] VSC 363 (repeated trespass by oversailing crane jib).

[38] See *Coventry v Lawrence (No 1)* (n 17 above) [149]–[152] (Lord Neuberger). These possible additional proceedings seem not to have taken place.

[39] *Coventry v Lawrence (No 1)* (n 17 above) [157]–[161].

[40] *Coventry v Lawrence (No 1)* (n 17 above) [173]. See the sequence of cases relating to land which start with *Wrotham Park Estate Co Ltd v Parkside Homes Ltd* [1974] 1 WLR 798, [1974] 2 All ER 321 (Ch); approved in *Attorney-General v Blake* [2001] 1 AC 268, [2000] 3 WLR 625, [2000] 4 All ER 385 (HL). Later examples in the construction field include *Horsfold v Bird* [2006] UKPC 3, (2006) 22 *Const LJ* 187; *Stadium Capital Holdings (No 2) Ltd v St Marylebone Properties Co Plc* [2010] EWCA Civ 952 and *Jones v Ruth* [2011] EWCA Civ 804, [2012] 1 WLR 1495, [2012] 1 All ER 490. This approach is in some cases called 'negotiating damages': what a reasonable defendant would have been willing to pay for the right to do the wrong activity, and what a reasonable claimant would have been willing to accept.

[41] Tim Bullimore, 'A Sound Analysis? Quantum in Noise Nuisance Cases' [2014] *Journal of Planning and Environment Law* 6, 9. He points out that the cost of instructing an expert valuer may well be greater than the damages likely to be awarded, let alone the costs at stake in dealing with this issue in court.

On this basis, the claimants' award from the Queen's Bench Division in *Coventry v Lawrence* of £20,850, based on diminution of the home's rental value between their arrival at 'Fenland' in 2006 and their having to move out in 2010, looks near the top of the range.

III. Leases, Gas Pipes, Trespass and Nuisance: *Yeung v Potel*[42]

A. Background

In this second Court of Appeal case, Jackson LJ was joined by Sharp and Arden LJJ, who both simply concurred with his seven-part judgment. The setting for the litigation was a nineteenth-century house in London W14, divided in the 1960s into four self-contained flats, each on a long lease.[43] The dispute concerned the negative impact on the top (second-floor) flat of renovations in the first-floor flat below, including work to install a new higher ceiling and a new gas pipe and meter.

B. At First Instance

As Part 3 of Jackson LJ's judgment lucidly summarised, in 2008 extensive remodelling work started in the first-floor flat; in 2009 the two lessees of the flat above started legal action, claiming that the defendant lessee below was committing trespass by his work on his ceiling and nuisance by the noise, dust, etc which the work was causing them. They asked the Chancery Division for an injunction, requiring him to stop the work under way and to reinstate his flat's original ceiling (the interim injunction they gained lapsed after seven days without being renewed, so work below must then have continued); they also claimed damages. The defendant in turn counterclaimed, asserting that he had a right of access to the top flat to re-route a gas pipe and meter; as part of that, he needed to turn off the gas to that flat for a short period.

The case was transferred to the Central London County Court and heard over four days in 2012 by District Judge Langley, assisted by expert evidence. Her reserved judgment found that, under the terms of the two leases, the new higher ceiling in the defendant's flat trespassed into space which was not part of his flat;[44] the claimants had a right to damages for past trespass and nuisance

---

[42] *Yeung* (n 5 above).

[43] At the time of the litigation, the freehold of the whole building was owned and managed by a company whose shareholders were the four lessees, though nothing in the case seems to turn on this.

[44] Had the defendant served a notice under the Party Wall etc. Act 1996, this might have enabled him legally to do at least part of the work planned.

(assessed at more than £87,000); and the defendant's counterclaims, including for damages, had no basis in law. The judge finally awarded the claimants 90 per cent of their costs so far.

C. On Appeal

The defendant lessee then appealed, on those grounds alone for which he had permission.[45] The only real issues in contention were two: (a) his intended gas supply changes; and (b) the first-instance judge's assessment of the cost of remedial works. Jackson LJ got to the nub of (a) by pointing out that, in the common form leases for the building, each lessee had a right to use the services 'which now are or may at any time hereafter be in under or passing through the Building or any part thereof'.[46] This therefore contemplated that the pipes, wiring, etc which provide these services may change over time, each lessee being given the right, under conditions, to enter other parts of the building for 'repairing, cleansing maintaining or renewing [the services] and of laying down any new [services]'. However, the corresponding reservation in every lease, permitting entry by another lessee, was on the face of it more limited, spelling out only 'repairing, cleansing maintaining or renewing [services]'. This, it seems, covered only substituting new pipes or wires for existing ones, not laying new or additional ones.[47] So should the words 'or laying new [services]' be added by implication to this reservation clause? The lessee of the first-floor flat reasonably argued that this is what the parties must have intended, as it would mean that the powers in one lease were mirrored by identical obligations in the other.

Jackson LJ noted that the law leans strongly against limiting by implication the freedoms normally associated with a legal estate in land (freehold or leasehold), unless necessity requires it.[48] A heavy burden lies on a party wishing to argue that a reservation is wider in scope than its express words, since it would permit a grantor to give with one hand but take back with the other:

> If the original lessor had wished to extend the reservations clause to cover laying new and additional pipes and wires, it would and should have said so expressly in paragraph 3 of schedule 2. A second opportunity arose in March 1985, when 50 Warwick Gardens Ltd [*a company controlled by the four lessees, which acquired the freehold from the original owner*] was the freeholder. If the parties considered that the reservations

---

[45] He attempted unsuccessfully twice to reinstate those grounds of appeal for which he was not originally given permission, and to add new grounds – all of this taking place beyond the normal time-limits: see *Yeung* (n 5 above) [32]–[33].

[46] Each of the relevant lease provisions in fact included a list of the individual services concerned, abbreviated to [services] in the text above.

[47] On this last point, see Buckley LJ in *Lurcott v Wakeley and Wheeler* [1911] 1 KB 905 (CA) 923–24.

[48] *Wheeldon v Burrows* (1879) 12 Ch D 31 (CA), where the court refused to recognise that the vendor of a plot of land had impliedly reserved an easement of light for the benefit of a building on the land retained.

clause was insufficiently wide, they could and should have amended it by means of the deed of variation [*extending the leases to 999 years at the same time*].[49]

Authority, too, suggested construing the words actually used in the lease here as not giving a right of entry to do what the defendant hoped: to install a completely new service.[50] The judge obviously reached this conclusion with regret, saying that to add the words proposed would certainly be desirable. However, as Jackson LJ said: 'the case for adding in the proposed phrase falls far short of necessity … It is not … the function of the court to rewrite carefully drawn leases and deeds of variation merely to eliminate oddities of this kind'.[51] At least the lease could still function without the extra words. So, even if the context been purely contractual, it is not certain that the court would have felt been able to invoke *The Moorcock* to justify implying the extra words put forward.[52]

The defendant wanted to install the new gas pipe above the original level of his ceiling, in a position which, as the first-instance judge held (Jackson LJ explicitly agreeing), was not part of his own flat, belonging to the flat above (or perhaps to the building's overall corporate landlord). The defendant could therefore carry out this plan only if the relevant leases gave him power to do so and imposed a corresponding duty on the lessee above to permit this work – which on their proper construction these provisions did not do. So the defendant could not request an injunction forcing the lessees of the top flat to allow him to re-route the gas pipe and meter; nor could he expect damages for his neighbours' refusal to permit this.

However, the first-instance judge did not require the defendant to reinstate his ceiling at its original height (ie bringing to an end his ongoing trespass); nor did she award the claimants damages instead. This issue not being 'live' on appeal, the result was a sort of stalemate, as Jackson LJ pointed out: the defendant's trespass could continue, at least until the claimants or the overall landlord brought proceedings for a mandatory injunction, when the cost of reinstating the original ceiling might encourage a judge to award damages instead.[53] At least the first-floor lessee learned in the Court of Appeal that he could not lawfully install a new gas pipe and meter as planned, in part because the law would not support him in turning off the gas supply to the top-floor flat in order to do so.

---

[49] *Yeung* (n 5 above) [47] (Jackson LJ).

[50] In *Trailfinders v Razuki* [1988] 2 EGLR 46 (Ch) [the year is misquoted as 1998 in the online report of Jackson LJ's judgment] the reservation clause, giving the landlord right of access, included a phrase close to that in *Yeung v Potel*: 'conduits which are now or may hereafter during the term hereby granted, be in under or over the said demised premises'. Despite this, Judge Finlay QC held that the linked right of entry authorised access only to replace existing services, not to install a new category of service (network cables).

[51] *Yeung* (n 5 above) [49] (Jackson LJ).

[52] *The Moorcock* (1889) LR 14 PD 64 (CA). Even here the test would have looked to business necessity: see *Marks & Spencer plc v BNP Paribas Securities Services Trust Co (Jersey) Ltd* [2015] UKSC 72, [2016] AC 742; also Joanna McCunn, 'Belize It Or Not: Implied Contract Terms in *Marks & Spencer v BNP Paribas*' (2016) 79 *MLR* 1091.

[53] *Yeung* (n 5 above) [56].

As the final point, Jackson LJ considered Issue (b) mentioned above: the challenges the defendant wished to make to the assessment of damages in the County Court below. Out of respect for the first-instance judge's findings of fact, as well as for her detailed analysis and computation, the Court of Appeal refused to interfere. It also made no costs award as part of its judgment on the merits.

IV. A Garden Shed, Trespass and Remedies:
Rashid v Sharif[54]

A. Background

The final case of this 'neighbour dispute' trio came before a two-judge Court of Appeal, Elias LJ simply concurring with Jackson LJ's relatively short four-part judgment. The dispute arose between two neighbours in Ilford, Essex about the position of a breeze-block shed built by the defendants at the far end of their north-facing garden, which backed on to the far end of the south-facing garden of the house owned by the claimants in a parallel street. Two questions arose: Did the north wall of the shed trespass into the far end of the claimants' garden? If it did, what remedy should the court order? To answer the first question required the court to decide where the boundary ran – as so often, not adequately defined on the title register, though the online report of the Court of Appeal judgment does include a helpful sketch plan.

B. At First Instance

In the Central London County Court, the judge was, as in the previous case, District Judge Langley. Following a site visit, she held that the north wall of the defendants' new shed had been built along the line of a brick wall which had once formed the boundary between the two properties. She also held that the whole of this wall belonged to the claimants' land, the boundary with the defendants therefore being its south face; or that the claimants and their predecessors had by adverse possession acquired title to the land on which the wall once stood. For the defendants to build on this line was therefore to trespass on the claimants' land by at least the thickness of that one-time brick wall (225mm).[55] As the remedy, she ordered the defendants to take down the north wall of their shed and reinstate the claimants' previous wall; she made no separate award of damages.

---

[54] *Rashid* (n 6 above).
[55] The defendants made other arguments in the County Court against the conclusion that the north wall of their shed was trespassing: that the claimants had consented to the new shed; that the defendants had an irrevocable licence to occupy the space; or that they had the benefit of a proprietary estoppel

C. On Appeal

Jackson LJ concentrated, in Part 4 of his judgment, on the defendants' challenge to Judge Langley's central finding that the claimants' predecessor in title, whose witness statement the claimants had included in the proceedings, had built the one-time wall entirely on his own land. Jackson LJ acknowledged the principle that findings of fact at first instance will not be re-opened on appeal, but in effect considered that part of this first-instance judgment fulfilled the 'plainly wrong' test recently laid down by the Supreme Court.[56] The witness suggested only that he built the wall on the line of an earlier wooden fence, which was itself the boundary. Judge Langley wrongly interpreted this to mean that the whole of that fence and wall were within the witness's own land.

'Since the historic brick wall was 225 mm thick and it went along the line of the former fence, the natural inference is that it was a party fence wall', said Jackson LJ.[57] This statutory phrase, paradoxically, does not apply to a fence but only to 'a wall (not being part of a building) which stands on lands of different owners and is used or constructed to be used for separating such adjoining lands'.[58] This analysis had been argued unsuccessfully at first instance, but its re-emergence on appeal and adoption by the court had a negative consequence for the defendants: they *shared* ownership of this 'party fence wall' with the claimants, so could not acquire ownership of the space occupied by the long ago fence, the old wall and now the north wall of their shed by adverse possession. As a result, the Court of Appeal dismissed their counterclaim.[59]

This approach also meant that the north wall of their new shed was in effect part of a new 'party fence wall', so the notice and counter-notice regime of the Party Wall etc. Act 1996 applied to any work on it or changes to it – which the defendants had failed to trigger. Technically, therefore, their new wall still constituted a trespass (though more limited than the County Court had held); but, as Jackson LJ noted, if the right statutory procedure had been followed, the shed might still have been built in exactly the same place.[60]

As for the remedy, Jackson LJ considered that to award the claimants damages would be adequate (though did not explain this exercise of discretion at any length, nor the basis for calculating the damages), so the County Court judge's injunction was replaced by a modest award of £300 to the claimants; each party was to bear its own costs throughout, as neither fully succeeded or lost.

---

enforceable against the claimants. None of these arguments, rejected at first instance, is discussed at length by the Court of Appeal.

[56] See *McGraddie v McGraddie* [2013] UKSC 58, [2013] 1 WLR 247 [1]–[6] (Lord Reed, giving the judgment of the whole Court in a case from Scotland); *Henderson v Foxworth Investments Ltd* [2014] UKSC 41, [2014] 1 WLR 2600 [58]–[68] (Lord Reed once again giving the Court's judgment); and *Watson Farley & Williams (a firm) v Ostrovizky* [2015] EWCA Civ 457 [8] (Burnett LJ).

[57] *Rashid* (n 6 above) [49].

[58] The Party Wall etc. Act 1996, s 20.

[59] *Rashid* (n 6 above) [54].

[60] *Rashid* (n 6 above) [61].

V. Conclusions

The trio of cases in this chapter illustrates a range of situations, including construction ones, in which the torts of trespass and nuisance may be the focus of litigation. It also gives examples of issues which parties may consider important enough to be worth pursuing to the Court of Appeal or beyond – or which they have failed to find simpler, quicker and cheaper ways to resolve.

It is easy to see the issues of principle which each side in *Coventry v Lawrence* thought worth fighting for, up to the summit of the court system if necessary. Of the three judgments analysed in this chapter, it seems safe to suggest that this case – like most which reach the Supreme Court – will have the greatest and most long-lasting impact, in part because few nuisance cases have reached the highest appeal court in recent times.[61] However, several of the changes which *Coventry v Lawrence* introduced need future litigation to add detail and greater precision to the new principles – notably on the interaction between the idea of an ongoing nuisance hardening into an easement and the system of registration of title.[62]

However, in finding that the claimants ought to have known that the neighbourhood they were buying into was noisy and that the planning position had set the bar higher for the law of nuisance, Jackson LJ in the Court of Appeal seemed to have as much common sense on his side as Lord Neuberger's alternative views in the Supreme Court. For the claimants themselves at 'Fenland', the outcome was a complete vindication of what they believed to be their rights (though they became newly vulnerable on remedy, if the defendants had chosen to litigate further); for the defendants in the final appeal, the result was a serious challenge to their commercial operations at the stadium and track, their ultimate costs liability driving their business into the arms of a bigger operator.

It is a bittersweet reflection that the funding model which allowed the claimants' lawyers to share their clients' risk in the eventual outcome (with a fee uplift on success), making the second appeal possible, was itself swept away by legislation for the future while *Coventry v Lawrence* was between Court of Appeal and Supreme Court. These changes came from proposals made in 2009 by Jackson LJ in his reports on costs in civil cases, discussed in Chapters three and four of this volume. The key reform both banned the success fee uplift under a winning party's

---

[61] Its main immediate predecessors on injury to amenity were *Hunter v Canary Wharf* (n 2 above), almost 20 years earlier, and *London Borough of Southwark v Mills, Baxter v Mayor etc of the London Borough of Camden* [2001] AC 1, [1999] 3 WLR 939, [1999] 4 All ER 449 (HL). See also Maria Lee, 'Private Nuisance in the House of Lords: Back to Basics' (2004) 15 *King's College Law Journal* 417.

[62] None of the Supreme Court judgments address this issue in any detail, Lord Neuberger (n 17 above) [34] saying simply: 'Subject to questions of notice and registration, the benefit and burden of an easement run with the land and, therefore, if a right to emit noise which would otherwise be a nuisance is an easement, it would bind successors of the grantor'. It looks as if the burden could run with the claimant's land as an overriding interest under the Land Registration Act 2002, Sch 3, para 3; the benefit could run with the defendant's land under the word-saving presumption of the Law of Property Act 1925, s 62(1).

conditional fee agreement and prevented that party's After-The-Event insurance premium (guaranteeing funds for its potential costs liability to the other party) from being recoverable from the loser. The Government's stated aim was to move the balance of power away from claimants and towards defendants, so reducing the final bill which might be payable by future defendants in the Coventry brothers' position.[63]

The other two cases, *Yeung v Potel* and *Rashid v Sharif*,[64] do not change the law significantly, but they do illustrate some common problems in relations between neighbours, both vertical and horizontal, and offer warnings on the consequences of failing to provide (or agree) clear physical boundaries between different owners or lessees. *Yeung v Potel* also shows what can go wrong where a set of leases fails to provide clear machinery allowing for the installation of new services in a multi-occupation leasehold building; in an ideal situation, rights to add new services would bring with them rights of entry, matched by reciprocal duties on other lessees or on the freeholder. Although the documentation was unhelpful and ambiguous, there must still have been scope, as Jackson LJ suggests, for sensible negotiation and an outcome that satisfied both parties. But once work started – perhaps without any warning at all to the neighbours upstairs – it is easy to see how goodwill might evaporate.

Another noteworthy feature of these two cases is the parties' eagerness to expose themselves to a second round of litigation risk (there being a counterclaim on appeal in *Rashid*): all the more unexpected, since both these situations turned out, after the event, to be ones where the statutory machinery of a notice under the Party Wall etc. Act 1996 could and probably should have been triggered. This would, in the absence of immediate agreement between the neighbours following the initial notice, have brought in at least one professional surveyor: its machinery is designed so far as possible to identify, and then resolve, possible uncertainties and disputes before work starts. So use of the statute might have defused the conflicts in both cases before they could get to entrenched positions and no real possibility of compromise.[65]

Although the 1996 Act machinery was not used in *Rashid*, Jackson LJ records that many attempts were made to resolve the dispute amicably, including with outside intervention, but his judgment does not give full details. This is the usual situation once a case has progressed to a 'day in court' before a judge – a fortiori once the first-instance decision is appealed: the ultimate reported judgment seldom gives a blow-by-blow account of all the ADR possibilities, formal and informal, which were in the frame, some perhaps having been attempted without success and others not even tried. This may be in part because judges remain unaware

---

[63] Ministry of Justice, 'Clarke announces major overhaul of civil justice' (29 March 2011): www.gov.uk/government/news/clarke-announces-major-overhaul-of-civil-justice. On costs in *Coventry v Lawrence*, see n 17 above.

[64] *Yeung* (n 5 above); *Rashid* (n 6 above).

[65] See Stephen Bickford-Smith, David Nicholls and Andrew Smith, *Party Walls: Law and Practice*, 4th edn (Bristol, Jordan, 2017).

of the 'without prejudice' stages the case has already been through, even where actively encouraged by the court itself as part of pre-trial. It's also true that to understand how a dispute arose by starting in the courtroom, then looking backwards in time, is to view events through the wrong end of a telescope. Nonetheless, these two cases and their outcomes illustrate vividly a point ruefully made not long ago by another Court of Appeal judge, Ward LJ:

> All disputes between neighbours arouse deep passions and entrenched positions are taken as the parties stand upon their rights, seemingly blissfully unaware or unconcerned that that they are committing themselves to unremitting litigation which will leave them bruised by the experience and very much the poorer, win or lose.[66]

It is a characteristic feature of the breadth and volume of the work of the Court of Appeal (Civil Division) that its judges are required to show familiarity with – or at least willingness to grasp – issues in disputes of kaleidoscopic variety. These three cases show, though within the relatively small 'neighbour dispute' context, the polymathic range and scope of Jackson LJ's activity. The final two also show his ability to deliver a clear and logically structured judgment (in numbered parts, of course) *ex tempore*: at the end of the hearing, with minimum time for preparation or research.[67]

Each of the cases discussed evidences his proper conception of the judicial role, which involves above all courtesy and respect to litigants and appreciation of a case well prepared and well argued by counsel.[68] A key part of this is that a judgment should accurately summarise the material each side has presented to the court, going on to explain carefully to one or more of the parties (and to their legal teams) why they are to win, and to the others why they must in the end be the losers. At the same time, his judgments evidence an economy which wastes no time on issues which have no impact on the ultimate outcome.

They also fulfil admirably the vital educational function of case law for the wider legal (sometimes non-legal) public: laying out with clarity and precision what the law is, where it has come from and why it is as it is. In the relatively rare case where a party disappointed in the Court of Appeal does take on the considerable extra risk and cost(s) of a final appeal, Jackson LJ's intellectual and drafting skills must make the job of the Supreme Court significantly easier – even when Parliament Square takes a different view on the law from the Royal Courts of Justice, as it did in *Coventry v Lawrence*.[69]

---

[66] *Oliver v Symons* [2012] EWCA Civ 267 [53] (a 'scope of express easement' dispute).

[67] In *MRH Solicitors Ltd v The County Court Sitting at Manchester* [2015] EWHC 1795 (Admin) [26], Nicol J, giving the judgment of the court, pointed out: 'it is common practice for a judge who gives an oral *ex tempore* judgment to refine it when asked to approve a transcript. Ordinarily, this is limited to tidying up the language, but in principle we see no reason why it may not include more significant changes.'

[68] And the opposite: exceptionally, he recorded understandable irritation with badly prepared documentation for an appeal hearing, as in *Yeung v Potel*, n 5 above, [33]; and did the same with greater forcefulness about skeleton arguments in *Inplayer Ltd v Thorogood* [2014] EWCA Civ 1511 [52]–[57].

[69] *Coventry v Lawrence*: text to n 17 above.

PART VII

Contract Administration

15

To Hold the Scales Even: The Duty of a Construction Contract Administrator

ANTHONY LAVERS

I. Introduction

It was in the House of Lords' decision of *RB Burden Ltd v Swansea Corporation*[1] that Lord Radcliffe advanced as an 'established principle of law' the proposition that 'in granting his certificate, the architect has a duty towards each party to hold the scales even'. At that level of generality, the 'established principle' set out in 1957 had been in existence since the previous century[2] and has survived a further 60 years to the present day. However, the effects of its application cannot be assumed to be constant. The purpose of this chapter is to consider the changes which have occurred in the position of the construction contract administrator in English law and internationally, especially under the standard forms of contract. Particular attention will be given to the contribution to the development of the modern law of the judgments of Mr Justice Jackson in *AMEC Civil Engineering Ltd v Secretary of State for Transport,*[3] *Costain Ltd v Bechtel Ltd*[4] and *Scheldebouw BV v St James Homes (Grosvenor Dock) Ltd.*[5] The chapter will focus specifically on the decision-making function, as in the granting of payment certificates, of the contract administrator (CA throughout).

II. The Role of the CA in a Construction/Engineering Contract

The status of the CA in a construction/engineering contract is, if not unique in manufacturing industry, sufficiently unusual to be regarded as something of

[1] *RB Burden Ltd v Swansea Corporation* [1957] 1 WLR 1167 at 1172.
[2] Certainly as far back as *Stevenson v Watson* (1879) 40 LT 485.
[3] *AMEC Civil Engineering Ltd v Secretary of State for Transport* [2004] EWHC 2339 (TCC).
[4] *Costain Ltd v Bechtel Ltd* [2005] EWHC 1018 (TCC).
[5] *Scheldebouw BV v St James Homes (Grosvenor Dock) Ltd* [2006] EWHC 89 (TCC).

an anomaly. There are few commercial situations where an individual or firm is identified in the body of the agreement, not as one of the parties, but as an integral part of the contractual machinery: an 'officer of the contract' was the traditional description,[6] and construction law has had to generate principles to govern the operation of this function. Inevitably, these principles operate in conjunction with contractual provision, but the latter is complicated by the tripartite nature of the relationship, between the parties to the contract and the CA appointed under it. The anomalous nature of this relationship can be illustrated by reference to one of its distinctive features, namely the physical location of the express contractual duties of the CA. Usually, it might be expected that the duties of a professional person would be set out in the contract for services under which they were retained by the client.[7] Yet in the current edition of the FIDIC Model Services Agreement[8] the treatment of the services to be provided by the Consultant is almost minimalist. Apart from one sub-clause[9] on Contract Administration and the Scope of Services,[10] which comprises five short paragraphs (three of a single sentence) on a largely blank page, the Consultant's duties are not expressed. It is true that this can be expanded by Particular Conditions, and Clients/Consultants are invited[11] to 'refer to the FIDIC Definition of Services' for guidance on preparing a scope of services, but tellingly the Contract Administration clause makes 12 references to the Works Contract ('defined function … under a Works Contract', 'as laid down in the Works Contract', 'to the extent provided in the Works Contract', 'authorised under the Works Contract to certify', 'its duties under the Works Contract', for example) and only four to the Scope of Services.

Accordingly, it is to the 'Works Contract', as the White Book describes it, that reference should be made for a much fuller appreciation of the activities of the CA. In the FIDIC Red Book,[12] over half of the 163 sub-clauses of the General Conditions contain references to the functions, powers or duties of the Engineer. The equivalent proportion of references to the Architect/Contract Administrator in the current JCT Standard Building Contract (SBC)[13] is just under half of the

---

[6] When this author worked in Singapore in the 1980s, government contracts routinely referred to the 'superintending officer': see, for example, *Engineering Construction Pte Ltd v Attorney General* [1993] 1 SLR 390. See n 34 below.

[7] 'Employer', 'owner' and 'client' are used synonymously in this chapter to mean the purchasing party. In a standard form construction contract, such as those produced by FIDIC, 'Employer' is typically a defined term. In a professional services context, 'client' may be more usual.

[8] Fédération Internationale des Ingénieurs Conseils (FIDIC), Client/Consultants Model Services Agreement, 5th edn (2017): The White Book.

[9] Sub-Clause 3.9.

[10] Appendix 1.

[11] ibid.

[12] FIDIC, Conditions of Contract for Construction of Building and Engineering Works Designed by the Employer, 1st edn (1999). See new 2017 edition at p 20.

[13] The example selected is the Joint Contracts Tribunal Standard Building Contract with Quantities 2016.

158 sub-clauses and in NEC 4,[14] there are references to the Project Manager in just over half of the 189 core clauses.

The content of the functions/powers/duties can be divided into two categories, which correspond approximately with items vii) and viii) on the 'Hudson's list of duties'[15] reproduced with commendable deference by the editors of *Keating*,[16] namely 'supervise the work, and see that the contractor performs the contract', and

> perform their duties to their employer as defined by any contract with their employer or by the contract with the builder, and generally to act as the employer's agent in all matters connected with the work and the contract, except where otherwise prescribed by the contract with the builder.

This is sometimes referred to as the 'duality' of the CA's role;[17] the categorisation of the activities of the CA into those where the CA is acting on behalf of the employer and those embodying a decision-making function under the contract as between employer and contractor.

Two caveats need to be observed before adopting these categories for the purposes of analysis of duties and liabilities. First, the term 'supervision' is no longer always apt to describe the function of ensuring the contractor's implementation of the design, at least in the UK. At one time, it was at the heart of the duty of an architect (or engineer), as the courts made clear in leading professional negligence cases. In *Jameson v Simon*,[18] the Lord Ordinary stated that he could not

> assent to the suggestion that an architect undertaking and being handsomely paid for supervision, the limit of his duty is to pay occasional visits ... to the work, and paying those visits to assume that all is right which he does not observe to be wrong,[19]

and as Lord Young said:

> He is not supposed to do all the supervision personally ... but if he undertakes to do it, he is bound either to do it himself, or to have it done by some person whom he employs and in whom he has confidence.[20]

This Scots authority was followed by the Ontario Court of Appeal in *Campbell Flour Mills Co Ltd v Bowes*[21] in holding that 'The architects failed to perform

---

[14] The example selected is Option A of the Engineering and Construction Contract, 4th edn (2017) Priced Contract with Activity Schedule.

[15] From L Mead, *Hudson's Building and Engineering Contracts*, 7th edn (London, Sweet & Maxwell, 1946), p 9.

[16] S Furst and the Hon Sir V Ramsey, *Keating on Construction Contracts*, 10th edn (London, Sweet & Maxwell, 2016) para 14-059.

[17] E Baker et al, *FIDIC Contracts Law and Practice* (London, Informa, 2009), p 280.

[18] *Jameson v Simon* (1899) 1 F (Ct of Sess) 1211.

[19] ibid, at 1216.

[20] ibid, at 1221.

[21] *Campbell Flour Mills Co Ltd v Bowes* (1914) 32 O.L.R. 270, otherwise cited as *Campbell Flour Mills v Ellis and Connery*.

their elementary duty to exercise a sufficient supervision over the building, and so broke their contract'.[22] By the time *Florida Hotels Pty v Mayo*[23] came on appeal from the Supreme Court of New South Wales to the High Court of Australia, Barwick CJ was able to conclude a passage of his judgment on the obligation 'at least to have made reasonable arrangements of a reliable nature to be kept informed of the general progress of the work' simply with the name: '*Jameson v Simon*'. The reason why the duty of supervision was viewed in much the same way across the common law jurisdictions was not solely due to the persuasive effect of judicial precedent. The wording of conditions of engagement was also a powerful influence. In *Florida Hotels*, Windeyer J noted that the Royal Australian Institute of Architects' standard contract documentation contained the words: 'The architect shall give such periodical supervision and inspection as may be necessary to ensure that the works are being executed in general accordance with the contract'.[24] This wording corresponded closely with that utilised by the RIBA and by the Singapore Institute of Architects; *Jameson v Simon* was also followed in Singapore in *Sim and Associates v Alfred Tan*,[25] where it again supported a duty of general supervision.

It was changes to standard form wording which produced major change in this area in the UK. As early as the 1970s,[26] the word 'supervision' disappeared from the RIBA's widely used conditions of engagement,[27] leaving in its place the concept of 'inspection'. The consequences have been significant but complex. Even well after the disappearance of the term 'supervision' from the standard forms, architects were still being held liable for breach of the duty of supervision, because, mainly through informality of contract formation, they allowed a duty of supervision to be implied. In *Alexander Corfield v David Grant*,[28] HH Judge Bowsher QC regarded it as essential to consider 'The difficult question of what is sufficient supervision by an architect', in the absence of express contractual provision to the contrary. Ten years later, in *Consarc Design Ltd v Hutch Investments Ltd*[29] the same judge reflected on the change:

> the older forms of contract required the architect to 'supervise'. The more recent contracts, including the contract in this case, require the architect to 'visit the Works to inspect the progress and quality of the Works.' It seems to me that inspection is a lesser responsibility than supervision.[30]

---

[22] ibid, at 276, per Riddell J.

[23] *Florida Hotels Pty v Mayo* (1965) 113 CLR 588.

[24] ibid, at 590.

[25] *Sim and Associates v Alfred Tan* [1994] 3 SLR 169.

[26] RIBA Conditions of Engagement 1971 (1979 Revision).

[27] See A Lavers, 'The Architect's Responsibility for Inspection or Supervision': Society of Construction Law Paper No 40 (1994) (www.scl.org.uk).

[28] *Alexander Corfield v David Grant* (1992) 59 BLR 102.

[29] *Consarc Design Ltd v Hutch Investments Ltd* (2001) 84 Con LR 36.

[30] ibid, at 88.

The architect could not be liable to the client for negligent supervision when, using modern RIBA conditions of engagement, there was no such duty. In some countries, by contrast, supervision is still routinely undertaken, typically to meet the requirements of a building control regime.[31] It is, of course, still possible for an architect to be held to be in breach of the lesser duty of inspection, as in the recent case of *West v Ian Finlay & Associates*,[32] where the Technology and Construction Court (TCC) held an architect liable for failure to inspect mechanical and electrical fittings, as part of the duty of inspection.[33]

The second caveat concerns the relationship between the 'supervision' and 'decision-making' functions. They cannot be regarded as unconnected. In *Jameson v Simon*, the Lord Justice Clerk explicitly linked supervision with certification, holding that the CA has to 'be able to give his certificates upon knowledge, and not on assumption, as to how work hidden from view had been done'. The issue of certificates without inspection is likely to constitute breach of the CA's duty of reasonable skill and care, as in the Malaysian case of *Chin Sin Motor Works Sdn Bhd v Arosa Development Sdn Bhd*.[34]

But there is a crucial distinction between these functions. In supervising or inspecting, the CA is acting purely as agent for the employer and in the employer's interests. This does not preclude the possibility of an action in the tort of negligence by a party suffering, for example, personal injury, as, for example, in *Clay v AJ Crump*,[35] where an architect's negligent inspection of a wall led to a workman being injured. But it does mean that the CA's only contractual obligation is to protect the employer's interest by undertaking with reasonable care and skill its tasks under the professional services contract and as set out in the works contract. In certification, and the exercise of other decision-making functions, the position is very different. That this fundamental difference is of long duration, even antiquity, is considered in the next section.

III. Acting for the Employer versus Holding the Scales Even: The Early Cases

In the last quarter of the nineteenth century, the courts had to contend with the propositions that the CA was both acting for the employer and engaged in

---

[31] Singapore, Malaysia and Hong Kong are examples.

[32] *West v Ian Finlay & Associates* [2013] EWHC 868, [2014] EWCA Civ 316.

[33] The Court of Appeal held the architect entitled to rely on a net contribution clause and did not disturb the primary finding of the TCC on liability.

[34] *Chin Sin Motor Works Sdn Bhd v Arosa Development Sdn Bhd* [1992] 1 *Malayan Law Journal* 23, discussed further below.

[35] *Clay v AJ Crump & Sons Ltd* [1964] 1 QB 533.

making decisions as between employer and contractor. Two lines of authority emerged, although in the absence of obvious judicial policy, it must have been very hard to follow their development contemporaneously. In *Armstrong v Jones*,[36] the defendant architect had certified payments to the builder and was sued successfully by the client on the ground that the house had not been constructed in accordance with contract. The judge's direction to the jury[37] was that the architect would be responsible if they found that the giving of the certificates arose from negligence and want of caution in the duty of superintending[38] the work. This would seem to sit uneasily with *Stevenson v Watson*,[39] where it was held that an action against an architect for negligent certification could not succeed because a person in this position would not be liable for want of care or skill. In the words of Denman J:

> I do not intend to hold that he is to all intents and purposes an arbitrator, but I think that his duties are very analogous to the duties of an arbitrator ... I think that he is a person exercising very important functions requiring skill and judgment in cases of this kind ... and, unless he gave the duty up altogether from the first appointment, he is from the first a person exercising judgment on a matter on which the parties cannot exercise judgment.[40]

In the Canadian case of *Badgley v Dickson*,[41] the Ontario Court of Appeal distinguished *Stevenson v Watson*, Osler J actually referring to it as an action against an 'arbitrator'. In finding against the architect on a counterclaim to a claim for unpaid fees, the judge held that he was not absolved from obligations under his professional services contract with the employer merely because he was performing a particular role under another contract, ie the works contract:

> It would be an extraordinary result if we were obliged to hold that the contract which the building owner makes with the architect for his own protection, is neutralised by or inconsistent with a provision introduced into a different contract between the owner and the builder for the purpose of preventing or settling disputes as between themselves.[42]

The following year, in *Young v Blake*,[43] the English Court of Appeal went to the length of holding that the architect's re-measurement function conferred a

---

[36] *Armstrong v Jones* (1869), reported in *Hudson's Building, Engineering & Ship Building Contracts*, 4th edn (London, Sweet & Maxwell, 1914) vol 2, p 6.

[37] In the days when civil actions were heard in this way.

[38] The early term for 'supervision' was 'superintendence', a term still used in Australia and other common law countries. See Julian Bailey, *Construction Law*, 2nd edn (London, Informa, 2016) pp 343–44 for a comprehensive summary of terminology.

[39] *Stevenson v Watson* (1879) 40 LT 485.

[40] ibid, at 161–62.

[41] *Badgley v Dickson* (1886) 13 A.R. 494.

[42] ibid, at 499.

[43] *Young v Blake* (1887), *Hudson's Building, Engineering & Ship Building Contracts*, 4th edn (London, Sweet & Maxwell, 1914) vol 2, p 110.

quasi-judicial immunity from suit by the builder; the architect had no liability in negligence or breach of contract.

In *Rogers v James*,[44] the Court of Appeal considered this issue for the first time.[45] Again, the case was an action for unpaid fees from the architect with a counterclaim for negligent supervision. Lord Esher MR held that the certificate was 'final as between the building owner and the builder'[46] but did not govern the relationship between the architect and the owner. The building owner could question the competence of the architect: as Lopes LJ held,

> The architect must not act negligently ... the contract gave the architect no jurisdiction to decide any question of negligence as between himself and the building owner and the building owner could bring an action of negligence against the architect.[47]

The Court of Appeal got the opportunity to consider the position fully in *Chambers v Goldthorpe*.[48] Again, the architect's unpaid fee claim was met with a counterclaim of negligent measurement and payment of the contractor. In *Restell v Nye*, heard at the same time, the allegation by executors was of improper certification by the architect. The majority[49] held that the architect, in ascertaining the amounts payable and/or certifying sums due, occupied the position of an arbitrator and so was not liable for negligence in the exercise of these functions.

The clarification of the law at the dawn of the twentieth century was achieved by the crystallisation of the authorities of the previous 30 years into two strands. *Armstrong v Jones*, *Badgley v Dickson* and *Rogers v James* concerned the relationship of the architect with the owner; they comprised negligence in performance of duties undertaken for the protection of the owner. AL Smith MR in *Chambers* specifically dealt with *Rogers v James* as a case of negligence in not properly supervising the work under a building contract. *Armstrong v Jones* is more difficult to analyse in that way except by reference to the relationship between supervision and certification;[50] it was negligence in performance of inspection rather than the act of certification which could ground the decision.

Chambers v Goldthorpe also extended the scope of the 'quasi-arbitral immunity' cases. *Stevenson v Watson* and *Young v Blake* were decisions on claims brought by contractors alleging negligent certification, holding that no such action would lie. Relying on the same 'quasi-arbitral immunity' rationale, the Court of Appeal held that no action could be brought by either party for this reason. Both *Chambers* and *Restell v Nye* were claims by owners/owners' representatives; the result was a blanket immunity for this element of the CA's functions. The courts had concluded that the fact that the CA was placed in a position to make decisions between the

---

[44] *Rogers v James* (1890) 8 TLR 67.
[45] The first time reported.
[46] ibid, at 67.
[47] ibid, at 67–68.
[48] *Chambers v Goldthorpe* [1901] 1 KB 624. Heard with *Restell v Nye*.
[49] Romer LJ dissenting.
[50] Discussed above.

two parties to the contract should mean that neither would have a right of action based on negligent performance of the decision-making function.

IV. *Sutcliffe v Thackrah* and the Removal of Immunity

Fewer than eight years had passed since the decision of *Sutcliffe v Thackrah*,[51] when the authors of the newly published text on 'Professional Negligence'[52] remarked that the effect of the House of Lords' decision was that an architect did not 'in the absence of specific agreement act as an arbitrator between the employer and the contractor and was not immune from an action in negligence at the suit of the employer for over-certification.'[53] They added that 'The question whether in the same circumstances the architect might owe a duty to the contractor was expressly left undecided.'[54] The first of these two elements of analysis, namely the CA's loss of immunity, leading to the immediate exposure to professional negligence claims by the employer, is clear enough. It had been coming. Donald Keating QC, in one of his greatest triumphs, had cited to the House of Lords in *Thackrah* the South African case of *Hoffman v Meyer*,[55] in which the Cape Province Divisional Court had roundly criticised the immunity concept in general and *Chambers v Goldthorpe* in particular.[56] Ogilvie Thompson J in *Hoffman* described the result of the latter case, by which the owner was bound by a certificate and yet had no redress against the party issuing it, as 'both inequitable and contrary to the true nature of the relationship between the building owner and the architect.'[57] He saw the false logic in proceeding from a requirement of impartiality to immunity:

> The circumstance that in determining these matters the architect must be impartial – in the sense that he must not cheat the contractor but must certify the amount to which the contractor is entitled – is not, in my judgement, any sufficient warrant for investing the architect with the character of an arbitrator or quasi-arbitrator.[58]

Lord Denning MR had given (obiter) due warning in *Hosier & Dickinson Ltd v P&M Kaye Ltd*,[59] where he held that the architect 'owes a duty to the employers to use due care in giving his final certificate. If he should negligently give a final certificate barring the employers from a good claim, he would, I think, be liable in damages.'[60] The example given by Lord Denning of a certificate barring a claim,

---

[51] *Sutcliffe v Thackrah* [1974] AC 727.
[52] RM Jackson and J Powell, *Professional Negligence* (London, Sweet & Maxwell, 1982), p 41.
[53] ibid, at 41, para 2.20.
[54] ibid, at 41, para 2.20.
[55] *Hoffman v Meyer* (1956) 2 SALR 752.
[56] The preference was for Romer LJ's dissenting view.
[57] (1956) 2 SALR 752 at 757.
[58] ibid, at 758.
[59] *Hosier & Dickinson Ltd v P&M Kaye Ltd* [1970] 1 WLR 1611.
[60] ibid, at 1616.

rather than 'mere' over-certification, was actually prophetic, given the subsequent decision of the Court of Appeal, holding that final certificates could do exactly that, in *Crown Estate Commissioners v John Mowlem and Co Ltd.*[61] The Court held that a final certificate under JCT 80 would provide a good defence for a contractor to allegations that its work did not satisfy the requirements of the contract. As a contemporary *Architects Journal*[62] commentary noted with some alarm: 'in the absence of an alternative target, the employer is likely to react to the subsequent emergence of defects by blaming the architect for wrongful certification.' The JCT subsequently addressed this issue in the later editions of its contracts, but a similar result was noted under the Institution of Chemical Engineers contracts in *Matthew Hall Ortech Ltd v Tarmac Roadstone.*[63] Where the final certificate actually determined the possibility of rights of recovery against the contractor, rather than merely acting as a payment mechanism,[64] the focus would inevitably shift to the professional who had issued it. See also *Oxford University Fixed Assets Ltd v Architects Design Partnership*[65] on the inability of the CA to recover from the contractor in respect of the negligent issue of a final certificate.

Lord Denning MR had given further warning of the likelihood of impending change in his powerful dissenting judgment in *Arenson v Arenson.*[66] He agreed that *Chambers v Goldthorpe* should be reconsidered in the light of *Hedley Byrne v Heller*[67] and quoted obiter remarks by Lord Coleridge CJ in *Clemence v Clarke*[68] to the effect that 'a professional man might be liable for misconduct in giving a certificate'.[69] The learned Chief Justice had said[70] that the plaintiff owner

> having got the certificates in good faith and without any suggestion of collusion or fraud has the right to rely upon them ... If his architect had been guilty of anything like misconduct ... I strongly think that [the owner] would have had an action against his architect to recover damages from the architect, and, amongst those damages, any sum that he had improperly to pay to a contractor in consequence of his architect's misconduct.[71]

The Law Lords in *Sutcliffe v Thackrah* dealt almost summarily with the majority decision of the Court of Appeal in *Arenson v Arenson* and with *Chambers*

---

[61] *Crown Commissioners v John Mowlem and Co Ltd* (1994) 70 BLR 1.
[62] Mark Klimt, 'The case of the final certificate' (February 1995) 201(7) *Architects Journal* 40.
[63] *Matthew Hall Ortech Ltd v Tarmac Roadstone Ltd* (1998) 87 BLR 96.
[64] The Singapore SIA and PSSCOC contracts made clear that no certificate would be conclusive evidence of completion of the works according to the contract; no doubt a lasting tribute to the powerful influence of Ian Duncan Wallace QC.
[65] *Oxford University Fixed Assets Ltd v Architects Design Partnership* [1999] EWHC 271 (TCC).
[66] *Arenson v Arenson* [1973] Ch 346.
[67] *Hedley Byrne & Co Ltd v Heller & Partners Ltd* [1964] AC 465.
[68] *Clemence v Clarke* (1880), Hudson's *Building, Engineering & Ship Building Contracts*, 4th edn (London, Sweet & Maxwell, 1914) vol 2, p 54.
[69] [1973] Ch 346, at 366.
[70] *Clemence v Clarke* (n 68 above) at 69, cited in *Arenson v Arenson* [1973] Ch 346 at 366.
[71] ibid, at 367.

v Goldthorpe. Lord Reid buried, presumably forever, the idea of the certifying CA as a quasi-arbitrator:

> Persons who undertake to act fairly have often been called 'quasi-arbitrators'. One might almost suppose that to be based on the completely illogical argument – all persons carrying out judicial functions must act fairly, therefore all persons who must act fairly are carrying out judicial functions. There is nothing judicial about an architect's function in determining whether certain work is defective. There is no dispute.[72]

Chambers v Goldthorpe, was 'virtually indistinguishable on its facts'[73] from *Sutcliffe v Thackrah* and was overruled.

Lord Morris of Borth-y-Gest agreed that:

> The circumstance that an architect in valuing work must act fairly and impartially does not constitute him either an arbitrator or a quasi-arbitrator. The circumstance that a building owner and contractor agree between themselves that a certificate of an architect showing a balance due is to be conclusive evidence of the works having been duly completed and that the contractor is entitled to receive payment does not of itself involve that the architect is an arbitrator or quasi-arbitrator in giving his certificate. *Chambers v Goldthorpe* was wrongly decided.[74]

It is interesting to note that two of the occupational groups with whom arbitrators were compared by Lord Salmon were to suffer significant losses of immunity: barristers (and solicitors) conducting advocacy[75] and expert witnesses.[76] The immunity of arbitrators survived but would not extend to a CA.

Potential liability to the employer was thereby established and is a part of the CA's risk exposure, as subsequent cases have repeatedly demonstrated. Oliver LJ stated that this position applied in the Court of Appeal's decision of *Townsend v Stone Toms & Partners*:[77]

> The whole purpose of certification is to protect the client from paying to the bidder more than the proper value of the work done, less proper retentions, before it is due. If the architect deliberately over-certifies work which he knows has not been done properly, this seems to me a clear breach of his contractual duty, and whether certification is described as 'negligent' or as 'deliberate' is immaterial. If, after certification and payment, Laings (the builder) had gone out of business leaving the work unrectified, I cannot see how the defendants could possibly have had any answer to a claim for damages … whether something is a breach of duty cannot depend upon whether the builder remained solvent or not. If it was a breach of duty when it occurred, it remains a breach of duty.

---

[72] *Sutcliffe v Thackrah* [1974] AC 727 at 737.
[73] ibid, at 738.
[74] ibid, at 753.
[75] *Arthur JS Hall and Co v Simons* [2000] UKHL 38.
[76] *Jones v Kaney* [2011] UKSC 13.
[77] *Townsend v Stone Toms & Partners* (1984) 27 BLR 32, 46.

The exposure to liability is not limited to the certification function. In *West Faulkner v London Borough of Newham*,[78] it was held to include interpretation and application of the termination provisions of the contract. Nor is it limited solely to CAs who belong to a professional group such as architects or engineers. In *Great Eastern Hotel Co Ltd v John Laing Construction Ltd*,[79] the project was based on the construction management method of procurement, and the responsibility of the defendant construction manager was 'managing, administering, planning and co-ordinating of the trade contracts.' The court held that it had been guilty of 'institutionalised misreporting' of delays: 'the defendants failed to comply objectively with their contractual obligation to report candidly and objectively as to the extent of the delay which was known to them.'[80]

An archetypal illustration of the modern position of the CA in this respect can be found in the TCC decision of *George Fischer Holding Ltd v Multi Design Partnership*,[81] in which it was held that there had been no adequate justification for the issue by the CA of a certificate of practical completion. HH Judge Hicks QC said that if the document issued was a certificate under clause 20 of the contract, the CA quantity surveyors

> were manifestly in breach of their duties as supervising officer in issuing it in view of the undisputed fact that practical completion had not been achieved. If it was not then [they] were equally in breach of duty in not making that plain to the parties and on the face of the document.

V. Potential Liability to Other Parties

Sutcliffe v Thackrah left open the possibility of liability for negligent certification to parties other than the employer. This could include the employer's purchasers and even the lenders financing the purchase. In *Chin Sin Motor Works Sdn Bhd v Arosa Development Sdn Bhd*,[82] purchasers had agreed to buy land and a house constructed on it from developers. The purchase price was to be advanced in stages by the lenders to the developers, on the basis of certificates issued by the developers' architect. When the developers went into liquidation, it was discovered that a number of certificates had been issued for work not completed or not done at all, notably the connection of utility services. The electricity supply was not connected until some four years after the architect had certified that it was done. It will be recalled that in *Arenson v Arenson*, Lord Denning MR had agreed with counsel that the CA's position should be reconsidered in the light of *Hedley Byrne v Heller*, and the Malaysian High Court utilised *Hedley Byrne* in holding that both

---

[78] *West Faulkner v London Borough of Newham* (1994) 71 BLR 1.
[79] *Great Eastern Hotel Co Ltd v John Laing Construction Ltd* (2005) 99 Con LR 45.
[80] ibid, at 201.
[81] *George Fischer Holding Ltd v Multi Design Partnership* (1998) 61 Con LR 85, 141.
[82] See n 34 above.

the purchasers and their lenders were entitled to rely upon the certificates provided to and relied on by them in advancing tranches of funding. It should be noted that to succeed in establishing a duty to parties other than the employer, it would be necessary to show reliance under normal *Hedley Byrne* principles. In *Hunt v Optima (Cambridge) Ltd*,[83] the Court of Appeal rejected claims by purchasers from a residential developer that they were entitled to rely on certificates from the project architect, because there had been no such reliance.

Hedley Byrne was also the basis of liability in the New Zealand case of *Day v Ost*,[84] where the New Zealand Court of Appeal gave judgment against an architect whose negligent assurance as to the soundness of the employer's financial position had led a subcontractor to undertake further work in the belief that it would be paid for; though the architect was undoubtedly the CA, the giving of the assurance is an example of stepping outside the duties laid down in the contract and thus incurring liability by acting gratuitously and without any obligation to do so.

The main possibility left open by the Law Lords in *Sutcliffe*, as specifically noted by Jackson & Powell in 1982,[85] was 'whether in the same circumstances the architect might owe a duty of [care to] the contractor'. At the time, there had been little enough indication of the answer. It will be recalled that the contractor's actions against the CA had failed in *Stevenson v Watson* and *Young v Blake*, but relying there on the rationale which was to reach fruition in *Chambers v Goldthorpe*.

There was a dissenting judgment by Grandpré J in the Supreme Court of Canada in *Vermont Construction Inc v Beatson*[86] to the effect that 'the architect's responsibility is not limited to the owner' and that a contractor suffering loss from the former's negligence should be able to recover. *Vermont* concerned design liability, but the prospect received a fillip in relation to contract administration in *Michael Salliss and Co Ltd v Calil*.[87] The architect was alleged by the contractors to have wrongfully granted an extension of time of 12 weeks, instead of the 29 weeks claimed, and to have accordingly failed to certify properly as to prolongation costs. The basis for this assertion was alleged failure by the architect, as CA, to act fairly and impartially as between owner and contractor.[88] HH Judge Fox-Andrews QC held that the contractor could have a right of action against a CA who failed to exercise reasonable care and skill in administering the contract[89] and certifying. He paid particular regard to dicta of Lord Salmon in *Arenson v Casson Beckman Rutley*[90] to the effect that as well as the architect's duty to the owner, there was 'a similar duty to the contractor arising out of their proximity'; the specific example

---

[83] *Hunt v Optima (Cambridge) Ltd* [2014] EWCA Civ 714.
[84] *Day v Ost* [1973] 2 NZLR 385.
[85] RM Jackson and J Powell, *Professional Negligence* (n 52 above) 41.
[86] *Vermont Construction Inc v Beatson* (1976) 67 D.L.R. (3d) 95.
[87] *Salliss and Co Ltd v Calil* (1987) 4 *Construction Law Journal* 125.
[88] The contract was the JCT 63 edition.
[89] JCT 63 in this case.
[90] *Arenson v Casson Beckman Rutley* [1977] AC 405.

cited being of an architect who 'negligently certified that less money was payable than was in fact due' because 'In a trade in which cash flow is especially important, this might have caused the contractor serious damage for which the architect could have been successfully sued'.[91]

HH Judge Fox-Andrews QC in *Salliss v Calil* sought to differentiate between those elements of the CA's function which were solely for the benefit of the owner and those which involved obligations to both parties. As to the former: 'He owes no duty of care to contractors in respect of the preparation of plans and specifications or in deciding matters such as whether or not he should cause a survey to be carried out'.[92] His Lordship made the interesting addition: 'He owes no duty of care to a contractor whether he should order a variation'.[93] However, insofar as concerned allegations by a contractor of failure to certify appropriately, these might be justified: 'if the architect is to be fair to both parties he has to exercise reasonable care and skill to achieve this'.[94]

The impression created by *Salliss v Calil* did not survive long, being overtaken by the Court of Appeal's leading decision of *Pacific Associates v Baxter*[95] and the High Court of Hong Kong case of *Leon Engineering and Construction Co Ltd v Ka Duk Investment Co Ltd*.[96]

Pacific Associates v Baxter can be viewed narrowly as part of the long-running direction of travel of the common law away from the superimposition of tortious duties in situations where the parties have by contract agreed their obligations and the means of their enforcement. Purchas LJ, in finding that no liability can be established in tort in circumstances where the engineer owes a direct duty to the contractor, as in this case, emphasised that this depended on the existence of 'contractual provisions in the contract which afforded an avenue enabling the contractor to recover from the employer'.[97] Purchas LJ could see no justification for superimposing on this contractual structure an additional liability in tort as between the engineer and the contractor. This approach was followed in the *Leon Engineering* case. The plaintiff contractors for a hotel project in Shatin argued that the project architects owed them a duty of care in considering claims and certifying. Bokhary J said that where, first, there is adequate machinery under the contract between the employer and a contractor to enforce the contractor's rights thereunder and, secondly, there is no good reason at tender stage to suppose that such rights and machinery would not together provide the contractor with an adequate remedy, then, in general, a certifying architect or engineer does not owe to the contractor a duty in tort coterminous with the obligation in contract owed

---

[91] *Arenson* at 438.
[92] ibid, at 131.
[93] ibid.
[94] ibid, at 130.
[95] *Pacific Associates Inc v Baxter* [1989] 2 All ER 159.
[96] *Leon Engineering and Construction Co Ltd v Ka Duk Investment Co Ltd* (1989) 47 BLR 139.
[97] [1989] 2 All ER 159 at 180.

to the contractor by the employer. Bokhary J's image of the CA 'shot at' from both sides[98] was a rather more colourful version of Lord Salmon's description of the architect as being exposed to the dual risk of being sued in negligence.

Certainly, the British Columbia Court of Appeal in *Edgeworth Construction Ltd v ND Lea and Associates*[99] regarded *Pacific Associates* as having decided that 'the web of contractual relationship in a complex construction project formed a crucial element in the whole context which governed the determination of the question of proximity'.[100] In reality, it is possible to see *Pacific Associates v Baxter* as having a much wider effect, despite the cautious formulation of principle by Purchas LJ. The contract in use for the dredging of Dubai Creek was the 2nd Edition of the FIDIC Red Book and it contained, at Clause 67, provision for ICC arbitration of all disputes or differences in respect of which the Engineer's decision had not become final and binding. It is true that it had a Particular Condition to the effect that 'Neither any member of the employer's staff nor the Engineer nor any of his staff, nor the Engineer's representative shall be in any way personally liable for the acts or obligations under the contract' but in giving to the Contractor contractual mechanisms for making claims challenging certificates and, if necessary, resolving disputes, it was completely typical of UK and international engineering contracts.

As Bailey[101] has summarised the result:

> where, as is often the case, parties to construction or engineering projects have gone to great lengths in spelling out their respective rights and obligations as against each other, it will be difficult to draw the conclusion that one party (scil, the contract administrator) has assumed an unstated liability towards another (scil, the contractor) for economic losses that the latter may suffer should the former not exercise due care.

In such circumstances, the contract will govern and the contractor's (sole) means of recourse for alleged under-certification will be to challenge the certificate via the mechanisms provided.

VI. Obligations of the CA Beyond Reasonable Care and Skill

If the CA's duty to the employer is that of reasonable care and skill, whether in the agency tasks or in the certifying/decision-making functions, and given that

---

[98] Perhaps redolent of Tennyson's 'Charge of the Light Brigade' who faced 'cannon to right of them, cannon to left of them'.
[99] *Edgeworth Construction Ltd v ND Lea and Associates* (1991) 54 BLR 11. Though see the revision of the role of contracts by McLachlin J in the Canadian Supreme Court in *Edgeworth Construction Ltd v ND Lea & Associates Ltd* [1993] 3 S.C.R. 206.
[100] (1991) 54 BLR 11 at 21.
[101] Bailey, *Construction Law* (n 38 above) vol 1, p 425.

no duty of care to the contractor will arise in the tort of negligence, save in rare cases of physical harm like *Clay v Crump*, or self-created advice situations like *Day v Ost*, the question remains as to the effect of a requirement in the main contract that the CA will treat its role in a particular way. Such requirements have long been found in the standard forms and continue to be so. They may be specific or general. In the 1999 FIDIC Red Book,[102] the Engineer's obligation was 'whenever these Conditions provide that the Engineer shall proceed ... to agree or determine any matter ... If agreement is not achieved, the Engineer shall make a fair determination'; 'fairness' replaced the concept of 'impartiality' in its predecessor, FIDIC 4th Edition:[103]

> Wherever, under the Contract, the Engineer is required to exercise his discretion by (a) giving his opinion, decision or consent, (b) expressing his satisfaction or approval, (c) determining value, or (d) otherwise taking action which may affect the rights and obligations of the Employer or the Contractor, he shall exercise such discretion impartially.[104]

In a modern JCT contract,[105] specific tasks are subject to such requirements, so a valuation of a variation 'shall be made on a fair and reasonable basis';[106] likewise an extension of time[107] shall be what the Architect/Contract Administrator 'estimates to be fair and reasonable'. Especially given that these duties are placed on the CA by a contract to which the CA is not a party, how, or whether, they are to be enforced is not straightforward, and the courts have played a crucial role in deciding on their application.

Historically, when the 'quasi-arbitral' analysis was in the ascendant, the expectation was that the CA would act 'impartially' or 'independently'. This would proscribe any form of collusion between CA and employer, in particular. In *Hickman & Co v Roberts*,[108] the employers had actually written to the architect instructing him to 'reduce the account as much as possible' and the architect's response to the contractor's claims was that 'in the face of their instructions to me I cannot issue a certificate whatever my own private opinion in the matter'. The House of Lords, while stopping short of a finding of fraudulent collusion on the facts, was very critical of the relationship between architect and employer: 'It is undoubted that the defendants Messrs Hickman tried ... to lead him astray in their own interests'.[109] It was noted that the architect 'was an intimate friend

[102] Sub-Clause 3.5.
[103] Conditions of Contract for Works of Civil Engineering Construction, 4th edn (1987) (1992 reprint).
[104] Sub-Clause 2.6.
[105] The example taken is the Standard Building Contract with Quantities (2016).
[106] Sub-Clause 5.3.3.
[107] Sub-Clause 2.28.2.
[108] *Hickman & Co v Roberts* [1913] AC 229.
[109] Per Lord Loreburn LC at 233.

of Mr Hickman, and a gentleman who had done as much as £100,000 worth of work for them',[110] which were just the kind of facts requiring the architect to maintain 'the confidence that is entertained by builders and by contractors in referring their disputes'. The position can be exacerbated in the public sector if the employer chooses to appoint as CA a member of its own staff. Fletcher Moulton LJ commented disapprovingly on this practice in *Robert W Blackwell & Co Ltd v Mayor of Derby*[111] as likely to result in a conflict of interest between their duties to the authority which employs them and their duties under the contract.[112] It is not necessary to go the length of proving fraudulent collusion between employer and CA,[113] although in principle such a finding could ground an action in the tort of deceit.[114] If the CA has failed to fulfil its duty towards the parties, this is capable of producing consequences as between them. Thus in *Hickman v Roberts* and in *Brodie v Cardiff Corporation*,[115] the effect would be that the decision in the former and absence of decision in the latter would not avail the employer and the contractor would be permitted to recover the amount of its claim.

Lord Hoffmann in *Beaufort Development (NI) Ltd v Gilbert Ash (NI) Ltd*[116] took a more pragmatic, even cynical, view of what could be expected of a CA:[117] 'The architect is the agent of the employer. He is a professional man but can hardly be called independent.' This recognition of the tension between the commercial and professional relationships of employer, CA and contractor may have the merits of realism, but it is seriously problematic for modern tribunals seeking to apply the appropriate test to the facts of the CA's conduct, and its effect on the contractor's entitlements.

VII. The Contribution of the Technology and Construction Court

AMEC Civil Engineering Ltd v Secretary of State for Transport[118] arose out of the Thelwall Viaduct renovation project, executed under the ICE 5th form of contract[119] (as amended). After practical completion, certain defects were identified in the

---

[110] Per Lord Alverstone at 237.

[111] *Robert W Blackwell & Co Ltd v Mayor of Derby* (1909) *Hudson's Building, Engineering & Ship Building Contracts*, 4th edn (London, Sweet & Maxwell, 1914) vol 2, p 401.

[112] Cited by Bailey, *Construction Law*, 2nd edn (n 38 above) p 370.

[113] Lord Atkinson in *Hickman v Roberts* (n 108 above) (p 238) refers to the words 'collusion, corruption or fraud' as 'rather extravagant terms to apply to the conduct that has been established'.

[114] This would be a high bar for the claimant to clear evidentially and it is unsurprising that it is rarely attempted.

[115] *Brodie v Cardiff Corporation* [1919] AC 337.

[116] *Beaufort Development (NI) Ltd v Gilbert Ash (NI) Ltd* [1999] 1 AC 266.

[117] ibid at 276.

[118] *AMEC Civil Engineering Ltd v Secretary of State for Transport* [2004] EWHC 2339 (TCC).

[119] ICE Standard Form of Civil Engineering Contract, 5th edn (1973).

works and AMEC referred a dispute[120] to the engineer for decision. The employer referred the dispute to arbitration and AMEC argued that the arbitrator lacked jurisdiction.

The case is perhaps most celebrated for the first ground of challenge, on the existence of a dispute, of which *Hudson*[121] says that the 'summary by Jackson J in *AMEC Civil Engineering Ltd v Secretary of State for Transport* has now been approved twice in the Court of Appeal'.[122] But the second ground of challenge raised questions about the behaviour of the engineer. It was argued for AMEC, based on *Sutcliffe v Thackrah*, that the engineer in making his decision fell into the category of a quasi-arbitrator. Jackson J rejected this submission, holding that the engineers were in 'the conventional position of certifiers' and 'did not have any additional duties flowing from or attaching to the label "quasi-arbitrator"'.[123] He followed the rejection by Megarry J in *Hounslow London Borough Council v Twickenham Gardens Developments*[124] of the importation of the rules of natural justice into the work of the certifying architect, as 'still broadly correct as a statement of the position of the architect or engineer under many of the standard form conditions which are in use'.[125]

When AMEC appealed to the Court of Appeal,[126] Lord Justice May, as well as supplementing Jackson J's 'seven propositions', upheld his views on the validity of the engineer's decision: 'I reach the same conclusion for much the same reasons.'[127] The concept of 'impartiality' would not 'overlay independence and honesty so as to encompass natural justice ... the engineer has to act "fairly" so long as what is regarded as fair is flexible and tempered to the particular facts and occasion.'[128]

The outcome of this element of the *AMEC* case is that

> in certifying or acting under Clause 13 here the engineer, though not bound to act judicially in the ordinary sense, was bound to act fairly and impartially ... Fairness is a broad and even elastic concept, but it is not altogether the worse for that. In relation to persons bound to act judicially, fairness requires compliance with the rules of natural justice. In other cases this is not necessarily so ...[129]

The engineer is not obliged to act judicially.[130]

---

[120] Under Clause 66.

[121] Atkin Chambers, *Hudson's Building and Engineering Contracts*, 13th edn (London, Sweet & Maxwell, 2015), p 1213.

[122] In *Collins (Contractors) Ltd v Baltic Quay Management (1994) Ltd* [2004] EWCA Civ 1757 and in May LJ's judgment in *AMEC* (see below).

[123] [2004] EWHC 2339 (TCC) at [84].

[124] *Hounslow London Borough Council v Twickenham Gardens Developments* [1971] Ch 223.

[125] [2004] EWHC 2339 (TCC) at [88].

[126] *AMEC Civil Engineering Ltd v Secretary of State for Transport* [2005] BLR 227.

[127] ibid, at [46].

[128] ibid, at [47].

[129] *Canterbury Pipe Lines Ltd v Christchurch Drainage Board* (1979) 16 BLR 76, cited in *AMEC Civil Engineering Ltd v Secretary of State for Transport* [2005] BLR 227 at [47].

[130] [2005] BLR 227 at [51].

Less than nine weeks after the Court of Appeal had dismissed AMEC's appeal, the decision of the TCC in *Costain Ltd v Bechtel Ltd*[131] was handed down. Costain, part of a contractor consortium on the Channel Tunnel Rail Link project, sought an interim injunction to stop the exercise by the project manager, a consortium led by Bechtel, of its assessment and certification functions 'otherwise than impartially or in good faith'. The allegation was that the project manager, and also individually its chairman, had instructed its staff to challenge and disallow applications for payment, in an attempt to reduce budget overruns. A major challenge presented by the case was that the contract which the project manager was appointed to administer was based on the New Engineering Contract[132] and did not expressly require the project manager to carry out its duties in any way more specific than 'as stated in this contract and in a spirit of mutual trust and co-operation',[133] which applied alike to Employer, Contractor, Project Manager and Supervisor.

From this absence of express provision, Counsel for Bechtel sought to argue a different approach from that of 'conventional contracts' like ICE and JCT, so that there would be no implied term, as contended for by Costain, that the project manager would act impartially. Jackson J[134] rejected the differentiation, holding that under NEC:

> there are still many instances where the project manager has to exercise his own independent judgement, in order to determine whether the criteria are met and what precisely should be paid to the contractor or deducted from payments made to the contractor ... When the project manager comes to exercise his discretion in those residual areas, I do not understand how it can be said that the principles stated in *Sutcliffe* do not apply. It would be a most unusual basis for any building contract to postulate that every doubt shall be resolved in favour of the employer and every discretion shall be exercised against the contractor.

In the contract provisions, Jackson J declared himself 'unable to find anything which militates against the existence of a duty upon the project manager to act impartially in matters of assessment and certification'.[135] The fact that 'in discharging many of its functions under the contract, the project manager acts solely in the interests of the employer' was accepted but 'I do not see how this circumstance detracts from the normal duty which any certifier has on these occasions when the project manager is holding a balance between employer and contractor'.[136] In the result, the injunction was refused, by an application of the 'balance of convenience test',[137] so these statements are not strictly *ratio*[138] but their importance is

---

[131] *Costain Ltd v Bechtel Ltd* [2005] EWHC 1018 (TCC).
[132] Engineering and Construction Contract, 2nd edn (1995).
[133] Core Clause 10.1. NEC 4 2017 has similar wording in Clauses 10.1 and 10.2.
[134] [2005] EWHC 1018 (TCC) at [43]–[44].
[135] ibid, at [46].
[136] ibid, at [48].
[137] *American Cyanamid Co v Ethicon* [1975] AC 396.
[138] R Wilmot-Smith QC, *Wilmot-Smith on Construction Contracts*, 3rd edn (London, Oxford University Press, 2014) p 111 'The conclusion is not definitive.'

undoubted. Reference to *Keating*[139] is sufficient on its own to make this clear.[140] The Infrastructure Conditions of Contract[141] form contains the provision that 'the Engineer shall act impartially where the Contract requires him to decide any matter as between the parties to the Contract'[142] and the *Keating* commentary[143] explicitly links this to the *Costain* decision: 'This clause now precludes any such argument.' Even more importantly, the case is used in the interpretation of provisions of the NEC form of contract from which it arose. This ranges from general principles to specific clauses. In the former category, 'The distinction between agency functions and decision-making functions applies to the Project Manager in the NEC form'[144] and 'the Employer will be in breach of an implied term of the Contract if the Project Manager or Supervisor acts in a biased or unfair manner in making assessments or other decisions.'[145] Support for the availability of implied terms is also provided by the judgment of Jackson J in *Costain v Bechtel*. In the latter category (of Sub-Clause 50.4): 'The Project Manager must also act fairly or impartially between Employer and Contractor in making assessments'[146] (of forecast of Defined Cost to Ascertain Price for Work Done to Date in Option C)[147] and in responding to a Contractor's quotation for a Compensation Event (in Sub-Clause 62.3).[148] The astringent criticism of the drafting style by Edwards-Stuart J as 'a triumph of form over substance'[149] may make *Anglian Water Services v Laing O'Rourke Utilities*[150] the best known case on NEC, but *Costain v Bechtel* has a claim to be the most influential decision to date on those forms.

Both *AMEC* and *Costain* were immediately on point in *Scheldebouw BV v St James Homes (Grosvenor Dock) Ltd*,[151] in which the contractor, Scheldebouw, alleged that the employer, St James Homes, had been guilty of repudiatory breach of the trade contracts between them in dismissing the construction manager and itself taking on the construction management function. Jackson J considered the body of authorities on the position of the decision-maker under a construction contract, which now included, as well as *Sutcliffe v Thackrah*, the TCC and Court of Appeal decisions in *AMEC* and the then-recent case of *Costain v Bechtel*.

His Lordship derived three propositions[152] from them:

(1) The precise role and duties of the decision-maker will be determined by the terms of the contract under which he is required to act.

---

[139] See *Keating on Construction Contracts* (n 16 above).
[140] See also N Jones and C O'Carroll, 'The Independence and Impartiality of Contract Administrators under Various Standard Forms of Construction Contracts' (2007) 23 *Construction Law Journal* 475.
[141] 2014 edition.
[142] Sub-Clause 5.4.
[143] By Prof John Uff QC in *Keating on Construction Contracts* (n 16 above) at p 967.
[144] *Keating on Construction Contracts* (n 16 above) p 1054.
[145] ibid, at 1055.
[146] Clause 50.2 is the equivalent in NEC 4 2017.
[147] Clause 11.2 in NEC 4 2017.
[148] Also 62.3 in NEC 4.
[149] *Anglian Water Services v Laing O'Rourke Utilities* [2010] EWHC 1529 (TCC) at [28].
[150] [2010] EWHC 1529 (TCC).
[151] *Scheldebouw BV v St James Homes (Grosvenor Dock) Ltd* [2006] EWHC 89 (TCC).
[152] [2006] EWHC 89 (TCC) at [34].

(2)   Generally the decision-maker is not, and cannot be regarded as, independent of the employer.

(3)   When performing his decision-making function, the decision-maker is required to act in a manner which has variously been described as independent, impartial, fair and honest. These concepts are overlapping but not synonymous. They connote that the decision-maker must use his professional skills and his best endeavours to reach the right decision, as opposed to a decision which favours the interests of the employer.

These propositions would apply to a construction manager as they would to a traditional CA, whether architect or engineer, and whether or not it was under a traditional JCT or ICE contract. Given that the employer was entitled to remove the construction manager, the crucial question was whether the employer itself could meet the requirement of the role. The employer as CA was relatively unusual in the UK at the time of *Scheldebouw*. Jackson J referred to *Balfour Beatty Civil Engineering Ltd v Docklands Light Railway Ltd*,[153] where ICE 5th Edition had been amended to allow an Employer's Representative to act in place of the Engineer. Of course, the FIDIC Silver Book[154] is an example of a contract administered by the employer,[155] but it had not come before an English court. However, these contracts expressly provided for such an arrangement. Scheldebouw had entered into the contract, and no doubt priced its tender accordingly, on the understanding that it would be administered (i) by a third party and (ii) independently, impartially, fairly and honestly. It was therefore a breach of contract to remove a 'layer of protection' from the contractor. Jackson J accepted that an employer was capable of performing the role of a CA as the law required, though it would be 'more difficult for the employer than it is for a professional agent'.[156] He agreed with Lord Hoffmann in *Beaufort*[157] that 'the architect is not independent, because he is employed by the employer' but that the fact that he 'is not independent is perfectly consistent with the proposition that he is required to act in an independent manner in certain situations'.[158]

The significance of the *Scheldebouw* decision is apparent from the references to it in the text books[159] and from the reception by the learned editors of the Building Law Reports in their Commentary:[160] 'There is little direct authority on what exactly a construction manager is, and what he or it does, and this case is one of the very few to analyse this in any detail and is to be welcomed.' Perhaps most telling

---

[153] *Balfour Beatty Civil Engineering Ltd v Docklands Light Railway Ltd* (1996) 78 BLR 42.

[154] Conditions of Contract for EPC/Turnkey Projects 1999.

[155] See Christopher Wade, 'The Silver Book: The Reality' (2001) 18(3) *International Construction Law Review* 497 on the removal of the 'venerable' Engineer.

[156] [2006] EWHC 89 (TCC) at [46].

[157] *Beaufort Development (NI) Ltd v Gilbert Ash (NI) Ltd* (n 116 above).

[158] [2006] EWHC 89 (TCC) at [31].

[159] Eight each in *Keating on Construction Contracts* (n 16 above) and *Bailey, Construction Law* (n 38 above) for example.

[160] [2006] BLR pp 114–15.

is its enduring relevance. When Fraser J gave judgment in July 2017 in *Imperial Chemical Industries Ltd v Merit Merrell Technology*,[161] he referred at length[162] to the 'three propositions' and the reasoning in *Scheldebouw*, concluding

> In my judgement, exactly the same analysis applies to the contract here between ICI and MMT and Jackson LJ's (sic) reasons apply to this contract too, and indeed to most if not all of the standard forms in this field.[163]

VIII. Conclusion

To obtain an accurate appreciation of the position of the construction contract administrator, it is necessary to understand that it is essentially dynamic. For over 70 years, the expression 'quasi-arbitral' was regarded as excluding any liability for negligent certification. The decision of the House of Lords in *Sutcliffe v Thackrah* overthrew that received wisdom: because an arbitral role connotes a duty of fairness, it does not follow that a duty of fairness denotes an arbitral role.

As well as establishing that the CA routinely owes a duty of care in respect of decision-making such as in the issue of certificates, as well as in supervision/ inspection and other functions on behalf of the employer, *Sutcliffe* left open the possibility of rights of action by a contractor, eg in the context of alleged under-certification. This was largely, though not comprehensively, closed off by *Pacific Associates v Baxter*. Insofar as duties to parties other than the client are concerned, they will largely depend on the development of *Hedley Byrne* principles, as in *Chin Sin v Arosa Developments* or *Day v Ost*.

Chin Sin, as a Malaysian case, and *Day v Ost*, a decision of the New Zealand Court of Appeal, are further reminders of the 'jurisdictional factor'. The Scots case of *Jameson v Simon* on liability for supervision and its linkage with certification, was followed by the Ontario Court of Appeal in *Campbell Flour Mills v Bowes*, by the High Court of Australia in *Florida Hotels Pty v Mayo*, and by the Singapore Court of Appeal in *Sim Associates v Alfred Tan*. The High Court of Hong Kong in *Leon Engineering v Ka Duk* came to a similar conclusion to that of the English Court of Appeal in *Pacific Associates v Baxter*. But it cannot be assumed that even all common law systems will proceed at the same pace or to identical conclusions. The Cape Province Divisional Court in *Hoffman v Meyer* had rejected the reasoning in *Chambers v Goldthorpe* some 18 years before the House of Lords did so in *Sutcliffe*. *Spandeck Engineering (S) Pte Ltd v Defence Science and Technology Agency*[164] and *Kane Construction Pty Ltd v Sopov*[165] are leading modern examples

---

[161] *Imperial Chemical Industries Ltd v Merit Merrell Technology* [2017] EWHC 1763 (TCC).
[162] ibid, at [128]–[131].
[163] ibid, at [128]–[132].
[164] *Spandeck Engineering (S) Pte Ltd v Defence Science and Technology Agency* [2007] 4 SLR (R) 100.
[165] *Kane Construction Pty Ltd v Sopov* [2005] VSC 237.

of distinctive approaches taken by the courts of Singapore and Victoria respectively. Wider differences still are to be expected and encountered as between civil law jurisdictions. A European Society of Construction Law study by this author[166] posed to eight member states the question 'Can the client appoint a junior employee of his as contract administrator of a traditional construction contract?', a practice long disapproved by the English courts,[167] and received (inter alia) the following very significant responses: 'In Austria, we do not know the typical position of an Engineer (as under FIDIC) as a more or less neutral actor'; and from Germany 'The architect cannot and will never take on the role of an intermediary or of a wholly independent person'.

In all legal systems, whether common law or civil law, which support party autonomy, the content of the contracts (both the construction contract and the contract for professional services between the CA and the client) will be crucial in regulating duty and liability. Here, too, the narrative has been, and continues to be, dynamic. The FIDIC contracts moved, as discussed above,[168] from the Engineer's duty of 'impartiality' in the 4th Edition of the Red Book to a duty to be 'fair' in the decision making function in the 1999 Edition. The 'fairness' concept is retained in the 2017 Edition, but is now in its turn supplemented by the provision that in carrying out his/her duties regarding agreement or determination 'the Engineer shall act *neutrally* between the Parties and shall not be deemed to act for the Employer' (emphasis added).[169] What FIDIC meant by this is indicated in the Guidance Notes:[170]

> By these statements it is intended that, although the Engineer is appointed by the Employer and acts for the Employer in most other respects under the Contract, when acting under this Sub-Clause the Engineer treats both Parties even-handedly, in a fair and unbiased way.

The meaning of 'neutrally' in any given legal system will have to be determined, with or without resort to 'even-handedly' and 'in a fair and unbiased way'.

In any legal system, and a fortiori in a common law system with a highly developed doctrine of precedent, ultimately CAs and arbitrators will look to judicial pronouncements to provide guidance on how they should fulfil their contract administration/decision-making functions and their liability in respect of failure to do so; future contract drafting will also have regard to them. The NEC forms of contract have never contained exact equivalents of the express JCT and FIDIC requirements of 'fairness' or 'impartiality', and this applies to the 2017 4th Edition. *Costain v Bechtel* established what is the 'normal duty' [ie absent clear express

---

[166] A Lavers, 'Ethics in Construction Law – European Society of Construction Law Study: Responses from Eight Member Countries' (2007) 24(4) *International Construction Law Review* 435.
[167] See n 109 above.
[168] See text to nn 102–104.
[169] Red and Yellow Books (2017) Sub-Clause 3.7.
[170] Red and Yellow Books p 21.

provision to the contrary] 'which any certifier has', in English law. The users of the NEC are forewarned and those drafting the Infrastructure Conditions of Contract have also taken note accordingly.

That there could be express provision for no third-party neutral at all is clear from *Scheledebouw v St James*, which would uphold the use of the FIDIC Silver Book (though the 2017 2nd Edition provides that in carrying out Agreement or Determination functions 'the Employer's Representative shall not be deemed to act for the Employer',[171] which is counter-intuitive to say the least).

But more importantly, *Scheldebouw* establishes limits to that possibility, so that it cannot be imposed unilaterally by one party of the other, or adopted subsequent to agreement being reached, to replace the 'third-party neutral' model. It does more, setting out in restatement format, the principles which have been developed in the English law cases, so that these could be turned to and adopted by the TCC over a decade later, as they were in the *ICI* case.

The development of the rules governing the duty of the contract administrator has been dynamic – at times, even dramatic. *AMEC, Costain* and *Scheldebouw* together constitute the contribution of the then Jackson J to that development. The construction industry and the legal profession which serves it must depend heavily on those who apply those rules to understand in every sense what it means 'to hold the scales even'.

---

[171] Sub-Clause 3.5.

PART VIII

Private Finance Initiatives (PFIs)

16

PFI Problems: The Emperor Claudius and the Tiger Tails

MRS JUSTICE JEFFORD DBE

In 43 AD four Roman legions led by Claudius invaded Britain and subdued the indigenous Celtic tribes.

I. Introduction

Thus, following the enumeration of its twenty-one parts, began the judgment of Jackson J in *Midland Expressway Limited v Carillion Construction Ltd.*[1] Well-versed in the history of Roman Britain, Jackson J went on to explain his memorable introduction. The Romans brought with them remarkable engineering skills which they deployed to construct a network of roads across Britain. The routes of many of those roads remain in use today. First and most important of those roads was Watling Street which ran from Kent through London – as it still does – on to St Albans, across the Midlands and finally into Wales.

Fast forwarding to modern times, plans were made to alleviate congestion on the M6 by the construction of a new stretch of motorway originally known as the Birmingham Northern Relief Road (the BNRR), this road following in part the route of Watling Street.

It was from the outset a controversial project attracting opposition from varied groups leading to a public inquiry in 1995 to 1996, the outcome of which was that the project was given the go-ahead. The BNRR was intended to be a privately-operated toll road, making it the UK's first modern toll road and, at the time, its largest Private Finance Initiative project. The concession to design, build and operate the BNRR, or the M6 toll road as it became known, had already been granted to a Special Purpose Vehicle (SPV), Midland Expressway Limited.

On 27 September 2000, Midland Expressway, as 'the employer', and a joint venture of four construction companies entered into a contract under which the contractors were engaged to design and construct the road. The four companies

---

[1] *Midland Expressway Limited v Carillion Construction Ltd and Others* [2005] EWHC 2810 (TCC).

were Carillion Construction Ltd, Alfred McAlpine Ltd, Balfour Beatty Group Ltd and Amec Capital Projects Ltd. They were commonly referred to as CAMBBA. In the ensuing proceedings, this contract to design and construct was referred to as the D&C contract.

Construction was completed on time and the M6 toll was opened to the public in 2003.

CAMBBA's final account was not due to be submitted until the expiry of the maintenance period in 2006. In the meantime, CAMBBA submitted an array of claims to Midland Expressway. As explained below, they included a number of claims of varying size arising out of discrete issues; a larger claim for the so-called direct costs of the tiger tails; and a claim in excess of £57 million for so-called indirect costs or mitigation measures. As Jackson J in due course observed,[2] the parties wanted to resolve their disputes in an orderly manner before the time came for the 'tackling the final account'.

II. Round One

In the first instance, both parties submitted contractual disputes to adjudication. Two adjudicators, John Marrin QC and Roger ter Haar QC, decided these disputes. Virtually every one of their decisions was challenged in litigation and, in due course, determined by Jackson J, giving him the opportunity to provide his judgment in twenty-one parts, which may or may not be a record.

The range of topics covered by the litigation was, if not unprecedented, at the least eclectic. There were purely factual issues (for example, whether an agreement reached at the Belfry Hotel precluded the making of certain claims); a dispute about responsibility for the appropriate speed limit on the approach to toll stations; the height of coin baskets; the entitlement of Midland Expressway to share in discounts under the New Roads and Streetworks Act 1991; and the construction of the provisions relating to Provisional Sums.

The last in this list was the only matter to reach the Court of Appeal.[3] In summary, an issue arose because the D&C contract provided for payment for the expenditure of provisional sums but failed to contain any express provision for the omission of the provisional sum included in the contract. CAMBBA therefore claimed to be entitled to be paid the provisional sums in any event and the amount expended – an argument that succeeded, on the strict construction of the contract, in adjudication. Jackson J and the Court of Appeal took a rather more pragmatic approach, May LJ concluding that the provisional sums were there to be used or

---

[2] *Midland Expressway Ltd (t/a M6 Toll) and Secretary of State for Transport v Carillion Construction Ltd and Others (No 3)* [2006] EWHC 1505 (TCC) at [39].
[3] *Midland Expressway Limited v Carillion Construction Ltd* [2006] EWCA Civ 936.

not in accordance with the employer's instruction: 'To the extent they are not used they are not payable.'[4]

Jackson LJ's more recent observations in *Amey Birmingham Highways Ltd v Birmingham City Council*[5] chime with the approach that he and the Court of Appeal took to the provisional sums issue. In the *Amey* case, there was a PFI contract intended to run for 25 years. Jackson LJ observed that such a contract is likely to be of massive length, containing 'infelicities and oddities' and the parties should adopt a reasonable approach rather than latching on to the infelicities and oddities to disrupt the project or maximise gain.

In the *Midland Expressway* case, in the Court of Appeal, Jackson J's opening line was one that also caught the attention of May LJ, himself a classicist, who appears to have been more engaged by the possibility of a case delving into Roman history than one concerned with provisional sums. In an equally memorable passage he said this:

> [T]his issue was one of many issues which Jackson J, sitting in the Technology and Construction Court, decided in a judgment running to 651 paragraphs on 14 November 2005. Mercifully, the part of the judgment dealing with the issue about provisional sums is limited to paragraphs 426 to 453. I say mercifully conscious that paragraph 1 of the judgment opened with the sentence: 'In 43 AD four Roman legions led by Claudius invaded Britain and subdued the indigenous Celtic tribes.' ... It is not Jackson J's fault that the intrinsic general interest and even excitement of the judgment's opening paragraph is not maintained beyond paragraph 2.[6]

This last remark is a little unfair at least to my personal favourite of the many claims – also possibly a favourite of the judge – namely the claim in respect of the impact of archaeological finds. As junior counsel for CAMBBA, I found myself cross-examining on Roman burial practices – not previously my specialist area – and the archaeological significance of the burial finds along the course of the new road. This part of the case gave the judge the backdrop against which to observe that 'This area was revived following Hadrian's visit to Britain in 122AD. That emperor's interest in British affairs is well known.'[7] Disappointingly, no further emperors featured in the judgment.

Given the breadth and complexity of the disputes, the most remarkable aspect of Jackson J's judgment was the speed with which it was delivered. As soon as counsel had completed their closing speeches, the judge began to give judgment, continuing the following day, and using the transcription service provided for trial as a means of dictating his judgment. It was a monumental achievement.

It was also one that demonstrated the charm and courtesy that won Jackson J so many admirers in the Technology and Construction Court. At the conclusion of

---

[4] [2006] EWCA Civ 936 at [31].
[5] *Amey Birmingham Highways Ltd v Birmingham City Council* [2018] EWCA Civ 264.
[6] [2006] EWCA Civ 936 at [10]–[11].
[7] [2005] EWHC 2810 (TCC) at [563].

the judgment and downplaying his own remarkable achievement, Jackson J took time to express his appreciation of the 'excellent work done by the lawyers on both sides'. He continued:

> 648. … The bundle, although running to about 70 ring files, is user-friendly and contains everything which the court needs. The witness statements of both parties are clear, concise and to the point. The solicitors on both sides have rendered valuable service both to their clients and to the court in the preparation of the material for this trial.
>
> 649. Furthermore, the advocacy throughout this trial has been of a high order. I am indebted to both leading counsel and junior counsel for the excellence of the oral and written submissions and for the economy with which examination of witnesses has been carried out.
>
> 650. As a result of all these matters it has been possible for this substantial trial to proceed from opening speeches to judgment with the space of a month.

All these disputes had been resolved by the Court by 14 November 2005.

The disputes and the judgment serve to illustrate the scope of the issues that may arise on a PFI project and the complexities of the contractual arrangements, even those at the design and construct level of the contractual chain. However, given the nature of the disputes, and despite its other merits, this was not a judgment from which any significant principles could be derived.

III. Round Two

Before the ink was dry on this judgment, the parties and the judge had returned to court for 'round two' and a judgment, this time in nine parts,[8] about tiger tails.

As May LJ might have observed, the excitement of a case about tiger tails was not borne out in this round either, for tiger tails are not as exotic as they sound and are merely road markings.

At two points the M6 toll road diverges from and rejoins the M6: the southern tie-in (near Birmingham International Airport); and the northern tie-in (near Cannock). As a result it was necessary to design a road layout where a three-lane motorway diverged into two three-lane motorways. At the southern tie-in, the design agreed and adopted was one in which the M6 was widened for a short distance to allow a gradual take-off of traffic onto the M6 toll road. At the northern tie-in there was a more complex arrangement involving a take-off lane on a large embankment. White lines on the motorways guide drivers diverging or converging. The stripes allegedly resemble tigers' tails and on this project and in the litigation 'tiger tails' was the shorthand used for the road layouts required at the two tie-ins.

---

[8] *Midland Expressway Limited v Carillion Construction Ltd and Others (No 2)* [2005] EWHC 2963 (TCC).

In 2002, the tiger tails layout was the subject of Department's Change no 11 (DC11). Under the contractual arrangements between the parties, this was a 'project relevant event' and binding on both Midland Expressway and CAMBBA. There was no dispute that CAMBBA was entitled to additional payment for this work. The amount was, however, hotly disputed. On an interim basis, the Secretary of State for Transport had paid Midland Expressway, and Midland Expressway had paid CAMBBA, £1.5 million plus VAT. CAMBBA asserted that a further £9.8m was due to it.

The sheer complexity of the contractual arrangements and interrelationships rendered what might have sounded like a straightforward valuation dispute anything but – as a result not least of the differences between the Concession Agreement and the D&C Contract.

Firstly, the Concession Agreement between the Secretary of State for Transport and Midland Expressway was, of course, a PFI contract. As such it was exempt from the provisions of the Housing Grants, Construction and Regeneration Act 1996.[9] Nonetheless the dispute resolution procedure did make provision for adjudication. The first step in the procedure was for there to be a meeting of nominated individuals to endeavour to resolve the dispute. If they failed to agree (or if the dispute was expressly stated to be referable to the dispute resolution procedure) then the dispute could be referred to adjudication. Provision was made for service on CAMBBA, as the contractor, of any notice to adjudicate: if the contractor then considered that the issues referred to adjudication were potentially relevant to its rights and obligations, it could become party to the reference and have its rights and obligations determined at the same time.

So far as payment was concerned, the D&C contract contained provisions for payment, including a price adjustment and payment for a department's change. As the judge in due course summarised the position, the Concession Agreement and the D&C Contract together established 'an elaborate machinery' under which department's changes were valued under the Concession Agreement and the sums due passed down the line to CAMBBA.

The terms of the D&C contract sought to protect the employer, Midland Expressway, from exposure to liability for a department's change that exceeded what would be passed down the line. Clause 39.4.5 provided that the employer should bear no risk or liability arising from a department's change and have no liability to make payment, subject to certain exceptions, which included a liability pursuant to clause 39.4.4.

Clause 39.6.1 provided for the method of valuing the price adjustment. Clause 39.6.2 continued:

> Subject only to Clause Seven (Contractor's Rights) and notwithstanding any other provisions of this contract, the contractor's rights to any price adjustment under or in connection with clause 39 (Changes) in respect of a department's change shall in

[9] The Construction Contracts (England and Wales) Exclusion Order 1998.

no event exceed the amounts, if any, to which the employer is entitled to be paid by the Secretary of State in respect of a corresponding change pursuant to clauses 8.1.3.1 and 8.1.3.3 of the Concession Agreement.

Importantly, CAMBBA's position was that, under this procedure, where its estimate of the value of the change was not agreed and the change was not withdrawn, it was entitled to interim payments pursuant to clause 39.4.4.

Clause 7, referred to in these clauses, was the equivalent project relief clause. Equivalent project relief was defined as follows:

Equivalent Project Relief means a benefit or relief under the concession agreement to which the employer is or becomes entitled from time to time, pursuant to or under the concession agreement … to the extent that it is equivalent to a benefit or relief claimed by the contractor under this contract in respect of the same circumstances.

Clause 7 then provided:

7.1.1 The contractor shall, subject to clauses 7.1.1(a) and 7.1.1(b) be entitled to such proportion of any equivalent project relief as may in all the circumstances be fair and reasonable, but …

7.1.3 Notwithstanding any other provision of this contract, in the case of a project relevant event, the contractor shall only be entitled to payment or recovery by any means (including means of set-off or abatement) of any price adjustment to the extent that the following conditions precedent have … been satisfied …

Those conditions precedent were, in summary, an agreement or determination as between the Secretary of State and Midland Expressway that Midland Expressway was entitled to equivalent project relief in respect of such price adjustment and had received those funds.

Clause 7.2 placed an obligation on Midland Expressway to use all reasonable endeavours to pursue rights and remedies under the Concession Agreement. Clause 7.4 then continued:

Subject to clause 7.2 (Enforcement of Rights under Concession Agreement)

7.4.1 Pending determination, agreement or resolution of any equivalent project relief under the concession agreement, the contractor shall take no steps to enforce any right, benefit or relief under this contract to the extent that such right, benefit or relief relates to the same circumstances as those to which the project relevant event to which that equivalent project relief relates.

7.4.2 Following the determination, agreement or resolution of the equivalent project relief under the concession agreement, the contractor shall be conclusively deemed to have waived any rights, benefit, or relief under or in connection with this contract in respect of the project relevant event that gave rise to the entitlement to equivalent project relief in excess of those arising from such determination, agreement, or resolution. Accordingly, the contractor shall not take steps under the disputes resolution procedure, or otherwise, with the objective that the project relevant event should be resolved under this contract in any different manner from that under the concession agreement, and the contractor hereby waives any right to do so.

In other words, although CAMBBA was entitled to a proportion of monies paid to Midland Expressway as a price adjustment for a project relevant event, CAMBBA was not entitled to be paid anything unless and until monies had been paid to Midland Expressway under the Concession Agreement. Moreover, CAMBBA was prohibited from taking any steps to pursue an entitlement to equivalent project relief while that claim was unresolved under the Concession Agreement.

Such equivalent project relief clauses were commonplace in the contractual chain below PFI contracts. Their purpose was to protect the concessionaire, usually an SPV, from having to pay out money before it had received it. But, at the same time, such clauses placed the 'sub-contractors' in the invidious position of having to wait for their money, a position that the Housing Grants, Construction and Regeneration Act had been intended to avoid by its adjudication provisions and payment provisions.

Under the D&C Contract, a construction dispute was defined by clause 1.1 as:

> a difference or dispute of whatever nature between the employer and the contractor arising under, out of, or in connection with this contract [including] (a) any claim, demand or assertion as to contractual entitlement under this contract made by either party against the other party, which is neither agreed nor disputed by such other party, (b) any dispute as to any decision, opinion, instruction, direction, certificate or valuation of the employer, the employer's agent or the certifying engineer …

A construction dispute was to be resolved in accordance with the dispute resolution procedure set out in appendix 6 to the contract. That procedure mirrored the procedure under the Concession Agreement, providing first for a meeting to seek to resolve the dispute. If that was unsuccessful, the dispute was to be referred to adjudication. There were provisions to enable or require the contractor to become party to an adjudication under the Concession Agreement. Under the D&C contract, the Secretary of State had the option to join in an adjudication but could not be compelled to do so.

Paragraph 11 of the appendix provided for the employer to give notice if the dispute to be referred to adjudication related to a project relevant event. If the employer did so, the employer was obliged, if it had not already done so, to refer the dispute for resolution or determination under the Concession Agreement. Meanwhile paragraph 11.3.3 prohibited the contractor from taking any steps to enforce any of its rights under the contract which might 'prejudice or be inconsistent with' the operation of paragraph 8, under which the employer could compel the contractor to be joined to an adjudication under the Concession Agreement.

That brief recitation of the complex contractual background is important to an understanding of the issues that then arose when CAMBBA sought to refer the dispute about the direct costs of the tiger tails to adjudication.

It is also important to bear in mind that the D&C contract between Midland Expressway and CAMBBA, unlike the Concession Agreement, was subject to the

Housing Grants, Construction and Regeneration Act 1996. In the litigation which followed the Court had to consider the impact of the following sections:

— section 108(1) which provides that a party to a construction contract has the right to refer a dispute arising under the contract for adjudication under a procedure complying with this section. Under section 108(2)(a), the contract shall 'enable a party to give notice at any time of his intention to refer a dispute to adjudication'.

— section 113, headed 'Prohibition of conditional payment provisions', which rendered ineffective 'a provision making payment under a construction contract conditional on the payer receiving payment from a third person'.

On 11 October 2005, CAMBBA gave notice of its intention to refer a construction dispute to adjudication. That dispute was 'CAMBBA's entitlement to an interim payment in respect of the Department's Change 11 dated 14 July 2002'. There followed correspondence between Midland Expressway and the Secretary of State in which the Secretary of State declined to participate in that adjudication and Midland Expressway took steps to pursue claims under the Concession Agreement, as it was required to do by clause 7.2, seeking a meeting to resolve the dispute.

On 31 October 2005, CAMBBA served its referral notice. On the same day, Midland Expressway commenced Part 8 proceedings. The claim form sought declarations and injunctions against CAMBBA and the adjudicator. In essence, Midland Expressway's position was that, in the face of the contractual provisions in relation to adjudication and equivalent project relief, the adjudication ought not to proceed.

Jackson J identified the issues he had to consider as follows:[10]

(1)   Was there a construction dispute between Midland Expressway and CAMBBA?

(2)   Did clause 7 of the D&C contract prevent CAMBBA from pursuing their adjudication claim at that time?

(3)   Was CAMBBA entitled to press on with the claim for interim payment against Midland Expressway before the dispute resolution procedure under the Concession Agreement had been fully operated?

(4)   Was Midland Expressway entitled to any of the relief which it sought?

On issue (1), Midland Expressway's argument was that the valuation of a department's change was determined under the Concession Agreement, so that

---

[10] [2005] EWHC 2963 (TCC) at [50].

any dispute was in reality between Midland Expressway and the Secretary of State, and there was no construction dispute between Midland Expressway and CAMBBA. Jackson J disagreed for four reasons. Firstly, the definition of a construction dispute in clause 1.1 was 'broad and compendious' and sub-paragraphs (a) and (b) did not limit its breadth. Secondly, there were exceptions to the procedure under which a department's change was valued solely under the Concession Agreement and, thirdly, CAMBBA might be right or wrong about whether the claim fell within the exception but there remained a disputed claim which was a construction dispute.

Fourthly, Jackson J explained that there was a dispute between Midland Expressway and CAMBBA as to whether the provisions of the D&C contract that prevented CAMBBA from pursuing the claim or receiving payment until the mechanism under the Concession Agreement was operated and/or Midland Expressway was paid fell foul of sections 108 and 113 of the Act. Accordingly, CAMBBA said they were entitled to pursue their claims. He expressed the view that those assertions themselves gave rise to a construction dispute. This last reason points to a conundrum that arose in these particular circumstances. A dispute as to the proper construction of a contract could be referred to adjudication. So, as in this case, could a dispute as to whether a contractual provision was contrary to law. This argument was inherent in CAMBBA's claim. If CAMBBA was wrong, then it could not pursue its financial claim but no more could it pursue a claim to a decision as to the meaning and effect of the contract which would enable it to pursue a claim. So, it could be argued, if the adjudicator decided that he could proceed with the claim, that decision would not be one he had jurisdiction to make if the claim itself was made in circumstances where CAMBBA was not entitled to commence an adjudication.

That jurisdictional conundrum was, perhaps thankfully, not one that needed to be delved into because the issue was already before the Court. The real issue, therefore, was whether clause 7 prevented CAMBBA from pursuing its claim.

Midland Expressway's argument hinged on clause 7.4, which clearly sought to prevent CAMBBA from taking any steps to enforce a claim in respect of a project relevant event. In response, CAMBBA argued that 'insofar as that clause purports to fetter CAMBBA's right to an immediate adjudication, that clause is contrary to section 108(2) of the 1996 Act.'

The Court agreed with CAMBBA. Section 108(2) requires the contract to provide the right to give notice *at any time* of a party's intention to adjudicate. Jackson J agreed with the reasoning of His Honour Judge Toulmin CMG QC in *John Mowlem & Co plc v Hydra-Tight Limited*[11] and His Honour Judge Thornton QC in *RG Carter Limited v Edmund Nuttall Limited*.[12] In each of these cases there

---

[11] *John Mowlem & Co plc v Hydra-Tight Limited* (TCC) 6 June 2000, [2000] Adj LR 06/0, (2001) 17 *Construction Law Journal* 358, available at: http://www.nadr.co.uk/articles/published/AdjLr/JOHNMOWLEMvHYDRA2000.pdf.

[12] *RG Carter Limited v Edmund Nuttall Limited* [2002] BLR 359.

was a provision that deferred the time at which the contractor could commence an adjudication and in each case, the judge held that the terms did not comply with the Act.

That decision led the judge to the following question of whether clause 7.4 should be construed narrowly and in a manner compatible with the Act or whether the contractual adjudication provisions fell away and were replaced by the Scheme for Construction Contracts. It was a question he did not need to decide and he did not do so.

Midland Expressway still argued, however, that CAMBBA could not proceed with its claim for interim payment because of the provisions of clause 39.6.2. CAMBBA's response again turned on the Act and, in this instance, the prohibition on conditional payment provisions in section 113. Jackson J again agreed with CAMBBA. He regarded the effect of clause 39.6.2 as being that CAMBBA could not be paid any money in respect of a department's change until Midland Expressway had established an entitlement to payment under the Concession Agreement and that, if the original evaluation was in error, CAMBBA could not be paid the correct sum due until the dispute resolution procedure in the Concession Agreement had been operated. As he put it 'The practical consequence of clause 39.6.2 is that CAMBBA will not be paid for department's changes unless and until [Midland Expressway] has received a corresponding sum from the department' and 'this state of affairs is precisely what s.113 of the 1996 Act is legislating against.'

In any event, clause 39.6.2 had to be read with clause 7.1.3. Jackson J concluded that 'clause 7.1.3 in conjunction with clause 39.6.2 constitute express and ineluctable "pay when paid" provisions.'

Finally, Jackson J had to consider the effect of paragraph 11.3.3 of the disputes resolution procedure in appendix 6. On the facts, it did not come into play because Midland Expressway had, in his view, not served the relevant notice but, if it had, paragraph 11.3.3 would then postpone the time at which CAMBBA could commence an adjudication. It was, therefore, contrary to section 108(2).

The decision, therefore, firmly asserted that the courts would take a rigorous approach to ensuring the effectiveness of both sections 108(2) and 113.

In the course of his judgment, Jackson J observed that it might be thought surprising that the D&C contract contained provisions that were non-compliant with the Act. He surmised that the explanation might lie in the fact that the D&C Contract was based on PFI forms but was not itself a PFI contract. To that extent the case proved an object lesson in the perils of passing down contractual provisions without sufficient regard to the regimes (statutory or otherwise) that apply at different rungs on the contractual ladder. That said, it is difficult to see what Midland Expressway could have done to achieve a position in which its liability to CAMBBA, at least on an interim basis, was conditioned on the Secretary of State's liability to Midland Expressway.

In effect, the application of both sections 113 and 108(2) rendered the equivalent project relief clause of little or no effect in terms of when an entitlement to payment arose and could be pursued. At the time, that conclusion provoked considerable interest amongst those dealing with PFI contracts but it did not result in any body of case law about such clauses. The case highlighted the problems for all parties but was not the forum to offer a solution. The dearth of further case law might well be attributable to the implementation of other contractual schemes that were already in play at the time.[13]

It is at least worth noting, however, that concern about the impact of this decision did not lead to any substantial change in the law in respect of 'pay when paid' provisions. When the Act was amended by the Local Democracy, Economic Development and Construction Act 2009, section 113 remained unchanged and continued to apply to sub-contracts under PFI arrangements. However, sections 110(1A) and 110(1D) were also inserted, providing that the requirement in section 110(1)(a) for an adequate payment mechanism in a construction contract (as defined) was not met in certain circumstances – effectively outlawing clauses that relied on such circumstances. Under section 110(1A), an adequate payment mechanism is not provided 'where a construction contract makes payment conditional on (a) the performance of obligations under another contract or (b) a decision by any persons as to whether obligations under another contract have been performed'. First-tier PFI sub-contracts are excluded from the operation of this sub-section[14] and the exclusion in effect saves some elements of equivalent project relief clauses. Under section 110(1D), the operation of which is not excluded, an adequate payment mechanism is not provided where a construction contract

> provides for the date on which a payment becomes due to be determined by reference to the giving to the person to whom the payment is due of a notice which relates to what payments are due under the contract.

IV. Round Three

Returning to tiger tails, Jackson J's involvement with the M6 toll road was not yet over and there was still one further piece of litigation to come before him resulting in the judgment in *Midland Expressway Ltd and the Secretary of State for Transport v Carillion*.[15] As the title of the action makes apparent on this occasion the Secretary of Statement for Transport was also directly involved in the action. That involvement came about as a result of a convoluted tactical game.

---

[13] Shortly following the decision, in August 2006 the City of London Law Society Construction Committee produced a Guidance note on best practice and alternative approaches, which remains available online and provides a robust discussion of such mechanisms: http://www.citysolicitors.org.uk/attachments/category/117/constmidlandexpressway.pdf.

[14] The Construction Contracts (England) Exclusion Order 2011 and the Construction Contracts (Wales) Exclusion Order 2011.

[15] *Midland Expressway Ltd (t/a M6 Toll) and the Secretary of State for Transport Carillion Construction Ltd and Others (No 3)* [2006] EWHC 1505 (TCC).

It will be recalled that it was common ground that both Midland Expressway and CAMBBA were entitled to payment in respect of Department Change no 11 (DC11). Both the Concession Agreement and the D&C Contract drew a distinction between what were described as direct costs and indirect costs.

The Concession Agreement provided as follows:

> 8.1.3 Where, in the opinion of the concessionaire, a department's change would require additional payment to the contractor or the grant of an extension to the period for completion for the purposes of the construction contract or lead to an additional expense to the concessionaire ... the concessionaire shall furnish the department's agent within 28 days of the request or, as the case may be, of agreement or final determination to proceed with the department's change ... with a statement of the order of magnitude of:
>
> 8.1.3.1 The value of the additional payment, if any, to the contractor and/or the concessionaire relating to the proposed works;
>
> 8.1.3.2 The length of any extension of time ...;
>
> 8.1.3.3 The amount of any direct loss and/or expense to which the contractor may be entitled under the construction contract.[16]

The costs referred to in clause 8.1.3.1 were 'direct' costs and those in clause 8.1.3.3 'indirect costs'.

If the concessionaire's estimate was not agreed the Secretary of State was either to withdraw the change or 'make payment therefor on an interim basis in accordance with the procedures contained in the construction contract'.[17] In that case, Midland Expressway was obliged to cause CAMBBA, in any application for an interim payment under the construction contract, to identify, as a separate item, the amounts claimed in respect of the change,[18] and was further obliged to provide relevant documentation evidencing the costs referred to in clauses 8.1.3.1, 8.1.3.4 and 8.1.3.5. Clause 8 then provided:

> 8.1.6.2 Evaluation of the value of the department's change shall be made by the department's agent within 21 days of submission of the documents referred to in clause 8.1.6.1:
>
> 8.1.6.2.1 Applying the principles contained in the construction contract, including but without limitation, those relating to costs incurred for delay and disruption, if any ...
>
> 8.1.6.3 Where the concessionaire has proceeded in accordance with clause 8.1.6 the Secretary of State shall pay to the concessionaire the amount determined pursuant to clause 8.1.6.2 or, if the concessionaire shall object to such determination, as determined by the disputes resolution procedure.

Under the D&C contract, payment for department's changes was dealt with under clause 39. To a large extent, and as might be expected, these provisions mirrored

---

[16] That is, the D&C contract.
[17] Clause 8.1.6.
[18] Clause 8.1.6.1.

those under the Concession Agreement so as to enable the concessionaire to operate the provisions under that agreement. This was the elaborate machinery the judge had already referred to in his earlier judgment. The same distinction between 'direct' and 'indirect' costs was drawn. Importantly for the dispute that emerged, clause 32.3 also provided that the contractor should constantly use its best endeavours to preclude or mitigate delay and allowed for the recovery of additional expenditure incurred in mitigation of delay caused by a delay event. That was to be achieved by a price adjustment. Such mitigation costs were also described as 'indirect costs'.

If the parties were unable to agree the contractor's estimates for a department's change, either the employer had to withdraw the notice 'upon withdrawal of the corresponding notice by the department's agent under clause 8.1.6 of the Concession Agreement' or the employer should agree to make interim payments. CAMBBA was then obliged to identify in any application for an interim payment, as a separate item, the amount claimed for the department's change and provide relevant documentation evidencing costs. The department's change was to be valued by the employer, applying the relevant principles in clause 39.6. Clause 39.6.2 provided for a cap on the contractor's entitlement to a price adjustment in respect of a department's change which 'shall in no event exceed the amounts, if any, to which the employer is entitled to be paid by the Secretary of State in respect of a corresponding change pursuant to clauses 8.1.3.1 and 8.1.3.3 of the Concession Agreement'.

Although there was agreement that Midland Expressway and CAMBBA were entitled to additional payment for DC11, the amount was disputed both in principle and as to quantification. At the heart of that dispute was a disagreement as to the scope of the work that CAMBBA would have had to undertake if DC11 had not been issued.[19]

By May 2003 and the submission of CAMBBA's application for payment no. 33, the estimate of direct costs was nearly £7 million and the estimate of indirect costs £19.25 million. In subsequent applications the estimate of direct costs increased to over £11 million (the figure that had been referred to in the earlier proceedings) but the estimate of indirect costs remained at £19.25 million.

Shortly after the parties issued the claim forms in respect of the adjudication decisions that led to the first trial in the Technology and Construction Court, CAMBBA made a claim in November 2004 for indirect costs in respect of numerous events which caused delay and disruption, including DC11. Since the motorway had opened on time, this was, in fact, a claim, pursuant to clause 32.3, for the costs of mitigation measures.

Referred to in the judgment as 'the November claim', the claim was in simple terms a total costs claim in which the contract sum plus various adjustments

---

[19] See [2006] EWHC 1505 (TCC) at [33].

(including the direct costs of DC11) was deducted from the total costs of the project and claimed as mitigation costs. The total sum so claimed was £56,248,317. In a further display of judicial courtesy, Jackson J politely described the claim as lengthy, detailed and 'no doubt the product of much industry' but also as 'somewhat optimistic in its conception'. That was something of an understatement for a claim that assumed that every event that caused delay and disruption was Midland Expressway's responsibility and made no attempt to identify costs incurred as a result of individual events or even to apportion costs to individual events.

As matters continued through 2005, there was a further payment to CAMBBA on account of the direct costs of DC11 and then the Price adjudication which gave rise to the second set of proceedings in the TCC. That adjudication ultimately proceeded and resulted in a decision that Midland Expressway was to pay CAMBBA £6,898,772 in respect of the direct costs of DC11.

Meanwhile, Midland Expressway had, as Jackson J put it, taken the initiative. That initiative concerned the claim for indirect costs. On 3 November 2005, around the same time as the parties were discussing the M6 toll road's Roman history in court, Midland Expressway took the rather more modern step of referring the November claim to adjudication. Midland Expressway sought declarations, amongst other things, that it had not delayed CAMBBA's works; had not prevented or impeded CAMBBA in completing the works in time; and had not rendered necessary any mitigation measures.

This was, therefore, what might be called a negative adjudication – instead of waiting for a claiming party to commence an adjudication, the recipient of the claim commenced the adjudication to seek a decision that the claim was ill-founded. It would seem that this step was taken in the not unreasonable hope and expectation that the adjudicator would decide that this global claim could not succeed. That would have left open to CAMBBA the option of challenging that temporarily binding decision in litigation or placed the onus on them to advance a further and different claim. The adjudicator appointed was Mr Anthony Bingham and this adjudication was dubbed 'the Bingham adjudication'.

On 28 November 2005, Midland Expressway gave notice to the Highways Agency, on behalf of the Secretary of State, referring to adjudication the dispute between them as to the price adjustment for DC11. The subsequent referral notice referred both to direct costs and indirect costs. The adjudicator appointed was Mr Nicholas Dennys QC (the Dennys adjudication). CAMBBA gave notice that it would join in the Dennys adjudication and that it required its claim for the direct and indirect costs of DC11 to be determined in that adjudication.

Meanwhile, back in the Bingham adjudication, Midland Expressway's solicitors wrote to the adjudicator withdrawing the indirect costs of DC11 from the scope of the Bingham adjudication. That followed from CAMBBA's joining in the Dennys adjudication where it seemed at this point that those costs would now be determined.

On 12 December 2005, CAMBBA sought to withdraw far more from the Bingham adjudication. CAMBBA's position was this: the November claim was only ever an interim claim; it had been affected by the outcome of the first round of litigation; there had been progress in claim recovery; there was now a response from Midland Expressway (served in the adjudication); and in light of all these matters, CAMBBA did not intend to pursue the November 2004 claim. There was, said CAMBBA, therefore no point in pursuing this adjudication. CAMBBA reserved the right to make further claims after due consideration of its claims.

At that point, it might have appeared that CAMBBA's claims in respect of DC11 would be resolved in the Dennys adjudication; the Bingham adjudication would come to an end; and all other claims would be dealt with at a later date. But the intricacy of the contractual relationships and dispute resolution procedures meant that nothing so straightforward would happen.

Firstly, on 14 December 2005, the Secretary of State informed the adjudicator, Mr Dennys QC, of its position that CAMBBA's claim for the indirect costs of DC11 had never been advanced by Midland Expressway against the Secretary of State and had not been through the stage of the dispute resolution procedure in paragraph 1.1 of Schedule 15 of the Concession Agreement (which dealt with the meeting to resolve the dispute). It was not, therefore, said the Secretary of State, a dispute that could be referred to adjudication. Further, it was argued, CAMBBA's claims for direct and indirect costs/mitigation measures, an alternative claim for an employer's change (under the D&C contract), and an extension of time claim could not be joined. CAMBBA responded that it was Midland Expressway which maintained that it was required to pass on CAMBBA's claims (including the indirect costs of DC11) and that CAMBBA did not require the indirect costs of DC11 to be determined at this stage, not least because CAMMBA had withdrawn the November claim.

At this point in this increasingly bewildering story, it is easiest to quote Jackson J:

> At this point in the story the consensus seemed to be emerging that CAMBBA's claim for indirect costs had no place in the Dennys adjudication. Four days later, however, the tide turned. On 19th December [Midland Expressway's solicitors] wrote to the adjudicator, taking issue with CAMBBA's letter dated 15th December and asserting that any claim by CAMBBA for the indirect costs of DC11 must remain part of the Dennys adjudication. On the same day, the Treasury Solicitor wrote to the adjudicator, abandoning her previous objections and contending that the indirect costs of DC11 must be addressed in the current adjudication.[20]

So by Christmas 2005, things had come full circle. Now it was common ground between the Secretary of State and Midland Expressway that CAMBBA's claims for the indirect costs of DC11 were in dispute between them and had been properly referred to the adjudication between them and joined by CAMBBA. That position was no doubt adopted for the same reason that Midland Expressway had referred

[20] [2006] EWHC 1505 (TCC) at [69].

the whole of the November claim to adjudication – the hope and expectation that the claim would be found to be unsubstantiated in its then form. But it appears from the arguments later advanced that Midland Expressway's intention was that that would do more than place the onus on CAMBBA to advance its claim in a more coherent form.

Mr Dennys QC concluded that there was no dispute as to CAMBBA's indirect costs of DC11 to be referred to him. Midland Expressway's 'game plan' became apparent from the arguments in the adjudication, which the adjudicator recited in his decision:

> The apparent purpose of this shadow-boxing was confirmed … as being relevant to any subsequent attempt by CAMBBA to adjudicate a new or revised mitigation costs claim. In other words, it was suggested that if I were to decide that the original claim was, on the basis presented, misconceived, then a subsequent adjudication in relation to a refor-mulated or new mitigation costs claim would be precluded. I express no views on the soundness of that premise, except to observe that it is common ground that CAMBBA would not be prevented from litigating such a revised claim.

Mr Dennys proceeded to decide the direct costs of DC11 and assessed these at £8,862,116. After taking account of sums paid, he directed that the balance should be paid by the Secretary of State to Midland Expressway and down the line to CAMBBA. The total was, however, less than the amount determined in the Price adjudication and, therefore, apparently of no benefit to CAMBBA.

The Secretary of State and Midland Expressway, having pinned their colours to the mast in so far as the indirect costs claim was concerned, did not leave matters there and in March 2006 commenced proceedings against CAMBBA for declara-tions. Thus at the end of this convoluted procedural story, the Secretary of State became a claimant in litigation against CAMBBA.

The terms of the declarations sought made clear what the claimants sought to achieve. Various declarations were sought, but all to the effect that the adjudicator ought to have decided the indirect costs of DC11. The fourth and final declaration sought was that 'CAMBBA's claim for indirect costs arising out of or in connec-tion with [DC11] stands no real prospect of success and should be dismissed in any adjudication or litigation'. Prior to the hearing, both the Secretary of State and Midland Expressway clarified that they asserted that any future claim for indirect costs of DC 11 would be defeated by a plea of res judicata or would be an abuse of the process of adjudication or litigation. Both claimants then made an amendment to the declaration they sought so that it referred to 'any present or future formula-tion of CAMBBA's claim for indirect costs'.[21]

On the issue of whether there was any dispute as to the indirect costs of DC11 to be referred to adjudication, Jackson J endorsed the decision of the adjudicator.

---

[21] By the time this argument came before Jackson J he had already decided the case of *Quietfield Ltd v Vascroft Contractors Ltd* [2006] EWHC 174 (TCC) (upheld on appeal at [2006] EWCA Civ 1737), dealing with the extent to which successive applications for an extension of time (on different bases) raised the 'same dispute'.

Crucially, everyone knew that there was a claim for indirect costs which would require considerable work to articulate and advance. CAMBBA's applications for an interim payment of £19.25 million 'could not remotely be regarded by anyone as CAMBBA's detailed case on the indirect costs arising from DC11' and the November claim did not even attribute a specific sum to DC11. Midland Expressway's notice of dispute did not refer to indirect costs which were first referred to in the referral notice and the Secretary of State had been right to say that this went beyond what could be referred. CAMBBA had mistakenly sought to join the claim for indirect costs but quickly realised this was wrong.

The judge was at pains to say that he was not laying down any new principle and was following established authority as to the meaning of dispute. The decision was, therefore, very much on its own facts and 'unusual' and 'convoluted' facts at that.[22]

The effect of that decision on the facts was that it was not necessary to decide the further issue of whether CAMBBA had been entitled to withdraw the claim made for indirect costs of DC11. This raised an issue of rather broader application and the judge did not miss the opportunity to express a view: 'I have come to the conclusion that it is impossible to read into either the 1996 Act or the Scheme any restriction prohibiting a party from withdrawing a disputed claim which has been referred to adjudication.'[23]

That view turned on the statutory purpose of adjudication to arrive at an interim resolution of a dispute. It would, Jackson J considered, be contrary to that purpose to prohibit a party from withdrawing a claim it did not wish to pursue and would have the 'bizarre' consequence that parties would be forced to press on with bad claims in adjudication.

This part of the decision was, for the reasons explained, obiter but it was a clear expression of the judicial view that a party was entitled to withdraw a claim that had been referred to adjudication whether it was the referring party or not. The rationale is obvious – why should a party be stuck with a bad claim if it recognises it is a bad claim? But the practical implications were potentially much further reaching and less obviously attractive. A party, like Midland Expressway, which attempted a pre-emptive strike on a bad claim against it might simply find the bad claim withdrawn after it had expended substantial costs in an adjudication. Equally a referring party, realising the flaws in its claim, might simply withdraw it with impunity and start again later.

The argument that the provisions of the contracts also prohibited the withdrawal of a claim from adjudication was also rejected. Moreover, Jackson J said that if the adjudicator's approval had been required for withdrawal of the claim, then the adjudicator effectively gave such approval and was right to do so. The judge pointed out that 'All parties to this litigation have been making their way through

---

[22] [2006] EWHC 1505 (TCC) at [98].
[23] [2006] EWHC 1505 (TCC) at [101].

a procedural minefield' and 'All parties have made tactical errors from which they have subsequently sought to escape' and 'adjudication should not become a game of chess in which the tactical skill of the players determines the outcome'.

It followed from both strands of this decision that Jackson J did not need to determine the issues in relation to res judicata. But he went so far as to say that he would be reluctant to transplant those principles into adjudication and that it would not be right to shut CAMBBA out from advancing an articulated claim for the indirect costs of DC11 which it had not yet put forward.

By the conclusion of this third outing, the Court had decided the minutiae of the claims relating to a cornucopia of aspects of motorway construction and the principles of the resolution of the dispute about tiger tails. CAMBBA's claim for the direct costs of the tiger tails had been determined in adjudication. Jackson J recorded that, at the time of his judgment, the Bingham adjudication had not resulted in a decision and had gone into abeyance pending the decision in the litigation. History, or at least the history of this litigation, does not relate the ultimate outcome of the indirect costs claims in that adjudication.

V. The End Game

It is easy to see the flurry of activity following completion of the M6 toll road and particularly around the end of 2005 as a clever procedural game. In a sense, that would be fair, but it was a game played to try to sort out as many claims and disputes as possible before the final account was due, it was one played in a procedural minefield and it was one in which all parties tried to take advantage of the time- and cost-effective decision-making process offered by the still relatively recent introduction of adjudication. The issues that then arose threw into stark relief the difficulties of interrelated contracts where one was subject to the Housing Grants, Construction and Regeneration Act 1996 and another was not. Clear decisions were reached on some issues but the more general PFI problems remained for future contractual negotiation and drafting with the benefit of the parties' experience on this fascinating project.

PART IX

Performance Bonds

17

Promises and Prejudice

RICHARD WILMOT-SMITH QC

I. Introduction

In considering the subject-matter of this chapter I realised that before discussing *Aviva*[1] in substance I had to refer to the structure of Lord Justice Jackson's judgments both at first instance and in the Court of Appeal and why they are an important model both for other judges and in *Aviva* itself.

I then realised that most readers of this chapter will have had little background in the recondite world of bonds and guarantees and there must be some understanding of the subject to understand *Aviva*. For me the subject has been something of a specialism and it is easy to drift into the vernacular and make assumptions. Therefore I give some explanation of 'the bond cases' and background in the history and legal background sections of this chapter. Those who are familiar with the special rules regarding the law of Principal and Surety (and there will not be many of them I hope) can skip those; although I think even those familiar with the bond cases will find something they do not know already.

Because I feature personally in the saga of *Aviva* and its background including the *Mercers*[2] case, I have occasionally taken refuge in the third person, just as 'this reporter' does in newsprint. This is to remove my ego, if not me, from the narrative which follows.

II. The Structure of Rupert Jackson's Judgments

Most of Rupert Jackson's judgments begin with the statement that it is in four, six or, in the case of *Aviva*, seven parts. This was one of his trademarks. Right at the beginning of his judgment he would say how many sub-headings or parts there were to the judgment and what the sub-headings were.

---

[1] *Aviva Insurance Ltd v Hackney Empire Ltd* [2012] EWCA Civ 1716, [2013] BLR 57.
[2] *The Mercers v New Hampshire Insurance Co Ltd* (see n 10 below).

This I understood to come from his first-instance practice of, whenever possible, giving an oral judgment in a matter of days after Counsel sat down, rather than reserving a written judgment for an indeterminate and lengthy time. It makes it much easier to give judgment soon after trying a case if you set out the headings of topics which must be dealt with in the judgment in your notes after reading the opening skeleton arguments. Then you can deal with the relevant topics in note form as you go along, giving the resultant oral judgment structure rather than creating the meander to which so many extempore judgments are prone.

By the time *Aviva* came to be argued the commencement of all his judgments, where he stated the number of parts it contained and their headings, was well-known and a source of wry amusement to practitioners and fellow judges alike. Thus it was that when I was opening the appeal in *Aviva*, Moses LJ said to me (and the courtroom) in a stage whispered aside as if under his breath: 'No doubt Jackson LJ will deliver a judgment in fourteen parts'. The aside was a combination of 'in joke' and a mild tease of Rupert Jackson. The unspoken point being made by Moses LJ was 'Why on earth does every Jackson judgment set out how many parts were contained within it? None of us do.'

That unspoken point is, and was, misguided. One of the things which is not taught or taught sufficiently, to aspirant and established judges is the art of judgment writing. It is a remarkable omission. In my 20 years as a part-time judge I attended not a single class on that subject. Newly appointed judges are often at sea as they gain familiarity with the new job and are under pressure from the bureaucracy (for that is what the Court Service is now) to produce a judgment and get on to the next case. Lists are packed and the pressure is high. When Rupert was judge in charge of the TCC, the pressure on him was to produce quick and excellent judgments in order to set an example to the other TCC judges at a time when that court was struggling.

The best advice that can be given to new judges (be they sitting in the relentless factories of the Administrative Court and the Court of Appeal Criminal Division or indeed the TCC) is: 'Read a Rupert Jackson judgment and see how he sets out its headings in the first paragraph of the judgment; adapt those headings to your case and there's your start. You may find it constricting to start with, but it gives discipline and structure to your judgment.'

One could add to that advice the word 'speed'. The sooner you deliver judgment, after Counsel have sat down having delivered all their submissions, the better. As you go on to the next case your memory will fade and the process will take longer. Have the structure in place at the outset and have your notes set to that; then you can deliver your judgment sooner.

I noticed that Rupert's extempore judgments in the TCC were delivered consistently quickly after the close of argument. The same could not be said for his brethren (and it was brethren only then). Indeed the problem of judgments having been reserved for a lengthy period by other judges was occasionally little short of scandalous. The sad case of *McAlpine Humberoak*[3] where the Court of Appeal had to deal with the first instance judgment, which came over one year after Counsel's closing submissions, showing every sign that the judge was overwhelmed and had forgotten the issues which he was to try and thus addressed questions which were not before him, is one example.

If the pressure at first instance is high, then it increases by an order of magnitude in the Court of Appeal where there is the added pressure of having three people whose schedules obtrude into the process. Here the shoe can pinch in two ways: in one, where the judge assigned to deliver the leading judgment is so slow that the other judges have forgotten the case by the time the first draft judgment is circulated to them; in another, when the lead judgment is e-mailed to the others quickly and one of them comes up with comments six months later.

The delivery of a speedy and fresh first judgment to the other justices in a court of appeal (intermediate or final) is aided by the Jackson method. The addition of late comments upon it by tardy appellate justices might need sterner and different measures, such as a rule of practice that you are deemed to concur with the lead judgment unless you provide your comments within, say, three weeks of receipt of it.

At all events the Jackson model is to be admired and followed.

Justice Sunil Ambwani in his article 'The Art of Writing a Judgment'[4] has said:

> The importance of [the] first paragraph of the judgment cannot be overemphasized. It must answer the questions as to how, when, where, what and why, which is an advise [sic] given to judicial cubs. The readability of the opinion improves if the opening paragraph answers three questions namely what kind of case is this, what roles plaintiffs and defendants had in the trial, and what are the issues, which the Court has to decide and answer, giving sufficient information to the reader to proceed with reading the judgment.

That is sound advice, but Rupert Jackson's headings give the signposts to the reader enabling her to ascertain the how, when, where, what and why quickly.

Finally under this topic, at first instance Jackson J introduced an almost ubiquitous section of each judgment where the legal principles to be followed in the case under consideration, were set out, so that, for the future in similar cases, a practitioner could see what the law was in an easily digestible form.

This practice appeared to this observer to be because the TCC judges, before Rupert Jackson was made judge-in-charge, regarded judicial comity askance. Not only were clear statements of principle a comparative rarity, but also, when they

---

[3] *McAlpine Humberoak Ltd v McDermott International Inc (No 1)* (1992) 58 BLR 1 (CA).

[4] Judge of the Allahabad High Court then Chief Justice of the Rajasthan High Court. The article can be found at: http://ijtr.nic.in/wejournal/3.htm. Commonwealth judges are less shy about giving advicg. See for example, 'Judgment Writing & Nature of Judgment by Justice (R) Shabbir Ahmed: http://sja.gos.pk/assets/articles/Judgment%20Writing.pdf.

came, they were at variance with other TCC judgments or (putting it charitably) appeared so. As judge-in-charge, Jackson J was, because of his seniority, able to ensure that the other TCC judges applied legal principle uniformly, because of his clear statements of principle.

The Jackson J model of TCC judgment, therefore, usually had one section entitled 'The law in relation to …' or similarly titled; and that section was identified at the outset in paragraph 1 of the judgment for easy discovery. This was to be a useful habit for an aspirant appellate judge to get into. In paragraph 1 of his judgment in *Aviva*, Part 5 is entitled: 'The law in relation to discharge of sureties.' To that we return, but first we need background.

III. History of the Archaic Language of Bonds

The law of principal and surety has been around for a long time. The Statute of Frauds 1677 is still referred to when it comes to guarantees because of its requirement that all guarantees, to be enforceable, must be evidenced in writing.[5]

Guarantees were originally given by family members or friends. But the eighteenth century brought about the professional bondsman. Those bondsmen issued standard forms of bond. The standard forms did not change with the times, and thus the language became antique. In *Trade Indemnity Company Limited v Workington Harbour and Dock Board*,[6] the House of Lords complained bitterly about the ancient language not making the job of judge any easier. Lord Atkin said:

> I may be allowed to remark that it is difficult to understand why business men persist in entering upon considerable obligations in old-fashioned forms of contract which do not adequately express the true transaction. The traditional form of marine policy is perhaps past praying for; but why insurance of credits or contracts, if insurance is intended, or guarantees for the same, if guarantees are intended, should not be expressed in appropriate language, passes comprehension.[7]

By the late twentieth century the professional bonds industry amounted to many millions of pounds annually. Thus the petition for leave to appeal to the House of Lords in *Trafalgar House Construction (Regions) Ltd v General Surety and Guarantee Co Ltd*[8] made reference to that point when the sum in issue in that case was small; although the principle (as with many appellate surety cases of relatively small amounts) was of great ambit. That case, over 60 years after *Trade Indemnity*, dealt with a bond in almost identical terms to that in *Trade Indemnity* and the same frustration as that expressed by Lord Atkin was remarked on by Lord Jauncey.[9]

---

[5] See for example *Actionstrength Ltd v International Glass Engineering* [2003] AC 541.
[6] *Trade Indemnity Company Limited v Workington Harbour and Dock Board* [1937] AC 1.
[7] ibid at 17.
[8] *Trafalgar House Construction (Regions) Ltd v General Surety and Guarantee Co Ltd* [1996] 1 AC 199; (1995) 73 BLR 35.
[9] ibid at 43.

Many bonds issued by professional bondsmen today (2018) are similarly worded to those on *Trade Indemnity* and *General Surety*. Eighty years of judicial complaint have not resulted in change. The reasons why this is the case is another subject.

So the law relating to bonds considered in this chapter must be set against the background that the language used in the instrument is ancient and has been unchanged, despite strong adverse judicial comment over many years.

IV. Legal Background to *Aviva*

The basic factual background to the cases considered by the Court of Appeal in *Aviva* involves a contractor undertaking work for an employer and, as part of the commercial arrangements, the contractor secures a bond from a third party (usually either a bank or professional bondsman) to guarantee its performance.

To define terms in this scenario, the employer is called the Creditor; the contractor the Debtor and the bondsman the Surety. The bond is the guarantee or promise made by the bondsman to the Creditor. The contract guaranteed is often called the 'underlying contract'.

The bonds cases come to court when the Debtor becomes insolvent and the Creditor calls upon the Surety to pay the damages the Debtor owes to it pursuant to the underlying contract. To state the obvious, the Surety is not required if there is a solvent Debtor. Thus in construction cases the contractor Debtor's insolvency and the subsequent termination of the underlying contract is the trigger to the Surety's liability.

Once a claim is made against a Surety and the Debtor's liability is established, the question is whether the Surety has a defence to the Creditor's claim. Since the Creditor's claim against the Debtor is established, the matter comes down to whether the Surety's legal promises pursuant to its bond have been discharged.

Aviva concerns the question of the circumstances giving rise to discharge of a Surety's obligations through the actions of the Creditor, namely the party guaranteed. In *Aviva* the question was whether advances of cash to the contractor (Debtor) by the employer (Creditor) caused the Surety's liability to the Creditor to be discharged.

Looked at generally, advances on payment instalments to a contractor Debtor by an employer Creditor prejudice the Surety by increasing the indebtedness of the Debtor to the Creditor (by the amount advanced) and thus the exposure of the Surety. If the contractor, as Debtor, receives early payment, then the state of account as between builder and client is *pro-tanto* and directly affected. Normally builders receive interim payments in arrears for work actually done. The value of work done operates as a credit to the builder's account between it (the Debtor) and the employer (Creditor). If an advance payment is made, that credit is reduced and the Surety's exposure is increased accordingly. That is not the only type of prejudice in this situation. Another prejudice involves the payment making the contractor Debtor less keen on earning its money, thus performing worse than if it were incentivised to earn it. Further prejudice could come about because the contractor Debtor, armed with the advance, would postpone its insolvency. Such a postponement frequently increases the amount of the Debtor's liabilities before the insolvency curtain comes down with the termination of the contractor Debtor's construction contract. In each case the amount of increase in the exposure of the Surety at the point of the advance payment being made is hard to ascertain, either prospectively or indeed retrospectively.

The cases dealing with the discharge of a bondsman are technical and have attracted multiple trips to appellate courts. *The Wardens and Commonality of the Mystery of Mercers of the City of London v New Hampshire Insurance Co Ltd*,[10] the case in which Rupert Jackson QC made his entrance into the law of Principal and Surety and to which we turn later, had two first instance hearings before it went to the Court of Appeal. But that was almost slender in its acquisition of court attention. *General Steam Navigation Company v Rolt*[11] (*Rolt*) had two first instance trials; two hearings before the Court of Common Pleas and two appeals to the Court of Exchequer. Similarly, *Trade Indemnity Company Limited v Workington Harbour and Dock Board*[12] had much first instance and appellate attention, with two first instance trials; two appeals to the Court of Appeal and two full hearings in the House of Lords.

Each of these cases concerned whether the Surety was discharged from its promise to guarantee the Debtor by the actions of the Creditor.

It may be obvious, but nevertheless is worth saying, that the defaults of the Debtor will not discharge a Surety. The whole point of a bond is to guarantee the Creditor against the depredations of the Debtor. The Debtor is almost expected to act in a way which is prejudicial to a Surety.

Rolt was a shipbuilding case where the purchaser of a ship, the Creditor, allowed the builder, the Debtor, an advance on the instalments to be paid for its construction. The shipbuilder went bankrupt and the Surety was sued under his guarantee.

Much of the report deals with the factual question of whether in fact the Surety knew of the advance in payment to the Debtor contractor by the employer Creditor. The Surety resisted liability successfully on the ground that his position was prejudiced by the advance payment. Importantly, the Surety did not consent to the advance payment. Thus the Surety's knowledge of the advance payment, which took up much trial time, was irrelevant. The simple facts were that the Creditor advanced money to the Debtor without the Surety's consent. Such an action, prejudicial to the Surety, discharged the Surety from its promise.

---

[10] *The Wardens and Commonality of the Mystery of Mercers of the City of London v New Hampshire Insurance Co Ltd* (1992) 60 BLR 26.
[11] *General Steam Navigation Company v Rolt* (1858) 6 CB (NS) 550; 144 ER 572.
[12] [1937] AC 1.

The grounds upon which each judge found the Surety's discharge require some analysis.

Crowder J said:

> It is obvious that a pre-payment must prejudice the surety in a case like this, inasmuch as it deprives him of the benefit of that which would be an inducement to the principal to perform the contract in due time.[13]

That is a clear statement of a doctrine that a pre-payment or an advance of money to a contractor provides a discharge of a Surety.

In the same case Willes J. said: 'It is clear, therefore there must be an assent by the surety to the creditor's dealing with the principal debtor otherwise than in the manner pointed out by the contract'.

But Willes J. said this, citing the case of *Samuell v Howarth*[14] where Lord Eldon said: 'A creditor has no right, – it is against the faith of his contract, – to give time to the principal, even though manifestly for the benefit of the surety, without the knowledge of the surety.' Accordingly Willes J looked at the advance payment as if it were akin to the giving of time and stated that it was irrelevant whether the advance decreased or increased the exposure of the Surety. It was enough for discharge that its position had been altered. Inquiry into whether the Surety's position was improved or prejudiced was not permitted. Mere alteration of the Surety's position was enough to discharge the Surety.

Cockburn CJ said 'His position as surety was equally prejudiced by the alteration of the contract for the performance of which he consented to be bound.'[15] Cockburn CJ started from the position that the advance payment was a prejudice to the Surety 'who loses, by that anticipatory payment to the principal, the strong inducement which otherwise would have operated on his mind to induce him to finish the work in due time.'[16]

On appeal Pollock CB held that this was a case where

> the withdrawal of a fund which is a security for the thing in respect of the not doing of which he is now called upon to pay damages is a prejudice to the surety ... he is deprived of the security of the fund out of which the company might in the first instance have indemnified themselves.[17]

That rationale agrees with Crowder J's analysis. It is in accord with the cases on injury to the Surety's security as, for example, in the earlier case of *Watts v Shuttleworth*.[18]

In *Watts* the Creditor did not insure fittings for a warehouse as he should have done under his contract. It was held that the Surety was discharged because

---

[13] (1858) 6 CB (NS) 550 at 597; 144 ER 572 at 590.
[14] *Samuell v Howarth* (1817) 3 Meriv 278; 36 ER 105.
[15] (1858) 6 CB (NS) 550 at 595; 144 ER 572 at 589.
[16] (1858) 6 CB (NS) 550 at 595; 144 ER 572 at 589.
[17] *General Steam Navigation Company v Rolt* (1858) 6 CB (NS) 550 at 604–05; 144 ER 572 at 593.
[18] *Watts v Shuttleworth* (1860) 5 H&N 234; 157 ER 1171.

of that failure, which was injurious to the Surety. The only question, in the end (on appeal), was whether the discharge was absolute or *pro tanto*. It was held to be absolute because the Creditor had so conducted himself as to alter the position of the Surety. Such an alteration of position meant that the discharge was absolute.[19] Pollock CB stated the rule at first instance:

> The substantial question in the case is, whether the omission to insure discharges the defendant, the surety. The rule upon the subject seems to be that if the person guaranteed does any act injurious to the surety, or inconsistent with his rights, or if he omits to do any act which his duty enjoins him to do, and the omission proves injurious to the surety, the latter will be discharged ... the rights of a surety depend rather on principles of equity than upon the actual contract.[20]

That statement was approved in the Privy Council in *China & South Sea Bank v Tan*.[21] Therefore it would appear from *Rolt* and *Watts* that the law would provide a discharge of a Surety if an advance payment is made because it is, of itself, an act injurious to the Surety.

The *locus classicus* relating to the discharge of a Surety is *Holme v Brunskill*.[22] It decides that a material variation of the underlying contract will provide a Surety with an absolute discharge.

Cotton LJ said:

> The true rule in my opinion is, that if there is any agreement between the principals with reference to the contract guaranteed, the surety ought to be consulted, and that if he has not consented to the alteration, although in cases where it is without enquiry evident that the alteration is unsubstantial, or that it cannot be otherwise than beneficial to the surety, the surety may not be discharged; yet, that if it is not self-evident that the alteration is unsubstantial, or one which cannot be prejudicial to the surety, the court, will not, in an action against the surety, go into an enquiry as to the subject of the alteration, or allow the question, whether the surety is discharged or not, to be determined by the finding of a jury as to the materiality of the alteration or on the question whether it is to the prejudice of the surety, but will hold that in such a case, the surety himself must be the sole judge whether or not he will consent to remain liable notwithstanding the alteration, and that if he has not so consented he will be discharged.[23]

---

[19] The other well-known advance payment case is *Re Warre and Calvert* (1837) 7 Ad & E 142; 112 ER 425. That suggests, but does not state, that there would be a *pro tanto* rule such as discussed in the *Mercers* case discussed below. But that case (from 1837) preceded *Watts* and *Rolt*.

[20] (1860) 5 H&N 234 at 247–48; 157 ER 1171 at 1176.

[21] *China & South Sea Bank v Tan* [1990] 1 AC 536 at 544. See also *Polak v Everett* (1876) 1 QBD 669 particularly Blackburn J's judgment. For light relief see the third interjection of Blackburn J in argument at the bottom of page 672, where Counsel suggests that where time is given or the agreement is varied in respect only of part of the debt or security the discharge rule does not apply. The judge simply says 'This point is quite new to me'.

[22] *Holme v Brunskill* (1878) 3 QBD 495.

[23] ibid at 505.

This dictum is often referred to as the rule in *Holme v Brunskill*.[24]

The rule in *Holme v Brunskill* led to the insertion of indulgence clauses into standard forms of bonds issued by professional bondsmen (archaic language and all). Their effect was designed to ensure that a guarantee remained in force despite the granting of time, payment of money or variation of contract terms. Thus the harshness of the rule in *Holme v Brunskill* could be avoided, should the contracting parties so choose. It would be a commercial decision for the parties (affecting the premium paid for the bond) whether such a clause was to be agreed. The bond industry's standard forms have, for 140 years, had indulgence clauses inserted into them as a matter of course.

It was the scope of the rule in *Holme v Brunskill* which was the subject-matter of the two Surety cases discussed below in which Rupert Jackson was Counsel in the first and an appellate judge in the second.

V. Rupert Jackson QC and *The Mercers* Case

We now come to Rupert Jackson QC's immersion in the law of Principal and Surety in *The Mercers* case.[25]

The Mercers Company was the Creditor. The ill-starred contractor Rush & Tompkins Limited (R&T) was the Debtor and New Hampshire Insurance was the Surety.

The Mercers, on 20 March 1989, contracted with R&T under a JCT Standard Form of Building Contract for work to its properties in Holborn. The contract price was £5m.

The Mercers and R&T then entered into a side agreement on 21 March 1989 whereby the Mercers would pay R&T just over £4.5m of the contract sum in advance. This was for tax purposes.

That advance payment was secured by a bond which (unusually) had no indulgence clause and the material part of the bond was in the following terms:

> [I]f the aforementioned advance so made is liquidated in accordance with the terms of … [the building contract] and is faithfully employed for the purposes of said contract, then this obligation shall be void; otherwise it remains in full force and effect.

Those terms were in just the kind of language which caused the judicial complaints we have already seen in *Trade Indemnity* and elsewhere. Parker LJ was moved to say 'The construction of the bond is not assisted by its archaic language or the fact that its recitals are factually inaccurate.'

Possession under the building contract was to be given by the Mercers no later than the end of June 1989. But pursuant to an Architect's Instruction no 20

---

[24] For an example of the rule's application see *Marubeni Hong Kong and South China Ltd v Mongolian Government* [2004] EWHC 472 (Comm).

[25] *The Mercers v New Hampshire Insurance Co Ltd* (1992) 60 BLR 26 (n 10 above).

(AI 20) dated 7 July 1989, possession was deferred until 24 July 1989. The building contract had no power within it to postpone possession of the site by way of a variation instruction. But in this case AI 20 was followed by the uncomplaining acceptance by the contractor of that new date for possession.

R&T became insolvent. Its employment under its contract was determined and the Mercers sued the Surety for the unliquidated part of the advance payment.

The case came before Hobhouse J. The writer of this chapter, acting for the Surety, was then being led by Simon Tuckey QC. The Surety's case was that the deferment of possession of the site pursuant to AI 20 involved the giving of time to the contractor Debtor or was a material variation of the underlying obligations of the Debtor and thus, in the absence of an indulgence clause, the Surety was discharged.

The parties agreed the facts, so no witnesses were called. One of the agreed facts was that the date for possession was consensually postponed by agreement between contractor and employer.

Hobhouse J (later Lord Hobhouse) thought little of the Surety's argument and ordered an interim payment of the whole of the claimed amount but gave the Surety leave to defend. Procedurally this was odd because it was not a witness action. The facts were agreed and the only decision which Hobhouse J had to make was in relation to the application of the law of Principal and Surety to those agreed facts. It, however, gave the Surety a second bite of the cherry (this cliché is, in the circumstances, permissible).

So the case came to trial before Phillips J (later Lord Phillips) who had to deal with identical arguments based upon the identical agreed facts and he took a different view to Hobhouse J and accepted the Surety's argument giving judgment for the Surety. The Mercers appealed.

Then Simon Tuckey was appointed to the High Court and thus Rupert Jackson entered the case to lead for the Surety in the Court of Appeal. It is doubtful he was helped much by his junior. The legal research was led by our instructing solicitors Richard White and Karen Spencer, two of the most acknowledged experts on bonds, whose expertise in Surety cases has been built up over many years. Perhaps his junior's discussion of the *pro tanto* rule, or rather its absence in English law, may have diverted him. That is doubtful somehow.

Contrary to his junior counsel's expectations that Rupert Jackson QC had a good judgment from Phillips J to uphold, he had a torrid time.

This was the sort of appeal every lawyer dreads appearing in. You have the law on your side. The facts are agreed and you think your case pretty much impregnable accordingly. This appeared to be a classic case of a material variation of the underlying contract's obligations by the Creditor giving time to the Debtor, thus discharging the Surety. The agreed facts were that there was a variation of the underlying contract postponing the date for possession and there had been no consultation of the Surety. The cases and dicta cited above, applied to the agreed facts, made Phillips J's first instance decision seem very strong and Hobhouse J's decision perverse.

But the Court of Appeal would have none of it. There was hostility from the beginning from a Court which clearly did not like what it saw, considering the bond cases to have produced an inflexible set of rules built up over centuries. Never mind that the commercial parties were taken to know the technical rules, and never mind that the presence of those technical rules would have an effect on the premium paid by those who wanted a Surety to execute a bond in their favour – the Court of Appeal did not like the Surety's position.

There were two primary discussions instigated by the Court when Rupert Jackson QC was on his feet.

The first discussion was whether instead of a discharge of the Surety there could be a *pro tanto* reduction in the Surety's obligations. As stated already, our researches had indicated that although some common law jurisdictions (New York for example) had a *pro tanto* rule, there was none in England and Wales (in spite of *Watts v Shuttleworth* and *Re Warre and Calvert*[26]). The law was clear on that subject, see *Holme v Brunskill*. But the Court of Appeal would not let go of it and a re-reading of the report supports this reporter's recollection that if they were driven to it they would have invented a *pro tanto* rule re the discharge of Sureties through the actions of the Creditor. Had it done so it would have reversed over 100 years of authority in order to achieve what it saw as a merits-based result.

The second discussion related to whether there had been a variation of the underlying obligations at all and whether the delayed possession was a breach of contract instead – contrary to the agreed facts.

Here the Court of Appeal dispensed with the agreed facts, embarked upon an on-the-hoof exploration of the 'facts' and decided that its own researches led to the conclusion that the delayed possession of the site was not, as agreed, a variation of the underlying contract but rather was a breach of contract by the Creditor which did not discharge the Surety.

The distinction was made between a consensual variation of the underlying contract by Creditor and Debtor which did discharge the Surety and a breach of contract by the Creditor, which did not. The rationale for the distinction being operative as a key to whether the Surety is discharged from its promise is not obvious. Each situation involves the Creditor acting in such a way as to prejudice the Surety. As already observed, the actions of a Debtor can never discharge the Surety; it is the actions of the Creditor which do. The distinction made by the Court of Appeal meant that if a Creditor employer agreed with the Debtor contractor that there would be a postponement of the possession of the site by the contractor, then the Surety would be discharged from its bond; but if possession was denied by the Creditor in breach of contract, then the Surety would not be discharged. Each action by the Creditor is equally detrimental to the Surety's interests, but the consent of the Debtor was held to be the operative distinction between discharge and non-discharge.

[26] See n 19 above.

The case, therefore, had an unhappy conclusion, with a result-oriented Court of Appeal which had its own view of the merits and was determined to impose them on the outcome.

Needless to say Rupert Jackson QC argued the case with an admirable combination of finesse and dogged persistence and he and his junior could only console themselves with the shared experience of a rampant Court of Appeal, which, in other circumstances, loudly hold themselves bound by a first instance judge's findings of fact – and therefore a fortiori agreed facts.[27]

VI. The *Aviva* Case and Lord Justice Jackson's Judgment

Aviva was a case involving the question of whether a Surety was discharged by advance payments being made by the Creditor. My researches do not disclose Rupert Jackson conducting a case relating to a bondsman's discharge at the Bar, aside from *The Mercers* case. Neither do they reveal a case where he considered the rule in *Holme v Brunskill* as a judge (first instance or appellate). So Jackson LJ must have had a bad feeling of déjà vu when *Aviva* came before him.

A reminder of his experience in *The Mercers* arrived in the living form of his old junior opening the appeal. There must not have appeared, to him, to have been any mitigating circumstances. Post-traumatic stress in the form of flashbacks must have been advancing upon his psyche.

His erstwhile junior was leading counsel for the Surety, Aviva, which was appellant against a TCC decision holding it liable under a bond.

As with so many projects finding their way to court, the (not necessarily legally relevant) background facts concerning the underlying construction contract were interesting. I hope I am forgiven for sharing them in a few lines in this chapter. The construction works involved the Hackney Empire Theatre which had seen great days in the Edwardian era, hosting stars like Charlie Chaplin, WC Fields, Stanley Holloway and Stan Laurel. In the 1950s it became a television studio, an outer sanctum of artistic Hades, where such 'classics' as *Take Your Pick* and *Emergency Ward Ten* were filmed. Then it fell on hard (and somewhat infra-dig) times in 1964, becoming a Bingo Hall – a status it held for over 20 years. It brings to mind *Sunset Boulevard* in North London, with the Norma Desmond part played by a theatre. There was then a brief revival when there was comedy performed, where stars such as Dawn French, Jennifer Saunders and Harry Enfield appeared. Finally the Theatre's former grandeur was remembered and its disrepair noticed, bringing about a scheme for its refurbishment and restoration under the auspices of Hackney Empire Limited (HEL).

Those are the interesting background facts in precis; now the legally relevant ones.

---

[27] One is reminded of the philosopher of the pragmatism school, Sidney Hook's statement about Mary McCarthy: 'People do what they want anyway. She at least admits it.'

On 24 April 2001 a letter of intent was sent to the contractor, STC, by HEL. The contract between HEL and STC was eventually let on 5 March 2002. On 6 August 2001 Aviva executed a bond in favour of HEL in the sum of £1.1m in standard archaic terms, including an indulgence clause guaranteeing the anticipated, and eventually executed, construction contract. Like in *Mercers* it was let on a JCT Standard Form of Building Contract and the Contract Sum was £11m.

STC's performance was poor and its claims optimistic – classic signs of a soon-to-arrive insolvency. The architect was resolute that the claims were unjustified. The contractor wanted payment on account of claims, it said, to ensure progress, which got slower and slower. Meetings were held to try and break the deadlock and on 16 December 2002 an oral agreement (described in the judgment as a side agreement) was made in which it was agreed that HEL would pay STC £1m on account of STC's claims pending the provision of proper particulars of their claims (which the architect continued to say were unjustified). The payment was to be in three instalments. The first payment was of £500,000 and the second and third were of £250,000 each. Each payment was made against the background of the classic insolvency signs I have referred to. It would be hard to see how the Surety's situation could have been more knowingly prejudiced by the Creditor.

The first instalment of £500,000 was paid on 30 December 2002 and the second of £250,000 was paid on 26 February 2003. Progress remained slow despite the payments and an administration order was made on STC on 2 July 2003. STC's employment was determined pursuant to the building contract's JCT Standard Form's terms on 21 July 2003 and on 8 March 2004 HEL made a claim against the Surety, Aviva, which rejected the claim stating that the advance payments to STC by HEL discharged it – relying upon *Rolt* and *Holme v Brunskill*.

There matters rested until 24 February 2010 when HEL issued proceedings in the TCC against Aviva. The TCC judge gave judgment for HEL and Aviva appealed to the Court of Appeal. The Court was Sir John Thomas P and Moses and Jackson LJJ.

Sir John Thomas was intrigued by the arguments and alternately benign and sharp, reminding leading counsel for the Surety of Alastair Sim playing the judge in the television adaptation of AP Herbert's *Misleading Cases*.

Moses LJ's remark, alluded to earlier in section II, did not suggest that his ink would be first to the page.

So it was obvious to Counsel that the junior member of that Court would be called upon to write the judgment and the two more senior members would wrestle with the intellectual problems raised by the case for fun but, in the end, would leave it to the professional. That observation by Counsel was amply borne out by the fact that the two concurring judgments mustered five words in all – the second being identical to the first save with the word 'also' inserted between the words 'I' and 'agree'.

Here we must go back to the beginning of this chapter and the structure of judgments leading to speed and clarity in the disposal of cases. The case was argued on 20 and 21 November 2012. Lord Justice Jackson's draft judgment came to Counsel on (as far as this correspondent can recall) 14 December 2012 for a hand-down on 19 December 2012. Thus the period between the end of argument and submission of the draft to Counsel was 17 working days.

Those lawyers concerned with bonds and their discharge find the law summarised in Part 5 of his judgment.[28] Here Lord Justice Jackson had to grapple with the circumstances in which a bondsman's obligations are discharged. *Rolt, Trade Indemnity* and *Holme v Brunskill* are cited and additionally the more ancient case of *Calvert v The London Dock Company*.[29] The facts of each case are pithily expressed; the essentials of each judgment are quoted – but not to excess. Jackson LJ does not fall into the cut-and-paste laziness of so many judges. So in those 24 paragraphs you have an excellent analysis of the law in relation to the discharge of Sureties in cases where the Creditor has made an advance payment.

The Mercers case was referred to and must have been very much in his mind. As stated above in relation to judgment structure, as a TCC judge Jackson J was astute to ensure that the principles which he had to apply in that case (the Court of Appeal and House of Lords cases being binding on him) were clearly set out so that they could be applied in that and future cases. As Jackson LJ in *Aviva*, he continued on this path (would that every appellate judge did). We can see this done in paragraphs 78–80 of the judgment:

> 78. There has been some debate between Mr. Wilmot-Smith and Mr. Thomas as to how one should reconcile *Trade Indemnity* with *Calvert* and *General Steam-Navigation Company*. I conclude that the proper reconciliation is as follows. Where the employer pays instalments of the agreed contract price before those instalments fall due under the terms of the original contract, then absent consent or an appropriate indulgence clause, those advance payments may result in discharging the liability of the surety. On the other hand where the employer pays sums to the contractor under a separate agreement, rather than under the contract which the surety is guaranteeing, the liability of the surety is not discharged. The surety remains liable in respect of the original contract, but not of course in respect of the separate payments or loans which have been made.
>
> 79. A number of other authorities have been cited by counsel and they are, of course, most illuminating. Nevertheless the principles which must be applied in the present case emerge clearly from the authorities cited above. I would summarise those principles as follows:
>
> i) The rule in *Holme v Brunskill* only applies where parties to the contract guaranteed have varied the terms of that contract without the consent of the surety.
>
> ii) Advance payments of the agreed contract price made by an employer to a contractor may have the effect of discharging the liability of the surety. On the other hand additional payments (whether by way of gift or loan) made by the employer to the contractor outside the terms of the original contract do not have that effect.
>
> iii) A surety will not be released from liability by reason of contractual variations or advance payments if (a) he has specifically consented to what was done or (b) there is an indulgence clause which covers what was done.

---

[28] *Aviva Insurance Ltd v Hackney Empire Ltd* [2012] EWCA Civ 1716, paragraphs 56–80.

[29] *Calvert v The London Dock Company* (1838) 2 Keen 638; 48 ER 774.

If the law as developed in the nineteenth century and early twentieth century does not accord with the needs of modern commercial life, the industry can of course amend the form of the bond.

80. Having identified the relevant principles, I must now revert to the present case and consider whether Aviva has been discharged from liability under the bond.

Cavil as I might, as Counsel, that the distinction drawn in paragraph 78 was without a substantive difference, the distinction is clearly set out and supported in his judgment by proper analysis of authority. Practitioners can see that one contractual movement (a variation of the contract guaranteed) heads in one direction, – discharge of the Surety; and the other contractual movement (a separate agreement) in another – non discharge. Commercial parties have legal certainty and can make arrangements, and their lawyers may advise, accordingly.

Paragraph 79 is classic Jackson. Practitioners want to know the principles to be applied more generally (with a distillation of the law) and here he does so, rendering the complicated and arcane easy for any layman to understand.

Then in paragraph 80 he applies those principles to the facts of the case in front of him – a task which engages the parties more than practitioners of the future who want to know what the principles are so they can be applied in their case. He decided firstly that the two payments made by HEL to STC did not discharge Aviva from liability under the bond, but secondly, Aviva's liability as surety only related to the original construction contract and did not extend to STC's failure to repay the £750,000 which it owed to HEL under the side agreement.

This was in the mode of the best appellate judgements. Firstly examine the background authorities, secondly distill the principles to be drawn from them and then, and only then, apply them to the facts of the individual case.

The appellate judgments of Lord Diplock have that hallmark – see particularly his judgments in *Hong Kong Fir Shipping Co Ltd v Kawasaki Kisen Kaisha Ltd*[30] and *Birkett v James*.[31] The appellate judge looks for principle first, expresses it clearly and then applies it. In *Aviva*, despite any post-traumatic stress he may have acquired from seeing his junior re-appear arguing about a Surety's discharge, Lord Justice Jackson did just that in a properly structured judgment which was issued timeously and which will stand the test of time.

---

[30] *Hong Kong Fir Shipping Co Ltd v Kawasaki Kisen Kaisha Ltd* [1962] 2 QB 26.
[31] *Birkett v James* [1978] AC 297.

PART X

Time and Liquidated Damages

18

Time Rolls On

VINCENT MORAN QC

This chapter is in six Parts. It considers the Court of Appeal's decision in *Carillion Construction Ltd v Emcor Engineering Services Ltd*.[1] This case concerned the operation of an extension of time provision in a common standard form sub-contract. I will set out the background to the underlying dispute, the reasoning of the decision and the possible wider implications of the case. I will also touch upon the wider issues thrown up by the *Chestermount* case,[2] which, although found to be distinguishable in relation to the issue of contractual construction arising on the appeal in *Carillion*, is well worth re-considering in light of it.

I. Introduction

The case arose out of the design and construction of the Rolls Building, where the TCC, Commercial Court and Chancery Division now sit. The claimant, Carillion, was the main contractor for the project. The second defendant, AECOM, was the sub-contractor for the provision of various Mechanical and Electrical (M+E) services. The third/fourth defendant, EMCOR, was another M+E sub-contractor for certain other services. Only Carillion and EMCOR were parties to the appeal.

The main contract was made on the JCT Standard Form of Building Contract with Contractor's Design, 1998 edition (incorporating Amendments 1:1999, 2:2001 and 4:2002) with bespoke amendments. The sub-contract between Carillion and EMCOR incorporated the Standard Form of Sub-Contract Conditions for use with the Domestic Sub-Contract DOM/2, 1981 edition (referred to simply as DOM/2). It was for the carrying out and completion of the sub-contract works, namely the design, manufacture, supply, installation, testing and commissioning of the M+E and associated works.

---

[1] *Carillion Construction Ltd v Emcor Engineering Services Ltd* [2017] EWCA Civ 65 [2017] BLR 203, 170 Con LR 1.
[2] *Balfour Beatty Building Ltd v Chestermount Properties Ltd* (1993) 62 BLR 1, 32 Con LR 139.

Clause 11.2 of the sub-contract conditions required the sub-contractor to give notice of delay or likely delay. Clause 11.3 provided as follows:

> 11.3 If on receipt of any notice, particulars and estimate under clause 11.2 the Contractor properly considers that:
>
> > .1 any of the causes of the delay is an act, omission or default of the Contractor, his servants or agents or his sub-contractors, their servants or agents (other than the Sub-Contractor, his servants or agents) or is the occurrence of a Relevant Event; and
> >
> > .2 the completion of the Sub-Contract Works is likely to be delayed thereby beyond the period or periods stated in the Appendix, part 4, or any revised such period or periods,
>
> then the Contractor shall, in writing, give an extension of time to the Sub-Contractor by fixing such revised or further revised period or periods for the completion of the Sub-Contract Works as the Contractor then estimates to be reasonable.

EMCOR were therefore required to complete their works in accordance with the details set out in part 4 of the appendix to the sub-contract. As a result of subsequent agreements between the parties, part 4 of the appendix underwent successive amendments. The final position arrived at was that EMCOR were required to complete both the section B and section C works by 28 January 2011, which was also the revised contractual completion date under the main contract.

In the proceedings, Carillion claimed damages in respect of their own costs and sums they alleged were levied under the main contract in respect of liquidated damages as a result of delay to the carrying out and completion of both the EMCOR and AECOM sub-contract works. EMCOR's case was that it was not liable for damages for delay to completion of its sub-contract works because it was entitled to an extension of time to complete them.

The preliminary issue that became the subject of the appeal was defined as follows:

> 1. On the assumption that EMCOR is entitled to an extension of time pursuant to clause 11.3 of the EMCOR Sub-Contract (as amended) by fixing such revised or further revised period or periods for the completion of its Sub-Contract Works, does the EMCOR Sub-Contract (as amended) require:
>
> (a) that such revised or further revised periods are added contiguously to the end of the current period, so as to provide an aggregate period within which EMCOR's Sub-Contract Works should be completed (as contended for by EMCOR); or
>
> (b) that such revised or further period or periods are fixed in which EMCOR can undertake its Sub-Contract Works, which are not necessarily contiguous but which reflect the period for which EMCOR has in fact been delayed and is entitled to an extension of time (as contended for by CCL)?

EMCOR's case was that any extension of time in accordance with clause 11.3 was to be made by adding time to the end of the period or periods set out in the Appendix, part 4, as amended by the later agreements or as previously revised under clause 11.3 (ie contiguously to a previously fixed period).

In contrast, Carillion contended that, as a matter of the proper construction of clause 11.3, the natural and ordinary meaning of the words used did not lead to the conclusion that an extension of time should be 'contiguous' but that the words used contemplated and allowed for the provision of additional but discontinuous periods of time for the carrying out and completion of the sub-contract works (ie a non-contiguous extension of time).

Carillion's case was therefore that EMCOR's approach only applied if the matter giving rise to the entitlement to an extension of time occurred before practical completion. If the date for practical completion had passed and EMCOR was in culpable delay, consideration had to be given to the effect of the matter relied upon at the time that it impacted progress, and any extension of time period need not be added to a previous fixed period. Rather, it could be a further discontinuous period of time and, under clause 11.3, it should be a discontinuous period if that properly reflected responsibility for delay.

II. The Decision of the Court of Appeal

Jackson LJ summarised the problem in this way in his judgment:

34. In this part I shall refer to the date upon which a contractor or sub-contractor is required to complete as 'date A'. That date may be specified in the contract or sub-contract. Alternatively, date A may be derived from the contract or sub-contract, for example because x weeks are allowed for carrying out the works. Alternatively, date A may be the consequence of one or more extensions of time granted by the person or body empowered to extend time.

35. I shall refer to a delaying event which occurs after date A as 'event B'. I shall refer to the date upon which event B actually causes delay to start to occur as 'date C'. Date C will usually postdate event B. For example, if the event B is an instruction to install additional lighting, date C may be the date when the electrical sub-contractor starts his first fix.

36. Carillion's case in relation to Emcor's sub-contract is that where a delaying event occurs after date A, the proper way to deal with the matter is to grant a non-contiguous extension of time. In other words, the sub-contractor is liable for all delay between date A and date C, but is not liable for delay during the period following date C. In this way the sub-contractor bears the consequences of the delay for which he is responsible. He does not bear the consequences of the delay caused by event B, which is not his fault.

Carillion's argument was that where a delay event occurred after date A, a non-contiguous extension of time should be awarded. This, Carillion contended, would have the effect of making commercial sense, as it would make the period of liability under the sub-contract coincide with the period of sub-contractor-culpable delay. The sub-contractor would be liable for all of the consequences of delay between dates A and C (and any related loses), but not liable for delay in the period after date C. This would generate a liability that reflected the sub-contractor's responsibility as a matter of fact for the respective periods of delay. EMCOR's approach, in contrast, would have the disadvantage of granting the sub-contractor an extension of time in a period in which it was in culpable delay.

The Court of Appeal rejected Carillion's case. Jackson LJ decided the issue of construction on the basis that the natural meaning of the words used in clause 11.3 was that the extension should be contiguous. Five reasons were provided at paragraph 39:

> a) The phrase 'any such revised period or periods' in clause 11.3.2 indicates that when the employer grants extensions of time he is revising the period or periods stated in part 4 of the appendix, not granting separate periods of justified delay with their own start and end dates.
>
> b) The simple phrase 'extension of time' in the last part of clause 11.3 has the natural meaning that the period of time which is allowed for the work is being made longer.
>
> c) The next phrase in the last part of clause 11.3 'by fixing such revised or further revised period or periods' naturally conveys the same meaning.
>
> d) The notice provision in clause 11.2.2.2 includes the telling phrase 'beyond the expiry of the period or periods stated in the appendix part 4 or <u>beyond the expiry of any extended period or periods previously fixed under clause 11</u>' (my underlining). Those words indicate that if the employer has granted an extension of time, he will have increased the length of the existing period or periods for doing sections of the work, not created new periods for doing the work, each with their own start and end dates.
>
> e) More generally, as I read and re-read the provisions of clauses 11 and 12, they all fit naturally with the assumption that any extensions of time granted will be contiguous.

As an exercise in contractual interpretation this all seems straightforward enough, especially given that the obvious intention of any extension of time entitlement, absent express contrary indication, is to provide a mechanism to extend the then applicable contractual completion date – which very strongly suggests that a contiguous approach must be the parties' presumed intention.

Although the Court of Appeal was plainly concerned about the possible practical implications of such an approach, Jackson LJ emphasised the importance of a traditional approach to the operation of extension of time provisions that was considered to have worked satisfactorily in practice in this respect to date:

> 47. I turn now to the substantive argument. Mr Reed points out that on the judge's interpretation of clause 11.3 Emcor may be exempted from liability under clause 12 during a period when Emcor is in culpable delay. Emcor would then be made liable to the employer under clause 12 during a period when Emcor is not in culpable delay, for example because it is complying with a late variation instruction. The loss and damage suffered by Carillion during those two periods is unlikely to be the same. Therefore one or other party will gain a windfall benefit.
>
> 48. I am unable to see any answer to this argument. It is, at the very least, an oddity. We pressed Mr Cowan with this point in argument. He too was unable to suggest any convincing answer to it.

49. *I am therefore bound to accept the logic of Mr Reed's argument. On the other hand, as Oliver Wendell Holmes famously observed in his lectures on The Common Law, 'the life of the law has not been logic: it has been experience'. In practice the system of awarding extensions of time contiguously has worked satisfactorily, even though it is open to the criticisms which Mr Reed advances. It appears that no contractor or sub-contractor in a reported case has ever before felt the need to argue that awards of time should be non-contiguous.*

50. *In the case of main contractors that omission is not surprising. Liquidated and ascertained damages are normally levied at a specified rate per week or per month. Therefore, it makes no difference whether any extension of time granted is contiguous or non-contiguous. In the case of sub-contractors, however, the position is different. Their liability for delay is often calculated (as in this case) by reference to the loss and damage which their delay has caused to the main contractor or to some other sub-contractor higher up the chain.*

51. *The judge accepted that anomalies of the kind identified by Carillion may arise. In her view, those possible scenarios were not sufficient to displace the natural interpretation of clause 11.3. I have come to the same conclusion. As the judge rightly observed, Emcor's interpretation of clause 11.3 is practicable and workable. It accords to what a reasonable person, with all the background knowledge of the parties, would have understood the clause to mean on the date when the sub-contract was made* (emphasis added).

Although perhaps the absence of analogous argument in previous authority is unsurprising, given the paucity of reported decisions in this field of the law these days, and the suggestion that the system had worked satisfactorily in the past is on its face difficult to reconcile with the acceptance that anomalies of the kind complained about could occur, this reasoning is compelling.

Thus, in spite of the (accepted) logic of Carillion's analysis, the possibility of 'anomalies' in the provision's operation, and the associated 'commercial common sense' of Carillion's approach to a non-contiguous operation of the provision, the Court of Appeal ultimately preferred the ordinary meaning of the language used in clause 11.3 to trump the risk of such potentially anomalous outcomes.

III. Analysis

On one view the decision represents a straightforward confirmation of what many practitioners would consider the natural approach to be taken to the operation of extension of time provisions, especially in light of the decision in *Chestermount*. But, as was made clear both at first instance (before Jefford J)[3] and by the Court of Appeal, in *Chestermount* there was no issue as to whether any extension of time should be awarded contiguously or non-contiguously and in any event that case concerned a different standard form (main) contract.

---

[3] *Carillion Construction Ltd v Woods Bagot Europe Ltd* [2016] EWHC 905 (TCC), [2016] BLR 382, 166 Con LR 52.

Carillion's argument was in fact a novel one, not previously made or considered in previous reported authority. It was also of special relevance in the context of a sub-contract, where loss and damage for a sub-contractor's delay is often assessed by reference to the loss actually suffered by the main contractor up the contractual chain, rather than on the basis of a liquidated damages regime. This distinction makes the assessment of damages exercise dependent upon the timing of the relevant breach of contract, rather than merely the period of any related extension of time entitlement. It is this interaction that creates the potential for anomalies in the application of the extension of time provisions in sub-contracts.

It is suggested that the real significance of the decision is threefold.

First, it is a good example in the context of the interpretation of contractual provisions of the triumph of clear wording, and the ordinary interpretation of the meaning of the language used, over alleged 'business common sense' or anomalies in operation in practice – even when the logic of the latter is acknowledged as likely to lead to potentially strange results. This reflects the continuing impact of the Supreme Court's decision in *Arnold v Britton*[4] and more generally the gentle demise of the role of supposed business common sense in the interpretation exercise (note also in this respect the decision of Hamblen J, as he then was, in *Cottonex Anstalt v Patriot Spinning Mills Ltd*).[5]

Secondly, the Court of Appeal recognised the importance of construing each provision and contract in its own relevant context. This was how the supposed relevance of the decision in *Chestermount* was so easily discarded. This point should of course be obvious, but is often lost in the construction law context as parties seek, almost always in vain, general guidance from the relatively infrequent decisions of higher courts on extension of time issues. The parties are of course free to agree an extension of time clause in any way they wish, and there are no principles of law that dictate how an extension of time mechanism should operate. A similar point was made, albeit in the context of an extension of time provision purporting to deal with the effect of concurrent delay events, by Fraser J in *North Midland Building Ltd v Cyden Homes*.[6]

Third, and really an offshoot to the previous point, the decision has, perhaps unintentionally, focused attention on one of the most revered first instance decisions in construction folklore, what exactly was decided by it and with what general application, namely Colman J's decision in *Chestermount*.

IV. *Chestermount*

Although ultimately having only a walk-on part in the Court of Appeal's reasoning in *Carillion*, quickly to be distinguished on its facts and discarded from the

---

[4] *Arnold v Britton* [2015] UKSC 36.
[5] *Cottonex Anstalt v Patriot Spinning Mills Ltd* [2014] EWHC 236, [2014] 1 Lloyd's Rep 615.
[6] *North Midland Building Ltd v Cyden Homes* [2017] EWHC 2414 (TCC) at [19].

analysis, this decision was relied upon by EMCOR as an authority supporting, effectively as a default position, the 'traditional' contiguous approach to the operation of extension of time provisions.

In the Court of Appeal, however, it was merely observed:

> 42. The important feature of *Chestermount* is that both parties accepted that the extension of time should be contiguous. The employer was arguing for a short contiguous extension, limited in length to the actual period of the delay caused by the variation instructions. The contractor was arguing for a long contiguous extension, namely covering the whole period up to event B plus four months thereafter for the actual delay caused by event B. Neither party invited the arbitrator or the judge to award a non-contiguous extension of time starting on date C.

There are, of course, only a few (first instance) construction law decisions that have considered in terms the operation of extension of time provisions and/or the nature of the causal test required to be satisfied under particular provisions. *Carillion* is concerned with the former. *Chestermount* considered both of these topics.

Chestermount is perhaps best known for the its consideration of the operation of the provision in question, namely whether a 'gross' or 'net' approach to operating an extension of time entitlement was required under the JCT Standard Form (1980 edn) wording. Colman J's judgment, however, also dealt with the nature of the causal criterion that had to be satisfied to generate a right to relief in the first place. This is, if anything, a much more tricky issue – albeit one that, like the 'contiguous' operation argument, ultimately depends upon the wording of the contract under consideration.

In relation to the causation criterion arising under the extension of time provision in *Chestermount*, Colman J stated as follows:

> [I]t is right to examine the underlying contractual purpose of the completion date/extension of time/liquidated/damages regime. *At the foundation of this code is the obligation of the contractor to complete the works within the contractual period terminating at the completion date* and on failure to do so to pay liquidated charges for the period of time for which practical completion exceeds the completion date. But superimposed on this regime is a system of allocation of risk. [1] *If events occur which are non-contractor's risk events and those events cause the progress of the works to be delayed, in as much as such delay would otherwise cause the contractor to become liable for liquidated damages or for more liquidated damages*, the contract provides for the completion date to be prospectively or, under clause 25.3.3, retrospectively, adjusted in order to reflect the period of delay so caused and thereby reduce pro tanto the amount of liquidated damages payable by the contractor...

> In view of the inherent difficulties in *predicting with precision the impact on the progress of the works of non-contractor risk events, particularly when operating simultaneously with contractors' risk events*, the architect is given a power of retrospective adjustment to the completion date. [2] *The underlying objective is to arrive at the aggregate period of time within which the contract works as ultimately defined ought to have been completed having regard to the incidence of non-contractor's risk events* and to calculate the

excess time if any, over that period, which the contractor took to complete the works. In essence, the architect is concerned to arrive at an aggregate period for completion of the contractual works, having regard to the occurrence of non-contractor's risk events and to calculate the extent to which the completion of the works has exceeded that period (emphasis added).[7]

Therefore the entitlement to an extension of time was reasoned on the basis of the proper construction of the relevant clauses and what is a fair and reasonable 'aggregate period for the completion of the works, having regard to the occurrence of non-contractor's risk events' – see my '[2]' in the quote above.

Although not elaborated upon in any detail, the suggestion was that in order to be causally relevant the employer risk events must be 'operating simultaneously with contractors' risk events' and 'cause the progress of the works to be delayed' in a way that would otherwise cause the contractor to become liable for liquidated damages (ie causing critical delay) – see my '[1]' above.

There was, however, no analysis or explanation of what 'operating simultaneously' in this context actually meant in terms of a causation test. On the facts of the case, although not stated in terms in the judgment, it would appear that the instruction to reintroduce previously omitted work seems to have caused *further* critical delay to completion of the works. It was not stated in Colman J's reasoning, however, that an employer risk event could *only* become causally relevant for the purpose of generating an extension of time entitlement if it caused *further* critical delay in the period of culpable contractor delay, ie in this 'but for' sense.

V. Causation and Extension of Time Provisions

Derived from *Chestermount*, at least in the context of employer risk events occurring during a period of culpable contractor delay, the relevant authorities suggest two approaches to the causal criterion which, at first sight at least, seem somewhat inconsistent with one another: namely that the contract requires that the contractor to be (i) provided with the overall time that the contractor reasonably requires to complete the works in light of the employer risk events, and/or (ii) required to demonstrate the impact of the employer risk event in terms of it causing *further* actual critical delay to the works during the culpable contractor delay period.

The issue of concurrency was not specifically under consideration in *Chestermount* which, of course, pre-dated the equally seminal decision in *Henry Boot v Malmaison*[8] where Dyson J, as he then was, described the causation test as follows:

> 15. I accept the submissions of Miss O'Farrell. *It seems to me that it is a question of fact in any given case whether a relevant event has caused or is likely to cause delay to*

---

[7] *Balfour Beatty Building Ltd v Chestermount Properties Ltd* (1993) 62 BLR 1 at 25.
[8] *Henry Boot Construction (UK) Ltd v Malmaison Hotel (Manchester) Ltd* (1999) 70 Con LR 32, [1999] All ER (D) 1118.

the works beyond the completion date in the sense described by Colman J in the Balfour Beatty case. In the present case, the respondent has what Miss O'Farrell calls both a negative and a positive defence to the EOT/I claim. The negative defence amounts to saying that the variations and late information etc relied on by the claimant did not cause any delay because the activities were not on the critical path, and on that account did not cause delay. The positive defence is that the true cause of the delay was other matters, which were not relevant events, and for which the contractor was responsible ... In my judgment it is incorrect to say that, as a matter of construction of clause 25 when deciding whether a relevant event is likely to cause or has caused delay, the architect may not consider the impact on progress and completion of other events (emphasis added).

Once again it is notable (albeit a tad unhelpful) that the Court did not elaborate upon exactly what was meant by the 'question of fact ... in the sense described by Colman J in the Balfour Beatty case'. It is suggested that the latter is not self-evident in this respect. Also the Court did not explain how this test was to be applied in practice, save by reference to the agreed notion of concurrency agreed by the parties in that case.

In *Royal Brompton Hospital NHS Trust v Hammond (No 7)*,[9] HHJ Richard Seymour QC dealt in terms with the meaning of the causal criterion in the context of concurrency as follows:

[I]t is, I think, necessary to be clear what one means by events operating concurrently. *It does not mean, in my judgment, a situation in which, work already being delayed, let it be supposed, because the contractor has had difficulty in obtaining sufficient labour, an event occurs which is a Relevant Event and which, had the contractor not been delayed, would have caused him to be delayed, but which in fact, by reason of the existing delay, made no difference.* In such a situation although there is a Relevant Event, 'the completion of the Works is [not] likely to be delayed *thereby* beyond the Completion Date.' The Relevant Event simply has no effect upon the completion date (emphasis added).[10]

This analysis emphasised: the centrality of the contractual wording to understanding the causal criterion that has to be satisfied (ie, in that case the requirement that 'the completion of the Works is likely to be delayed thereby'); the importance of timing to the legal significance of competing delay events (with only the first in time being capable of satisfying the causal requirement under the relevant provision); and the need for 'pure concurrency' (in the sense of multiple delay events occurring and impacting the works at the same time) for there to be a legally relevant concurrent cause of delay.

It should be noted, however, that this strict approach to the meaning of concurrent delay is now doubted,[11] and that this relaxation in the generally accepted

---

[9] *Royal Brompton Hospital NHS Trust v Hammond (No 7)* (2001) 76 Con LR 148.
[10] (2001) 76 Con LR 148 at [31].
[11] *Keating on Construction Contracts*, 10th edn (London, Sweet & Maxwell, 2016) at paragraph 8-025 and *City Inn Ltd v Shepherd Construction Ltd* [2010] BLR 473, per Lord Osborne at [33]–[38].

definition of concurrency in turn undermines the notion that what should be considered an 'actual' cause of critical delay simply depends upon which delay event becomes operative first in time (in the sense of beginning to push completion of the Works beyond the Completion Date) – because it is concurrency in the delaying effect of the respective causes that now appears to be relevant to the existence of concurrent delay.

In *De Beers UK Limited v Atos Origin IT Services UK Limited*,[12] a more relaxed approach to the causal criterion was articulated. Edwards-Stuart J described the approach as follows:[13]

> The general rule in construction and engineering cases is that *where there is concurrent delay to completion* caused by matters for which both employer and contractor are responsible, *the contractor is entitled to an extension of time* but he cannot recover in respect of the loss caused by the delay. In the case of the former, this is *because the rule where delay is caused by the employer is that not only must the contractor complete within a reasonable time but also the contractor must have a reasonable time within which to complete. It therefore does not matter if the contractor would have been unable to complete by the contractual completion date if there had been no breaches of contract by the employer* (or other events which entitled the contractor to an extension of time), *because he is entitled to have the time within which to complete which the contract allows or which the employer's conduct has made reasonably necessary* (emphasis added).

This reasoning seems to emphasise Colman J's approach as summarised in the highlighted passage at '[2]' above, but without express reference for the need for *further* critical delay to be established beyond that which would occur in any event as a result of the concurrent contractor delay events and without explaining what was meant by 'concurrent delay to completion' or 'where delay is caused by the employer'.

The most authoritative decision in this field is probably that of Hamblen J (as he then was) in *Adyard Abu Dhabi v SD Marine Services*.[14] The decision analysed most of the key authorities and concluded, albeit in obiter dicta, as follows:

> 270. It was held in *Balfour Beatty* that the net basis was the correct approach. In his judgment Colman J analysed the 'contractual purpose of the completion date/extension of time/liquidated damages regime' (page 25) …
>
> …
>
> 272. Colman J then went on to make it clear that *delay (to the completion date) must be therefore assessed by reference to the progress of the works (to the then-projected completion date)* …
>
> 273. As the editors of the BLR commented at the time (at 10):
>
> > 'The practical value of the judgment of Colman J is that it should put an end to hypothetical questions about the potential as opposed to the actual effect of causes of

[12] *De Beers UK Limited v Atos Origin IT Services UK Limited* [2010] EWHC 3276 (TCC).
[13] [2010] EWHC 3276 (TCC) at [177].
[14] *Adyard Abu Dhabi v SD Marine Services* [2011] EWHC 848 (Comm).

delay which entitle a contractor to an extension of time. In many cases it will be a simple exercise to determine whether, for example, a variation did in fact *further delay completion in a period of culpable delay*. It may be found that no such delay can be established. *If it can, then a fair period is added to the then applicable date to produce the requisite extension of time...*'

...

277. It is to be noted that this example involves a relevant event which *caused a period of actual delay to the progress of the works* – no work could be done for a week due to the weather. If that is established then the contractor is entitled to his extension of time even if there is another concurrent cause of that same delay ...

278. A similar approach was taken by HHJ Seymour QC in *Royal Brompton Hospital NHS Trust v Hammond (No 7)* (2001) 76 Con LR 148 ...

279. This makes it clear that *there is only concurrency if both events in fact cause delay to the progress of the works and the delaying effect of the two events is felt at the same time*. In HHJ Seymour QC's first example, the relevant event did not in fact cause any delay to the progress of the works. His first example is consistent with Colman J's comments as to the situation in which a variation is instructed during a period of culpable delay at pages 30–31 of the report in *Balfour Beatty* (emphasis added).

On this analysis, there is therefore only legally relevant concurrency when 'the delaying effect of the two events is felt at the same time'. There is a reference to the commentary on this case in the BLR, describing the causal criterion in these situations as being one requiring the relevant event to cause *further* delay to completion in a period of culpable delay. This is a matter, however, as explained above, that is not identified in terms by Colman J in *Balfour Beatty v Chestermount* as representing a causal requirement – although, admittedly, it was implicit on the facts of that case. It is also unclear why the causal test should be different depending upon when the delay event occurs – ie pre or post the existing contractual completion date.

Also, and contrary to Hamblen J's conclusion, HHJ Seymour's first example is not entirely consistent with Colman J's analysis at pages 30–31 of the report in *Chestermount*. This is because Colman J's analysis seems primarily to depend upon a consideration of 'the total number of working days starting from the date of possession within which the contractor ought fairly and reasonably to have completed the works'. This approach, whether or not a delay event occurs in a period of culpable contractor delay, does not seem to depend upon whether as a matter of fact *further* critical delay is caused to the completion date.

It is difficult to see why a combination of Colman J's approach in *Chestermount* and the concept of concurrency as introduced in and generally accepted since *Malmaison* should not ordinarily justify an extension of time entitlement where the delaying effect of an employer risk event is felt prior to or during a period of contractor culpable delay – even if its effect is merely to coincide or overlap with or reinforce the cause of the existing critical delay to the works.

The nature of the causal criterion was also considered in *Walter Lilly v Mackay and DMW*.[15] In this case Akenhead J, after reviewing *Balfour Beatty, City Inn, Malmaison, De Beers* and *Adyard*, found as follows:[16]

> In any event, I am clearly of the view that, where there is an extension of time clause such as that agreed upon in this case and *where delay is caused by two or more effective causes*, one of which entitles the Contractor to an extension of time as being a Relevant Event, the Contractor is entitled to a full extension of time. Part of the logic of this is that many of the Relevant Events would otherwise amount to acts of prevention and that it would be wrong in principle to construe Clause 25 on the basis that the Contractor should be denied a full extension of time in those circumstances. More importantly however, *there is a straight contractual interpretation of Clause 25 which points very strongly in favour of the view that, provided that the Relevant Events can be shown to have delayed the Works, the Contractor is entitled to an extension of time for the whole period of delay caused by the Relevant Events in question.* There is nothing in the wording of Clause 25 which expressly suggests that there is any sort of proviso to the effect that an extension should be reduced *if the causation criterion is established.* The fact that the Architect has to award a 'fair and reasonable' extension does not imply that there should be some apportionment in the case of concurrent delays. *The test is primarily a causation one.* It therefore follows that, although of persuasive weight, the *City Inn* case is inapplicable within this jurisdiction (emphasis added).

This analysis is significant for a number of reasons. First, it confirms that the relevant test 'is primarily a causation one'. Next, no mention is made in it of the relevance of the so-called 'dominant cause' test in this context – reinforcing the impression that this test is increasingly redundant. There is, however, no explanation of what exactly the 'causation criterion' or 'causation test' consists of. There is also no explanation of how it can be established that delay has been 'caused by' a Relevant Event in the event of concurrent alleged delay events in the required sense. If anything, it is suggested that the reference to 'effective causes' connotes a less onerous causation requirement or an 'effective cause' test – consistent with *De Beers*.

Akenhead J elaborated upon the test as follows:[17]

> In the context of this contractual based approach to extension, one cannot therefore do a purely retrospective exercise. What one can not do is to identify the last of a number of events which delayed completion and then say it was that last event at the end which caused the overall delay to the Works. *One needs to consider what critically delayed the Works as they went along. For instance in this case, it would be wrong to say that the problem with the Courtyard Sliding Doors delayed the Works until it emerged as a problem in April 2008.* Put another way, *it did not delay the Works (if at all) until it emerged as a problem which needed to be addressed* (emphasis added).

---

[15] *Walter Lilly v Mackay and DMW Developments Ltd* [2012] EWHC 1773 (TCC).
[16] [2012] EWHC 1773 (TCC) at [370].
[17] [2012] EWHC 1773 (TCC) at [365].

The requirement for a delay event to have 'emerged' is a helpful reminder that to be legally relevant alleged concurrent delay events must be operating so as to cause actual delay to the works – a point also emphasised by Hamblen J in *Adyard* at paragraph 292.

VI. Conclusions

To coin a phrase, I should now draw the threads together.

First, *Carillion* demonstrates the importance of considering each contract in light of its own wording and context – and the need to put previous authority dealing with extension of time issues in its proper context, which will rarely be decisive.

Secondly, the key issues to consider in relation to any extension of time provision (especially where relied upon in periods of contractor culpable delay) are (i) how was it intended to operate (*Carillion*)?; and (ii) what is the causal criterion that needs to be satisfied in order to generate an entitlement to relief (*Chestermount*)?

Thirdly, the ordinary meaning of the words used in a relevant provision is likely to be given paramount importance – although these provisions are often opaquely worded and, certainly in standard form contracts, unlikely to be terribly helpful in resolving these issues.

Fourthly, the parties are free to agree any method of operation and/or causation test they wish.

Fifthly, it needs to be acknowledged that generally the authorities in this area are not especially helpful, in that (i) they are inevitably fact sensitive, and (ii) they do not analyse or explain clearly (or sometimes even at all) the nature of the relevant causal criterion in the extension of time provisions under consideration.

Sixthly, the current state of the law on the issues of concurrency and the causal criterion in typical extension of time provisions may be summarised as follows:[18]

a.   A relevant event must be shown to be the effective cause of actual critical delay to the works to generate an entitlement.

b.   An effective cause may be a sole or concurrent cause.

c.   To be an effective cause the delay event must act alone or in combination with other delay events to critically delay the progress of the works.

d.   It will be taken to have this effect if it operates so as to impinge on the works in the required sense and would, if operating alone, have caused the same amount of critical delay.

e.   A delay event that has not emerged and/or does not impact on an activity or activities on the critical path is not an effective legal cause for these purposes.

---

[18] See generally *Keating on Construction Contracts*, 10th edn (n 11 above) at paragraphs 8-023 and 9-096.

f.   Delay to the completion date must be assessed by reference to the progress of the works to the then-projected completion date.

An 'effective' cause in this sense is probably best understood as a cause, by itself or in combination with other matters, of a period of critical delay – and 'effective cause' has been held, albeit in a slightly different context (per Beldam LJ in *County Ltd v Girozentrale Securities*)[19] to potentially mean something less than 'of equal causative potency' with another cause, or at least there is no clear authority to suggest that it cannot in the case of building contracts.

As to how this test is to be applied, at least during periods of contractor culpable delay, the *Adyard* approach (to the effect that *further* actual critical delay must be shown to have been caused by the employer risk event) is likely to be followed by the courts, certainly at first instance, because this is the most considered and recent of the relevant decisions in this area of the law – and has been approved in other decisions.

My own view, however, is that this is probably too onerous an approach to the causal criterion test in such a situation. It is unclear, given the current consensus understanding of the meaning of concurrent delay, why a legally relevant cause should only be recognised in such a situation where it has the 'but for' consequence described in the reasoning set out above.

However, the limits of this more relaxed causal criterion should also be recognised. Even if a more relaxed 'effective cause' causation test were established to be of more general application, this would nevertheless require any alleged concurrent impact of an employer risk event to be a joint cause of actual critical delay – in the sense that it has emerged as an operable cause of delayed progress of the relevant works.

There would still be, therefore, a need to distinguish between concurrent causes of actual critical delay and matters that have not, as a matter of fact, yet emerged as problems which impact the progress of the works at all and/or that do not affect the critical path and may therefore be ignored as only theoretical causes of delay.

Ultimately, perhaps the lasting impact of Jackson LJ's decision in *Carillion* will be to encourage the taking of 'novel' points in this whole field of construction law and to re-focus attention on the wider issues that arise in considering the impact of extension of time provisions and the continued significance, in particular, of the decision in *Chestermount*.

---

[19] *County Ltd v Girozentrale Securities* [1996] 3 All ER 834 at 849b–d.

19

Prevention, Time-Bars and *Multiplex Constructions (UK) Ltd v Honeywell Control Systems Ltd (No 2)*

DOUG JONES AO[1]

I. Introduction

Consider the situation where an Employer provides critical documentation late to the Contractor, relevantly causing a delay of two weeks. The Contractor has access to extension-of-time provisions under the contract, but only upon providing notice within 28 days. For whatever reason, whether forgetfulness or otherwise, the Contractor does not do so. Now, not only is the Contractor not entitled to an extension of time, but is also in breach of contract for completing the project later than the contractually stipulated date. The Employer rubs its hands with glee: the Contractor's failure to provide notice not only deprived the latter of its ability to claim costs for the Employer's delay; it also allows the Employer to be paid liquidated damages for the period of delay which the Employer caused.

This conclusion is based on the prevailing understanding of the prevention principle, as expressed by Lord Justice Jackson in *Multiplex*.[2]

In a different context, in 2016 the United Kingdom Supreme Court overturned the settled law of extended joint criminal enterprise for over 30 years.[3] In so doing, the Court held that the law had then taken a 'wrong turn' which now needed correction.[4] The purpose of this chapter is to examine whether the prevailing position in *Multiplex* should be reconsidered for situations arising at the intersection of the prevention principle and contractual notice and time-bar provisions.

---

[1] www.dougjones.info. I would like to thank the contributions of my legal assistants, Jonathon Hetherington and George Pasas, for their assistance in preparing this chapter.
[2] *Multiplex Constructions (UK) Ltd v Honeywell Control Systems Ltd (No 2)* [2007] BLR 195, [2007] EWHC 447 (TCC), 111 Con LR 78 (*Multiplex*) (in obiter).
[3] *R v Jogee* [2016] UKSC 8.
[4] *R v Jogee* [2016] UKSC 8, [87].

I was delighted to accept the invitation to contribute to this *Festschrift* for Lord Justice Jackson. I join with the many other authors in this book in lauding his great contributions to the law. It would not be putting it too highly to say that he is one of the great construction law judges in England in recent decades, and his retirement will be sorely missed (though doubtless very well earned). On a personal level, I have known Lord Justice Jackson for many years, and he has always touched me with his character, his humour, his prodigious work ethic, and his integrity. This chapter proposes to continue the debate[5] on the prevention principle, which it is hoped will be welcomed by Jackson LJ in view of his renowned intellectual enthusiasm for the development of the law both in England and internationally.

The chapter is structured as follows:

1.   First, I set out what is conventionally understood as the prevention principle, and attempt to crystallise the problem at hand: a party cannot prevent someone from meeting their obligations, and then punish them for not doing so;

2.   Second, I summarise the two primary cases with which this chapter deals, namely *Gaymark*[6] and *Multiplex*;

3.   Third, I analyse the arguments commonly used to support the view expressed by Jackson LJ, namely the role of notice provisions, the allocation of risk under contract, and the importance of certainty of contract. In doing so, I argue that a more internally consistent approach is to draw a distinction between delays caused by the Employer and delays caused by the Contractor; and

4.   Fourth, I propose an alternative formulation which perhaps partly reconciles the presently differing positions advanced in this area. I suggest attaching the prevention principle to the 'remedy' of liquidated damages, and not to the 'obligation' of the Date for Practical Completion. Doing so would allow delay to be apportioned according to who was at fault, leading to a more intuitive and just outcome.

I now turn to a discussion of the prevention principle and its underlying purpose.

II. The Foundations – An Overview of the Prevention Principle

As presently formulated, the prevention principle states that if an Employer contributes or causes a delay to the Contractor then, absent any relevant extension of time being granted, the Employer is unable to claim liquidated damages for *any* delay.

---

[5] Begun in the 2008 TECBAR lecture: Doug Jones, 'Can Prevention Be Cured by Timebars' (2009) 26 *International Construction Law Review* 57.

[6] *Gaymark Investments Pty Ltd v Walter Construction Group Ltd* [1999] NTSC 143 (Supreme Court of the Northern Territory).

Before proceeding to the meatier (and more controversial) section of analysis in this chapter, it is useful to say some words regarding the operation of this principle. Rather than pretend to be a comprehensive summary of all the nuances of this area, this section instead chooses to focus on two aspects of the prevention principle which are critical to note for the remainder of this chapter: first, the roots of the principle in considerations of justice and fairness and, secondly, the fact that the principle operates on the obligation of the date of completion, and not the remedy of liquidated damages.

A. Rationale for the Prevention Principle

Whilst the prevention principle is often considered to be unique to construction law, its origins derive from a more fundamental principle of contract law: a party may not rely upon the non-performance of another party to the contract where it is its own actions that have been the cause of this non-performance.[7] Effectively, if the Employer prevents the Contractor from completing on time, it is simultaneously prevented from suing the Contractor and claiming liquidated damages for that delay.

Thus, in *Multiplex*, Jackson J (correctly, with respect) described the essence of the prevention principle as:[8] 'the promisee cannot insist upon the performance of an obligation which he has prevented the promisor from performing'.[9] This aligns with one of the earliest formulations of the prevention principle in *Holme v Guppy*:[10] 'there are clear authorities, that if the party be prevented, by the refusal of the other contracting party, from completing the contract within the time limited, he is not liable in law for the default'. The emergence and existence of this general position is not difficult to understand, and it is rooted in notions of fairness and justice.[11] Unfortunately, as will soon become apparent, it appears that these roots have been abandoned in recent judicial pronouncements.

---

[7] This principle is also reflected in international commercial law: see, eg, Article 7.1.2 UNIDROIT Principles of International Commercial Contracts 2010, which provides 'A party may not rely on the non-performance of the other party to the extent that such non-performance was caused by the first party's act or omission or by another event as to which the first party bears the risk'; see also *Perini Pacific Ltd v Greater Vancouver Sewerage and Drainage District* (1966) 57 DLR (2d) 307.

[8] *Multiplex* [2007] BLR 195, [47].

[9] *Multiplex* [2007] BLR 195, [47].

[10] *Holme v Guppy* (1838) 3 M&W 387, 389.

[11] *SMK Cabinets v Hili Modern Electrics Pty Ltd* [1984] VR 391, 397; see also Crispin Winser, 'Shutting Pandora's Box, The Prevention Principle after Multiplex v Honeywell' (2007) 23 *Construction Law Journal* 512; Jeremy Coggins, 'The application of the prevention principle in Australia – part one' (2009) 21(3)–(4) *Australian Construction Law Bulletin* 30; Damien Cremean, Michael Whitten and Michael Sharkey, *Brooking on Building Contracts*, 5th edn (London, LexisNexis Butterworths, 2014) p 104.

B. Obligation and Not Remedy

Another interesting, and technical, aspect of the prevention principle is exactly *why* it operates to disable the liquidated damages clauses. It is necessary to explain this in some depth, not least because it provides a crucial springboard for the conclusion to this chapter.

The prevention principle operates in contracts where there is a date of completion specified. If the Employer relevantly delays the Contractor, this means that the contractually stipulated date of completion is no longer enforceable (for the reasons discussed above). As a consequence, all liquidated damages are similarly unenforceable, because there is no reference date of completion from which they are to be calculated.[12] Thus, the prevention principle effectively operates to set 'time at large' in the contract, meaning that the contractual date of completion is replaced with an obligation to complete within a 'reasonable time'.[13]

It is this 'peculiarity' which I suggest has led to the judicial disfavour into which the prevention principle has fallen.

Importantly, the principle does not operate to conclusively bar the Employer from remedy or redress. The Employer can still bring an action claiming that the Contractor finished even later than a reasonable time.[14] The consequence, however, is that the Employer must resort to the more challenging approach of proving loss and damages, from a date uncertain, in accordance with general common law rules, and not with the simplicity which liquidated damages offers in those common law jurisdictions where valid clauses are applied to the period of delay calculated by reference to the extension of time provisions in the contract.[15]

In order to avoid this outcome, the Employer can include extension-of-time provisions for Employer-caused delay within the contract. This allows the Employer to move the contractual date of completion to accommodate for the delays for which they are responsible and therefore claim liquidated damages for Contractor-caused delay occurring beyond this new date of completion.[16] Effectively, the preventing conduct of the Employer is 'cured' by its granting of additional time through creating a new contractual obligation from which time

---

[12] *Sattin v Poole* (1901), *Hudson's Building and Engineering Contracts*, 4th edn (London, Sweet & Maxwell, 1914) vol 2, 306, 310.

[13] *Gaymark* [1999] NTSC 143, [54]; *Multiplex* [2007] BLR 195, [48]; see also paras [5] and [103] of the same judgment; John Dorter and JJA Sharkey, *Building and Construction Contracts in Australia*, 2nd edn (Sydney, Law Book Co, 1990); see eg *Rapid Building Group Ltd v Ealing Family Housing Association* (1984) 29 BLR 5.

[14] *Peak Construction (Liverpool) Ltd v McKinney Foundations Ltd* (1970) 1 BLR 114, 121 ('Peak'); Julian Bailey, *Construction Law*, 2nd edn (London, *Informa*, 2016) p 1204.

[15] *Peak* (1970) 1 BLR 114, 121. But it must be remembered that in some common law jurisdictions such as India and Malaysia actual loss must still be proven even though liquidated damages are provided for (effectively as a limit on liability).

[16] Stephen Rae, 'Prevention and Damages: who takes the risk for employer delays?' (2006) 22 *Construction Law Journal* 307, 307; Ian Duncan Wallace, *Hudson's Building and Engineering Contracts*, 11th edn (London, Sweet & Maxwell, 1994) paragraph [10.0204].

can be measured. The mechanisms for granting extensions of time are thus of critical importance, and it is for this reason that the *Multiplex* judgment considered the construction of these terms, and how they are operated, in such depth.[17]

There are two further factors which make extension-of-time provisions essential for the Employer. The *first* is that the preventing conduct sufficient to invoke the principle does not need to be a breach of contract, but includes any conduct which prevents the Contractor from reaching the date of completion.[18] In practice, this means that even in contracts which provide for orders for variation and modification, these orders, if they cause delay, will be considered to be preventing conduct.[19] Thus, in *Multiplex*, directions and instructions given by Multiplex to Honeywell were part of the relevant delaying conduct. This delay, however, must actually occur.[20]

The *second*, and more important, factor is that the prevention principle does not distinguish between situations where it was *only* the Employer which caused delay, and situations where *both* the Employer and the Contractor caused delays.[21] The reason for this is that the courts cannot apportion delay,[22] meaning that regardless of how significant the Employer's actions were to the overall delay, liquidated damages cannot be claimed. For instance, if there is a delay of 12 weeks for which the Employer was only responsible for one week of delay, then, in the absence of an extension-of-time provision, the prevention principle prevents the Employer from claiming liquidated damages for any of the 12 weeks.

These conclusions follow from the fact that the prevention principle attaches to the obligation of the date of completion, and not the remedy of liquidated damages.[23] Consequently, any period of Employer-caused delay, even if small, will make the contractually stipulated date unenforceable absent any appropriate extension of time.

At the outset, it can be seen that this position is unsatisfactory and indeed anomalous, and it would be intuitively preferable to allow courts to apportion liability for different causes of delay, in a similar manner to how apportionment

---

[17] *Multiplex* [2007] BLR 195, [16]–[28].

[18] Ian Duncan Wallace, *Hudson's Building and Engineering Contracts*, 11th edn (London, Sweet & Maxwell, 1994) (vol 2) paragraph [10.0204]; *Dodd v Charlton* [1897] 1 QB 562; *Percy Bilton Ltd v Greater London Council* [1982] 1 WLR 794, 801; *SBS International Pty Ltd v Venuti Nominees Pty Ltd* [2004] SASC 151, [12]; *Multiplex* [2007] BLR 195, [48].

[19] *SMK Cabinets v Hili Modern Electronics Pty Ltd* [1984] VR 391.

[20] *Turner Coporation Ltd (in prov liq) v Co-Ordinated Industries Pty Ltd* (1995) 11 *Building and Construction Law Journal* (BCL) 202, 217; Julian Bailey, *Construction Law*, 2nd edn (London, Informa, 2016) p 1206.

[21] *Peak Construction (Liverpool) Limited v McKinney Foundations Limited* (1970) 1 BLR 111, 121: See also *SMK Cabinets v Hili Modern Electronics Pty Ltd* [1984] VR 391, 398–400.

[22] *Rapid Building Group Ltd v Ealing Family Housing Association Ltd* (1984) 29 BLR 5; See also Julian Bailey, *Construction Law*, 2nd edn (London, Informa, 2016) p 1204.

[23] As I noted in my earlier article the link of authority traced by Brooking J in *SMK Cabinets v Hili Modern Electrics Pty Ltd* [1984] VR 391, 398 clearly indicates that the principle attaches to the obligation: see Doug Jones, 'Can Prevention Be Cured by Timebars' (2009) 26 *International Construction Law Review* 57, 72.

is carried out in the area of contributory negligence. This is not a revolutionary concept; the idea of 'time at large' and an obligation-focused approach is one exclusive to English law and its descendants. Indeed, civil law traditions have no issues, either conceptual or practical, with apportioning liability for delay caused by Employers and Contractors. I return to this later in this chapter.

III. A Fork in the Road – '*Gaymark v Multiplex*'

With these preliminary remarks in mind, I will consider the two titular cases, that of *Gaymark* in the Northern Territory Supreme Court, and that of *Multiplex*, in the English High Court. What will become immediately apparent is that, for all its hype, the ratio of *Gaymark* is quite narrow and turns on some very unique adjustments to a standard form contract.[24] Consequently, this chapter does more than seek to justify *Gaymark* on its facts; it also seeks to justify the proposition for which it is often cited. Namely, that the prevention principle remains enlivened in cases of Employer-caused delay, even where a Contractor has failed to comply with notice provisions which are conditions precedent to the granting of an extension of time.

   Multiplex disagrees with this position, with Jackson LJ relevantly opining that 'if the facts are that it was possible to comply with clause 11.1.3 [the extension-of-time clause] but Honeywell simply failed to do so (whether or not deliberately), then those facts do not set time at large'.[25] The disagreement thus being squarely identified, it is necessary to note that the typically persuasively judgment of Jackson LJ also deals with a number of issues relating to the prevention principle, including arguments regarding the construction of extension-of-time clauses, and in what circumstances they become inoperable. In light of the scope of this chapter being limited to the death or otherwise of *Gaymark*, it leaves for another day discussion of those issues to the extent that they are not directly involved in the present analysis.

A. The *Gaymark* Decision

Gaymark v Walter Constructions considered a request for leave to appeal from an arbitration pursuant to section 38 of the Commercial Arbitration Act. The arbitration involved a dispute between the Contractor, Walter Construction Group Ltd (formerly known as Concrete Constructions Group Ltd) and the Employers; Gaymark Investments Pty Ltd and Darwin Central Nominees Pty Ltd, as part of the construction of the Darwin Central Hotel.[26] The arbitrator was the highly

---

[24] *Gaymark* [1999] NTSC 143, [68]–[71].
[25] *Multiplex* [2007] BLR 195, [105].
[26] *Gaymark* [1999] NTSC 143, [2].

respected engineer arbitrator Mr Max McDougall (father of Justice McDougall of the NSW Supreme Court). The arbitrator found that Gaymark had delayed Concrete Constructions by 77 days, and that these delays 'constituted "acts of prevention" by Gaymark with the result that there was no date for practical completion and Concrete Constructions was then obliged to complete with a reasonable time (which the arbitrator found that it in fact did)'.[27]

Importantly, and contentiously, the arbitrator found as a matter of fact that Concrete Constructions had failed to meet the appropriate notice requirements requisite to an extension of time,[28] but still held that the prevention principle was enlivened in any event.

In an appeal to the Northern Territory Supreme Court, Gaymark did not contest the arbitrator's findings on the facts but appealed the arbitrator's application of the prevention principle. The contract in question was a standard form public sector building contract – NPWC Edition 3 (1981), which had been significantly amended.[29] To understand this decision, it is unfortunately necessary to identify some provisions of the contract:

1. Clause 35.5 provided for the payment of liquidated damages in the sum of AUS$6,500 per calendar day.[30]

2. Clause 35.2 provided that the contractor was obliged to complete the works by a stipulated date of completion, or any extended date as allowed by the Superintendent.[31]

3. In the standard form template, clause 35.4 provided that where a Contractor notified of a claim for delay the Superintendent was entitled to grant extensions of time. It also provided that the Superintendent could grant extensions of time at will, regardless of any notice provided by the Contractor. However, in the contract in question, clause 35.4 was replaced by a new clause 19 which automatically entitled the Contractor to extensions of time if they gave notice, and deleted the unilateral power of the Superintendent to grant an extension.[32]

The arbitrator held that he could interpret the contract in three ways:

1. That a term could be implied, similar to that of the standard form 35.4 that allowed the employer to unilaterally provide an extension of time. The arbitrator noted that this would be difficult given the conscious efforts to replace clause 35.4;[33]

[27] ibid [50].
[28] ibid [49].
[29] ibid [47].
[30] ibid [48].
[31] ibid [56].
[32] ibid [59].
[33] ibid [62].

2.   That a failure by the Contractor to comply with clause 19 has exposed them to the risk of liquidated damages. The arbitrator noted that this led to the absurd result that not only did the Employer avoid the Contractor's costs of delay but also entitled them to liquidated damages; or

3.   That by amending the contract the Employer had assumed the risk that it would cause a delay and that the Contractor would not comply with the notice requirements, resulting in time being set at large.

The arbitrator adopted the third option, holding that an intention that the Employer would bear the risk was clearly manifest. Bailey J concurred with this reasoning and in the ratio of *Gaymark* held:

> I agree with the arbitrator that the contract between the parties fails to provide for a situation where Gaymark caused actual delays to Concrete Constructions achieving practical completion by the due date coupled with a failure by Concrete Constructions to comply with the notice of SC19.1.[34]

This conclusion was clearly correct in the absence of the unilateral power to extend time. In my view, the answer should remain the same even if such a power were there and unexercised.

B.   The *Multiplex* Decision

Eight years later in the English High Court, Mr Justice Jackson (as he then was) in *Multiplex* offered a critique of *Gaymark*, stating that, 'whatever may be the law of the Northern Territory of Australia, I have considerable doubt that *Gaymark* represents the law of England.'[35]

Multiplex v Honeywell concerned the construction of the new Wembley Stadium. Honeywell contended that in its sub-contract with Multiplex, Multiplex's delays had set time at large. At the outset, it is worth noting that Jackson J concluded that the factual circumstances were distinct from those of *Gaymark*, as unlike in *Gaymark*, non-compliance with the notice clause did not expose the Contractor to automatic liability. This was because liquidated damages could only be recovered for the failure of the sub-Contractor, which Multiplex, as the perpetrator of the alleged delay, was not.[36]

In obiter, Jackson J canvassed several then-recent authorities,[37] including *Gaymark*, and dismissed the appellant's attempts to set time at large, stating that notice provisions 'serve a valuable purpose' and were necessary to allow matters to

---

[34] ibid [71].

[35] *Multiplex* [2007] BLR 195, [103].

[36] ibid [104].

[37] Jackson J particularly focused upon the two *Turner* decisions: *Turner Corporation Ltd (Receiver and Manager Appointed) v Austotel* (1997) 13 BCL 378; and *Turner Corporation Ltd (in provisional liquidation) v Coordinated Industries Pty Ltd* (1995) 11 BCL 202.

be investigated.[38] He also noted with concern that if *Gaymark* were good law, the Contractor would be able to disregard notice provisions with impunity.[39]

This critique was later endorsed by HHJ Stephen Davies in *Steria Ltd v Sigma Wireless Communications Ltd*, in which it was stated:[40]

> Although on the facts of that case Jackson J did not, due to the particular wording of the extension of time and liquidated damages clauses employed, need to express a final decision on the point, nonetheless I gratefully adopt his analysis and agree with his preliminary conclusion. Generally one can see the commercial absurdity of an argument which would result in the Contractor being better off by deliberately failing to comply with the notice provision.

IV. A Change in Direction – Returning to First Principles

Recall that the conventional position, which Jackson J adopted, is that where a Contractor fails to comply with notice provisions which are conditions precedent to an extension of time, the Employer may still claim liquidated damages. This is irrespective of whether the relevant delay was caused by the Contractor, by a neutral factor, or by the Employer. At this juncture, it is useful to reflect on the example given in the introduction. One cannot help but feel a sense of disquiet about forcing a Contractor to pay compensation for a delay caused by the Employer. The simple solution to this problem is to draw a bright-line distinction between Contractor-caused delay, neutral delay, and Employer-caused delay.

This part of the chapter seeks to establish the validity of this distinction, as one that is in conformity with both the rationale for the prevention principle, and broader policies of contract law. It does so through critically examining the traditional rationales for the conventional position.

It is instructive to set out the relevant paragraph justifying Jackson J's view in *Multiplex*:

> Contractual terms requiring a contractor to give prompt notice of delay serve a valuable purpose; such notice enables matters to be investigated while they are still current. Furthermore, such notice sometimes gives the employer the opportunity to withdraw instructions when the financial consequences become apparent. If *Gaymark* is good law, then a contractor could disregard with impunity any provision making proper notice a condition precedent. At his option the contractor could set time at large.[41]

It will be seen that this paragraph reflects three traditional underlying themes: first, the issue of 'causation' and its relationship with notice provisions; secondly,

---

[38] *Multiplex* [2007] BLR 195, [103].
[39] ibid.
[40] *Steria Ltd v Sigma Wireless Communications Ltd* [2007] EWHC 3454 (TCC), [95].
[41] *Multiplex* [2007] BLR 195, [103].

the supposed intentions of the parties in utilising extension-of-time principles; and thirdly, the desirability of certainty in contractual relations. I suggest that none of these provides a compelling justification for disabling the operation of the prevention principle in the case of Employer-caused delay.

A. The 'Cause' of the Delay?

If the Contractor fails to meet its obligations, for example through delayed mobilisation or the mobilisation of insufficient labour, then it is the Contractor who has caused the delay. Similarly, in cases of 'neutral' delays, such as weather events, unless the contract allows the Contractor relief, it will bear the risk of delays thereby arising. The relevant issue relates to delays caused by the Employer, for example through giving a variation order or providing insufficient site access, which are not the subject of extensions of time.

The judicial view with which I join issue is that if a Contractor fails to comply with the notice requirement, it is *this* failure which is the proximate cause of any delay. Consequently, the Employer's conduct is no longer relevant, and thus there is nothing for the prevention principle to attach itself to. I suggest that this view is in error through ascribing to notice provisions a greater power than they possess, and ignoring the original wrongdoing by the Employer. Before demonstrating this, however, it is necessary to discuss what this position is.

B. Notice Failure as Causation?

The starting point is the obiter of Justice Cole in *Turner Corporation Ltd (Receiver and Manager Appointed) v Austotel Pty Ltd*, where his Honour states: 'A party to a contract cannot rely upon the preventing conduct of the other where it *failed to exercise a contractual right which would have negated the preventing conduct*' (emphasis added).[42]

To understand this argument, it is necessary to first consider the importance of notice provisions with regards to contract management in the construction world. These provisions allow the Contractor to inform the Employer of the effects of its actions, as well as any associated delay and financial repercussions.[43] In his oft-cited article (including several citations in *Multiplex*),[44] the late Professor Wallace emphasises that Employer-caused delay commonly manifests itself in orders for

---

[42] *Turner Corporation Ltd (Receiver and Manager Appointed) v Austotel Pty Ltd* (1997) 13 BCL 378, 384. As Stephen Rae notes, this passage is merely obiter dicta, as compliance with notice provisions was not in issue in *Austotel*: Stephen Rae, 'Prevention and Damages: Who Takes the Risk for Employer Delays?' (2006) 22 *Construction Law Journal* 311–12.

[43] *Multiplex* [2007] BLR 195, [103]; *Zhoushan Jinhaiwan Shipyard Co Ltd v Golden Exquisite Inc* [2014] EWHC 4050 (Comm), [54].

[44] *Multiplex* [2007] BLR 195, [100].

variation and modification.[45] He submits that, in the majority of these cases, the Contractor will be better positioned to determine whether an Employer's action impacts upon the critical path and will cause delay. Take, for instance, an Employer's variation of the positioning of a set of electrical wires. There the Contractor will likely have unique knowledge of changed material sourcing requirements, labour availability and on-site obstacles impacting on the critical path. Notice provisions thus provide an opportunity for dialogue between the parties to determine the scale of delay and whether it should be incurred or can be mitigated or avoided.

Thus, Jackson J writes of the opportunity given to the Employer to withdraw instructions.[46] Crispin Winser notes that such 'early warning' as a form of dispute avoidance has become an increasingly featured focus of standard form contracts, particularly in the New Engineering Contract (NEC).[47] Further, several commentators have also suggested that notice provisions offer a valuable incentive to prevent meritless claims, contributing to their dispute avoidance value.[48]

It is for this reason that it is often argued that a Contractor's failure to comply with notice provisions provides the cause of the delay, and not the Employer's actions themselves. In *Multiplex*, therefore, the implied position would be that it was the failure of Honeywell to provide notice of delay and not Multiplex's variation of the communication systems. This position received some endorsement in the New South Wales Court of Appeal in *Peninsula Balmain v Abrigroup Contractors*, where Hodgson JA appeared to refer positively to this line of reasoning and Professor Wallace's views.[49]

C. Response

The approach to causation suffers two major defects.

First, it can be noted that it deals with a very favourable example. Professor Wallace, for example, considers the plight of the Employer who gives instructions in blissful ignorance of any delay caused, whilst the Contractor has knowledge of this.[50] Although on its face this situation has appeal, upon deeper inspection it raises some challenging questions. As Stephen Rae highlights, for example, what

---

[45] Ian Duncan Wallace, 'Prevention and Liquidated Damages: A Theory too Far' (2002) 18 *Building and Construction Law Journal* 82.

[46] *Multiplex* [2007] BLR 195, [101]–[103].

[47] Crispin Winser, 'Shutting Pandora's Box: The Prevention Principle after Multiplex v Honeywell' (2007) 23 *Construction Law Journal* 511.

[48] For a detailed discussion of this question: See E Baker, J Bremen and A Lavers, 'The Development of the Prevention Principle in English and Australian Jurisdictions' [2005] *International Construction Law Review* 198.

[49] *Peninsula Balmain Pty Limited v Abigroup Contractors Pty Limited* [2002] NSWCA 211, (2002) 18 BCL 322. The position was also later endorsed: see *Beckhaus v Brewarrina Shire Council (No 2)* [2004] NSWSC 1160, [34].

[50] Ian Duncan Wallace, 'Prevention and Liquidated Damages: A Theory too Far' (2002) 18 *Building and Construction Law Journal* 82.

happens in the situation where an Employer is aware of the ramifications of their actions.[51] Should they still be entitled to rely upon a failure of compliance with the notice provisions to be paid for their own preventing conduct?

Introducing an element of knowledge into this equation is not the solution for two reasons.[52] First, on a practical level, the prevention principle is too blunt an instrument to engage effectively with these challenging factual questions. Second, on a legal level, the prevention principle is just that – to do with *prevention*. Its underlying rationale, as previously set out, is to stop the Employer in preventing the Contractor with one hand, and then punishing it with the other. Questions of knowledge or fault are not relevant in this respect. Thus, the burden is not placed on the Contractor to establish a malicious breach of contract, or to establish knowledge on behalf of the Employer. To understand why this is the case, it is necessary to consider in a little more depth questions of risk allocation under construction contracts, which I discuss later in this chapter.

In this respect, it is challenging to observe Jackson J's reasoning where, on the one hand, he affirms the prevention principle as extending to all cases of prevention (and not just culpable prevention), and on the other he denies the application of the principle in cases where the Contractor did not give notice even if it was prevented.[53]

Second, and more troubling, the conventional approach subverts ordinary and accepted principles of causation. Recalling again the distinction between Employer-caused delay and Contractor-caused delay, the conventional approach is to treat even Employer-caused delay as a result of the Contractor's failure to provide notice.[54] This is surely erroneous: any relevant delay was set into motion (and hence caused), by the Employer, not the Contractor. At best, the Contractor who failed to give notice could be considered to have not stopped the delay, but in no way was it causative of it.

Further, it is inconsistent for it to be accepted, as a matter of law, that delay partly caused by the Contractor and partly caused by the Employer still permits the use of the principle of prevention, whereas delay entirely caused by the Employer, and allowed to continue by the Contractor, bars its use altogether. Even if a causation argument was to be attempted in this regard, at best the Contractor in the latter example could be considered to be partially causing the delay, and hence the rationale for not applying the principle as normal is by no means clear.

---

[51] Stephen Rae, 'Prevention and Damages: Who Takes the Risk for Employer Delays' (2006) 22 *Construction Law Journal* 307.

[52] Against: Morris Ross, 'The Status of the Prevention Principle: good from far, but far from good?' (2011) 27 *Construction Law Journal* 15.

[53] *Multiplex* [2007] BLR 195, [47]–[48], [103].

[54] *Turner Corporation Ltd (Receiver and Manager Appointed) v Austotel Pty Ltd* (1997) 13 BCL 378, 384; Ian Duncan Wallace, *Hudson's Building and Engineering Contracts*, 11th edn, 1st Supp (London, Sweet & Maxwell, 2004) paragraph [10.026]; *Hsin Chong Construction (Asia) Ltd v Henble* [2006] HKCFI 965, [132]–[135].

V. Parties' Intentions and Risk Allocation

Turning to the second key issue, in any construction contract there is considerable uncertainty and risk which must be contractually allocated. These include matters within the control of one party (such as the Contractor's employees), or outside the control of either party (such as weather events). Accordingly, it makes sense to speak of Contractor-caused delay, neutrally-caused delay, and Employer-caused delay. It is uncontroversial that a Contractor should accept the risk of any delay that it causes, or of any neutral delay, if that has been so agreed. What is more contentious, in my view, is the situation of Employer-caused delay.

As previously noted, in the case of a combination of Employer- and Contractor-caused delay, the total delay will not be apportioned and the prevention principle will operate to set time at large and negate all claims for liquidated damages.[55] To avoid this blanket effect of the prevention principle, extension-of-time clauses are included in contracts to allow the amendment of the date of completion to accommodate Employer-caused delay, and thus allow the Employer to claim liquidated damages from the new date of completion. However, consider again the circumstance in the Introduction. The Employer is the cause of any relevant delay. The Contractor has failed to give notice. The relevant question is to whom this risk has been allocated to under the contract. In my view, most of the judicial comments, including those in *Multiplex*, unfortunately do not engage squarely with this question.

A. Extension-of-Time Provisions and the Prevention Principle

The proposition of concern is that the inclusion of extension-of-time clauses, expressly contemplating Employer-caused delay, displaces the prevention principle. The argument goes as follows: the parties have carefully negotiated and expressly agreed on extension-of-time clauses, along with associated notice provisions and time-bars. Consequently, there is no scope for the prevention principle to operate, as it has been entirely subsumed by the parties' agreement. This perspective appears to have been endorsed in *Turner Corporation v Coordinated Industries*, which states that where an extension-of-time clause is present, 'there is no room for the prevention principle to operate.'[56] Professor Wallace agrees, stating:

> [T]here is no reason to doubt that a ground of permitted extension of time which expressly includes acts of prevention or breach by the Employer will successfully avoid

---

[55] *CMA Assets Pty Ltd v John Holland Pty Ltd* [2015] WASC 217, [864]; *Spiers Earthworks Pty Ltd v Landtec Projects Corporation Pty Ltd (No 2)* [2012] WASCA 53, [49].
[56] *Turner Corp Ltd (in liq) v Co-ordinated Industries Pty Ltd* (1994) 11 BCL 202, 217.

application of the *Peak* prevention principle, and so preserve the contract liquidated damages machinery intact.[57]

For proponents of this view, the presence of an extension-of-time clause for Employer-caused delay therefore sufficiently indicates a displacement of the prevention principle for such delay. Such a finding was implicit in *Multiplex*.

B. Response

This approach suffers from a critical flaw, which was expressed by Chitty LJ in *Dodd v Churton*: '[It would] require very clear language to shew that a man has undertaken a responsibility which very few men would undertake with their eyes open'. The conventional position leads to a Contractor *paying damages* for a period of delay which was caused by the Employer. Phrased another way, the Employer is allowed to directly financially benefit from its act of prevention. Or a third way, the risk of the Employer's conduct has been shifted absolutely to the Contractor.

This is an extraordinary position, and one which is not only inconsistent with the rationale of the prevention principle, but contrary to ordinary norms of contractual interpretation. At the outset, it can be readily accepted that this result can be achieved *if the Parties so desire*. But in order to contract out of the prevention principle to this degree, and to achieve such an astonishing displacement of risk from the Employer to the Contractor, very clear language to this effect is required. The language in each of the established cases does not reach this level. The simplest way to see that fact is to imagine the situation where a provision explicitly wrote:

> The Contractor assumes the risk and liability for all delay caused by the Employer, and agrees to pay liquidated damages for such delay caused by the Employer, except in circumstances where it applies for an extension of time in accordance with the notice requirements and time-bars specified in the Contract.

I would postulate that it would be a rare Contractor who would accept such a provision. Consequently, there are conceptual difficulties in effectively implying such a term in the context of ordinary extension-of-time and notice clauses.

I do not wish, by this, to imply that notice and time-bar provisions are of limited importance. Clearly they are, as Jackson J correctly recognised.[58] They are just not of such importance that a failure to comply with them leads to the absolute imposition of liability for consequences of the other party's behaviour.

The solution is to more clearly draw a distinction between Employer-caused delay and Contractor-caused delay. In *Multiplex*, Jackson J held that if *Gaymark* was good law, a Contractor could disregard with impunity any notice provision.

---

[57] Ian D Wallace, 'Prevention and Liquidated Damages: A theory too Far?' (2002) 18 *Building and Construction Law Journal* 82.

[58] *Multiplex* [2007] BLR 195, [100], [103].

However, this does not pay appropriate regard to this distinction. If the delay is caused by neutral events for which the contract gives the Contractor relief, then non-compliance with a notice provision means that it will not receive an extensive of time, placing it at peril of a liquidated damages claim. It is only in the instance of Employer-caused delay that a Contractor can achieve the same result without notice. However, Jackson J does not explain why that result is unsatisfactory, particularly when it is considered that his conclusion leads to the Contractor being entirely liable for delay caused by the Employer, in the absence of an express acceptance of that risk.

As clauses which make no provision for an extension of time based on an Employer's delay require clear words to make the Contractor liable (in keeping with the principle of 'fairness'), this should also be true for a time-bar which wipes out an Employer's capacity to excise from periods of delay those of its own making.

Instead, the better position is that each party is responsible for its own conduct, absent some clear provision, or positive action, to the contrary.

VI. Certainty in Contractual Relationships

Finally, it is apposite to consider the issue of contractual certainty. Although certainty is a powerful virtue in the commercial world, it is not to be pursued at any and all costs.

A. Certainty View

This approach, namely that notice provisions and time-bars are effective even in the case of Employer-caused delay, is said to lead to greater contractual certainty. This is because, if it were otherwise, a Contractor could disregard the notice provisions of a contract with impunity, setting 'time at large' at will.[59] The application of the prevention principle has therefore been presented as an escape hatch through which a Contractor can quickly duck to avoid the date of completion.[60] Julian Bailey, for example, notes that if a breach of a condition precedent could set time at large it would subvert 'the utility and purpose of the Contractor being expressly required to follow the relevant mechanism for an extension of time.'[61]

In the English decision of *Steria Ltd v Sigma Wireless Communications Ltd*, referring to *Multiplex*, *Gaymark* was said to represent the commercial absurdity that a Contractor could benefit by disregarding the notice machinery.[62] Further

---

[59] *Multiplex* [2007] BLR 195, [103].
[60] Crispin Winser, 'Shutting Pandora's Box: The Prevention Principle after *Multiplex v Honeywell*' (2007) 23 *Construction Law Journal* 511, 512.
[61] Julian Bailey, *Construction Law*, 2nd edn (London, Informa, 2016) p 1203.
[62] *Steria Ltd v Sigma Wireless Communications Ltd* [2008] BLR 79, [95].

in *Multiplex*, Jackson J looked towards the case of *City Inn v Shepard Construction* where it was held that where a notice provision is included a 'contractor could not obtain an extension of time if it did not comply with that provision.'[63]

The argument is therefore that the preferred and certain position is that the risk of Employer-caused delay sits with the Contractor until such time that it utilises its contractual rights. While it is acknowledged that this can cause the seemingly unconscionable result that an Employer benefits from its own wrong, Jeremy Coggins finds that this is the 'lesser of two evils' and is to be preferred over depriving the Employer of a remedy in a case of Contractor non-compliance with the condition precedent.[64]

It is also often noted that the roots of the prevention principle derive from the courts' history of suspicion of liquidated damages. While such a position did exist, courts certainly no longer hold this attitude now, with several contemporary cases preserving liquidated damages.[65] Critics of *Gaymark* therefore often posit that the decision to preclude liquidated damages and require the Employer to seek damages reflects an antiquated and lingering distrust of agreements for liquidated damages.[66] They submit that liquidated damages should rather be lauded in providing commercial and case management value and that courts should be slower to intervene in valid liquidated damages agreements.[67]

B. Response

It can be recognised, of course, that certainty in contracts is an important virtue. However, once again, the arguments logically suffer from an erroneous conflation of Employer-caused delay with Contractor-caused delay. Consider the 'commercial absurdity' argument raised by HHJ Stephen Davies in *Steria*,[68] whereby a Contractor is placed in a better position through failing to comply with a notice provision. This proposition can surely be accepted with regard to neutral delays, as an extension of time gives the Contractor an *extra right which it did not otherwise have*, namely, the right to complete the Contract later than originally promised. Hence, in order to obtain that additional right, the Contractor should comply with the contractual terms. If it does not, it can be considered to have waived that right. It is unclear, however, why that proposition applies with the same force to

---

[63] *City Inn Limited v Shepherd Construction Limited* [2003] SLT 885; *Multiplex* [2007] BLR 195, [102].

[64] Jeremy Coggins, 'The Application of the Prevention Principle in Australia – Part 2' (2009) 21(5) *Australian Construction Law Bulletin* 45.

[65] Crispin Winser, 'Shutting Pandora's Box: The Prevention Principle after *Multiplex v Honeywell*' (2007) 23 *Construction Law Journal* 511; *Phillips Hong Kong v Att-Gen of Hong Kong* (1993) 61 BLR 41.

[66] Crispin Winser, 'Shutting Pandora's Box: The Prevention Principle after *Multiplex v Honeywell*' (2007) 23 *Construction Law Journal* 511.

[67] ibid.

[68] *Steria Ltd v Sigma Wireless Communications Ltd* [2008] BLR 79, [95].

Employer-caused delay. If non-compliance with a notice provision defeats a claim for prevention, this effectively means that non-compliance with the notice provision operates so as to place all of the Employer-caused risk on the Contractor. Adopting the words of HHJ Stephen Davies, it could well be said that it is, instead, this position which is commercially absurd.[69]

Instead, the virtue of contractual certainty can be equally well achieved by leaving responsibility where it was created, and imposing an obligation on *that* party to take some consequential action. So, for the situation of neutral delay, it is for the Contractor to establish an entitlement to an extension of time, and its failure to do so is at its own peril. Likewise, for the situation of Employer-caused delay, it is for the Employer to grant an extension of time and its failure to do so is likewise at its own peril. For this reason, if the Employer wishes to issue a variation order and request extra works, it should ensure that there will either be no delay, or that it grants an appropriate extension as a result. This is not a draconian result. The commercial reality is that most Employers are highly sophisticated, and should be aware of what is happening on their projects.

Finally, the criticism with regards to changing perceptions of liquidated damages lacks merit. At no point in *Gaymark* does Justice Bailey evince a presumption against the enforceability of liquidated damages.

VII. Embarking on a Future Journey?

For the reasons set out in the previous section, it is clear that the current development of the law pays inadequate regard to the underlying policy of the prevention principle, and its role in ensuring fairness. In my view, there are two responses to this situation.

The first, and less satisfactory, response is to retain the current focus of the prevention principle on the obligation of the date of completion. In order to alleviate the injustice of forcing a Contractor to pay damages for delay caused by an Employer, appropriate regard should be paid to the distinction between Contractor-caused delay and Employer-caused delay. This regard would have a *Gaymark*-like effect, allowing Employer-caused delay to still enliven the prevention principle even in the absence of compliance with notice conditions precedent.

The reason why this is not a satisfactory solution is evident from the tensions underlying the issues above. It is not satisfactory that a Contractor can cause multiple weeks of delay, and yet avoid liquidated damages simply because the Employer also caused some of the delay. The adage 'two wrongs don't make a right' immediately springs to mind. Another source of dissatisfaction is the result of

---

[69] ibid.

the prevention principle's inherent bluntness. The matter is phrased most clearly by Winser:[70]

> If the employer obstructs the contractor, yet the contractor fails to apply for an extension of time, there is something unconscionable in the employer levying liquidated damages for the consequent delay. Yet if the employer entirely unknowingly causes delay, what fairness is there in the contractor sitting back, failing to apply for an extension of time in accordance with a mechanism he agreed to, and then invoking the prevention principle to avoid the liability to pay liquidated damages.

A. A Logical Approach

The solution is to change the focus on the obligation, and instead turn attention to the remedy of liquidated damages. In circumstances where the Employer caused four weeks of delay, and the Contractor caused three weeks, the Employer is simply prevented from claiming liquidated damages for the four weeks which it caused. Matthew Bell has advocated for such a development, stating:

> It is submitted that such a middle path may be found in the ability to apportion responsibility for delay in calculating the liquidated damages payable where an act of prevention has rendered time 'at large' under a building contract.[71]

This position is more in accordance with the fairness underlying the prevention principle in any event, and leads to a more intuitive outcome.

This is not as revolutionary as it initially appears, or as has been described in the literature.[72] Happily, such an approach will likely see universal acceptance, as it fairly apportions liability for wrongdoing, and thus any difference of opinion between myself and Jackson LJ will vanish. As long as a contract is drafted with a provision which allows an arbitral tribunal or court to retrospectively exercise a power for extension of time upon proven grounds, and obliges its exercise in cases of Employer-caused delay, the same result would be achieved. This is because a court or arbitrator could simply step in the shoes of the relevant decision-maker, extend the date of completion to take into account all of the Employer-caused delay, and then hold the Contractor liable for the residual delay. Such an approach also avoids difficult questions of the burden and onus of proof, as the contract would specifically allocate these.

---

[70] Crispin Winser, 'Shutting Pandora's Box: The Prevention Principle after *Multiplex v Honeywell*' (2007) 23 *Construction Law Journal* 511.

[71] Matthew Bell, 'Scaling the Peak: The Prevention Principle in Australian Construction Contracting' (2006) 23 *International Construction Law Review* 318, 335, 354.

[72] Jeremy Coggins, 'The Application of the Prevention Principle in Australia – Part 2' (2009) 21(5) *Australian Construction Law Bulletin* 45, 49; Matthew Bell, 'Scaling the Peak: The Prevention Principle in Australian Construction Contracting' (2006) 23 *International Construction Law Review* 318, 335, 354.

B. Parallels in Civil Systems

This approach would have the same practical effect as that contained within Article 7.4.13, of the UNIDROIT Principles, which allows for the re-adjustment of damages in light of the actual damage suffered and therefore would, in cases of concurrent delay, allow liquidated damages to be apportioned. Article 7.4.13 provides that:

> (2) However, notwithstanding any agreement to the contrary the specified sum *may be reduced to a reasonable amount* where it is grossly excessive in relation to the harm resulting from the non-performance and to the other circumstances (emphasis added).[73]

While this does seem an unusual step from the 'traditional' common law view, such an apportionment of damages is a common feature in civil law systems: present in many legal systems, including China, South Korea and France.[74] For instance, in French Law, Article 1147 of the French Civil Code provides that:[75]

> A debtor shall be ordered to pay damages, if appropriate, either by reason of the non-performance of that obligation, or by reason of delay in performance, in circumstances where the non-performance does not result from an external cause which is non-attributable to the debtor, so long as there is no lack of good faith on his part.

French case law has interpreted 'external causes' to include Employer acts of delay. Article 1147 therefore operates to preclude recovery of damages to the extent that the owner was responsible for the delay, tying the preclusion of damages to the remedy rather than the date of completion.

Chinese law reaches a similar conclusion, albeit adopting a different approach. In the People's Republic of China Contract Law, Article 114 provides:[76]

> If the stipulated penalty for breach of contract is lower than the loss caused by the breach, the party concerned may apply to a people's court or an arbitration institution for an increase. If the stipulated penalty for breach of contract is excessively higher than the loss caused by the breach, the party concerned may apply to a people's court or an arbitration institution for an appropriate reduction.

While the reference to 'penalties' here will perplex some readers from common law systems, the phrase, in this context, should simply be taken to equate to 'liquidated damages'. Thus, from the provision, in cases of concurrent delay, recourse may be had to the actual loss suffered by each party when evaluating the sum of

---

[73] UNIDROIT, UNIDROIT Principles of International Commercial Contracts (2010) art 7.4.13.

[74] Doug Jones, 'The Prevention Principle Across the Common and Civil Law Divide and the Maritime Construction Industry' (Conference Paper, Nineteenth International Congress of Maritime Arbitrators Conference, 2015).

[75] France Civil Code, art 1146.

[76] Contract Law of the People's Republic of China (Adopted at the Second Session of the Ninth National People's Congress on 15 March 1999 and promulgated by Order No 15 of the President of the People's Republic of China on 15 March 1999).

liquidated damages. This will potentially facilitate an apportionment of damages that reflects the Employer's contribution to the delay. This conclusion was reflected in the case of *Baiti Real Estate v Zhao et al* (2011) which considered an appeal of an arbitral award, relying upon Article 114 and the principle of good faith. The Court found that as actual losses could not be proved, a reduction in liquidated damages would be appropriate.[77]

Thus, whilst differences do exist, the civil law approach generally resists the common law blanket application of the prevention principle in setting 'time at large'. Rather, it presents a more nuanced approach to the norm Jackson J recounted,[78] that a promisee cannot require performance from a promiser that it itself has prevented. By rendering liquidated damages referrable to the losses that have actually been suffered, the civil law effectively allows an apportionment of liquidated damages. While outlandish to those practising within the common law, it is a proposition not to be lightly dismissed.

VIII. Conclusion

The law surrounding the prevention principle has evolved significantly since its early-nineteenth-century roots. At times, however, it is useful to step back and consider the issue from first-principles. This chapter has sought to argue that, in cases of Employer-caused delay, greater regard needs to be paid to principles of risk allocation in order to not hold the Contractor liable for risks that it did not contractually assume.

From a legal perspective, it is instructive to reflect on the enduring words of Lord Justice Salmon in *Peak*, where his Lordship said

> If the failure to complete on time is due to the fault of both the employer and the contractor, in my view, the clause does not bite. I cannot see how, in the ordinary course, the employer can insist on compliance with a condition if it is partly his own fault that it cannot be fulfilled.[79]

Like his Lordship, I struggle to see how a delay caused by the Employer somehow becomes the entire responsibility of the Contractor simply because of a failure to comply with a notice provision. For this reason, in my view, the law surrounding the prevention principle has long journeyed on a dangerous path away from its origins in principles of fairness and justice. For all the criticisms levelled at *Gaymark*, it remains the only high-profile decision to successfully balance the

[77] *Baiti Real Estate v Zhao et al* [2011] Huaian IPC, 28 March 2011.
[78] *Multiplex* [2007] BLR 195, [47]; See also UNIDROIT, UNIDROIT Principles of International Commercial Contracts (2010) art 7.1.2.
[79] *Peak Construction (Liverpool) Ltd v McKinney Foundations Ltd* (1970) 1 BLR 114, 121.

difficult questions that these cases raise. It is time for the courts to now take a stand and follow a path of righteousness.

Of course, the best solution is to avoid all of these difficult questions altogether. A reformulation of the principle to focus on the remedy and not the obligation would resolve the tension between *Multiplex* and *Gaymark*, and provide greater fairness to all in the construction world.

20

Penalties in the Box

RIAZ HUSSAIN QC

I. Introduction

Following the Supreme Court's judgment in *Cavendish*[1] the issue of what constitutes a penalty clause as opposed to a legitimate liquidated damages clause has given lawyers and academics much to talk about. One question which in my opinion remains unanswered is how, if at all, the judgment in *Cavendish* moves the law away from Lord Dunedin's formulations in *Dunlop*[2] with regard to delay damages?

Pre-*Cavendish* at least, Lord Dunedin's four principles in *Dunlop* were a starting point for the discussion; the 'classic statement' of the law on penalties.[3] Lord Neuberger PSC lamented in *Cavendish* that 'Lord Dunedin's speech in the Dunlop case achieved the status of a quasi-statutory code in the subsequent case law.'[4]

In that light, Jackson J's (as he then was) judgment and exposition of the law on penalties in *Tilebox*[5] was referred to as the 'second seminal case' after *Dunlop* in a paper presented by Dr Hamish Lal to the Society of Construction Law in April 2009.[6]

My contribution to this *Festschrift* arises from being junior counsel for the defendant in *Tilebox*. I was led by Robert Akenhead QC (now Sir Robert, who of course became judge in charge of the TCC some years after). The claimant, McAlpine, was represented by Paul Darling QC and Paul Sutherland.

---

[1] *Cavendish Square Holdings BV v Talal El Makdessi* and *ParkingEye Ltd v Beavis* [2015] UKSC 67.

[2] *Dunlop Pneumatic Tyre Co Ltd v New Garage and Motor Co Ltd* [1915] AC 79 at 86–88. In this chapter I call these the Dunedin propositions or principles. This is shorthand. I appreciate the note in *Cavendish* that Lord Dunedin did not see these propositions or 'four tests' as an immutable code.

[3] Per Arden LJ in *Murray v Leisureplay plc* [2005] EWCA Civ 963, at paragraph 34.

[4] See n 1 above at paragraph 22.

[5] *Alfred McAlpine Capital Projects Ltd v Tilebox* [2005] EWHC 281 (TCC), [2005] BLR 271.

[6] *Liquidated Damages*, Dr Hamish Lal, April 2009, A paper presented to a meeting of the Society of Construction Law at the University of Central Lancashire, Preston on 15 October 2008 (Paper no D099) (see www.scl.org.uk).

I discuss the substantive issues raised later in this chapter. There are other aspects of the case that stand out.

First is the remarkable efficiency and co-operation shown by Jackson J and leading counsel. The claim form seeking a declaration that the liquidated damages clause was a penalty was issued the week before Christmas on 20 December 2004. It is fair to assume that at least some of the lawyers involved would have been at Christmas drinks that afternoon. There was no putting things off till after the holiday period. We had a directions hearing on 21 December 2004. Robert Akenhead QC and Paul Darling QC were at this time the leading construction silks at the Bar.

Pleadings, and evidence were exchanged, disclosure completed and skeletons served. Without the need for any further case management hearings the matter proceeded to hearing as listed on 22 February 2005. It was heard over two days with hard-nosed cross-examination on both sides. The nuanced and full judgment was handed down on 25 February 2005. Sir Robert recalled that it was a great credit to the emerging competence and efficiency of the TCC that this sort of case involving a relatively heavy issue about the enforceability of liquidated damages clause could be dealt with so quickly in less than a couple of months.

Second, although we reserved our position in this regard, ultimately there was no point taken that this matter was unsuitable for a Part 8 hearing. Such a position would be highly unlikely now given a general timidity about what constitutes a dispute that is 'unlikely to involve a substantial dispute of fact' under CPR r. 8.1. This was a fact-heavy dispute that ultimately involved seven witnesses, four of whom gave oral evidence. Much of this was down to both counsel's utter faith in the judge to give them a full, proper and fair hearing in the time allotted. To give credit to the solicitors on record there were no stern letters or ultimatums between the two sides. The parties got on with the task at hand. The same can be said of the witnesses who, as Jackson J noted in his judgment, without exception gave helpful and engaged evidence:

> I have formed the view that all of the witnesses in this case were entirely honest in their evidence. They made concessions where they felt it appropriate to do so. They are experienced professional people who have done their best to assist this court in resolving some quite difficult issues.

Third, the advocacy was a pleasure to witness. The contrast between leading counsel, both indomitable but very different in style, was fascinating to see. Robert Akenhead QC has the perfect radio voice and a very gentle touch in submissions. Paul Darling QC is a very punchy advocate and has a take-no-prisoners approach. I was a new entrant to Robert's set, Atkin Chambers, and very much in awe of his gravitas. The hearing was in the less than glamorous venue of St Dunstan's House, the former home of the Technology and Construction Court (which I understand is now a luxury residential development). We were suitably robed. These were still the days when TCC trials were in full court robes.

I vividly remember my shock and guilty admiration as Paul Darling at one point leaned back in his chair to guffaw in the middle of Robert's submissions. Admittedly it was our less meritorious submission. Robert good naturedly acknowledged the noise and indicated that he probably would move on from the point.

I was 26 years old at the time; some two years in tenancy. It was a lifelong lesson to see the very good humour between these two stalwarts of the bar and the judge and the immaculate politeness displayed in a hard-fought case.

This January (2018) with the publication deadline for this chapter looming, I appeared in the much smarter Rolls Building with Mr Darling QC, now Mr Darling OBE QC. We were representing the two defendants in the case. I mentioned to Paul that I was still amazed at how quickly and smoothly the *Tilebox* case was decided – he replied 'that's Jackson for you.'

II. The Background

The claim we were served with at Christmas 2004 was to do with Onslow House; still today somewhat of a landmark in Guildford. In 1998 Tilebox purchased a leasehold interest in Onslow House and planned to strip out the 50,000 sq ft Property to its core and re-fit it as a 90,000 sq ft, Grade-A commercial premises. It was to be marketed as a suitable headquarters for a big corporation.

There were negotiations for Tilebox and McAlpine to carry out the Works as a joint venture but these fell through. Tilebox then undertook the development itself. Tilebox entered two relevant agreements.

In the summer of 2000, Tilebox entered into negotiations for a funding agreement with Standard Life Association Company (SLAC). Detailed appraisals of the property market and the likely return on the development were produced by property agents. These appraisals were seen as relevant to deciding whether the liquidated damages for delays to the Works under the Building Contract were a penalty; being seen as the best indicator of anticipated revenue from the development.

On 12 February 2001, Tilebox and SLAC entered into the Development Funding Agreement (DFA). The DFA provided that Tilebox would transfer the head lease for the Property to SLAC for £10 million plus VAT. Tilebox would, as Developer of the Property, undertake to carry out and complete the Works. SLAC would be obliged to fund the Works, subject to certain limitations, including a Maximum Commitment of £26,473,276. Further, under the DFA Tilebox had to secure the letting of each Lettable Unit.

Tilebox's profit or remuneration under the DFA was in the form of the development completion payment or 'DCP', calculated as defined in the DFA. Delays in completion of the Works under the Building Contract could reduce Tilebox's entitlement to the DCP. The precise pricing mechanism is not necessary to set out in this chapter; the summation of the parties' positions at paragraphs 67 through 69 of Jackson J's judgment will suffice.

With regard to the time for completion the relevant terms of the DFA included:

The Developer hereby covenants with the Fund: …

6.8.1 Without prejudice to any other rights and remedies of the Fund … the Works and each part of them have been and shall be carried out and completed in accordance with the various engagements under which the Works have been instructed;

6.8.2 As soon as reasonably practicable after the Unconditional Date to commence the Works and thereafter to take all reasonable steps to ensure that Practical Completion is achieved on or before 30th November 2002 but so that [] the date shall be extended by the period of any delay due to any cause in respect of which the Employer's Agent (acting properly) shall have issued a certificate authorizing an extension of time under the Building Contract and for which cause neither the Developer nor any of the Consultants is responsible.

After signing the DFA, Tilebox continued negotiations with McAlpine for the Building Contract. One matter discussed in negotiations was the level of liquidated ascertained damages (LADs) for late completion. Tilebox proposed £45,000 per week and it was accepted by Jackson J that this figure represented what Tilebox saw as the minimum weekly rental value of the Building.[7] On 27 April 2001, Tilebox and McAlpine entered into a written Building Contract in the JCT Standard Form of Building Contract with Contractor's Design (1998 edition). The contract sum was £11,573,076. The date for completion was 12 July 2002. Clause 24.2 of the Building Contract provided that McAlpine should pay LADs for delay at the rate of £45,000 per week or part thereof.

As noted in the judgment there was substantial delay to completion under the Building Contract. The Works were not completed by the extended Completion Date of 14 August 2002, and indeed were incomplete at the time of the trial some two and a half years later, with the anticipated time for completion being the summer of 2005. Shortly prior to issue of the claim form, having understood the likelihood that it would be liable for at least some delay, McAlpine wrote to Tilebox on 7 December 2004 asserting that the liquidated damages provision was a penalty clause and therefore invalid. Tilebox denied that clause 24.2 was a penalty clause and initiated a claim under clause 24.2 for liquidated damages.

III. The Rule Against Penalties

Jackson J noted that the rule against penalties is an anomalous feature of the law of contract going against the general move under English Law from the nineteenth century of freedom to bargain as parties see fit. He noted the

---

[7] *Tilebox*, see n 5 above, at paragraph 18.

discussion of the origins of the rule per Kay LJ in *Law v Redditch Local Board*,[8] having been developed by the courts of equity and then taken over by the courts of law, which looked behind phrases used, such as 'penalty' or 'liquidated damages' and considered the substance of each clause. Kay LJ's judgment in *Redditch* provides a useful summary of the development of the rule as does the joint Opinion of Lords Sumption JSC and Neuberger PSC in *Cavendish* at paragraphs 4–8.[9]

Jackson J then set out the classic formulation of the four tests for a penalty by Lord Dunedin in *Dunlop*:

1. Though the parties to a contract who use the word 'penalty' or 'liquidated damages' may prima facie be supposed to mean what they say, yet the expression used is not conclusive. The Court must find out whether the payment stipulated is in truth a penalty or liquidated damages. This doctrine may be said to be found passim in nearly every case.

2. The essence of a penalty is a payment of money stipulated as in terrorem of the offending party; the essence of liquidated damages is a genuine covenanted pre-estimate of damage (Clydebank Engineering and Shipbuilding Co v Don Jose Ramos Yzquierdo y Castaneda ([1905] AC 6, [1904–7] All ER Rep 251)).

3. The question whether a sum stipulated is penalty or liquidated damages is a question of construction to be decided upon the terms and inherent circumstances of each particular contract, judged of as at the time of making of the contract, not as at the time of the breach (Public Works Commissioner v Hills ([1906] AC 368, [1904–7] All ER Rep 919) and Webster v Bosanquet ([1912] AC 394)).

4. To assist this task of construction various tests have been suggested, which if applicable to the case under consideration may prove helpful, or even conclusive. Such are:

(a) It will be held to be a penalty if the sum stipulated for is extravagant and unconscionable in amount in comparison with the greatest loss that could conceivably be proved to have followed from the breach. (Illustration given by Lord Halsbury in Clydebank case) …

(c) There is a presumption (but no more) that it is a penalty when, 'a single lump sum is made payable by way of compensation, on the occurrence of one or more or all of several events, some of which may occasion serious and others but trifling damage' (Lord Watson in Lord Elphinstone v Monkland Iron and Coal Co Ltd (1886) 11 App Cas 332).

On the other hand:

(d) It is no obstacle to the sum stipulated being a genuine pre-estimate of damage, that the consequences of the breach are such as to make precise pre-estimation almost an impossibility. On the contrary, that is just the situation when it is probable that pre-estimated damage was the true bargain between the parties (Clydebank case, Lord Halsbury ([1905] AC 6 at 11); Webster v Bosanquet, Lord Mersey ([1912] AC 394 at 398)).

---

[8] *Law v Redditch Local Board* [1892] 1 QB 127.
[9] Note 1, above.

Jackson J also considered[10] the Privy Council's judgment in *Philips Hong Kong Ltd v A-G of Hong Kong*[11] and particularly Lord Woolf's statement that it would not suffice, in order to establish that a clause was objectionably penal, to identify a potential situation where the LADs might vastly exceed the actual damage arising from the breach. The comparator would be the range of losses that could be reasonably anticipated as arising from the breach.[12]

Jackson J also noted[13] the observation in *Hudson on Building and Engineering Contracts*[14] that there were virtually no reported cases whereby a liquidated damages provision in a building contract had been struck down as penal.

Having reviewed the authorities Jackson J made four observations about the rule against penalties:[15]

(1) There seem to be two strands in the authorities. In some cases judges consider whether there is an unconscionable or extravagant disproportion between the damages stipulated in the contract and the true amount of damages likely to be suffered. In other cases the courts consider whether the level of damages stipulated was reasonable. Mr Darling submits, and I accept, that these two strands can be reconciled. In my view, a pre-estimate of damages does not have to be right in order to be reasonable. There must be a substantial discrepancy between the level of damages stipulated in the contract and the level of damages which is likely to be suffered before it can be said that the agreed pre-estimate is unreasonable.

(2) Although many authorities use or echo the phrase 'genuine pre-estimate', the test does not turn upon the genuineness or honesty of the party or parties who made the pre-estimate. The test is primarily an objective one, even though the court has some regard to the thought processes of the parties at the time of contracting.

(3) Because the rule about penalties is an anomaly within the law of contract, the courts are predisposed, where possible, to uphold contractual terms which fix the level of damages for breach. This predisposition is even stronger in the case of commercial contracts freely entered into between parties of comparable bargaining power.

(4) Looking at the bundle of authorities provided in this case, I note only four cases where the relevant clause has been struck down as a penalty ... In each of these four cases there was, in fact, a very wide gulf between (a), the level of damages likely to be suffered, and (b), the level of damages stipulated in the contract.

As Dr Lal notes,[16] Jackson J's approach was to recognise a judicial predisposition to uphold liquidated damages clauses at least where they were freely negotiated, to allow a large margin of appreciation in applying the genuine pre-estimate test and to make the test less intrusive and more broad-brush. The question was not

---

[10] *Tilebox*, see n 5 above, paragraphs 44–45 of the judgment.
[11] *Philips Hong Kong Ltd v Attorney-General of Hong Kong* (1993) 61 BLR 41.
[12] (1993) 61 BLR 41, per Lord Woolf at 58–59.
[13] *Tilebox*, see n 5 above, paragraph 47 of the judgment.
[14] I Duncan Wallace (ed), *Hudson's Building and Engineering Contracts*, 11th edn (London, Sweet & Maxwell, 1995) at para 10-021.
[15] *Tilebox*, see n 5 above, paragraph 48 of the judgment.
[16] See n 6 above.

whether the damages were right as a pre-estimate or arithmetically correct but whether they were a reasonable pre-estimate given the facts known at the time. The yardstick was a *substantial discrepancy* between the damages set and the objectively likely damages foreseeable from the breach. Thereafter at least until *Cavendish*, the approach in *Tilebox* has been a benchmark for construction law practitioners.

Mathias Cheung[17] notes that Jackson J's decision in *Tilebox* is a 'crystallisation' of the recognition of the fundamental principle of *pacta sunt servanda* and freedom of contract, necessitating greater caution before striking down a liquidated damages clause as a penalty.

Interestingly, *Tilebox* does not appear to have been cited to the Supreme Court in *Cavendish* and is not referred to in any of the judgments. However the later case of *Murray*[18] is cited by the judges in *Cavendish* variously as a 'broader' approach and a case that escapes from the straitjacket of a strict dichotomy between a genuine pre-estimate of loss on the one hand and a penalty on the other.[19]

It is correct that in *Murray* the judges referred variously to a party being permitted to show a justification (other than deterrence) if a clause was held not to be a genuine pre estimate of loss.[20] However it would be incorrect in my view to suggest that the TCC was applying the Dunedin principles or the genuine pre estimate of loss test slavishly or was unduly restrictive of the freedom of contract.

IV. The Evidence and Findings

A. Tilebox's Liability to SLAC for Delays

In respect of clause 6.8.2 Jackson J concluded that the words 'take all reasonable steps' to ensure completion of the Works by 30 November 2002 or any extension to the date did not constitute a strict obligation. Tilebox was not liable in damages under clause 6.8.2 of the DFA if, despite its reasonable steps the builder did not complete by this date. Jackson J held that the term take 'all reasonable steps'

> is regularly used in contractual documents to connote a low level obligation. It is the antithesis of a contractual provision requiring the promisor to achieve a particular result. In my judgment, it is not possible read clause 6.8.2 of the DFA in such a way as to disregard the phrase 'take all reasonable steps'.[21]

However, crucially Jackson J held that clause 6.8.1 of the DFA did oblige Tilebox under the DFA to procure completion in accordance with the Building Contract

---

[17] Mathias Cheung, 'Shylock's construction law: the brave new life of liquidated damages?' (2017) 33 *Construction Law Journal* 173 at 179.

[18] *Murray v Leisureplay plc*, see n 3 above.

[19] *Cavendish*, n 1 above, see for instance paragraphs 224 and 225, per Lord Hodge JSC.

[20] *Murray*, see n 3 above, at paragraph 54 per Arden LJ.

[21] *Tilebox*, see n 5 above, paragraph 52 of the judgment.

and this obligation included procuring completion of the Works by the Completion Date under the Building Contract (which had not yet been agreed at the time of the DFA).

The meaning of clause 6.8.1 was argued at some length by both parties. Jackson J explained the reasons why he preferred Tilebox's construction of clause 6.8.1. Under clause 6.8.1 Tilebox covenanted that 'the Works and each part of them have been and shall be carried out and completed in accordance with the various engagements under which the Works have been instructed'. There was no basis to exclude from 'various engagements' the Building Contract on the basis that it was not yet agreed. In particular Jackson J emphasised that ownership of Onslow House was passing from Tilebox to SLAC and clause 6.8.1 was needed to avoid a 'black-hole' argument being raised by the Building Contractor.

> The obvious commercial purpose of cl 6.8.1 was to create back-to-back liability. This would enable Standard Life to recover its losses through the medium of Tilebox. If back-to-back liability was not created, it was clearly foreseeable that there would be a variety of 'no loss' arguments in the event of future claims.[22]

Therefore at the date of the Building Contract the reasonably foreseeable losses from delays to completion under the Building Contract would include Tilebox's liability to SLAC for the delays. This would be the loss of rent less a credit to SLAC for not having to pay the DCP to Tilebox. Arithmetically, on either side's case, that would mean the LADs under clause 24.2 of the Building Contract were within the range of losses that could be estimated to arise from delays to completion. This was conceded by Mr Darling QC for the applicant.[23] As Jackson J noted:

> There is no dispute between the parties that it was foreseeable in April 2001 that lost rental income would be somewhere in the region of £45,000 per week. Tilebox would say that the true figure is higher but this contention is not relevant for present purposes.[24]

B. Tilebox's Other Foreseeable Losses

Jackson J proceeded to consider if he were incorrect in his construction of the DFA and if Tilebox were not liable to SLAC for delays under the Building Contract; what Tilebox's foreseeable losses would have been at the date of the Building Contract as the result of delays to the Completion Date. He used the phrases 'foreseeable' and 'reasonable to foresee' interchangeably. These other losses fell into two broad heads: (1) the more contentious erosion of recovery of the DCP under the DFA and (2) Tilebox's own costs of prolongation.

Tilebox's case was that the DCP would be at least £1.67 million which would be eroded at the rate of £38,182 per week. Of course, the anticipated DCP would

---

[22] *Tilebox*, see n 5 above, at paragraph 59(iv).
[23] *Tilebox*, see n 5 above, at paragraph 96.
[24] *Tilebox*, see n 5 above, at paragraph 91.

after some time (in this case 43 weeks) be entirely eroded. However, in 2001 no one had reasonably thought the completion of the Works under the Building Contract would be delayed by that long. McAlpine disputed that there would be any recovery of the DCP or in this amount. Further that the weekly erosion of the DCP, if any, would be at a lower rate. McAlpine submitted that this erosion would be in a range between £17,300 per week and £36,000 per week depending upon the stage at which delay occurs.

Jackson J set out the key factual issues that went to the reasonably anticipated DCP[25]

(i)   What rent per square foot would be achieved.
(ii) How soon after completion the whole of Onslow House could be let to one or more tenants upon a lease or leases of 15 years.
(iii) What rent-free period, if any, would be granted to the tenants.
(iv) What other incentives, if any, would be given to the tenants.
(v)   What would be the net internal area of the building.
(vi) The amount of the total costs of the development.

He then considered the evidence on each of items (i) through (vi). Jackson J concluded that

> it would have been reasonable in April 2001 to expect the weekly loss attributable to erosion of the DCP to be in the region of £30,000. The actual figure may be somewhat higher or it may be somewhat lower. This could not be foretold at the time when the building contract was executed.[26]

Thereafter, for Tilebox's own costs of prolongation, Jackson J concluded on the evidence that 'it would have been reasonable in April 2001 to foresee a weekly loss falling somewhere within the range between £5,000 and £10,000 under this head.'[27]

From the above, on his alternative hypothesis (no liability owed by Tilebox under the DFA to SLAC for delay damages), Jackson J concluded on the facts:[28]

> From the viewpoint of April 2001, it was most unlikely, although just conceivable, that the total weekly loss would be as high as £45,000. Against that background, should cl 24.2 be struck down as a penalty? In my judgment, it should not, for five reasons.
>
> 1.   The figure of £45,000 was at or slightly above the top of the range of possible weekly losses flowing from delay. Whether one takes the top of the range or the middle of the range of possible future losses as the yardstick, it seems to me that the gap between that yardstick and £45,000 was not nearly wide enough to warrant characterising this clause as a penalty.
> 2.   Mr Hutley did make a genuine attempt to estimate the losses which would flow from future delay ...

---

[25] *Tilebox*, see n 5 above, at paragraph 69.
[26] *Tilebox*, see n 5 above, at paragraph 85.
[27] *Tilebox*, see n 5 above, at paragraph 89.
[28] *Tilebox*, see n 5, at paragraph 95.

3.   The difficulty which was inherent in the exercise of estimating future losses makes it particularly sensible in this case for the parties to have agreed upon a weekly figure …

4.   This court, following the lead set by higher courts, is predisposed where possible to uphold contractual terms which fix the level of damages. This predisposition is somewhat stronger in the present case for the following reason: the building contract dated 27 April 2001, is a commercial contract made between two parties of comparable bargaining power.

5.   During the course of the pre-contract negotiations, the level of liquidated damages was the subject of specific debate. A figure of £45,000 was considered not only by the parties, but also, as can be seen from the documents, by their legal advisors. The fact that cl 24.2 and its appendix survived such scrutiny is further evidence that, as at April 2001, the liquidated damages provision was reasonable.

It is interesting to see the tension between considerations one and two above. The first looks objectively at the substance of the clause; the rate of liquidated damages. The second looks at the particular conditions of the parties and their subjective intent, ie the genuineness or bona fides of Tilebox's intent to estimate losses arising from delay. Considerations three and four operate very strongly in most large-scale construction contracts. It is usually difficult to predict with certainty the losses that could accrue from delay and indeed the nature of such losses would vary depending on the extent of the delay.

As noted in a recent article,[29] it is not clear why if the test is objective, the courts would consider subjective factors such as the reasoning of the parties at the time the clause were agreed or the comparable bargaining power of the parties. It is unlikely that a clause that was found objectively not to be a genuine pre-estimate of loss would survive under the Dunedin principles because it was subjectively a genuine pre-estimate or was freely negotiated. It appears that the relevance is in terms of the margin of appreciation or latitude to be given to the payee or beneficiary of the clause in the objective exercise. In such cases a wider margin or gap would be allowed between the objectively anticipated losses and the level of damages under the clause. This also shows, in my view, that the Dunedin principles and the 'genuine pre-estimate of loss' test were not being applied under a straitjacket.

V. *Cavendish* and the Way Forward on Penalties – Whither the Dunedin Principles?

Much has been written on *Cavendish* and its impact on the rule on penalties. In this chapter I consider if *Cavendish* leaves the door open to apply the Dunedin principles and the genuine pre-estimate of loss test to delay damages clauses.

---

[29] Thomas Ho, 'Against *Cavendish*: Towards a Procedural Conception of the Penalty Doctrine' [2016] *International Construction Law Review* 451.

The facts of the two appeals are important and the relevant clauses and circumstances are far removed from the everyday delay damages clause in a construction contract.

The *Makdessi* appeal related to a share purchase agreement; Mr El Makdessi was transferring his shares in an underlying company to Cavendish. Clause 11.2 of the agreement was a clause prohibiting Mr El Makdessi from various competitive or potentially competitive activities. Clauses 5.1 and 5.6 provided that, if he breached clause 11.2, he would not be entitled to receive the interim and/ or final payments due, and could be required to sell Cavendish the rest of his shares at a 'Defaulting Shareholder Option Price', based on a straight asset value and so ignoring any goodwill value. Cavendish's claim was for declarations that Mr El Makdessi's breach of clause 11.2 meant that clauses 5.1 and 5.6 now had the effect stated. Mr El Makdessi argued that they were unenforceable penalty clauses.

In the *ParkingEye* appeal, Mr Beavis parked in a retail car park owned by BAPF. BAPF had appointed ParkingEye to operate the car park, applying a 'traffic space maximisation scheme'. This involved a notice stating a two-hour maximum stay with a parking charge of £85 for any overstay. Mr Beavis was charged the £85 for overstaying and challenged it as an unenforceable penalty. Alternatively, he alleged the charge was unfair and invalid within the meaning of the Unfair Terms in Consumer Contracts Regulations 1999.

The Supreme Court reversed the decisions of the Court of Appeal that the clauses in each case were unenforceable as penalties. Lord Neuberger PSC and Lord Sumption JSC (with Lord Carnwath JSC agreeing) in a joint judgment described the penalty rule as an 'ancient, haphazardly constructed edifice which has not weathered well'.[30] They declined to abolish the law against penalties[31] whilst at the same time holding that it should not be extended judicially.[32]

Lords Neuberger PSC and Sumption JSC stated that it was wrong to treat Lord Dunedin's propositions in *Dunlop* as 'almost immutable rules of general application which exhaust the field' and stated that the fact that a clause is not a 'genuine pre-estimate of loss' does not 'without more' mean it is penal:

> 31. In our opinion, the law relating to penalties has become the prisoner of artificial categorisation, itself the result of unsatisfactory distinctions: between a penalty and genuine pre-estimate of loss, and between a genuine pre-estimate of loss and a deterrent. These distinctions originate in an over-literal reading of Lord Dunedin's four tests and a tendency to treat them as almost immutable rules of general application which exhaust the field ... The real question when a contractual provision is challenged as a penalty is whether it is penal, not whether it is a pre-estimate of loss. These are not natural opposites or mutually exclusive categories. A damages clause may be neither or both. The fact that the clause is not a pre-estimate of loss does not therefore, at any rate

---

[30] *Cavendish*, see n 1 above, at paragraph 3.
[31] *Cavendish*, see n 1 above, at paragraph 36.
[32] *Cavendish*, see n 1 above, at paragraph 42.

368 Riaz Hussain QC

without more, mean that it is penal. To describe it as a deterrent (or, to use the Latin equivalent, in terrorem) does not add anything. A deterrent provision in a contract is simply one species of provision designed to influence the conduct of the party potentially affected. It is no different in this respect from a contractual inducement. Neither is it inherently penal or contrary to the policy of the law. The question whether it is enforceable should depend on whether the means by which the contracting party's conduct is to be influenced are 'unconscionable' or (which will usually amount to the same thing) 'extravagant' by reference to some norm.

At the same time Lords Neuberger and Sumption expressed a preference for what they termed a broader approach, suggested in Lord Atkinson's judgment in *Dunlop*:[33]

> 23. ... Lord Atkinson was making substantially the same point as Lord Robertson had made in *Clydebank*. The question was: what was the nature and extent of the innocent party's interest in the performance of the relevant obligation. That interest was not necessarily limited to the mere recovery of compensation for the breach. Lord Atkinson considered that the underlying purpose of the resale price maintenance clause gave Dunlop a wider interest in enforcing the damages clause than pecuniary compensation. £5 per item was not incommensurate with that interest even if it was incommensurate with the loss occasioned by the wrongful sale of a single item.

They held that the true test is whether the material provision is a secondary obligation which imposes a detriment on the contract-breaker out of all proportion to any legitimate interest of the innocent party in the enforcement of the primary obligation.

So far, so good. However, importantly, Lords Neuberger and Sumption stated that in a 'straightforward' clause Lord Dunedin's four tests would usually be perfectly adequate:

> 32. ... In the case of a straightforward damages clause, that interest will rarely extend beyond compensation for the breach, and we therefore expect that Lord Dunedin's four tests would usually be perfectly adequate to determine its validity. But compensation is not necessarily the only legitimate interest that the innocent party may have in the performance of the defaulter's primary obligations.[34]

At paragraph 22 of the judgment their Lordships similarly stated: 'The four tests are a useful tool for deciding whether these expressions can properly be applied to simple damages clauses in standard contracts. But they are not easily applied to more complex cases.'

Continuing at paragraph 25:

> 25. The great majority of cases decided in England since *Dunlop* have concerned more or less standard damages clauses in consumer contracts, and Lord Dunedin's four tests have proved perfectly adequate for dealing with those. More recently, however, the

---

[33] *Cavendish*, see n 1 above, at paragraphs 22–24.
[34] *Cavendish*, see n 1 above, at paragraph 32.

courts have returned to the possibility of a broader test in less straightforward cases, in the context of the supposed 'commercial justification' for clauses which might otherwise be regarded as penal.

Much has been made in academic and practitioner writing of how the concept of 'legitimate interest' is ill defined and could be uncertain. However, possibly an equally fundamental uncertainty following *Cavendish* is: do courts and parties apply the Dunedin propositions at all, and if so when and how?

Lords Neuberger and Sumption (with Lord Carnwath agreeing) state that the Dunedin propositions are not determinative but can be 'perfectly adequate'. On their joint judgment one could say that the Dunedin propositions or the genuine pre-estimate of loss test continue to apply to a 'straightforward' liquidated damages clause. This of course begs the question in each case as to what a 'straightforward' liquidated damages clause is?

It is not necessarily the case that construction contracts and indeed even standard form clauses will be straightforward. Lord Hodge in *Cavendish*[35] referred to the House of Lords decision in *Gilbert-Ash (Northern) Ltd v Modern Engineering (Bristol) Ltd*,[36] which considered a clause in a construction sub-contract that allowed the main contractor to suspend or withhold payment of any moneys due to the sub-contractor if the sub-contractor failed to comply with any of its conditions. The contractor conceded that this part of the contractual clause was a penalty. It is clear that the Court agreed with the concession. Would this be a 'straightforward' damages clause?

Lord Hodge JSC, although he did not refer specifically to the Dunedin propositions, stated that the yardstick of foreseeable losses arising from breach would apply to a 'clause fixing the level of damages to be paid on breach' (he did not refer to the clause being 'simple' or 'straightforward'):

> 255. I therefore conclude that the correct test for a penalty is whether the sum or remedy stipulated as a consequence of a breach of contract is exorbitant or unconscionable when regard is had to the innocent party's interest in the performance of the contract. Where the test is to be applied to a clause fixing the level of damages to be paid on breach, an extravagant disproportion between the stipulated sum and the highest level of damages that could possibly arise from the breach would amount to a penalty and thus be unenforceable. In other circumstances the contractual provision that applies on breach is measured against the interest of the innocent party which is protected by the contract and the court asks whether the remedy is exorbitant or unconscionable.

Lord Mance emphasised case law following the decision in *Lordsvale Finance plc v Bank of Zambia*,[37] a case concerning a common form provision in a syndicated loan agreement for interest to be payable at a higher rate during any period when the borrower was in default. Interestingly this case was not cited to the Court in

---

[35] *Cavendish*, see n 1 above, at paragraph 226.
[36] *Gilbert-Ash (Northern) Ltd v Modern Engineering (Bristol) Ltd* [1974] AC 689.
[37] *Lordsvale Finance plc v Bank of Zambia* [1996] QB 752.

Tilebox, its facts and clause being so far removed from the delay damages clause in *Tilebox*. Lord Mance referred to cases considering *Lordsvale*, including *Murray v Leisureplay plc*.[38] That case concerned a clause in a chief executive's employment contract entitling him to payment of a year's gross salary in the event of wrongful termination of his employment without a year's notice. However, unlike Lords Neuberger, Sumption and Hodge, Lord Mance did not indicate that a different test or approach would apply to 'straightforward' clauses that expressly designate damages for breach:

> 152. In my opinion, the development of the law indicated by the authorities discussed in paras 145 to 151 above is a sound one. It is most easily explained on the basis that the dichotomy between the compensatory and the penal is not exclusive. There may be interests beyond the compensatory which justify the imposition on a party in breach of an additional financial burden … What is necessary in each case is to consider, first, whether any (and if so what) legitimate business interest is served and protected by the clause, and, second, whether, assuming such an interest to exist, the provision made for the interest is nevertheless in the circumstances extravagant, exorbitant or unconscionable. In judging what is extravagant, exorbitant or unconscionable, I consider (despite contrary expressions of view) that the extent to which the parties were negotiating at arm's length on the basis of legal advice and had every opportunity to appreciate what they were agreeing must at least be a relevant factor.

From the judgments of Lords Neuberger, Sumption and Mance one could venture that for delay damages clauses in construction contracts, *Cavendish* does not displace the Dunedin principles and the genuine pre-estimate of loss approach. Indeed, that was the view of at least some construction law commentators. Dr Hamish Lal in an article shortly following noted that:[39]

> The Supreme Court has removed reliance on commercial purpose as an excuse for inserting what would otherwise be a penalty.

> Readers may think there is no real difference between the new test and how the industry has applied the so called Lord Dunedin test, as set out in the 1915 case of *Dunlop Pneumatic Tyre Company Ltd vs New Garage and Motor Company Ltd*. Such readers would be correct and indeed the Supreme Court recognises that in the case of a straightforward damages clause (as in typical building contracts), the employer's interest would rarely extend beyond compensation for the breach, and their lordships would expect that Lord Dunedin's four tests would usually be adequate to determine validity. A lazy reader could stop here and presume that the Supreme Court's decision has changed nothing for the construction industry.

> However, where monetary compensation was not the only legitimate interest which the innocent party might have in the performance of the defaulter's primary obligations, the new test makes several subtle adjustments. First, it removes debate on whether the sum stated to be the liquidated damage was a genuine pre-estimate of the loss that the employer would suffer as consequence of a delay to completion. Second, it removes

---

[38] [2005] EWCA Civ 963.
[39] Dr Hamish Lal, 'A new test for penalties', *Building Magazine*, 16 November 2015.

debate on whether the clause was inserted as a deterrent. Third, the Supreme Court has removed reliance on commercial purpose as an excuse for inserting what would otherwise be a penalty.

Mathias Cheung[40] notes that

> In demolishing the *Dunlop* dichotomy and holding that '[t]he real question when a contractual provision is challenged as a penalty is whether it is penal, not whether it is a pre-estimate of loss', the entire inquiry risks becoming circular and tautologous. There is little concrete guidance for the construction industry on whether or not a clause is penal.

However, whether the genuine pre-estimate of loss test continues to apply to delay damages clauses and if so, how, is not clear given the overall judgment.

At paragraph 31 in their joint judgment, Lords Neuberger and Sumption stated that a deterrent provision *is not inherently penal*. At paragraph 28, they stated politely that they had some misgivings with the approach in *Lordsvale*,[41] *Murray*[42] and the strand of authority following those cases which saw the question as whether the impugned clause was intended to deter breach.

> 28. Colman J in *Lordsvale* and Arden LJ in *Murray* were inclined to rationalise the introduction of commercial justification as part of the test, by treating it as evidence that the impugned clause was not intended to deter. Later decisions in which a commercial rationale has been held inconsistent with the application of the penalty rule, have tended to follow that approach … It had the advantage of enabling them to reconcile the concept of commercial justification with Lord Dunedin's four tests. But we have some misgivings about it. The assumption that a provision cannot have a deterrent purpose if there is a commercial justification, seems to us to be questionable.

In the *ParkingEye* appeal the fine was intended to have a deterrent effect in order to achieve and uphold an overriding commercial justification – keep the cars moving so more customers can come. Their Lordships accepted deterrence as a legitimate intent of a clause:

> 98. Against this background, it can be seen that the £85 charge had two main objects. One was to manage the efficient use of parking space in the interests of the retail outlets, and of the users of those outlets who wish to find spaces in which to park their cars. This was to be achieved by deterring commuters or other long-stay motorists from occupying parking spaces for long periods or engaging in other inconsiderate parking practices, thereby reducing the space available to other members of the public, in particular the customers of the retail outlets. The other purpose was to provide an income stream to enable ParkingEye to meet the costs of operating the scheme and make a profit from its services, without which those services would not be available. These two objectives appear to us to be perfectly reasonable in themselves. Subject to the penalty rule and the Regulations, the imposition of a charge to deter overstayers is a reasonable mode of

---

[40] See n 17 above, (2017) 33 *Const LJ* 173 at 184.
[41] *Lordsvale Finance plc v Bank of Zambia* [1996] QB 752.
[42] See n 3 above.

achieving them. Indeed, once it is resolved to allow up to two hours free parking, it is difficult to see how else those objectives could be achieved. ...

99. In our opinion, while the penalty rule is plainly engaged, the £85 charge is not a penalty ...

100. None of this means that ParkingEye could charge overstayers whatever it liked. It could not charge a sum which would be out of all proportion to its interest or that of the landowner for whom it is providing the service. But there is no reason to suppose that £85 is out of all proportion to its interests. The trial judge, Judge Moloney QC, found that the £85 charge was neither extravagant nor unconscionable having regard to the level of charges imposed by local authorities for overstaying in car parks on public land.

The relevance of what other authorities are charging as fees for overstaying is not immediately apparent. As their Lordships themselves accepted[43] the penalties rule does not concern itself with the fairness of men's bargains[44] either at law or in equity. It is difficult to see how an agreed remedy is not part of the bargain. Looking at what other authorities charge comes very close to looking at the fairness of the bargain.[45]

More fundamentally, if deterrence of breach is a legitimate intent (whether as a purpose on its own or to serve a broader purpose) then it is difficult to sustain the position in the joint judgment that the Dunedin test is 'perfectly adequate' in 'straightforward' clauses. If a deterrent purpose or intent is permitted, how can the Dunedin principles apply at all? Deterrence would relate to what would sufficiently pain and deter the potential contract breaker from breach. The Dunedin propositions measure the losses that could follow from the breach. The outcome of these two measures may or may not be coincident in some cases but they are very different measures and starting points.

To give a hypothetical but realistic example, let's take a building contract to build a spare bathroom. Delays to the works will not cause the occupying owner financial loss, she has a bathroom that she can continue to use. She does, however, have a legitimate interest in wanting to have the disruption of building works finished and she wishes to have the spare bathroom ready for Christmas so her family can enjoy it. She knows the propensity of builders to do the cost heavy work and then rather than press on with completion to go on to a more lucrative work heavy job and leave the crucial finishing to as and when they have a moment to spare. To get the builder to focus on finishing the job, rather than finish the job in

---

[43] *Cavendish*, see n 1 above, at paragraph 13.

[44] The curiously gendered language aside, the focus on the judgment is on commercial moneyed interests. It is a narrow focus and a narrow view of the law of contract – big money bargains. Their Lordships and the other judges in the case focus on clauses protecting commercial or business interests with the occasional unspecified reference to 'other' interests. See for instance *Cavendish*, n 1 above, at paragraphs 75, 145, 152, 227 and 248. It would be interesting to see how they would approach the example of the residential works contract I refer to below.

[45] See for instance, Cheung, n 17 above, at 184: 'Further, the *Makdessi* test could effectively become a test of unconscionability and substantive fairness'.

dribs and drabs, she needs a sufficient deterrent in place under a delay damages clause. So she puts in place a delay damages clause that for each week of delay after Christmas the builder will pay her £4,000. That figure is selected by her to be greater than the profit the builder would make on another job and is her best estimate of a deterrent.

In such a case we have on its face a 'straightforward' damages clause protecting the interest of performance. On the genuine pre-estimate of loss test the clause would be a penalty. Objectively the employer faces no financial loss from delays, and the courts do not value loss of amenity, inconvenience and so on as high as £4,000 a week. Do the Dunedin principles and the genuine pre-estimate of loss test apply here at all? The joint judgment of Lords Neuberger and Sumption states that they are perfectly adequate for 'straightforward' *clauses*, so the barometer is the clause rather than the circumstances surrounding the contract. Likewise, in terms of Lord Hodge's distinction, this is a clause (expressly) *fixing the level of damages to be paid on breach*.[46] But why should the stricter parameters apply here? Is the employer less entitled to rely on her legitimate interest in performance than the media conglomerate in *Makdessi*?

That is not to suggest that the answer would necessarily be different under the legitimate interest test but it certainly would be a very different measure of this 'straightforward' clause.

See in this regard the non-construction case of *Vivienne Westwood Ltd v Conduit Street Development Ltd*,[47] where HHJ Timothy Fancourt QC, sitting as a Deputy High Court Judge, applied the legitimate interest test and found that a clause which allowed the lessor to terminate for any non-trivial (or more than de minimis) breach of a lease agreement for a reduced rate of rent, and recover rent at the original rate both prospectively and retrospectively, was a penalty. HHJ Timothy Fancourt QC held in particular there were two factors that made the termination clause exorbitant and unconscionable in comparison with any legitimate interest in full performance: the termination of the reduced rent applied retrospectively and prospectively for even a minor breach; and it applied additionally to a claim for unliquidated damages and contractual interest for the minor breach.

VI. Conclusion

The TCC has applied the Dunedin principles and the genuine pre-estimate of loss test with consistency, clarity and with proper regard to respecting the will of the parties. Jackson J's approach in *Tilebox*, and his reference to the need for a substantial discrepancy or a wide gulf between the range of losses foreseen from

---

[46] See *Cavendish*, n 1 above, at paragraph 255.
[47] *Vivienne Westwood Ltd v Conduit Street Development Ltd* [2017] EWHC 350 (Ch).

the breach and the level of delay damages, is a crystallisation of that approach. The fact remains that the construction courts have rarely, if at all, struggled with applying the rule on penalties. The clear dicta of Lords Neuberger, Sumption and Hodge in *Cavendish*, as identified above, point to the Dunedin propositions and the genuine pre-estimate of loss approach remaining the measure, or at least the starting point, for determining whether a delay damages clause is a penalty clause. However, that is a fundamentally different approach from the legitimate interest approach. It is difficult to see how the two can be squared up, and if there is a dividing line in the approach or measure, what the justification for the same will be. It may be that another court will have to decide how much of a departure *Cavendish* is from the established wisdom in previous building contract cases.

INDEX

NB Those cases given main headings in this index are the cases in which Jackson LJ played a direct part.

Lightning Source UK Ltd.
Milton Keynes UK
UKHW020207180620
365083UK00006B/214